DU BOIS
ON REFORM

8-20-20

Dear Bill,

Thank you for being a steward of your grace and place here at Warner Pacific University!

8th President Warner Pacific University

DU BOIS ON REFORM

Periodical-based Leadership for African Americans

Edited by Brian Johnson

ALTAMIRA
PRESS

A DIVISION OF
ROWMAN & LITTLEFIELD PUBLISHERS, INC.
Lanham • New York • Toronto • Oxford

AltaMira Press
A division of Rowman & Littlefield Publishers, Inc.
A wholly owned subsidary of The Rowman & Littlefield Publishing Group, Inc.
4501 Forbes Boulevard, Suite 200
Lanham, MD 20706
www.altamirapress.com

P.O. Box 317, Oxford, OX2 9RU, UK

British Library Cataloguing in Publication Information Available

Library of Congress Cataloging-in-Publication Data

Johnson, Brian, 1973–
  Du Bois on reform : periodical-based leadership for African Americans /
edited by Brian Johnson.
    p. cm.
  Includes bibliographical references and index.
  ISBN 0-7591-0804-8 (cloth : alk. paper)—ISBN 0-7591-0805-6 (pbk. : alk. paper)
  1. Du Bois, W. E. B. (William Edward Burghardt), 1868–1963—Political and
social views. 2. African American leadership. 3. African Americans—Social
conditions—To 1964. 4. Social problems—United States—History—19th century.
5. Social problems—United States—History—20th century. 6. American periodicals—History—19th century. 7. American periodicals—History—20th century. I.
Title.

  E185.97.D73J64 2005
  305.896'073'0092—dc22
                                                                    2005009745

Printed in the United States of America

♾™ The paper used in this publication meets the minimum requirements of
American National Standard for Information Sciences—Permanence of Paper for
Printed Library Materials, ANSI/NISO Z39.48-1992.

For my sons, Brian Asa and
Nathan Morgan Qodesh

CONTENTS

**PART III   PERIODICAL WRITINGS APPEARING IN
            *CRISIS MAGAZINE: A RECORD OF THE
            DARKER RACES*, 1910–1934**

INTRODUCTION   195

ACKNOWLEDGMENTS

There are several persons and institutions I would like to thank for their assistance while researching this project.

The research for this project was funded at various points by the University of South Carolina at Columbia's African American Professors Program, (UNCF) SSRC/Mellon-Mays Pre-Doctoral Grants, and a Woodrow Wilson Travel/Research Grant. The staff in the manuscript division of the Library of Congress (Washington, D.C.) also provided invaluable assistance with my research.

Ezra Greenspan, Kwame Dawes, James Miller, and Leon Jackson served on my dissertation committee at the University of South Carolina at Columbia. The administration, faculty, and English department colleagues at Gordon College (Wenham, Mass.) have encouraged me tremendously in my first year there. Ron Mahurin at Council for Christian Colleges and Universities (CCCU) in Washington, D.C., has also provided tremendous encouragement. Vanessa Crooks and Charis Bynum, who provides administrative assistance to the Gordon College Humanities Division, have gone beyond the call of duty in assisting me. And without my teaching assistant, Anne Colpitts, this project would not have been possible. Special thanks to Grace Ebron and AltaMira Press, Adam Biggs, and, especially, the Souls of Black Folk—my folk.

Most importantly, I would like to thank my wife, Shemeka, whose encouragement, patience, support, wisdom, and love toward me is simply immeasurable.

The editor finally wishes to thank the Crisis Publishing Co., Inc., the publisher of the magazine of the National Association for the Advancement of Colored People, for authorizing this use of the *Crisis Magazine* articles. For the remaining articles, the editor wishes to thank David Graham Du Bois and the W. E. B. Du Bois estate.

INTRODUCTION

*Du Bois on Reform: Periodical-based
Leadership for African Americans*

Progress in human affairs is more often a pull than a push, a surging forward of the exceptional man, and the lifting of his duller brethren slowly and painfully to his vantage-ground.

—W. E. B. Du Bois[1]

So then the Negro group leader not only sets present standards, but he supplies in a measure the lack of past standards, and his leading is doubly difficult, since with Emancipation there came a second partial breaking with the past. The leader of the masses must discriminate between the good and bad in the past; he must keep the lesson of work and reject the lesson of concubinage; he must add more lessons of moral rectitude to the old religious fervor; he must, in fine, stand to this group in the light of the interpreter of the civilization of the twentieth century to the minds and hearts of people who, from sheer necessity, can but dimly comprehend it. And this man—I care not what his vocation may be—preacher, teacher, physician or artisan, this person is going to solve the Negro problem; for that problem is at bottom the clash of two different standards of culture and this priest it is who interprets the one to the other.

—W. E. B. Du Bois[2]

I n 1956, six years before W. E. B. Du Bois's death in Ghana, Africa, the Vienna World Peace Council asked him to write a biographical account of Benjamin Franklin's life. The biography was to commemorate the 250th anniversary of Franklin's birth. While Du Bois's *The Story of Benjamin Franklin* consisted of only 39 pages, this was indeed a noteworthy, unprecedented moment in American print history: the most looming figure in African American letters was requested to document the life of one of the most formative figures in the whole of American letters. In considering Franklin's life and letters alongside Du Bois's, one notices several striking parallels—parallels that would not have escaped Du Bois's shrewd perception. Like Franklin, Du Bois (albeit a century later) was reared in the New England Congregationalist tradition and later disavowed it. As teenagers, both men undertook their first printed efforts, in the form of moralizing columns—Franklin for his brother's *New England Courant* newspaper, and Du Bois for T. Thomas Fortune's *New York Globe*. Also, both shared a devotion to scientific and rational pursuits of truth throughout their long careers in public life. However, the most provocative link between these writers, found throughout their various labors in print media, is their consistent choice of theme: reforming behavior.

Many of Franklin's moralizing commentaries were designed to reform his eighteenth-century American compatriots, and Du Bois's reform writings were directed toward his fellow compatriots as well—late-nineteenth-century and early-twentieth-century African Americans. Although it is difficult to determine decisively whether or not Benjamin Franklin figured prominently in Du Bois's conceptions of periodical authorship (Du Bois does, however, reference Poor Richard in a writing appearing in *Crisis* entitled "Thrift," January 1921, Vol. 21, No. 3, pp. 101–2), the Franklin biography is an intriguing place to consider Du Bois's little-discussed career as a reformer via periodical authorship.

Situating African American scholars as authors is not a foreign idea in African American studies. Since Harold Cruse's *The Crisis of the Negro Intellectual*, contemporary African American scholars have also commented upon a separate and distinct tradition of African American scholars as writers.[3] Among their commentaries, Cornel West's "The Dilemma of the Negro Intellectual" draws the clearest link between African American scholarship and authorship. Sharing Cruse's recognition of African American scholars' dual commitments to their professional occupations and larger ethnic communities, West describes their dilemma thus: "black intellectuals have little choice: either continued intellectual lethargy on the edges of the academy and literate subcultures unnoticed by the black community, or insurgent creative activity on the margins of the mainstream ensconced within bludgeoning new infrastructures."[4] Although West's observations point to creating future possibilities for uniting African American scholarship and authorship for larger communal purposes, the suggestion also provides a rather remarkable opportunity for history of the book scholars to look retrospectively at the ways in which the most prominent African American scholar engaged in an unconventional form of print authorship to impact African American readership.

Robert Darnton's seminal articulation of history of the book studies in "What Is the History of Books?" has provided the framework for such a task. By arguing that history of the book's purpose is to concern itself with how a book "comes into being" and "spread[s] through society," Darnton allows history of the book scholars to unearth and contemplate varying forms of African American print authorship to make manifest a print tradition not unlike America's overarching print landscape.[5] Elizabeth

McHenry's *Forgotten Readers: Recovering the Lost History of African American Literary Societies* (2002) is one of the first studies to apply what Darnton describes to African American literature. McHenry's project uncovers a "lost history" relating to nineteenth-century African American reading and writing practices. In doing so, McHenry's project applies book history scholarship to the assumption shared by "students of African American literature, history and culture" that viable sources of African American intellectual print production have been rendered "historically invisible" because of the academic tendency "to push aside facts surrounding other [African American] language usages—especially those related to reading and writing."[6] The significance of *Forgotten Readers* is that it widens what scholars have normally considered as "insurgent creative [print] activity" in African American social, cultural, and literary history. And this anthology shares McHenry's assumptions and goals—along with history of the book's evolving methodological considerations—but presses in the opposite direction.

This anthology recognizes that Darnton's "communications circuit" need not only consider how a text "comes into being" and "spread[s] through society."[7] Similar to Michael Warner's history of the book analysis, *The Letters of the Republic* (1990), which has a chapter examining Benjamin Franklin's reliance upon varying print media to make manifest a republican eighteenth-century authorship, this anthology considers how W. E. B. Du Bois utilized a specific form of print—magazine and newspaper periodicals—to bring a more utilitarian sense of authorship "into being" and "through[out] society." Du Bois's extensive authorship included 20 single-authored books, 33 pamphlets, 19 edited books, and 58 edited studies, yet 2000 of his periodical writings—particularly those appearing in *Crisis Magazine: A Record of the Darker Races*, the place of Du Bois's most prolific periodical record—have gone virtually unstudied in African American literature, although they were clearly his preferred genre and also demonstrated a distinct type of authorship.

To be sure, African American periodical writing—especially Du Bois's career as a periodical writer—is hardly a novel conception. Historians have already described Du Bois's use of the periodical to commingle his scholarly vocation as a sociologist and his activist concerns into "scholastic activism."[8] Du Bois wrote in a long periodical writing tradition including African American intellectual and cultural icons such as Frederick Douglass, Pauline Hopkins, Ida B. Wells, and William Monroe Trotter, who used the periodical to promulgate abolitionist and racial protest rhetoric. Penelope Bullock's *The Afro-American Periodical Press* (1981) describes this tradition's genesis: "The overall development of the Afro-American periodical press was influenced by the status of Negroes in American society during the years between

1838–1909. This press began in the 1830s as a part of the organized activities of black people who were working for the emancipation of the slave and for the liberation of the free Negro from inequities and restrictions."[9] In spite of this more widely recognized tradition, Du Bois's status as an African American scholar appearing within the pages of periodical publication was much more than "a career as a scientist swallowed up in the role of master of propaganda."[10] Du Bois's periodical writings—partly due to his academic background in sociology—existed within a *forgotten* stream of late-nineteenth-century and early-twentieth-century African American reform writing. Donald Franklin Joyce's "Reflections on the Changing Publishing Objectives of Secular Black Book Publishers, 1900–1986" provides a useful framework for considering late-nineteenth-century and early-twentieth-century African American reform writing. Joyce suggests:

> [B]lack book publishers have seldom published books that might be classified as escape reading. Books published by black publishers have been and continue to be utilitarian, in the sense that they foster moral, social or practical values. Since the early years of the twentieth-century, when black secular book publishing began to flourish in a meager way, the objectives of black secular publishers have involved satisfying definite intellectual and cultural needs within the black community. Often these needs reflected the reaction of blacks to the larger society's hostility or indifference toward the black community. In other instances the needs arose from changes within the black community.[11]

Although Joyce's study is primarily concerned with twentieth-century secular African American book publishers and their principal motivations, his commentary provides two powerful ideas for a broader consideration of African American authorship in general. Joyce insightfully recognizes a "utilitarian" tradition of African American writing—appropriately distinguishing it from most contemporaneous white writing—and his comments speak to a tradition of African American writing that was not singularly devoted to protest. Since Maria W. Stewart's *Productions of Maria W. Stewart* (1835)—perhaps the first compilation of African American reform essays, which included essays like "Religion and the Pure Principles of Morality, the Sure Foundation on Which We Must Build"—a significant number of late-nineteenth-century and early-twentieth-century African American writers have also written in a variety of genres to provide reform commentary to African American community members. In a rather curious moment in African American letters, W. E. B. Du Bois and Booker T. Washington approved a book containing their speeches, entitled *The Negro in the South: His Economic Progress in Relation to His Moral and Religious Development* (1907). Du Bois and Washington—along with other African American intellectual figures such as Alexander Crummell,

Francis Grimke, Archibald Grimke, T. Thomas Fortune, Paul Laurence Dunbar, Anna Julia Cooper, James Corrothers, Hubert H. Harrison, William Hannibal Thomas, and Charles Chesnutt—used either speeches, essays, sermons, fiction, autobiography, journalism, or organizational activities to help remedy African American moral deficiencies because it was one of the most pressing concerns in the post-slavery south and the early twentieth century.[12] Kevin Gaines suggests about the reformers' motivation: "Against the Post-Reconstruction assault on black citizenship and humanity, black ministers, intellectuals, journalists and reformers sought to refute the view that African-Americans . . . could not be completely assimilated into American society."[13] Although the writings and activities of secular African American reformers are more widely noted, it was the local black minister—due to his longstanding presence in the institutional life of black churches and black religious organizations—who was the African American community's best-known leader in reform matters.

Eddie S. Glaude Jr.'s *Exodus! Religion, Race, and Nation in Early Nineteenth-Century Black America* (2000) argues that nineteenth-century black churches and black religious organizations focused almost exclusively on issues of moral reform. Black religious organizations such as the American Moral Reform Society believed that moral reform was the best "strategy for the improvement of all human beings regardless of complexional distinctions."[14] Noting what other historians like E. Franklin Frazier, C. Eric Lincoln, Carter G. Woodson, Benjamin Mays, and Joseph Washington have already observed, Glaude explains that black churches and religious organizations "circumscribed social activity and provided vocabularies for moral and ethical judgments" for the African American community.[15] And, in many ways, this "vocabulary" was precisely what a more scholarly reformer like W. E. B. Du Bois hoped to offer an alternative to when writing in periodicals during the late nineteenth and early twentieth century. Unlike much of the dogma and didacticism associated with late-nineteenth-century and early-twentieth-century black churches and religious organizations, Du Bois insisted that an absence of education contributed to most of the immoral and unethical behavior in the larger African American community. African American churches and religious organizations had as their reform pretext—mirroring sermons pronounced from their pulpits—a vague religious dogma that did not provide the kind of practical instruction that Du Bois's sociological background offered.

Reverend Crawford Jackson of Atlanta, Georgia, typified the late-nineteenth-century reform ideals of most black churches and religious organizations when speaking at the Negro Young People's Christian and Educational Congress held August 6–11, 1902: "We want our [reform] movement to be Christian to the core. If God the Father through Christ is not to be its very Alpha and Omega, then I must be counted out."[16] Du Bois disagreed with this reform ideology, arguing that dogma alone could not eradicate contemporary social problems that derived from slavery. Instead, he believed African Americans needed a firm historical and sociological grasp of a distinct African American phenomenon that black ministers could not offer due to an inadequate educational background. Du Bois believed that such anti-intellectual positioning by black ministers played a crucial role in crippling the moral and ethical development of African American citizens. When Du Bois suggested that "a moral question" is nothing "more than a psychological and social question; and above all a field where our churches should get busy," Du Bois effectively likened African American moral concerns to a sociological field of activity; for Du Bois, this provided grounds for reform writings appearing in periodicals that his scholarly occupation uniquely qualified him to offer.[17]

Manning Marable is one of the few commentators to mark this persistent theme in Du Bois's writings. Marable proposes in *W. E. B. Du Bois: Black Radical Democrat* (1986) that "culture and ethics rather than politics dominated Du Bois's concerns."[18] African American cultural studies scholar Karla Holloway provides a helpful definition for the nominative term "ethics." In *Codes of Conduct: Race, Ethics, and the Color of Our Character* (1995), Holloway suggests, "ethics practices a moral imperative that is subject to narratives of community and culture."[19] To Du Bois—whose sociological studies on African Americans were the first to document social problems with systemic roots in immoral and unethical behavior—"ethical practices" in late-nineteenth-century and early-twentieth-century African American communities were faulty because their "moral imperatives" were shaped by primitive religious beliefs that omitted advanced liberal arts education and training. In "Of the Faith of the Fathers," an essay appearing in *The Souls of Black Folk* (1903)—though first appearing as a periodical writing entitled "Religion of the American Negro," *New World: A Quarterly Review of Religion, Ethics and Theology (Boston)*, Vol. 9, No. 36, pp. 614–25—Du Bois writes:

> This deep religious fatalism, painted so beautifully in "Uncle Tom," came soon to breed, as all fatalistic faiths will, the sensualist side by side with the martyr. Under the lax moral life of the plantation, where marriage was a farce, laziness a virtue, and property a theft, a religion of resignation and submission degenerated easily, in less strenuous minds, into a philosophy of indulgence and crime. Many of the worst characteristics of the Negro masses of today had their seed in this period of the slave's ethical growth. Here it was that the Home was ruined under the very shadow of the Church, white and black; here habits of shiftlessness took root, and sullen hopelessness replaced hopeful strife.[20]

Although black churches and religious organizations were historically recognized as the African American community's salient leaders, Du Bois found these groups to be largely ineffective when addressing persistent African American social problems that were rooted in immoral and unethical behavior. Du Bois believed that their refusal to rely upon liberal arts training to prepare for an increasingly civilized American culture necessarily limited African American moral and ethical possibilities in an advancing modern age. And the periodical became Du Bois's point of entry into tightfisted southern—and primarily religious—African American communities in the late nineteenth and early twentieth centuries. African American preachers had their wooden pulpits, and with the periodical, Du Bois had his paper pulpit; in effect, the periodical was the most expedient and most widely accessible means of communicating clipped knowledge for reform purposes as he envisioned it.

With the exception of Marable's commentary and Kevin Gaines's *Uplifting the Race* (1996), very little has been written in either historical or literary studies about Du Bois's desires to reform immoral and unethical behavior within the African American community. Kevin Gaines's history calls Du Bois's reform writings "racial uplift," which Gaines suggests was part of an early-twentieth-century African American middle-class anxiety fueled by white societal expectations.[21] Gaines's work bases its case upon Du Bois's moralizing sociological study, *The Philadelphia Negro* (1899)—which was the first sociological study describing social conditions within an African American urban community—and Gaines treats Du Bois's work alongside of other Negro social leaders of the period. Although Gaines's work uncovers a grossly overlooked subject in Du Bois's writings, his history fails to examine Du Bois's most frequently used genre for reform writing. To be certain, Gaines uses some of Du Bois's periodical writings to supplement his commentary upon *The Philadelphia Negro*. However, by neglecting to distinctly examine the primary site of Du Bois's reform writings—thus ignoring a genre significantly different from his academic publications—he fails to fully explain Du Bois's complete configuration of reform authorship, which most frequently appeared at the site of periodical publication before and after (and not primarily in) *The Philadelphia Negro*. Moreover, Du Bois's reform writings appearing primarily in periodicals were influenced as much by—if not more than—black churches and religious organizations as white societal expectations. The proximity between late-nineteenth-century and early-twentieth-century African American moral and ethical practices and the ministerial leadership of its dominant moral institutions—black churches and religious organizations—was such that it was difficult for Du Bois to introduce his reform writings into the public arena without intruding upon or contending with the reform work of these institutions. In keeping with Holloway's definition, Du Bois believed late-nineteenth-century and early-twentieth-century immoral and unethical practices among African Americans were due to moral imperatives shaped by the narratives of uneducated black ministerial leadership.

In the main, the periodical provided Du Bois's scholarly opinion on African American reform matters—prior to that time, a discourse generally reserved for ministers in black churches and religious organizations—a public sphere of influence. Du Bois innovatively used a form of print authorship to reform late-nineteenth-century and early-twentieth-century African American citizens who represented those affected by social problems rooted in immoral and unethical behavior. This periodical-based leadership offered a platform where an alternative to the anti-intellectual leadership of black churches might be communicated. Du Bois's use of the periodical for providing a more scholarly alternative to the leadership of Negro churches and religious organizations in reform matters evolved over three pivotal phases between 1883 and 1934. In each of the periodicals he communicated through during these three phases, Du Bois relied upon his uncommon academic background as the basis for a periodical-based leadership for reforming immoral and unethical behavior in the African American community.

Du Bois's employment of periodical-based reform can be traced to his New England Congregationalist experiences and his first periodical writings as a teenage Great Barrington correspondent at T. Thomas Fortune's *New York Globe (Freeman)* (1883–1885). It was during those years that Du Bois sought to reform Great Barrington's African American citizens. Du Bois possessed the advantage of New England common-school training, and he followed Fortune's model for African American public writing. Du Bois's earliest reform writings were intended for a newly transplanted group of religious black citizens from the south.

Secondly, as a newly graduated Ph.D. from Harvard, Du Bois became a proponent of Alexander Crummell's desire to provide educated and scholarly leadership in African American reform matters as an alternative to uneducated African American ministry. Encouraged by his connection within Crummell's American Negro Academy (1897–1903) and its *Occasional Papers*—a utilitarian periodical designed to transmit this leadership—Du Bois used his growing national reputation as a scholar to secure opportunities to publish these more inoffensive writings in progressive and religious white periodicals. These reform writings, which were some of Du Bois's earliest ventures into a national public domain, had the effect of establishing his reputation as a leading African American social leader.

Finally, Du Bois's organizational work within the National Association for the Advancement of Colored People (NAACP) from 1910 to 1934 (which led to the founding of *Crisis Magazine: A Record of the Darker Races*) is the most substantive place for analyzing his pioneering periodical-based leadership in African American reform matters. While working within the NAACP, he served as the group's cofounder, director of pub-licity and research, executive board member, and editor and chief writer of the organization's periodical, *Crisis*. At the core of Du Bois's periodical authorship within the pages of *Crisis* was a powerful interplay between the NAACP's desire to provide the African American community with leadership and Du Bois's longstanding ideals as a professional scholar providing leadership via periodical authorship. Although social protest against racial discrimination was the chief preoccupation of the NAACP during the period of Du Bois's periodical authorship, a latent, yet insistent desire to advance the social and moral dimensions of the national African American community existed among its executive board members. This desire partly allowed Du Bois to realize his career-long ambitions to secure institutional support for a utilitarian periodical devoted to reform-ing African Americans as well as protesting on behalf of them.

NOTES

1. William Edward Burghardt Du Bois, *The Souls of Black Folk* (New York: Bantam, 1989), 67.

2. Du Bois, "The Development of a People," *International Journal of Ethics (Philadelphia)* vol. 14 (April 1904): 308.

3. Harold Cruse, *The Crisis of the Negro Intellectual* (New York: William Morrow, 1967), 451. Cruse's work argues that African American intellectuals and scholars have a unique obligation to both the predominant ethos of the European academy and the particular needs of the African American community.

4. Cornel West, *Keeping Faith* (New York: Routledge, 1993), 70–71.

5. Robert Darnton, "What Is the History of Books?" *Reading in America: Literature and Social History*, ed. Cathy Davidson (Baltimore: Johns Hopkins University Press, 1989), 29.

6. Elizabeth McHenry, *Forgotten Readers: Recovering the Lost History of African American Literary Societies* (Durham: Duke University Press, 2002), 4–5.

7. Darnton, "What Is the History of Books?" 30.

8. Some of the more recent readings of Du Bois's scholarly activism are Adolph L. Reed, *W. E. B. Du Bois and American Political Thought* (New York: Oxford University Press, 1997), and Rutledge M. Dennis, ed., *W. E. B. Du Bois: The Scholar as Activist/Editor* (Greenwich: Jai Press, 1996). One of the earliest studies is Elliott M. Rudwick, *Propagandist of the Negro Protest* (New York: Athenaeum, 1968).

9. Penelope L. Bullock, *The Afro-American Periodical Press: 1838–1909* (Baton Rouge: Louisiana State University Press, 1981), 11.

10. William Edward Burghardt Du Bois, *Dusk of Dawn* (New York: Schocken, 1968), 94.

11. Donald Franklin Joyce, "Reflections on the Changing Publishing Objectives of Secular Black Book Publishers, 1900–1986," *Reading in America: Literature and Social History*, ed. Cathy Davidson (Baltimore: Johns Hopkins University Press, 1989), 226–27.

12. Du Bois's brief tenure within Alexander Crummell's American Negro Academy, which is discussed briefly in part II, was also due to these reasons.

13. Kevin Gaines, *Uplifting the Race* (Chapel Hill: University of North Carolina Press, 1996), xiv.

14. Eddie S. Glaude Jr., *Exodus! Religion, Race, and Nation in Early Nineteenth-Century Black America* (Chicago: University of Chicago Press, 2000), 126–27.

15. Glaude, *Exodus! Religion, Race, and Nation,* 19. Also see Carter G. Woodson, *The History of the Black Church* (Washington, D.C.: Associated Publishers, 1972); Hart M. Nelsen, Raytha L. Yokley, et al., *The Black Church in America* (New York: Basic, 1971); Joseph R. Washington, *Black Religion: The Negro and Christianity in the United States* (Boston: Beacon, 1964); C. Eric Lincoln, *The Black Church Since Frazier* (New York: Schocken, 1974); Albert J. Raboteau, ed., *Slave Religion: The "Invisible Institution" in the Antebellum South* (Oxford: Oxford University Press, 1980); Gayraud S. Wilmore, *Black Religion and Black Radicalism* (Garden City, NY: Doubleday, 1972). All of these studies suggest that the black church was the central point of Negro life and moral reform efforts.

16. Reverend Crawford Jackson, "The Neediest Class in the South," *The United Negro: His Problems and His Progress,* ed. I. Garland Penn and J.W.E. Bowen (Atlanta: D.E. Luther Publishing, 1902), 289.

17. Du Bois, "As the Crow Flies," *Newspaper Columns by W. E. B. Du Bois (1883–1944),* ed. and comp. Herbert Aptheker, vol. 2 (White Plains, N.Y.: Kraus-Thomson Organization, 1986), 477.

18. Manning Marable, *W. E. B. Du Bois: Black Radical Democrat* (Boston: Twayne, 1986), 37.

19. Karla Holloway, *Codes of Conduct: Race, Ethics, and the Color of Our Character* (New Brunswick, N.J.: Rutgers University Press, 1995), 6.

20. Du Bois, *The Souls of Black Folk* (New York: Bantam, 1989), 140.

21. Gaines, *Uplifting the Race,* xiv.

– PART I –

PERIODICAL WRITINGS APPEARING IN

NEW YORK GLOBE (FREEMAN),

1883–1885

INTRODUCTION

Reform and Periodical-based Leadership in Great Barrington (1883–1885)

One could hardly suggest that Du Bois's future reform efforts directed toward late-nineteenth-century and early-twentieth-century African Americans were due only to Fortune's newspaper since many other important figures and experiences helped shape his philosophy of social and moral reform; furthermore, none of Du Bois's writings appearing in *New York Globe (Freeman)* contains his more mature views. However, one would be remiss to deny that an impressionable fifteen year old might have been influenced by Fortune's idea that intelligent secular African American opinion in African American moral and ethical matters would receive a public hearing in spite of its disassociation from explicit religious efforts. A rather curious communiqué written by Du Bois to the First Congregational Church of Great Barrington in 1892, seven years after his last writings appeared in Fortune's newspaper, suggests this as well.

This revealing letter was written to the then superintendent of the increasingly mixed First Congregational Church of Great Barrington's Sunday school. At the time, Du Bois was a Harvard student studying abroad in Germany. He was apparently making his first distinctions between the suitability of liberally educated opinion appearing in periodical-based media versus that of primarily religious sectors. With a degree of trepidation, Du Bois informed Mr. Van Lennep, "I send enclosed a letter to the Sunday-school—after having written it I have had doubts as to its appropriateness, but I shall send it at any rate—perhaps it would be better for the *Berkshire Courier*, if so I should like to see a copy."[1] Du Bois's description of the town of Eisenach—a town famously known because of its ties to Martin Luther—is written from the standpoint of a detached historian and sociologist rather than of an ardent participant in the Protestant faith. The letter reads in part:

> To the Congregational Sunday-School, I venture to send you a few words about the German town in which I have been spending the summer,

because it is so intimately connected with the life of Martin Luther . . . It is however of the rich legacy of history and legend which belongs to these hills that I wish to speak. It is ever a strange experience for an American to walk for the first time in a land, the natural beauty of which is surrounded and enhanced by the thought, legends, and deeds of a thousand years. Such is the case here, and the deeds are all the more interesting because they furthered that freedom of conscience and deeper religion, which is the heritage of Gt. Barrington and of the world.

Du Bois's letter—which goes on to describe his experience sitting in the pews of the church where Martin Luther preached and the historical context of Luther's radical stance and excommunication—leaves conspicuously absent the kind of adulation and praise for the spiritual components of Protestantism that Du Bois's Sunday school audience probably would have preferred. Instead, the letter focused upon Luther's "deeds" in hopes of inspiring the kind of practical efforts that Du Bois believed the Sunday school communicants were most in need of. Du Bois's concern that the letter should be published through a secular medium instead of being read before a Protestant congregation is equally telling. It points to Du Bois's earliest inclinations to utilize public, rather than religious, print for more secular methods of reform. While it is not known whether the church's superintendent read Du Bois's letter either in private or in front of the Sunday school, it does appear that the letter represents a partial break from the Congregationalism of his Great Barrington rearing, for that letter is one of Du Bois's last recorded communications to the church.

If the 1892 Great Barrington Congregational Church would not have considered giving Du Bois's developing intellectual opinion a hearing within its doors—there is no record of them doing so—Fortune's *New York Globe (Freeman)* did because Fortune always considered such writings to be a public service.[2] Fortune thought the value of intelligent African American periodical writing to be not only equal to that of any public servant in the African American community, but even more necessary. One of Fortune's editorials affirms this idea:

> The editors of the great newspapers are more absolutely the servants of the people than any of the servants placed in positions of trust and profit and power by their votes. They are more faithful to the people's interests, they are more inaccessible to the allurements of corruptionists, they have generally a clearer and more thorough understanding of the rights of the people and voice their demands with greater accuracy and force than any other class of men in the Republic, simply because they live nearer to the people and are in many respects the servants in a more general sense of the public opinion to which they give voice . . . An editor, with no readers of his paper, is in a much more pitiable plight than a lawyer without briefs, or a preacher without a charge.[3]

Thus, for Fortune, editorial writing was tantamount to serving in a public office—including a pastoral one—because of its close proximity to and services rendered on behalf of people, particularly African Americans. One important service he rendered with his editorials was to give an intelligent "voice" to the desires and wants of African American citizens who were generally ignored or silenced. His singular ability to express himself so intelligently was due, in part, to the education he received as a youth. Fortune possessed strong Anglo-American physical features, which had enabled him to blend in with whites and obtain early school training in the south; this was an extraordinarily rare opportunity for most late-nineteenth-century African Americans in the south. Du Bois's reverence for Fortune's exceptional writing abilities and the training he received mimicking Fortune at the site of periodical publication were probably his chief inspirations when he wrote his own periodical writings for Fortune's newspaper. Although still a teenager, Du Bois understood that his New England Congregationalist experiences and common school training afforded him a distinct role among a group of newly transplanted Great Barrington African Americans from the south, and his first reform commentaries in T. Thomas Fortune's *New York Globe* (*Freeman*) relied upon this exceptional background.

The juxtaposition of these two formative influences—the First Congregational Church of Great Barrington and Fortune's *New York Globe* (*Freeman*)—provides an all-important blueprint for understanding Du Bois's later utilization of the periodical for African American reform purposes. Fortune's periodical was used to disseminate Du Bois's first reform commentaries and gave Du Bois—who possessed an unusual academic standing in the Great Barrington community while yet a teenager—an opportunity to exercise influence over an impressionable and largely uneducated African American public. In addition, these commentaries were coincident with the rising liberal sentiment within the First Congregational Church of Great Barrington; a prominent church member, judge Justin Dewey (who would later become infamous for his adjudication at Lizzie Borden's murder trial) contended that church's refusal to consider "new scientific studies" in the church's response to "rising social problems" was inexcusable.[4] Though Judge Dewey's liberalism was probably not as hostile as that of his namesake, philosopher-pragmatist John Dewey (whom Du Bois would eventually work with during his affiliation with the NAACP and *Crisis*), Evarts Scudder, minister at First Congregational Church while Du Bois, his mother, and Dewey attended, severely denounced him from the pulpit. Although the effect of Judge Dewey's liberalism and scholarly ideas upon Du Bois is purely speculative, Du Bois's familiarity with Dewey is without question.

All of these observations concerning Du Bois's first periodical writings would be repeated throughout his entire periodical career, although Du Bois's disaffection for the First Congregational Church of Great Barrington would extend to all dogma associated with African American churches and religious organizations. Over his lifetime, Du Bois's local periodical writing would expand into a national periodical writing career that would establish his reputation as the foremost African American leader in America; the local Great Barrington African American audience would become a national African American audience and, finally, Du Bois's scholastic and educational acumen would be unrivaled by any African American in the United States.

NOTES

1. Du Bois, "To Mr. Van Lennep," 29 September 1892, *The Correspondence of W. E. B. Du Bois: Volume I (Selections, 1877–1934)*, ed. and comp. Herbert Aptheker, vol. 1 (Amherst: University of Massachusetts Press, 1973), 18.

2. There is no record of Du Bois's remarks from Germany appearing in either the *Berkshire Courier* or Fortune's *New York Globe*.

3. I. Garland Penn, *The Afro-American Press and Its Editors* (New York: Arno Press, 1969), 481–83.

4. Howard Conn, *The First Congregational Church of Great Barrington* (Great Barrington, Mass.: Berkshire Courier, 1943), 38.

~ **1** ~

Great Barrington Notes: April 14, 1883

It is very pleasant here now and the merchants are fitting up their stores and getting in goods for the Spring trade. A number of families from the city have taken up their residence for the summer. The ladies of the AME Zion Sewing Society gave their monthly supper at the house of Mr. Jason Cooley. The table was well filled and a very enjoyable time was had. The Society will meet next week with Mrs. E. Lee. Misses Anna and Louise Piper of Sheffield have just returned from a four weeks visit to friends in Hartford. The Citizens of the town are forming a Law and Order Society to enforce the laws against liquor selling which have been sadly neglected for the past year or two. It would be a good plan if some of the colored men should join it. By the way I did not notice many colored men at the town meeting last month; it seems that they do not take as much interest in politics as is necessary for the protection of their rights. Mr. Wm. Chin is to be congratulated on the birth of a daughter. Mr. and Mrs. Joseph Smith of Norfolk, Conn., spent the Sabbath in town. I. N. Burghart of Albany, N.Y. was in town for a few days last week. There have been but few removals this Spring on account of the scarcity of houses.

⁓ 2 ⁓

Great Barrington Notes: May 5, 1883

The ladies of the AME Zion Society will hold their monthly supper at the residence of Mrs. L. Gardner on Wednesday. All are invited to attend. There was a large attendance at the Bible Reading last Sunday evening, which was held at Mr. J. Cooley's house. A party came down from Lee, Sunday afternoon, and are expected again on Wednesday. The family of Mr. Chinn leave town today for Cleveland, Ohio, including his sister, Mrs. Peterson who has been visiting them for some time past. Mr. G. F. Jackson will leave the Moore House to go to the Brunswick House at Troy, N.Y. And Mr. C. F. Jackson will succeed him in the culinary department. We are sorry to lose so many colored people from our town but they have "_____ wishes of all." At last week's Sewing Society it was proposed by some to form a literary society but there was not much interest manifested. It would be the best thing that could be done for the colored people if such a society could be formed here.

⁓ 3 ⁓

Great Barrington Notes: September 8, 1883

Your correspondent having been away on vacation no items have appeared for some time. During my trip I visited Providence, New Bedford, and Albany, and was pleased to see the industry and wealth of many of our race. But one thing that struck me very forcibly was the absence of literary societies, none of which did I meet in any of the cities. It seems to me as if this of all things ought not to be neglected.

The weather is growing cold here now and it seems as if winter is near at hand. A singing school has been organized here with Mrs. J. McKinsly as leader. The class meets next Thursday at Mr. Mason's.

On Thursday, Aug. 23, the A.M.E. Zion sewing circle took a ride to Lake Buel. On account of its storming in the early part of the evening a great many who intended, did not go, but those who did reported a very enjoyable time.

Mrs. F. Portland of New York is the guest of Mr. Wm. Crosley. Mr. Egbert Lee took his departure for Springfield last week to attend the Masonic lodge of which he is a member.

There is to be a debate soon before the sewing society upon the question "Should Indians be educated at Hampton?" Messrs. Cooley and Du Bois, affirmative, Messrs. Mason and Crosley, negative. A lively time is expected.

Mr. Wm. Chinn departs Saturday next for Washington, his former home. Your correspondent was pleasantly surprised upon his return, at having his subscription list for The Globe doubled through the exertions of Mr. Crosley, who kindly consented to distribute them during his absence and to whom he wishes to return thanks.

Mrs. A. Thompson and daughter of Amherst, Mass., and Mrs. L. Brown of Providence, RI., arrived today as guests of Mrs. L. Sumea. The Rev. James Anderson also of Providence is expected here to preach sometime this month. Mr. John Williams, who has been quite sick, has recovered.

~ **4** ~

Great Barrington Briefs: September 29, 1883

The political contest is near at hand, and the colored men of the town should prepare themselves accordingly. They should acquaint themselves with the political Status and attitude of the candidates toward them, particularly their representatives. The choice of Governor should also demand a good share of their attention. Those who voted for Gen. Butler last year "just to see what he would do," have found it a pretty costly experiment. They will see that while preaching economy and refusing the necessary appropriations to charitable institutions, he has spent an immense sum of money on needless investigations, such as Tewksbury and the like. The colored men may well ask themselves how they have been benefitted by his administration, although he professes to be their friend.

A political office should not be the goal of one's ambitions, but still if anyone wishes an office and is worthy of it, it should not be denied him on account of his color. We had an example of this here a short time ago, when a colored man, along with a number of white men, applied for the position of night watchman. After an examination the applicants melted down to one white man, a strong Democrat, and the colored man, a Republican. A committee, composed wholly of Republicans was chosen to decide between the two candidates, and they selected the white man.

The colored men of Great Barrington hold the balance of power, and have decided the election of many officers for a number of years. If they will only act in concert they may become a power not to be despised. It would be a good plan if they should meet and decide which way would be most advantageous for them to cast their votes.

The debate which I spoke of in my last letter took place last Wednesday evening at the house of Mr. William Crosley. It was contested warmly on both sides and strong arguments were brought up. It was finally decided in favor of the affirmative. After the debate the ladies of Zion Church held their monthly supper.

Mr. Wm. Chinn has returned from Washington. The First Congregational Church, which, was dedicated here last Friday, is the handsomest church in the county, and compares with any in the State. The organ, which was given by Mr. Timothy Hopkins of San Francisco, is one of the most complete in the world.

Miss Francis Newport has returned from Pittsfield, where she has been during the Summer. Miss Hattie Sumea returned to Providence last Tuesday. Mr. R. Hines and wife of Norfolk, Conn., were visiting friends in town last week. Mr. William Adams of Hartford, Conn., stopped here a short time and departed for Petersburg, Va. last Thursday. Messrs. Cooley and Mason will have an eating house at the Agricultural Fair, which is held here the 26th, 27th, and 28th inst.

∽ 5 ∽

Berkshire Hills: May 17, 1884

Miss Delphine Crosley recently entertained the members of the Mite Society with a supper and general good time, the occasion being her fourth birthday. Among her guests were Miss Julia Williams, and the Misses Lepyon, all of Canaan, Ct. Mr. Egbert Lee returned last week from an extended trip South. The youngest son of Mr. William Chinn is quite sick with a fever. Miss Francis Newport returned from Pittsburg, the 2nd inst.

The ladies of Westfield recently gave a leap year ball to their gentlemen friends of Lee, to the music of Oliver's orchestra. A few weeks ago there was a pleasant gathering at the residence of Mr. Jason Cooley, in honor of his guest, Miss Nehbie Jackson of Lee. The time was pleasantly divided between games, dancing and supper, and the participants in the feast retired about 2 a.m.

The Bible readings held every Sunday night are very interesting and have a large attendance, which however it is hoped may still increase. The reading will be held next Sunday at the residence of Mr. Wm. Crosley. Mr. J. Q. Williams is visiting in Stockbridge.

Those intending to replenish their libraries are advised to consult *The Globe* correspondent, before so doing.

↭ 6 ↭

Great Barrington Items: October 18, 1884

A party of nine from this place spent the evening very pleasantly with Mr. H. Jackson of Lee on the 9th inst. The trustees of the A.M.E. Zion Church have succeeded in making an advantageous exchange of land for the site of the church with Dr. Samuel Camp. The piece has a fine situation on Elm Street, in the heart of the town. Quarterly conference will be held here on the first Sunday in November, Rev. Mr. J. F. Floyd of Waterbury, Conn., presiding.

Mrs. M. Newport returned recently from a visit to Amherst. Singing schools are now held at Mrs. McKinley's on Thursday evenings. All are invited to join and have a good time.

In the political parade held here recently the colored voters marched with the white, and were neither tucked in the rear nor parcelled off by themselves.

There was a colored ball held in Sanford's Hall, under the management of Gilbert Don and C. F. Jackson, on the second night of the Agricultural Fair. It was a complete success, financially and otherwise. Mr. James T. Burghardt, of Amherst, paid us a visit a short time ago.

PART II

WRITINGS APPEARING IN VARIOUS PROGRESSIVE, LIBERAL, COLLEGE, RELIGIOUS, AND NEGRO PERIODICALS, 1897–1910

INTRODUCTION

Reform Writing and Periodical-based Leadership within the American Negro Academy and Progressive, Liberal, College, Religious, and Negro Periodicals (1897–1910)

A fter completing the most impressive educational career of any nineteenth-century African American—culminating in 1895 in becoming the first African American Ph.D. recipient at Harvard University—Du Bois became a professor at Wilberforce University in Ohio. It was there he first met Reverend Alexander Crummell (1819–1898), a man whose credentials as an African American theologian, pastor, scholar, author, lecturer, essayist, and organizer were rivaled only by Frederick Douglass.[1] Wilson Jeremiah Moses explains Crummell's unique qualifications: "He was a disconcerting anomaly, a black man of letters before the Civil War, knowledgeable in the classics at a time when the average black American was an illiterate slave."[2] Although Du Bois was certainly aware of Crummell's distinction as a scholar, he was also equally alert to his intriguing African American reform ideals; soon after making his acquaintance, Du Bois would ally himself with Crummell's American Negro Academy. While Crummell's pessimistic assessment that African American communities had "suffered in the whole domain of morals" differed little from the general consensus of most nineteenth-century African American social and church leaders, Du Bois believed Crummell's scholarly approach for combating these shortcomings—including his insistence upon a scholarly utilitarian periodical—offered the only real solution.[3]

Bearing these aims in mind, Crummell founded the American Negro Academy in 1897 with the support of notable African Americans such as Paul Laurence Dunbar, Francis J. Grimke, Dr. W.S. Scarborough, Dr. Kelly Miller, William Ferris, and John Cromwell, as well as Dr. W. E. B. Du Bois. By all historical accounts, Crummell's American Negro Academy was the first learned society of its kind. The American Negro Academy had its inaugural meeting on March 5 at the Lincoln Memorial Church in the District of Columbia. Crummell was specific about the terms of membership in the academy; the American Negro Academy was open only to college graduates or professors, authors, artists, and distinguished writers.

However, some exceptions were permitted in order to include literate ministers who shared Crummell's ideals and possessed strong affiliations with religious organizations.[4] To his expressed chagrin, the elderly Crummell (who died the following year) was elected as the organization's first president; Du Bois was appointed its first vice-president, later assuming the presidency after Crummell's death in 1898, a position he held until 1903. Before expiring, Crummell spelled out the aims that he hoped the organization would accomplish in his inaugural address, "Civilization, The Primal Need of the Race." The address would not only lay the foundation for the new organization, but it would also leave a lasting and discernible impression upon Du Bois's periodical career. Crummell proclaimed:

> Who are to be the agents to lift up this people of ours to the grand plane of civilization? Who are to bring them up to the height of noble thought, grand civility, a chaste and elevating culture, refinement and the impulses of irrepressible progress? It is to be done by the scholars and thinkers . . . But every man in a race cannot be a philosopher: nay, but few men in any land, in any age can grasp ideal truth. Scientific ideas however must be apprehended else there can be no progress, no elevation. Just here arises the need of the trained and scholarly men of a race to employ their knowledge and culture and teaching and to guide both the opinions and habits of the crude masses . . . [W]e can spread abroad and widely disseminate that culture and enlightenment which shall permeate and leaven the entire social and domestic life of our people and so give that civilization which is the nearest ally of religion.[5]

Crummell's address argued that educated African Americans and scholars must lead reform efforts amidst their uneducated African American community members by supplementing—perhaps even supplanting—traditional African American religious practices; this was what all advanced civilizations required, he believed. The corollary to Crummell's argument, then, meant that regular communication to uneducated African American community members was imperative. Crummell's concern about this ignorance was so earnest that it straightaway led him to form the American Negro Academy's *Occasional Papers* during the afternoon session of the inaugural meeting. Because educated African Americans and literate clergymen were without a suitable print medium of expression in either their community or the white one, Crummell's American Negro Academy tried to fashion an alternative print mode—minus the bulky scholastic documentation—that would convincingly adhere to their respective academic backgrounds while simultaneously facilitating a forum for moral and ethical leadership in the African American community.

Although Crummell's plan for the academy's *Occasional Papers* modeled itself after other cultured societies while simultaneously attempting to carry out the reform aims that Du Bois's "The Conservation of Races" promoted, it was clear that the question of how to infuse scholarly knowledge into a quasi-religious reform rhetoric was never entirely resolved.[6] The quandary became particularly tricky to unravel after Crummell's unexpected death occurred the following year on September 10, 1898. However, with Du Bois's appointment as American Negro Academy president in December 1898, as well as his preceding achievement in August 1897 of becoming, along with Frederick Douglass and Booker T. Washington, one of the few late-nineteenth-century African Americans to have his nonfictional prose appear in a major white periodical, Du Bois— at least for himself—reconciled this difficulty. Du Bois utilized his academic credentials and reform ideals proposed in "The Conservation of Races" and cultivated within the American Negro Academy to secure publishing opportunities in major periodicals to address reform concerns within the African American community.

Instead of concealing his scholarly credentials, as he was forced to do in the academy's *Occasional Papers*—Crummel made a provision in the academy's first constitution, which disallowed members from using their degree titles in publications—Du Bois was able to rely heavily upon his academic credentials to secure publishing opportunities in major white periodicals. Ingeniously, Du Bois decided to diffuse the whole range of his interests as a scholar, activist, writer, and reformer by disseminating reform articles through newspaper and magazine periodicals between 1898 and 1910. Beginning in 1920, Du Bois intermittently used "As the Crow Flies" as his signature editorial title for editorials appearing in *Crisis*, *The Brownies' Book*, the *Amsterdam News*, and the *Chicago Globe*. Although he would begin using it in 1920, the crow remarkably demon-·strates Du Bois's authorship between 1898 and 1910 in two significant ways. The crow is an unnested figure that reflects Du Bois's restlessness about an institutional location that would support his ambitions as a scholar and an author; Du Bois remained with the NAACP for 24 years as a *Crisis* editor, and this tenure represented his longest stint at any one institution during his life span of 95 years. Secondly, the crow's coloration represents the prophetic leadership role that he would occupy via periodical authorship when interpreting African American social maladies to readers and prescribing reform measures for African American communities throughout the nation. It should also be pointed out that all of his editorial columns appearing in the *Horizon*, which he founded in 1907 and edited until 1910, were headed with the caption "The Over-Look."

It was in *The Brownies' Book*—a children's periodical Du Bois founded and edited briefly while still editing *Crisis*—that Du Bois first introduced "As the Crow Flies" to readers. He described the crow as "black and o so beautiful, shining with dark blues and purples with little hints of gold in his mighty wings. He flies far above the Earth, looking downward with his sharp eyes. What a lot of things he must see and hear and if he could only talk—and lo! The Brownies' Book has made him talk for you."[7] In the July 1920 issue, Du Bois wrote, "I suppose you'd like to be a Crow and fly over the world and see just everything as I,—and maybe I wouldn't like to be a dear Brownie!—but since Crows must be Crows and Folks must be folks, I'll try to tell you about some things I've seen on my flight over the seas!"[8] Two years later he wrote, "But on and up I fly and fly to find the bits of news for my sweet babies. . . ."[9] Then in the October column of "As the Crow Flies," Du Bois personified the figure by saying, "I, the crow, am Eyesight. I am eyes. I see!"[10] In June 1921 Du Bois offered a rather telling description of the crow: "Terrible is sunshine out of the endless steel blue sky. I am afraid of sunshine for it glitters hard and sends its sharp shafts against my bright eyes. If all were sunshine and there were no rain I could not fly and caw. I should droop and weep."[11] Also in September 1921, Du Bois wrote, "Though I fly high, high up in the air, I, the Crow, can see the turmoil of human-folks."[12] Finally, in his first editorial column written for the *Chicago Globe* on April 1, 1950, he wrote, "Since this particular Crow began his wandering and muttering in 1920 he has found many and varied nests and answering winds and hurricanes. His cries have been interspersed with silences and shoutings and even with threats; still my restless meandering has continued."[13]

While Du Bois's own descriptions of the crow's travels through "many and varied nests" easily explain his quixotic search for a centralized place for his unique and innovative concerns as an author, the crow's prophetic symbolism in relation to the periodical is far more enigmatic. As an embodiment of Du Bois himself, the black crow bore a conspicuous resemblance to that of an Old Testament seer or prophet with only one distinction: a biblical seer or prophet possessed a providential mandate for his oracles and writings, whereas Du Bois's authority—manifested most profoundly in periodical writing—proceeded from his standing as an African American scholar. Du Bois addressed African American social maladies using truths derived from sociological investigations in the African American community, which heretofore had never been attempted by an African American. Du Bois had the unique advantage of being the most qualified African American to pursue African American social questions from an academic standpoint, and among qualified sociologists, Du Bois was among the few whose work was wholly devoted to African American social problems for reform purposes. The black crow also embodies the periodical's unique ability to tersely disperse Du Bois's enormous academic breadth for reform purposes. By situating the "black" crow "high above," "looking downward with sharp eyes" and dropping "bits of news" to the ordinary "folks," Du Bois was able to metaphorically describe his uniqueness as an African American scholar relaying pertinent historical and contemporary knowledge for the purposes of reforming African Americans. Although the imagery surrounding the crow remains cryptic in terms of periodical writing, it is certain that Du Bois had enough fortuitous insight to know that this figure would personify an African American with unparalleled possibilities as a periodical author that few could ignore, including major white editors.

To be sure, Du Bois's reform writings did not always give explicit instructions to African American audiences about proper behavior; Du Bois's writings had to take an entirely different and far less controversial shape when appearing in progressive, liberal, and religious white periodicals. His purpose in writing for these periodicals was to inform white Americans about those historical and contemporary social problems in the African American community that made his reform ideas necessary. Du Bois's commingling of scholarly knowledge and reform commentary relieved white periodical editors—secular and religious—from endorsing racial protest writings that would eventually make Du Bois infamous at *Crisis*. While these writings clearly echoed his work as a sociologist through their tone, they also played a crucial role in facilitating his appearances in white periodicals. Du Bois published at least 50 reform writings between 1897 and 1910 within white periodicals categorically described as ethical cultural journals, progressive general weeklies and monthlies, college periodicals, literary journals, magazine supplements, daily newspapers, social work magazines, and varying religious periodicals.[14] Some of these included *Independent Weekly*, (Chicago) *Dial*, (New York) *World's Work*, (New York) *Charities, Booklover's Magazine, New York Times Magazine Supplement, Conservator, International Journal of Ethics*, (Chicago) *World Today, Annals of the American Academy of Political and Social Science*, (New York) *Survey, New York Evening Post, Church Review*, (New York) *Outlook*, (Boston) *New World, Missionary Review of the World, Advance, Boston Transcript, Christian Register*, and *Bibliotheca Sacra*. In fact, Du Bois's most renowned work, and perhaps the most recognizable work in the African American literary canon, *The Souls of Black Folk* (1903), provides the most discernible example of Du Bois's reliance upon sympathetic white periodical editors for African American reform purposes. Nine of the fourteen essays contained within *The Souls of Black Folk* first appeared in progressive and religious white periodicals.

During this same period, some of the African American periodicals Du Bois published in were *The Voice of the Negro*, mainly a medium of communication for the Niagara Movement; *Southern Workman*, a periodical sponsored by a Negro college, Hampton Institute; the *A.M.E. Church Review*, a nationally circulated church-sponsored periodical; the little-known *Scroll*; and Negro college newspapers like *Spelman Messenger* and *Talladega College Record*, which printed some of Du Bois's commencement addresses and other speeches. Until Du Bois founded *Crisis* in 1910, there was no African American periodical with an impressive enough circulation to satisfy his desire to reach a national audience. In many ways, the white American periodical was the only organization that would enable Du Bois to realize his ambitions to become an author without sacrificing his aspirations as a scholar or reformer between 1897 and 1910.

NOTES

1. Wilson Jeremiah Moses, *Alexander Crummell: A Study of Civilization and Discontent* (New York: Oxford University Press, 1995) is the definitive biography of Crummell's life. Other studies or compilations that provide additional information on either Crummell or the founding of the American Negro Academy are Alfred A. Moss, *The American Negro Academy* (Baton Rouge: Louisiana State University Press, 1981); Wilson Jeremiah Moses, *The Golden Age of Black Nationalism: 1850–1925* (New York: Oxford University Press, 1988); Wilson Jeremiah Moses, ed., *Destiny and Race: Selected Writings 1840–1898: Alexander Crummell* (Amherst: University of Massachusetts Press, 1992); and Gregory U. Rigsby, *Alexander Crummell: Pioneer in Nineteenth-Century Pan-African Thought* (New York: Greenwood Press, 1987).

2. Moses, *Alexander Crummell*, 5.

3. Alexander Crummell, *Civilization and Black Progress: Selected Writings of Alexander Crummell on the South*, ed. J.R. Oldfield (Charlottesville: University of Virginia Press, 1995), 130.

4. Moss, *The American Negro Academy*, 24–29.

5. Moses, *Destiny and Race*, 287.

6. Moss, *The American Negro Academy*, 24. Du Bois's "The Conservation of Races" was more concerned with the role that the academy could play in cultivating morality and ethics in the African American community. Moss also suggests, "It was the most important statement on the place and role of the academy to emerge from this meeting."

7. Du Bois, "As the Crow Flies," *Writings in Periodicals Edited by W. E. B. DuBois: Selections from the Brownies' Book*, ed. and comp. Herbert Aptheker (White Plains, NY: Kraus-Thomson, 1980) 5. All "As the Crow Flies" citations from *The Brownies' Book* will be taken from Aptheker's collection.

8. Du Bois, "As the Crow Flies," 58.

9. Du Bois, "As the Crow Flies," 55.

10. Du Bois, "As the Crow Flies," 69.

11. Du Bois, "As the Crow Flies," 117.

12. Du Bois, "As the Crow Flies," 131.

13. Du Bois, "As the Crow Flies," *Newspaper Columns by W. E. B. Du Bois (1883–1944)*, ed. and comp. Herbert Aptheker, vol. 2 (White Plains, NY: Kraus-Thomson, 1986), 768.

14. Du Bois's writings also appeared in federal labor bulletins and academic journals. This anthology does not include these writings because the writings

appearing in these periodicals contained substantial academic documentation, which was consistent with Du Bois's explicit sociological investigations. The generic descriptions for these periodicals are taken from Frank Luther Mott's *A History of American Magazines 1886–1905*, vols. 1–5 (Cambridge: Harvard University Press, 1957).

∼ 7 ∼

A Program of Social Reform

The evils of our present social organization may roughly be classified under three heads: (a) Lack of Work, (b) Poverty, (c) Crime. In an ideal State we would expect that (a) most people would be employed according to their ability as developed by the best training; (b) that the wants of each person would be so far satisfied as to promote normal physical, mental and moral development, and (c) that crime should be at a minimum. What, then, are the chief causes of the failure of our present social organization to approximate these ideals? Lack of work on any considerable scale does not mean that there is no work to be done—that is unthinkable—but merely that efforts have been misdirected and time is required to redirect them. This misdirection may arise through bad training of workmen as is the case with the Southern freedmen; or because the best ability was not selected for certain sorts of work, as is the case often in business failures; or by pure accident, as in the case of inventions that substitute machines for laborers. Poverty is the inadequate satisfaction of the essential wants of human beings. When in a complex society like ours a thousand men unite their efforts, with varying efficiency, for varying periods, to produce a house, no mathematical calculation can determine what part of the price paid for that house shall go to each of these men. In the long run, in every community, the common standard of justice finally determines the share of the finished products which each worker shall receive. If the standard of justice is low, if selfishness and greed prevail, then the powerful, sharp and bold will often overreach the weak, dull and timid. Only where the common weal is the high ideal of the community will the interests of all find proper protection. Crime is an indication of social disorder, which may arise from misfortune, disease, carelessness, selfishness or vice, or from a combination of these causes. Ignorance of the cause is the greatest cause. For these evils this program of social reform offers these remedies: (a) Better training of workers in home and school, and a more impartial selection of ability, regardless of color, race or condition. (b) The raising of the present popular ideal from mere money-getting to that of common property—common weal. (c) Increased systematic knowledge of society. Briefly stated this means better training, broader aims, greater knowledge. Its keynote is individual regeneration aided by ability and knowledge. It is social opportunism which strives toward social science as its goal.

~ **8** ~

Strivings of the Negro People

Between me and the other world there is ever an unasked question: unasked by some through feelings of delicacy; by others through the difficulty of rightly framing it. All, nevertheless, flutter round it. They approach me in a half-hesitant sort of way, eye me curiously or compassionately, and then, instead of saying directly, how does it feel to be a problem? they say, I know an excellent colored man in my town or, I fought at Mechanicsville; or, Do not these Southern outrages make your blood boil? At these I smile, or am interested, or reduce the boiling to a simmer, as the occasion may require. To the real question, how does it feel to be a problem? I answer seldom a word.

And yet, being a problem is a strange experience,—peculiar even for one who has never been anything else, save perhaps in babyhood and in Europe. It is in the early days of rollicking boyhood that the revelation first bursts upon one, all in a day, as it were. I remember well when the shadow swept across me. I was a little thing, away up in the hills of New England, where the dark Housatonic winds between Hoosac and Taghanic to the sea. In a wee wooden schoolhouse, something put it into the boys' and girls' heads to buy gorgeous visiting cards—ten cents a package—and exchange. The exchange was merry, till one girl, a tall newcomer, refused my card,—refused it peremptorily, with a glance. Then it dawned upon me with a certain suddenness that I was different from the others; or like, mayhap, in heart and life and longing, but shut out from their world by a vast veil. I had thereafter no desire to tear down that veil, to creep through; I held all beyond it in common contempt, and lived above it in a region of blue sky and great wandering shadows. That sky was bluest when I could beat my mates at examination-time, or beat them at a foot-race, or even beat their stringy heads. Alas, with the years all this fine contempt began to fade; for the world I longed for, and all its dazzling opportunities, were theirs, not mine. But they should not keep these prizes, I said; some, all, I would wrest from them. Just how I would do it I could never decide: by reading law, by healing the sick, by telling the wonderful tales that swam in my head,—some way. 'With other black boys the strife was not so fiercely sunny: their youth shrunk into tasteless sycophancy, or into silent hatred of the pale world about them and mocking distrust of everything white; or wasted it self in a bitter cry, Why did God make me an outcast and a stranger in mine own house? The "shades of the prison-house" closed round about us all: walls strait and stubborn to the whitest, but relentlessly narrow, tall, and unscalable, to sons of night who must plod darkly on in resignation, or beat unavailing palms against the stone, or steadily, half hopelessly watch the streak of blue above.

After the Egyptian and Indian, the Greek and Roman, the Teuton and Mongolian, the Negro is a sort of seventh son, born with a veil, and gifted with second-sight in this American world,—a world which yields him no self-consciousness, but only lets him see him self through the revelation of the other world. It is a peculiar sensation, this double-consciousness, this sense of always looking at one's self, through the eyes of others, of measuring one's soul by the tape of a world that looks on in amused contempt and pity. One ever feels his two-ness,—an American, a Negro; two souls, two thoughts, two unreconciled strivings; two warring ideals in—one dark body, whose dogged strength alone keeps it from being torn asunder.

The history of the American Negro is the history of this strife,—this longing to attain self-conscious manhood, to merge his double self into a better and truer self. In this merging he wishes neither of the older selves to be lost. He does not wish to Africanize America, for America has too much to teach the world and Africa; he does not wish to bleach his Negro blood in a flood of white Americanism, for he believes—foolishly, perhaps, but fervently—that Negro blood has yet a message for the world. He simply wishes to make it possible for a man to be both a Negro and an American without being cursed and spit upon by his fellows, without losing the opportunity of self-development.

This is the end of his striving: to be a co-worker in the kingdom of culture, to escape both death and isolation, and to husband and use his best powers. These powers, of body and of mind, have in the past been so wasted and dispersed as to lose all effectiveness, and to seem like absence of all power, like weakness. The double-aimed struggle of the black artisan, on the one hand to escape white contempt for a nation of mere hewers of wood and drawers of water, and on the other hand to plough and nail and dig for a poverty-stricken horde, could only result in making him a poor craftsman, for he had but half a heart in either cause. By the poverty and ignorance of his people the Negro lawyer or doctor was pushed toward quackery and demagogism, and by the criticism of the other world toward an elaborate preparation that overfitted him for his lowly tasks. The would-be black savant was confronted by the paradox that the knowledge his people needed was a twice-told tale to his white neighbors, while the knowledge which would teach the white world was Greek to his own flesh and blood. The innate love of harmony and beauty that set the ruder souls of his people a-dancing, a-singing, and a-laughing raised but seclusion and doubt in the soul of the black artist; for the beauty revealed to him was the soul-beauty of a race which his larger audience despised, and he could not articulate the message of another people.

This waste of double aims, this seeking to satisfy two unreconciled ideals, has wrought sad havoc with the courage and faith and deeds of eight thousand people, has sent them often wooing false gods and invoking false means of salvation, and has even at times seemed destined to make them ashamed of them selves. In the days of bondage they thought to see in one divine event the end of all doubt and disappointment; eighteenth-century Rousseauism never worshiped freedom with half the unquestioning faith that the American Negro did for two centuries. To him slavery was, indeed, the sum of all villainies, the cause of all sorrow, the root of all prejudice; emancipation was the key to a promised land of sweeter beauty than ever stretched before the eyes of wearied Israelites. In his songs and exhortations swelled one refrain, liberty; in his tears and curses the god he implored had freedom in his right hand. At last it came,—suddenly, fearfully, like a dream. With one wild carnival of blood and passion came the message in his own plaintive cadences:—

> Shout, O children!
> Shout, you free!
> The Lord has bought your liberty!

Years have passed away, ten, twenty, thirty. Thirty years of national life, thirty years of renewal and development, and yet the swarthy ghost of Banquo sits in its old place at the national feast. In vain does the nation cry to its vastest problem,—

> Take any shape but that, and my firm nerves Shall never tremble!

The freedman has not yet found in freedom in his promised land. Whatever of lesser good may have come in these years of change, the shadow of a deep disappointment rests upon the Negro people,—a disappointment all the more bitter because the unattained ideal was unbounded save by the simple ignorance of a lowly folk.

The first decade was merely a prolongation of the vain search for freedom, the boon that seemed ever barely to elude their grasp,—like a tantalizing will-o'-the-wisp, maddening and misleading the headless host. The holocaust of war, the terrors of the Ku Klux Klan, the lies of carpet-baggers, the disorganization of industry, and the contradictory advice of friends and foes left the bewildered serf with no new watchword beyond the old cry for freedom. As the decade closed, however, he began to grasp a new idea. The ideal of liberty demanded for its attainment powerful means, and these the Fifteenth Amendment gave him. The ballot, which before he had looked upon as a visible sign of freedom, he now regarded as the chief means of gaining and perfecting the liberty with which war had partially endowed him. And why not? Had not votes made war and emancipated millions? Had not votes enfranchised the freedmen? Was anything impossible to a power that had done all this? A million black then started with renewed zeal to vote themselves into the kingdom. The decade fled away,—a decade containing, to the freedman's mind, nothing but suppressed votes, stuffed ballot-boxes, and election outrages that nullified his vaunted right of suffrage. And yet that decade from 1875 to 1885 held another powerful movement, the rise of another ideal to guide the unguided, another pillar of fire by night after a clouded day. It was the ideal of "book-learning;" the curiosity, born of compulsory ignorance, to know and test the power of the cabalistic letters of the white man, the longing to know. Mission and night schools began in the smoke of battle, ran the gauntlet of reconstruction, and at last developed into permanent foundations. Here at last seemed to have been discovered the mountain path to Canaan; longer than the highway of emancipation and law, steep and rugged, but straight, leading to heights high enough to over look life.

Up the new path the advance guard toiled, slowly, heavily, doggedly; only those who have watched and guided the faltering feet, the misty minds, the dull understandings, of the dark pupils of these schools know how faithfully, how piteously, this people strove to learn. It was weary work. The cold statistician wrote down the inches of progress here and there, noted also where here and there a foot had slipped or some one had fallen. To the tired climbers, the horizon was ever dark, the mists were often cold, the Canaan was always dim and far away. If, however, the vistas disclosed as yet no goal, no resting-place, little but flattery and criticism, the journey at least gave leisure for reflection and self-examination; it changed the child of emancipation to the youth with dawning self-consciousness, self-realization, self-respect. In those sombre forests of his striving his own soul rose before him, and he saw himself,—darkly as through a veil; and yet he saw in himself some faint revelation of his power, of his mission. He began to have a dint feeling that, to attain his place in the world, he must be himself, and not another. For the first time he sought to analyze the burden he bore upon his back, that dead weight of social degradation partially masked behind a half-named Negro problem. He felt his poverty; without a cent, without a home, without land, tools, or savings, he had entered into competition with rich, landed, skilled neighbors. To be a poor man is hard, but to be a poor race in a land of dollars is the very bottom of hardships. He felt the weight of his ignorance,—not simply of letters, but of life, of business, of the humanities; the accumulated sloth and shirking and awkwardness of decades and centuries shackled his hands and feet. Nor was his burden all poverty and ignorance. The red stain of bastardy, which two centuries of systematic legal defilement of Negro women had stamped upon his race, meant not only the loss of ancient African chastity, but also the hereditary weight of a mass of filth from white whoremongers and adulterers, threatening almost the obliteration of the Negro home.

A people thus handicapped ought not be asked to race with the world, but—allowed to give all its time and thought to its own social problems. But alas! while sociologists gleefully count his bastards and his prostitutes, the very soul of the toiling, sweating black man is darkened by the shadow of a vast despair. Men call the shadow prejudice, and learnedly explain it as the natural defense of culture against barbarism, learning against ignorance, purity against crime, the "higher" against the "lower" races. To which the Negro cries Amen! and swears that to so much of this strange prejudice as is founded an just homage to civilization, culture, righteousness, and progress he humbly bows and meekly does obeisance. But before that nameless prejudice that leaps beyond all this he stands helpless, dismayed, and well-nigh speechless; before that personal disrespect and mockery, the ridicule and systematic humiliation, the distortion of fact and wanton license of fancy, the cynical ignoring of the better and boisterous welcoming of the worse, the all-pervading desire to inculcate disdain for everything black, from Toussaint to the devil,—before this there rises a sickening despair that would disarm and discourage any nation save that black host to whom "discouragement" is an unwritten word.

They still press on, they still nurse the dogged hope,—not a hope of nauseating patronage, not a hope of reception into charmed social circles of stock-jobbers, pork-packers, and earl-hunters, but the hope of a higher synthesis of civilization and humanity, a true progress, with which the chorus "Peace, good will to men,"

> May make one music as before,
> But faster.

Thus the second decade of the American Negro's freedom was a period of conflict, of inspiration and doubt, of faith and vain questionings, of *Sturm und Drang*. The ideals of physical freedom, of political power, of school training, as separate all-sufficient panaceas for social ills, became in the third decade dim and overcast. They were the vain dreams of credulous race childhood; not wrong, but incomplete and over-simple. The training of the schools we need today more than ever,—the training of deft hands, quick eyes and ears, and the broader, deeper, higher culture of gifted minds. The power of the ballot we need in sheer self-defense, and as a guarantee of good faith. We may misuse it, but we can scarce do worse in this respect than our whilom masters. Freedom, too, the long we still seek,—the freedom of life and limb, the freedom to work and think. Work, culture, and liberty,—all this we need, not singly, but together; for today these ideals among the Negro people are gradually coalescing, and finding a higher meaning in the unifying ideal of race,—the ideal of fostering the traits and talents of the Negro, not in opposition to, but in conformity with, the greater ideals of the American republic; in order that some day, on American soil, two world races may give each to each those characteristics which both so sadly lack. Already we come not altogether empty-handed: there is today no true American music but the sweet wild melodies of the Negro slave; the American fairy tales are Indian and African; we are the sole oasis of simple faith and reverence in a dusty desert of dollars and smartness. Will America be poorer if she replace her brutal, dyspeptic blundering with the light-hearted but determined Negro humility; or her coarse, cruel wit with loving, jovial good humor; or her Annie Rooney with Steal Away?

Merely a stern concrete test of the underlying principles of the great republic is the Negro problem, and the spiritual striving of the freedmen's sons is the travail of souls whose burden is almost beyond the measure of their strength but who bear it in the name of an historic race, in the name of this the land of their fathers' fathers, and in the name of human opportunity.

⌁ 9 ⌁

A Negro Schoolmaster in the New South

Ancient our suit is. Present it.
Who rights us, desolate?
Man's is the crime: we arraign him.
God's is the bar: we wait.
. . . .
Compassionate of soul! Fused from an iron race,
Elect of heaven and thine own heart, sustain the case.
Peace, conquering, warred with war within thy regal veins;
The bounding artery of mercy strong remains.
Be blest! For grateful tears of living and of dead
Shall melt and mist into a rainbow round thy head.
Crown of the Romanoffs on colder brows has shone;
But this, of all thy House, thou proudly wear'st alone.

—*Elizabeth Stuart Phelps*

Once upon a time I taught school in the hills of Tennessee, where the broad dark vale of the Mississippi begins to roll and crumple to greet the Alleghanies. I was a Fisk student then, and all Fisk men think that Tennessee—beyond the Veil—is theirs alone, and in vacation time they sally forth in lusty bands to meet the county school commissioners. Young and happy, I too went, and I shall not soon forget that summer, ten years ago.

First, there was a teachers' Institute at the county-seat; and there distinguished guests of the superintendent taught the teachers fractions and spelling and other mysteries,—white teachers in the morning, Negroes at night. A picnic now and then, and a supper, and the rough world was softened by laughter and song. I remember now—But I wander.

There came a day when all the teachers left the Institute, and began the hunt for schools. I learn from hearsay (for my mother was mortally afraid of fire arms) that the hunting of ducks and bears and men is wonderfully interesting, but I am sure that the man who has never hunted a country school has something to learn of the pleasures of the chase. I see now the white, hot roads lazily rise and fall and wind before me under the burning July sun; I feel the deep weariness of heart and limb, as ten, eight, six miles stretch relentlessly ahead; I feel my heart sink heavily as I hear again and again, "Got a teacher? Yes." So I walked on and on,—horses were too expensive,—until I had wandered beyond railways, beyond stage lines, to a land of "varmints" and rattlesnakes, where the coming of a stranger was an event, and men lived and died in the shadow of one blue hill.

Sprinkled over hill and dale lay cabins and farmhouses, shut out from the world by the forests and the rolling hills toward the east. There I found at last a little school. Josie told me of it,—she was a thin, homely girl of twenty, with a dark brown face and thick, hard hair. I had crossed the stream at Watertown, and rested under the great willows; then I had gone to the little cabin in the lot where Josie was resting on her way to town. The gaunt farmer made me welcome, and Josie, hearing my errand, told me anxiously that they wanted a school over the hill; that but once since the war had a teacher been there; that she herself longed to learn,—and thus she ran on, talking fast and loud, with much earnestness and energy.

Next morning I crossed the tall round lull, lingered to look at the blue and yellow mountains stretching toward the Carolinas; then I plunged into the wood, and came out at Josie's home. It was a dull frame cottage with four rooms, perched just below the brow of the hill, amid peach trees. The father was a quiet, simple soul, calmly ignorant, with no touch of vulgarity. The mother was different,—strong, bustling, and energetic, with a quick, restless tongue, and an ambition to live "like folks." There was a crowd of children. Two boys had gone away. There remained two growing girls; a shy midget of eight; John, tall, awkward, and eighteen; Jim, younger, quicker, and better looking; and two babies of indefinite age. Then there was Josie herself. She seemed to be the centre of the family: always busy at service or at home, or berry-picking; a little nervous and inclined to scold, like her mother, yet faithful, too, like her father. She had about her a certain fineness, the shadow of an unconscious moral heroism that would willingly give all of life to make life broader, deeper, and fuller for her and hers. I saw much of this family afterward, and grew to love them for their honest efforts to be decent and comfortable, and for their knowledge of their own ignorance. There was with them no affectation. The mother would scold the father for being so "easy;" Josie would roundly rate the boys for carelessness; and all knew that it was a hard thing to dig a living out of a rocky side hill.

I secured the school. I remember the day I rode horseback out to the commissioner's house, with a pleasant young white fellow, who wanted the white school. The road ran down the bed of a stream; the sun laughed and the water jingled, and we rode on. "Come in," said the commissioner,— "come in. Have a seat. Yes, that certificate will do. Stay to dinner. What do you want a month?" Oh, thought I, this is lucky; but even then fell the awful shadow of the Veil, for they ate first, then I—alone.

The schoolhouse was a log hut, where Colonel Wheeler used to shelter his corn. It sat in a lot behind a rail fence and thorn bushes, near the sweetest of springs. There was an entrance where a door once was, and within, a massive rickety fireplace; great clunks between tile logs served as windows. Furniture was scarce. A pale blackboard crouched in the corner. My desk was made of three boards, reinforced at critical points, and my chair, borrowed from the landlady, had to be returned every night. Seats for the children,—these puzzled me much. I was haunted by a New England vision of neat little desks and chairs, but, alas, the reality was rough plank benches without backs, and at times without legs. They had the one virtue of making naps dangerous,—possibly fatal, for the floor was not to be trusted.

It was a hot morning late in July when the school opened. I trembled when I heard the patter of little feet down the dusty road, and saw the growing row of dark solemn faces and bright eager eyes facing me. First came Josie and her brothers and sisters. The longing to know, to be a student in the great school at Nashville, hovered like a star above this child woman amid her work and worry, and she studied doggedly. There were the Dowells from their farm over toward Alexandria: Fanny, with her smooth black face and wondering eyes; Martha, brown and dull; the pretty girl wife of a brother, and the younger brood. There were the Burkes, two brown and yellow lads, and a tiny haughty-eyed girl. Fat Reuben's little chubby girl came, with golden face and old gold hair, faithful and solemn. 'Thenie was on hand early,—a jolly, ugly, good-hearted girl, who slyly dipped snuff and looked after her little bow-legged brother. When her mother could spare her, 'Tildy came,—a midnight beauty, with starry eyes and tapering limbs, and her brother, correspondingly homely. And then the big boys: the hulking Lawrences, the lazy Neills, unfathered sons of mother and daughter; Hickman, with a stoop in his shoulders; and the rest.

There they sat, nearly thirty of them, on the rough benches, their faces shading from a pale cream to a deep brown, the little feet bare and swinging, the eyes full of expectation, with here and there a twinkle of mischief, and the hands grasping Webster's blue-back spelling-book. I loved my school, and the fine faith the children had in the wisdom of their teacher was truly marvelous. We read and spelled together, wrote a little, picked flowers, sang, and listened to stories of the world beyond and were stowed away in one great pile the hill. At times the school would dwindle away and I would start out. I would visit Mun Eddings, who lived in two very dirty rooms, and ask why little Lugene, whose flaming face seemed ever ablaze with the dark red hair uncombed, was absent all last week, or why I missed so often the inimitable rags of Mack and Ed. Then the father, who worked retired Colonel Wheeler's farm on shares, would tell me how the crops needed the boys; and the thin, slovenly mother, whose face was pretty when washed, assured me that Lugene must mind the baby. "But we'll start them again next week." When the Lawrences stopped, I knew that the doubts of the old folks about book-learning had conquered again, and so, toiling up the hill, and getting as far into the cabin as possible, I put Cicero pro Archia Poeta into the simplest English with local applications, and usually convinced them—for a week or so.

On Friday nights I often went home with some of the children; sometimes to Doc Burke's farm. He was a great, loud, thin Black, ever working, and trying to buy the seventy-five acres of hill and dale where he lived; but people said that he would surely fail, and the "white folks would get it all." His wife was a magnificent Amazon, with saffron face and shining hair, uncorseted and barefooted and the children were strong and beautiful. They lived in a one-and-a-half-room cabin in the hollow of the farm, near the spring. The front room was full of great fat white beds, scrupulously neat; and there were bad chromos on the walls, and a tired centre-table. In the tiny back kitchen I was often invited to "take out and help" myself to fried chicken and wheat biscuit, "meat" and corn pone, string beans and berries. At first I used to be a little alarmed at the approach of bedtime in the one lone bedroom, but embarrassment was very deftly avoided. First, all the children nodded and slept, and were stowed away in one great pile of goose feathers; next, the mother and the father discreetly slipped away to the kitchen while I went to bed; then, blowing out the dim light, they retired in the dark. In the morning all were up and away before I thought of awaking. Across the road, where fat Reuben lived, they all went outdoors while the teacher retired, because they did not boast the luxury of a kitchen.

I liked to stay with the Dowells, for they had four rooms and plenty of good country fare. Uncle Bird had a small, rough farm, all woods and hills, miles from the big road; but he was full of tales,—he preached now and then—and with his children, berries, horses, and wheat he was happy and prosperous. Often, to keep the peace, I must go where life was less lovely; for instance, 'Tildy's mother was incorrigibly dirty, Reuben's larder was limited seriously, and herds of untamed bedbugs wandered over the Eddingses' beds. Best of all I loved to go to Josie's, and sit on the porch, eating peaches, while the mother bustled and talked: how Josie had bought the sewing-machine; how Josie worked at service in winter, but that four dollars a month was "mighty little" wages; how Josie longed to go away to school, but that it "looked like" they never could get far enough ahead to let her; how the crops failed and the well was yet unfinished; and, finally, how "mean" some of the white folks were.

For two summers I lived in this little world; it was dull and humdrum. The girls looked at the hill in wistful longing, and the boys fretted, and haunted Alexandria. Alexandria was "town,"—a straggling, lazy village of houses, churches, and shops, and an aristocracy of Toms, Dicks, and Captains. Cuddled on the hill to the north was the village of the colored folks, who lived in three or four room unpainted cottages, some neat and homelike, and some dirty. The dwellings were scattered rather aimlessly, but they centred about the twin temples of the hamlet, the Methodist and the Hard-Shell Baptist churches. These, in turn, leaned gingerly on a sad-colored schoolhouse. Hither my little world winded its crooked way on Sunday to meet other worlds, and gossip, and wonder, and make the weekly sacrifice with frenzied priest at the altar of the "old-time religion." Then the soft melody amid mighty cadences of Negro song fluttered and thundered.

I have called my tiny community a world, and so its isolation made it; and yet there was among us but a half-awakened common consciousness, sprung from common joy and grief, at burial, birth, or wedding; from a common hardship in poverty, poor land, and low wages; and, above all, from the sight of the Veil that hung between us and Opportunity. All this caused us to think some thoughts together; but these, when ripe for speech, were spoken in various languages. Those whose eyes thirty and more years before had seen "the glory of the coming of the Lord" saw in every present hindrance or help a dark fatalism bound to bring all things right in His own good time. The mass of those to whom slavery was a dim recollection of childhood found the world a puzzling thing it asked little of them, and they answered with little, and yet it ridiculed their offering. Such a paradox they could not understand, and therefore sank into listless indifference, or shiftlessness, or reckless bravado. There were, however, some such as Josie, Jim, and Ben,—they to whom War, Hell, and Slavery were but childhood tales, whose young appetites had been whetted to an edge by school and story and half-awakened thought. Ill could they be content, born without and beyond the World. And their weak wings beat against their barriers,—barriers of caste, of youth, of life; at last, in dangerous moments, against everything that opposed even a whim.

The ten years that follow youth, the years when first the realization comes that life is leading somewhere,—these were the years that passed after I left my little school. When they were past, I came by chance once more to the walls of Fisk University, to the halls of the chapel of melody. As I lingered there in the joy and pain of meeting old school friends, there swept over me a sudden longing to pass again beyond the blue hill, and to see the homes and the school of other days, and to learn how life had gone with my school-children; and I went.

Josie was dead, and the gray-haired mother said simply, "We've had a heap of trouble since you've been away." I had feared for Jim. With a cultured parentage and a social caste to uphold him, he might have made a venturesome merchant or a West Point cadet. But here he was, angry with life and reckless; and when Farmer Durham charged him with stealing wheat, the old man had to ride fast to escape the stones which the furious fool hurled after him. They told Jim to run away; but he would not run, and the constable came that afternoon. It grieved Josie, and great awkward John walked nine miles every day to see his little brother through the bars of Lebanon jail. At last the two came back together in the dark night. The mother cooked supper, and Josie emptied her purse, and the boys stole away. Josie grew thin and silent, yet worked the more. The hill became steep for the quiet old father, and with the boys away there was little to do in the valley. Josie helped them sell the old farm, and they moved nearer town. Brother Dennis, the carpenter, built a new house with six rooms; Josie toiled a year in Nashville, and brought back ninety dollars to furnish the house and change it to a home.

When the spring came, and the birds twittered, and the stream ran proud and full, little sister Lizzie, bold and thoughtless, flushed with the passion of youth, bestowed herself on the tempter, and brought home a nameless child. Josie shivered, and worked on, with the vision of schooldays all fled, with a face wan and tired—worked until, on a summer's day, someone married another; then Josie crept to her mother like a hurt child, and slept—and sleeps.

I passed to scent the breeze as I entered the valley. The Lawrences have gone; father and son forever, and the other son lazily digs in the earth to live. A new young widow rents out their cabin to fat Reuben. Reuben is a Baptist preacher now, but I fear as lazy as ever, though his cabin has three rooms; and little Ella has grown into a bouncing woman, and is ploughing corn on the hot hillside. There are babies a plenty, and one half-witted girl. Across the valley is a house I did not know before, and there I found, rocking one baby and expecting another, one of my schoolgirls, a daughter of Uncle Bird Dowell. She looked somewhat worried with her new duties, but soon bristled into pride over her neat cabin, and the tale of her thrifty husband, the horse and cow, and the farm they were planning to buy.

My log schoolhouse was gone. In its place stood Progress, and Progress, I understand, is necessarily ugly. The crazy foundation stones still marked the former site of my poor little cabin, and not far away, on six weary boulders, perched a jaunty board house, perhaps twenty by thirty feet, with three windows and a door that locked. Some of the window glass was broken, and part of an old iron stove lay mournfully under the house. I peeped through the window half reverently, and found things that were more familiar. The blackboard had grown by about two feet, and the seats were still without backs. The county owns the lot now, I hear, and every year there is a session of school. As I sat by the spring and looked on the Old and the New I felt glad, very glad, and yet—

After two long drinks I started on. There was the great double log house on the corner. I remembered the broken, blighted family that used to live there. The strong, hard face of the mother, with its wilderness of hair, rose before me. She had driven her husband away, and while I taught school a strange man lived there, big and jovial, and people talked. I felt sure that Ben and 'Tildy would come to naught from such a home. But this is an odd world; for Ben is a busy farmer in Smith County, "doing well, too," they say, and he had cared for little 'Tildy until last spring, when a lover married her. A hard life the lad had led, toiling for meat, and laughed at because he was homely and crooked. There was Sam Carlon, an impudent old skinflint, who had definite notions about niggers, and hired Ben a summer and would not pay him. Then the hungry boy gathered his sacks together, and in broad daylight went into Carlon's corn; and when the hard-fisted farmer set upon him, the angry boy flew at him like a beast. Doc Burke saved a murder and a lynching that day.

The story reminded me again of the Burkes, and an impatience seized me to know who won in the battle, Doc or the seventy-five acres. For it is a hard thing to make a farm out of nothing, even in fifteen years. So I hurried on, thinking of the Burkes. They used to have a certain magnificent barbarism about them that I liked. They were never vulgar, never immoral, but rather rough and primitive, with an unconventionality that spent itself in loud guffaws, slaps on the back, and naps in the corner. I hurried by the cottage of the misborn Neill boys. It was empty, and they were grown into fat, lazy farmhands. I saw the home of the Hickmans, but Albert, with his stooping shoulders, had passed from the world. Then I came to the Burkes' gate and peered through; the inclosure looked rough and untrimmed, and yet there were the same fences around the old farm save to the left, where lay twenty-five other acres. And lo! the cabin in the hollow had climbed the hill and swollen to a half-finished six-room cottage.

The Burkes held a hundred acres, but they were still in debt. Indeed, the gaunt father who toiled night and day would scarcely be happy out of debt, being so used to it. Some day he must stop, for his massive frame is showing decline. The mother wore shoes but the lion-like physique of other days was broken. The children had grown up. Rob, the image of his father, was loud and rough with laughter. Birdie, my school baby of six, had grown to a picture of maiden beauty, tall and tawny. "Edgar is gone," said the mother, with head half bowed,—"gone to work in Nashville; he and his father couldn't agree."

Little Doc, the boy born since the time of my school, took me horseback down the creek next morning toward Farmer Powell's. The road and the stream were battling for mastery, and the stream had the better of it. We splashed and waded, and the merry boy, perched behind me, chattered and laughed. He showed me where Simon Thompson had bought a bit of ground and a home; but his daughter Lana, a plump, brown, slow girl, was not there. She had married a man and a farm twenty miles away. We wound on down the stream till we came to a gate that I did not recognize, but the boy insisted that it was "Uncle Bird's." The farm was fat with the growing crop. In that little valley was a strange stillness as I rode up; for death and marriage had stolen youth, and left age and childhood there. We sat and talked that night, after the chores were done. Uncle Bird was grayer, and his eyes did not see so well, but he was still jovial. We talked of the acres bought,—one hundred and twenty-five,—of the new guest chamber added, of Martha's marrying. Then we talked of death: Fanny and Fred were gone; a shadow hung over the other daughter, and when it lifted she was to go to Nashville to school. At last we spoke of the neighbors, and as night fell Uncle Bird told me how, on a night like that, 'Thenie came wandering back to her home over yonder, to escape the blows of her husband. And next morning she died in the home that her little bow-legged brother, working and saving, had bought for their widowed mother.

My journey was done, and behind me lay hill and dale, and Life and Death. How shall man measure Progress there where the dark-faced Josie lies? How many heartfuls of sorrow shall balance a bushel of wheat? How hard a thing is life to the lowly, and yet how human and real! And all this life and love and strife and failure,—is it the twilight of nightfall or the flush of some faint-dawning day?

Thus sadly musing, I rode to Nashville in the Jim Crow car.

∽ 10 ∽

The Negro and Crime

The development of a Negro criminal class after emancipation was to be expected. It's impossible for such a social revolution to take place without giving rise to a class of men, who, in the new stress of life, under new responsibilities, would lack the will and power to make a way, and would consequently sink into vagrancy, poverty and crime. Indeed it is astounding that a body of people whose family life had been so nearly destroyed, whose women had been forced into concubinage, whose labor had been enslaved and then set adrift penniless, that such a nation should in a single generation be able to point to so many pure homes, so many property-holders, so many striving law abiding citizens. "The vast majority of the colored people," says *The Atlanta Constitution*, "would no more commit heinous crime than would the corresponding white class," and the Rev. Dr. Hoss declares in the *Nashville Christian Advocate*, of which he is editor:

The negroes on the whole have done astonishingly well. Their record since the War has been almost as honorable as the one they made while the conflict was Raging. To hold the entire race responsible for the outrages committed by a few Thousands, or a few score thousands of its members, is not just or right.

In the town of Palmetto, where the recent disturbance began, it was only last December that a Methodist conference declared:

> We observe with gratitude the sympathetic and cordial relations between the white and colored people of this village and community, and the mutual co operation between them in Christian work and in civil life.

If one thing is certain then it is that the Negro criminal in no Southern community represents the mass of the race, or can rightly be mistaken for it. Even in the matter of sexual crime the most prominent paper in the South declared editorially that "ninety-five per cent" of the Negro men "are as respectful toward white women as any people on earth." And whenever the terrible crime of rape has been beyond reasonable doubt proven upon a Negro he has been found to be among the most ignorant and degraded of his people. The sexual looseness among the Negroes themselves, which the nation that taught them now taunts them with, is slowly but surely disappearing. The rate of illegitimacy among them is probably less than in Austria or Italy, and it would be still smaller if law and public opinion in the South gave the defenseless black girl half the protection it throws about the white girl.

Granting then, as every fair-minded man must, that "in almost all the elements of civilization the race, as a whole, has made distinct and gratifying progress," to quote Dr. W. W. Landrum, Pastor First [white] Baptist Church of Atlanta, Ga., the question then comes—and this is the crucial question—What is chiefly responsible for crime among Southern Negroes, outside the economic effects of emancipation?

The first and greatest cause of Negro crime in the South is the convict-lease system. States which use their criminals as sources of revenue in the hands of irresponsible speculators, who herd girls, boys, men and women promiscuously together without distinction or protection, who parade chained convicts in public, guarded by staves and pistols, and then plunge into this abyss of degradation the ignorant little black boy who steals a chicken or a handful of peanuts—what can such States expect but a harvest of criminals and prostitutes? Does it not seem natural that the State which produced Sam Hose is guilty, as *The Atlanta Constitution* declared March 22, of "the burning shame of converting our penal establishments into schools for crime"? and we are prepared to hear, notwithstanding the awful revelations of Governor William Y. Atkinson's prison commission:

> Georgia has not even made a beginning yet in the right direction. The provision of our new penal law will prove the veriest sham. We must get at the issue straight and separate juvenility from crime.

The next greatest cause of Negro crime in the South is the attitude of the courts. The Southern courts have erred in two ways: One, in treating the crime of whites so leniently that red-handed murderers walk scot-free and the public has lost faith in methods of justice. The other, in treating the crimes and misdemeanors of Negroes with such severity that the lesson of punishment is lost through pity for the punished. When, therefore, the number of Negroes in Southern penal institutions is cited as evidence of their lawlessness, students must not forget this double standard of justice, which can best be illustrated by the following clippings from *The Atlanta Constitution* of January 22d:

> Egbert Jackson [colored], aged thirteen, was given a sentence of $50, or ten months in the chain gang lot larceny from the house. . . . The most affecting scene of all was the sentencing of Joe Redding, a white man, in the killing of his brother, John Redding. . . . Judge is a most tender-hearted man, and heard the prayers and saw the tears, and tempered justice with moderation, and gave the modern Cain two years in the penitentiary.

Of course Jackson could pay no such fine and went to the chain gang.

The third cause of crime is the increasing lawlessness and barbarity of mobs. Let a Negro be simply accused of any crime from barn-burning to rape and he is liable to be seized by a mob, given no chance to defend himself, given neither trial, judge nor jury, and killed. Passing over the acknowledged fact that many innocent Negroes have thus been murdered, the point that is of greater gravity is that lawlessness is a direct encouragement to crime. It shatters the faith of the mass of Negroes in justice; it leads them to shield criminals; it makes race hatred fiercer; it discourages honest effort; it transforms horror at crime into sympathy for the tortured victim; and it binds the hands and lessens the influence of those race leaders who are stringing to preach forbearance and patience and honest endeavor to their people. It teaches eight million wronged people to despise a civilization which is not civilized.

Finally, the last cause of Negro crime is the exaggerated and unnatural separation in the South of the best classes of whites and blacks. A drawing of the color line, that extends to street-cars, elevators and cemeteries, which leaves no common ground of meeting, no medium of communication, no ties of sympathy between two races who live together and whose interests are at bottom one—such a discrimination is more than silly, it is dangerous. It makes it possible for the mass of whites to misinterpret the aims and aspiration of the Negroes, to mistake self-reliance for insolence, and condemnation of lynch-law for sympathy with crime. It makes it possible for the Negroes to believe that the best people of the South hate and despise them, and express their antipathy in proscribing them, taunting them and crucifying them. Such terrible misapprehensions are false, and the sooner some way is made by which the best elements of both races can sympathize with each other's struggles and in a calm Christian spirit discuss them together—the sooner such conferences can take place all over the South the sooner the lynch-law will disappear and crime be abated.

~ 11 ~

The Present Outlook for the Dark Races of Mankind

In bringing to you and your friends the official greetings of the American Negro Academy at this their third annual meeting, it is my purpose to consider with you the problem of the color line not simply as a national and personal question but rather in its larger world aspect in time and space. I freely acknowledge that in the red heat of a burning social problem like this, when each one of us feels the bitter sting of proscription, it is a difficult thing to place one's self at that larger point of view and ask with the cold eye of the historian and social philosopher: What part is the color line destined to play in the twentieth century? And yet this is the task I have laid out for you this evening, and one which you must take up for yourselves; for, after all, the secret of social progress is wide and thorough understanding of the social forces which move and modify your age.

It is but natural for us to consider that our race question is a purely national and local affair, confined to nine millions Americans and settled when their rights and opportunities are assured, and yet a glance over the world at the dawn of the new century will convince us that this is but the beginning of the problem—that the color line belts the world and that the social problem of the twentieth century is to be the relation of the civilized world to the dark races of mankind. If we start eastward tonight and land on the continent of Africa we land in the centre of the greater Negro problem—of the world problem of the black man. The nineteenth century of the Christian era has seen strange transformation in the continent where civilization was born twice nineteen centuries before the Christ-child. We must not overlook or forget the marvelous drama that is being played on that continent today, with the English at the North and on the cape, the Portuguese and Germans on the East and West coast, the French in Guinea and the Saharah, Belgium in the Congo, and everywhere the great seething masses of the Negro people. Two events of vast significance to the future of the Negro people have taken place in the year 1899—the recapture of Khartoum and the Boer war, or in other words the determined attempt to plant English civilization at two centres in the heart of Africa. It is of interest to us because it means the wider extension among our own kith and kin of the influence of that European nation whose success in dealing with underdeveloped races has been far greater than any others. Say what we will of England's rapacity and injustice, (and much can be said) the plain fact remains that no other European nation—and America least of all—has governed its alien subjects with half the wisdom and justice that England has. While then the advance of England from the cape to Cairo is no unclouded good for our people, it is at least a vast improvement on Arab slave traders and Dutch brutality. Outside of America the greatest field of contrast between whites and Negroes today is in South Africa, and the situation there should be watched with great interest. We must not forget that the deep-lying cause of the present Boer war is the abolition of Negro slavery among the Cape Dutch by England. The great Trek or migration of the Transvaal Boers followed and in the Free State no Negro has today a third of the rights which he enjoys in Georgia—he cannot hold land, cannot live in town, has practically no civil status, and is in all but name a slave. Among the English his treatment is by no means ideal and set there he has the advantage of school, has the right of suffrage under some circumstances, and has just courts before which he may plead his cause. We watch therefore this war with great interest and must regard the triumph of England as a step toward the solution of the greater Negro problem. In the Congo Free State we see the rapid development of trade and industry, the railroad has crept further in toward the heart of Africa and the slave trade has at least been checked. Liberia stands hard pressed by France but she has begun to pay interest on the English debt and shows in some ways signs of industrial development along with her political decline. Leaving our black brothers of Africa we travel northward to our brown cousins of Egypt: rescued from war and rapine, slavery and centuries of misrule they are today enjoying stable government under England and rapid industrial advancement. Crossing the Red Sea we come upon the brown and yellow millions of Asia. Those who have left their maps in their school days would best, in curiosity, look now and then at the modern development of the mother continent. On the north Russia creeping down far beyond the limits set by your school day geographies. On the south English India creeping up. On the west the still lively corpse of Turkey, the still wild deserts of Arabia and dreary Persia; on the east the vast empire of China and the island kingdom of Japan. This continent deserves more than a passing notice from us for it is a congeries of race and color problems. The history of Asia is but the history of the moral and physical degeneration which follows the unbridled injustice of conquerors toward the conquered—of advanced toward underdeveloped races—of swaggering braggadocio toward dumb submission. The brown Turanians of India were overborne by their yellow conquerors and the resulting caste system to keep the despised down was the very cause of that widespread discontent and internal dissension which welcomed the armies and government of England. So too when the case was reversed and the dark Turks swept over the white, inhabitants of Asia Minor and southern Europe, it was the unjust determination to keep down the conquered, to recognize among Armenians no rights which a Turk was bound to respect. It was this that ultimately paralyzed the pristine vigor of the Ottoman and leaves them today beggars at the gates of Europe. And finally if we turn to China we have again an example of that marvelous internal decay that overcomes the nation which trifles with Truth and Right and Justice, and makes force and fraud and dishonesty and caste distinction the rule of its life and government. The one bright spot in Asia today is the island empire of Japan, and her recent admission to the ranks of modern civilized nations by the abolition of foreign consular courts within her borders is the greatest concession to the color line which the nineteenth century has seen. Outside Japan we see in English India alone a fairly honest attempt to make in some degree the welfare of the lowest classes of an alien race a distinct object of government. A system of education with a well-equipped university at the head has long been established for the natives and in the last few years some natives have been admitted to administrative positions in government. The cordial sympathy shown toward Queen Victoria's black and brown subjects at the late jubilee has borne golden fruit.

Crossing the Pacific we come to South America where the dark blood of the Indian and Negro has mingled with that of the Spaniard and the whole has been deluged by a large German and Italian migration. The resulting social conditions are not clear to the student. The color line has been drawn here perhaps less than in any other continent and yet the condition of the dark masses is far from satisfactory. We must not forget these dark cousins of ours, for their uplifting, and the establishment of permanent government and for industrial conditions is the work of the new century.

At last, after this hasty and inadequate survey we come back to our own land. The race question in America has reached an acute and in some respects a critical stage. Tracing the Negro question historically we can divide it as follows:

Up to about 1774 there was on the whole acquiescence in Negro slavery.
From the inception of the Revolution up until 1820 or 1830, the best thought of the nation believed in the abolition of slavery and were casting about for the best way to accomplish this.
From 1830 to 1850 economic revolution led to apathy on the part of the nation and a growing disposition to defend the institution.
From 1850 to 1865 came the rise and triumph of the abolition movement.
From 1865 to 1880 an attempt was made to clothe the Negro with full civil and political right.
From 1880 to 1890 there was a growing sympathy with the South and apathy toward the Negro.
1890—Today the era of criticism and the beginning of the movement for social reform and economic regeneration.

In this we can see progress—tremendous progress from the times when New England deacons invested their savings in slave trade ventures, passed the Dred Scott decision and the fugitive slave act down to the lynchings and discriminating laws of today. To be sure the actual status today far from being ideal is in many respects deplorable and far beyond those ideals of human brotherhood which from time to time have animated the nature; and yet we must be prepared in the progress of all reformatory movements for periods of exhalation and depression, of rapid advance and retrogression, of hope and fear. The Negro problem in America curiously is this. Away back in the seventeenth century Massachusetts arose in wrath and denounced the slave trade, and the Pennsylvanian Quakers asked: "Is slavery according to the Golden Rule?" and yet 50 years later, Massachusetts slave traders swarmed on the coast of Africa and the Quakers held 10,000 slaves. Toward the end of the eighteenth century the conscience of the nation was again aroused. Darien, Georgia, where the Delegall riot recently occurred, declared its abhorrence of the unnatural practice of slavery. Jefferson denounced the institution as a crime against liberty, and the day of freedom seemed dawning; and yet fifty years later a cargo of black bondsmen were landed near Darien, Georgia, and the Vice President of the Confederacy declared Negro slavery the corner-stone of the new-born nation. So again the dreams of Garrison, Brown, Phillips and Sumner seemed about to be realized after the war when the Negro was free, enfranchised and protected in his civil rights, and yet a generation later finds the freedman in economic serfdom, practically without a vote, denied in many cases common law rights and subject to all sorts of petty discrimination. Notwithstanding all this the progress of the nation toward a settlement of the Negro is patent—the movement with all its retrogression is a spiral not a circle, and as long as there is motion there is hope. At the same time we must indulge in no fantastic dreams, simply because in the past this nation has turned back from its errors against the Negro and tardily sought the higher way is no earnest for the future. Error that ends in progress is none the less error—none the less dangerously liable to end in disaster and wrong. It behooves us then here, to study carefully and seek to understand the present social movement in America as far as it affects our interests and to ask what we can do to insure the ultimate triumph of right and justice. There is no doubt of the significance of the present attitude of the public mind toward us; it is the critical rebound that follows every period of moral exhalation; the shadow of doubt that creeps silently after the age of faith; the cold reasoning that follows gloomy idealism. Nor is this a thing to be unsparingly condemned. The human soul grasping—striving after dearly conceived ideals, needs ever the corrective and guiding power of sober afterthought. Human fancy must face plain facts. This is as true of nations as of men. We find great waves of sympathy seizing mankind at times and succeeded by cold criticism and doubt. Sometimes this latter reaction chokes and postpones reform or even kills it and lets the blind world flounder on. At the other times it leads to more rational and practical measures than mere moral enthusiasm could possibly offer. It is not the critic as such that the idealist must oppose but only that attitude of human criticism and doubt which neglects and denies all ideals. This is curiously illustrated in the modern world's attitude toward poverty: first came stern unbending morality: the pauper, the tramp, it said rascals and drones every one of them—punish them. Then came the century of sympathy crying as it saw dumb toil and hopeless suffering and the paradox of progress and poverty:

> Down all the stretch of Hell to its fast gulf
> There is no shape more terrible than this—
>   More tongued with censure of the world's blind greed
> More filled with signs and portents for the soul,
> More fraught with menace to the universe.

So the world sympathized until there came the era of calm criticism and doubt. Are all paupers pitiable? What makes men poor? Is the cause always the same? Is poverty or the fear of it an unmixed evil? Will not sympathy with the failures in the race of life increase the number of failures? Will not the strengthening of the weak weaken the strong and the enriching of the poor pauperize the rich? Today, in the world of social reform, we stand as it were between these two attitudes seeking some mode of reconciliation. The ideals of human betterment in our day could ill afford to lose the scientific attitude of statistics and sociology and science without ideas would lose half its excuse for being.

This then is the state of mind of the age that is called to settle the Negro problem in America and in the world. The abolitionists with their pure and lofty ideals of human brotherhood and their fine hate of dark damnation of national wrong and injustice, have left this generation a priceless heritage, and from their heights of enthusiasm was bound to come a reaction, and the natural recoil was hastened by sympathy with the stricken and conquered South, by horror at the memory of civil strife, by growing distrust of universal suffrage, and by deep-seated doubt as to the capabilities and desert of the Negro. Here then we have the ideal and the criticism—the still persistent thrust for a broader and deeper humanity, the still powerful doubt as to what the Negro can and will do. The first sign of reconciliation between these two attitudes is the growth of a disposition to study the Negro problem honestly, and to inaugurate measures of social reform in the light of the scientific study. At the same time this disposition is still weak and largely powerless in the face of the grosser and more unscrupulous forces of reaction, and the vital question is: which of these two forces is bound to triumph?

In our attitude toward this battle we must make no tactical mistake, we must recognize clearly the questions at issue. They have changed since the abolition controversy and arguments suited to that time run strangely by the point today; the question is now not as to slavery, not as to human equality, not as to universal suffrage, but rather as to individual efficiency, the proper utilization of the manifestly different endowments of men, and the proper limitation to-day is not so much of rights as of duties—not so much of desires as of abilities, not so much of leveling down the successful to the dead level of the masses as of giving to individuals among the masses the opportunity to reach the highest.

Here we must take our stand. We must inveigh against any drawing of the color line which narrows our opportunity of making the best of ourselves and we must continually and repeatedly show that we are capable of taking hold of every opportunity offered. I need hardly advert to the fact that denial of legal rights and curtailment of industrial opening does make our opportunities today exceptionally narrow. At the same time widespread laziness, crime, and neglect of family life, shows that we fall far short of taking advantage of the opportunities we have.

But most significant of all at this period is the fact that the colored population of our land is, through the new imperial policy, about to be doubled by our own ownership of Porto Rico, and Hawaii, our protectorate of Cuba, and conquest of the Philippines. This is for us and for the nation the greatest event since the Civil War and demands attention and action on our part. What is to be our attitude toward these new lands and toward the masses of dark men and women who inhabit them? Manifestly it must be an attitude of deepest sympathy and strongest alliance. We must stand ready to guard and guide them with our vote and our earnings. Negro and Filipino, Indian and Porto Rican, Cuban and Hawaiian, all must stand united under the stars and stripes for an America that knows no color line in the freedom of its opportunities. We must remember that the twentieth century will find nearly twenty millions of brown and black people under the protection of the American flag, a third of the nation, and that on the success and efficiency of the nine millions of our own number depends the ultimate destiny of Filipinos, Porto Ricans, Indians and Hawaiians, and that on us too depends in a large degree the attitude of Europe toward the teeming millions of Asia and Africa.

No nation ever bore a heavier burden than we black men of America, and if the third millennium of Jesus Christ dawns, as we devoutly believe it will upon a brown and yellow world out of whose advancing civilization the color line has faded as mists before the sun—if this be the goal toward which every free born American Negro looks, then mind you, my hearers, its consummation depends on you, not on your neighbor but on you, not on Southern lynchers or Northern injustice, but on you. And that we may see just what this task means and how men have accomplished similar tasks, I turn to the one part of the world which we have not visited in our quest of the color line—Europe.

There are three significant things in Europe of today which must attract us: the Jew and Socialist in France, the Expansion of Germany and Russia, and the race troubles of Austria. None of these bring us directly upon the question of color; and yet nearly all touch it indirectly. In France we have seen the exhibition of a furious racial prejudice mingled with deep-lying economic causes, and not the whole public opinion of the world was able to secure an entirely satisfactory outcome. The expansion of military Germany is a sinister thing, for with all her magnificent government and fine national traits, her dealings with undeveloped races hitherto have been conspicuous failures. Her contact with the blacks of east and west Africa has been marked by a long series of disgraceful episodes, and we cannot view with complacency her recent bullying of Haiti and her high-handed seizure of Chinese territory. The development of Russia is the vast unknown quantity of the European situation and has been during the 19th century. Her own great population of Slavs stands midway racially between the white Germans and the yellow Tartar, and this makes the whole progress of the Bear a faint reflection of the color line. With the advance of Russia in Asia, the completion of the great trans-Siberian railway, and the threatened seizure of Korea, comes the inevitable clash of the Slav with the yellow masses of Asia. Perhaps a Russia-Japanese war is in the near future. At any rate a gigantic strife across the color line is impending during the next one hundred years. In Austria we see today the most curious and complicated race conflict between Germans, Hungarians, Czechs, Jews and Poles, the outcome of which is puzzling. Finally in the lesser countries of Europe the race question as affecting the darker peoples is coming to the fore. In the question of the status of Turkey and the Balkan States, in the ventures of Italy in Africa and China, in the black membership of the Catholic church, indeed a survey of the civilized world at the end of the 19th century but confirms the proposition with which I started—the world problem of the 20th century is the Problem of the Color line—the question of the relation of the advanced races of men who happen to be white to the great majority of the undeveloped or half developed nations of mankind who happen to be yellow, brown or black.

I have finished now my view of the race problem in space, and now come to the crucial question: What in the light of historical experience is the meaning of such a world problem and how can it best be solved? The world has slowly but surely learned that few of its social problems are really new. New phases, new aspects may come to light, the questions may change and grow, but in most cases we are able to time them backward through the centuries to see how other nations regard them and how other ages failed and prospered in their solution. So today, in many respects the Negro question—the greater Negro question—the whole problem of the color line is peculiarly the child of the 19th and 20th centuries, and yet we may trace its elements, may trace the same social questions under different garbs back through centuries of European history.

We stand to-night on the edge of the year 1900. Suppose in fancy we turn back 100 years and stand at the threshold of the year 1800. What then could be called the Problem of the Century? Manifestly it was the Political Rights of the masses—the relation of the modern state to the great mass of its ignorant and poor laboring classes. To us this does not seem much of a problem and we have a smile of superiority for the age that puzzled itself with so simple a matter: universal suffrage. The rule of the people is our solution, the basing of all legitimate government upon the ultimate consent of the governed, however humble and lowly, is a proposition so widely accepted, that the nations who deny it are without exception placed beyond the pale of civilization. And yet the matter did not seem so clear in 1800. There were men—and honest men too—who saw in the orgies of the French mob the destruction of all that was decent in modern European civilization. There were men—and wise men, too—who believed that democratic government was simply impossible with human nature in its present condition. "Shall the tail wag the dog?" said they; shall a brutish mob sway the destinies of the intelligent and well-born of the nation? It was all very well for Rousseau to sing the Rights of Man, but this civic idealism must make way for calm criticism. What were the abilities of the mob anyway? Must there not in the very nature of the case be a mass of ignorant inefficiency at the bottom of every nation—a strata of laborers whose business it was (as the German princeling said) to honor the king, pay their taxes, and hold their tongues?

Over this the world struggled through the French Revolution, through the English chartist and reform movements, past the Frankfort Parliament and the upheavals of '48 down to the overthrow of the Federalists and the rise of Andrew Jackson, and today we have not to be sure a full realization of the dreams of the political philosophers of the 18th century, nor have we found the critic's distrust of the working classes justified. All civilized nations have found that the great mass of grown men can safely be given a voice in government and be represented in its deliberations, and that taxation without representation is tyranny. This is the revolution of one hundred years of thought and striving.

But this is but one century. Suppose instead of stopping with 1800 we had gone back past Napoleon, past the French Revolution, past the day of DuBarry and Pompadour—back to this bowed and stricken old man with his hooked nose and piercing eyes, his majestic figure and hands that grasped half the world—the 14th Louis, King of France. What was the problem of the year that dawned on 1700, almost the last year of the greatest monarch the world has known? It was the problem of the privileged class—the question as to whether or not the state existed for the sole privilege of the king and the king's friends; whether after all ordinary people not well born were really men in the broader meaning of that term. We who were born to sing with Burns "The rank is but the guineas stand, the man's the gawd for a' that," have faint conception of the marvellous hold which the idea of rank, of high birth once held on earth. How narrow and confined were the lives of all who were not their fathers' sons, and how hard a battle the world fought before the low born had a right to go where he pleased, to work as he pleased, to be judged according to his deserts and to be held and treated as a man.

And so I might journey on back in the world to 1600 when only those who went to your church were worthy of life and liberty and you roasted the others alive to the glory of God and the salvation of your own soul. Back to 1500 when Spaniards looked on Englishmen as Englishmen now look on Hottentots, and Frenchmen regarded Italians as Americans look on Filipinos, when the hatred and dislike of foreigners made war a holy pastime, and patriotism meant the murder of those who did not speak your language. But the world has grown. Till at last we acknowledge the brotherhood of men in spite of the fact that they may profess another creed or no creed at all; in spite of the fact that their fathers were nobodies; in spite of the fact that they belong to the mass of uncultivated laborers who toil for daily bread. And if the world has taken all this journey in 600 years may we not hope that another century will add to our victories of civilization by spreading the boundaries of humanity so wide that they will include all men in spite of the color of their skins and physical peculiarities?

We may to be sure hope for this, and we can find much in our surroundings to encourage this hope. First in the undoubted decadence of war. This may seem a strange declaration in view of the armed court of Europe, the impending clash in the East and the struggle in Africa, and yet it is true. No age has shown such genuine dislike of war and such abhorrence of its brutalities as this, and the 20th century is destined to see national wars, not disappear to be sure, but sink to the same ostracism in popular opinion as the street fight and the brawl among individuals; at the same time the expansion and consolidation of nations today is leading to countless repetitions of that which we have in America today—the inclusion of nations within nations—of groups of undeveloped peoples brought in contact with advanced races under the same government, language and system of culture. The lower races will in nearly every case be dark races. German Negroes, Portuguese Negroes, Spanish Negroes, English East Indian, Russian Chinese, American Filipinos—such are the groups which following the example of the American Negroes will in the 20th century strive, not by war and rapine but by the mightier weapons of peace and culture to gain a place and name in the civilized world.

In this vast movement then we are pioneers: on our success or failure hangs the success of many a people and largely the fate of the 20th century. Let us then quit ourselves like men, refusing to be discouraged, drawn away by no petty attractions, strong in the might of our strength not simply to follow but to lead the civilization of the day—pressing onward with him who never followed but marched breast forward.

> Never dreamed tho' right were vanquished, wrong would
>   triumph,
> Held we fall to rise, are baffled to fight better,
> Sleep to wake.

But how shall we strive? What shall be our weapons in the warfare and what our plan of battle? I fear that a brutal past and a materialistic present has bequeathed to many of us the medieval idea that the way to strive in this world is by knocks and blows—to hit somebody, to inflict personal injury, to wade through war to peace, through murder to love, and through death to life. And perhaps if we lived in the 15th or 16th centuries or even later our only hope of rising would be by a display of physical force. Even today there is no doubt but that much of the disdain with which the unthinking masses regard the average Negro is because he is not a brawler and fighter ready to give an eye for an eye and tooth for a tooth. But beware my fellows how the ideals of the rabble seduce you from the one true path to victory: the moral mastery over the minds of men—true desert, unquestioned ability, thorough work and purity of purpose—these things and these alone will ensure victory to any group of men if the 20th century fulfil its promise; and it is for the white races of mankind now in the ascendency to see to it that the culture they have developed is not debauched by the Philistine The Fool and the Lyncher—by wholesale murder falsely called expansion, and by retail torture falsely called race pride, and it is for us as the advance guard of that renaissance of culture among the black races of men to build up our strength, efficiency and culture. And right here let me continue to insist,—right here lies our danger—we have less to fear from lynchers and legislation than from the plain flat fact that, first, we are developing alarming criminal tendencies. Second, we are not as a race doing thoroughly excellent work, and thirdly, the spirit of personal sacrifice for greater ultimate good of all has not thoroughly permeated our best men.

In regard to the prevalence of Negro crime, I care not how great the provocation or how widespread the excuse; how large a figure prejudice may play or how natural it is for freemen to steal and fight—in spite of all this, the fact remains that we are guilty of widespread crimes and that the problem we are to face is not that of finding excuses for ourselves but it is rather the question of saving our youth from debauchery and wrongdoing in the face of temptation and in the very teeth of prejudice and excuse. As president of "The American Negro Academy" I hail as the greatest event of the past year the permanent establishment of a Reformatory in Virginia for black boys; I congratulate Maryland and Carolina on their new Negro orphanages, and I beg the Negroes of the nation to follow these pioneers.

But after all it is in the Negro home where the great revolution must come—in the right rearing of children—the protection of youth and the purity and integrity of family life.

Second, I notice continually a lack on the part of our best trained classes of a determination to do thorough efficient work wherever they have the chance. The desire of notoriety rather than of excellence continually spoils the efforts and cheapens the deeds of so many of us. A man will throw away ten years of his life writing careless essays and catchy addresses when this time put on a serious thorough book might have given the world something of permanent value instead of a heap of trash. A woman will play musical fireworks and catchy nothings all her life when half her day persistently and doggedly put into study and practice might have made her a musician instead of a hand organ. Young men and women continually graduate from our schools, and then satisfy their souls not with a masterpiece, a thoroughly excellent bit of work, but with a cut in the newspaper and a column of lies. Excellence, thoroughness, though it be in sweat and poverty, in obscurity, or even in ridicule, this must characterize the work of Negroes whether they plough or preach. And here again it is with infinite pleasure that I note some evidences of this in the rise of a real literature among us—the continued popularity of Dunbar, the excellent workmanship of Chesnutt, the new book by Booker Washington and the lines of the new poet, James David Corrothers.

And finally, we need in larger measure the spirit of sacrifice. I do not mean by this anything maudlin or sentimental; I mean the clear, calculating decision on the part of Negro men and women that they are going to give up something of their personal wealth, their own advancement and ambition, to aid in the ultimate emancipation of the nine millions of their fellows in this land and the countless millions the world over. Without this we cannot co-operate, we cannot secure the greatest good of all, we cannot triumph over our foes.

I know that the question, Why? floats before the vision of yonder dark-faced boy, who looks forth on life as a world of wailing waters and cries to the dim and silent hills. I, I, why should I be called to sacrifice all that life calls beautiful to forward the staggering footsteps of an unlovely horde—why—the everlasting why, and yet

> Tho' love repine and reason chafe,
> There came a voice without reply,
> 'Tis man's perdition to be safe
> When, for the truth he ought to die.

∾ **12** ∾

Religion of the American Negro

It was out in the country, far from home, far from my foster home, on a dark Sunday night. The road wandered from our rambling log house up the stony bed of a creek, past wheat and corn, until we could hear dimly across the fields a rhythmic cadence of song,—soft, thrilling, powerful, that swelled and died sorrowfully in our ears. I was a country school teacher then, fresh from the East, and had never seen a southern Negro revival. To be sure, we in Berkshire were not perhaps as stiff and formal as they in Suffolk of olden time; yet we were very quiet and subdued, and I know not what would have happened those clear Sabbath mornings had some one punctuated the sermon with a wild scream, or interrupted the long prayer with a loud Amen! And so most striking to me, as I approached the village and the little plain church perched aloft, was the air of intense excitement that possessed that mass of black folk. A sort of suppressed terror hung in the air and seemed to seize us—a pythian madness, a demoniac possession, that lent terrible reality to song and word. The black and massive form of the preacher swayed and quivered the words crowded to his lips and flew at us in singular eloquence. The people moaned and fluttered, and then the gaunt-cheek brown woman beside me suddenly leaped straight into the air and shrieked like a lost soul, while round about came wail and groan and outcry, and a scene of human passion such as I had conceived before.

Those who have not thus witnessed the frenzy of a Negro revival in the untouched backwoods of the South can but dimly realize the religious feeling of the slave; as described, such scenes appear grotesque and funny, but as seen they are awful. Three things characterized this religion of the slave—the Preacher, Music and the Frenzy. The Preacher is the most unique personality developed by the Negro on American soil. A leader, a politician, an orator, a "boss," an intriguer, an idealist—all this he is, and ever, too, the centre of a group of men, now twenty, now a thousand in number. The combination of a certain adroitness with deep-seated earnestness, of tact with consummate ability, gave him his preeminence, and helps him maintain it. The type, of course, varies according to time and place, from the West Indies in the sixteenth century to New England in the nineteenth, and from the Mississippi bottoms to cities like New Orleans or New York.

The Music of Negro religion is that plaintive rhythmic melody—with its touching minor cadences, which, despite caricature and defilement, still remains the most original and beautiful expression of human life and longing yet born on American soil. Sprung from the African forests, where its counterpart can still be heard it was adapted, changed and intensified by the tragic soul-life of the slave, until, under the stress of law and whip, it became the one true expression of a people's sorrow, despair and hope.

Finally the Frenzy or "Shouting," when the Spirit of the Lord passed by, and, seizing the devotee, made him mad with super natural joy, was the last essential of Negro religion and the one more devoutly believed in than all the rest. It varied in expression from the silent rapt countenance or the low murmur and moan to the mad abandon of physical fervor—the stamping, shrieking and shouting, the rushing to and fro and wild waving of arms, the weeping and laughing, the vision and the trance. All this is nothing new in the world, but old as religion, as Delphi and Endor. And so firm a hold did it have on the Negro that many generations firmly believed that without this visible manifestation of the god, there could be no true communion with the Invisible.

These were the characteristics of Negro religious life as developed up to the time of Emancipation. Since under the peculiar circumstances of the black man's environment, they were the one expression of his higher life, they are of deep interest to the student of his development, both socially and psychologically. Numerous are the attractive lines of inquiry that here group them selves. What did slavery mean to the African savage? What was his attitude toward the World and Life? What seemed to him good and evil—God and Devil? Whither went his longings and strivings, and wherefore were his heart-burnings and disappointments? Answers to such questions can come only from a study of Negro religion as a development, through its gradual changes from the heathenism of the Gold Coast to the institutional Negro church of Chicago.

Moreover, the religious growth of millions of men, even though they be slaves, cannot be without potent influence upon their contemporaries. The Methodists and Baptists of America owe much of their condition to the silent but potent influence of their millions of Negro converts. Especially is this noticeable in the South, where theology and religious philosophy are on this account a full half century behind the North, and where the religion of the poor whites is a plain copy of Negro thought and methods. The mass of "Gospel" hymns which has swept through American churches and well-nigh ruined our sense of song, consists largely of debased imitations of Negro melodies made by ears that caught the jingle but not the music, the body but not the soul, of the Jubilee songs. It is thus clear that the study of Negro religion is not only a vital part of the history of the Negro in America, but no uninteresting part of American history.

The Negro church of today is the social centre of Negro life in the United States, and the most characteristic expression of African character. Take a typical church in a small Virginian town: it is the "First Baptist"—a roomy brick edifice seating five hundred or more persons, tastefully finished in Georgia pine, with a carpet, a small organ and stained-glass windows. Underneath is a large assembly room with benches. This building is the central clubhouse of a community of a thousand or more Negroes. Various organizations meet here—the church proper, the Sunday school, two or three insurance societies, women's societies, secret societies and mass meetings of various kinds. Entertainments, suppers and lectures are held beside the five or six regular weekly religious services. Considerable sums of money are collected and expended here, employment is found for the idle, strangers are introduced, news is disseminated and charity distributed. At the same time this social, intellectual and economic centre is a religious centre of great power. Depravity, Sin, Redemption, Heaven, Hell and Damnation are preached twice a Sunday with much fervor, and revivals take place every year after the crops are laid by; and few indeed of the community have the hardihood to withstand conversion. Back of this more formal religion, the Church stands as a real conserver of morals, a strengthener of family life, and the final authority on what is Good and Right.

Thus one can see in the Negro church today, reproduced in microcosm, all that great world from which the Negro is cut off by color prejudice and social condition. In the great city churches the same tendency is noticeable and in many respects emphasized. A great church like the Bethel of Philadelphia has 1104 members, an edifice seating 1500 persons and valued at $100,000, an annual budget of $5000 and a government consisting of a pastor with several assisting local preachers, an executive and legislative board, financial boards and tax collectors; general church meetings for making laws; subdivided groups led by class leaders, a company of militia, and twenty-four auxiliary societies. The activity of such a church is immense and far-reaching, and the bishops who preside over these organizations throughout the land are among the most powerful Negro rulers in the world.

Such churches are really governments of men, and consequently a little investigation reveals the curious fact that, in the South, at least, practically every American Negro is a church member. Some, to be sure, are not regularly enrolled, and a few do not habitually attend services; but, practically, a proscribed people must have a social centre, and that centre for this people is the Negro church. The census of 1890 showed nearly 24,000 Negro churches in the country, with a total enrolled membership of over two and a half millions, or ten actual church members to every twenty-eight persons, and in some Southern States one in every two persons. Besides these there is the large number who, while not enrolled as members attend and take part in many of the activities of the church. There is an organized Negro church for every sixty black families in the nation, and in some States for every forty families, owning, on an average, $1000 worth of property each, or nearly $26,000,000 in all.

Such, then, is the large development of the Negro church since Emancipation. The question now is, What have been the successive steps of this social history and what are the present tendencies? First, we must realize that no such institution as the Negro church could rear itself without definite historical foundations. These foundations we can find if we remember that the social history of the Negro did not start in America. He was brought from a definite social environment—the polygamous clan life under the headship of the chief and the potent influence of the priest. His religion was nature-worship, with profound belief in invisible surrounding influences, good and bad, and his worship was through incantation and sacrifice. The first rude change in this life was the slave ship and the West Indian sugar-fields. The plantation organization replaced the clan and tribe, and the white master replaced the chief with far greater and more despotic powers. Forced and long-continued toil became the rule of life, the old ties of blood relationship and kinship disappeared, and instead of the family appeared a new polygamy and polyandry, which, in some cases, almost reached promiscuity. It was a terrible social revolution, and yet some traces were retained of the former group life, and the chief remaining institution was the Priest or Medicine-man. He early appeared on the plantation and found his function as the healer of the sick, the interpreter of the Unknown, the comforter of the sorrowing, the supernatural avenger of wrong, and the one who rudely but picturesquely expressed the longing, disappointment and resentment of a stolen and oppressed people. Thus, as bard, physician, judge and priest, within the narrow limits allowed by the slave system, rose the Negro preacher, and under him the first Afro-American institution, the Negro church. This church was not at first by any means Christian nor definitely organized; rather it was an adaptation and mingling of heathen rites among the members of each plantation, and roughly designated as Voodooism. Association with the masters, missionary effort and motives of expediency gave these rites an early veneer of Christianity, and after the lapse of many generations the Negro church became Christian.

Two characteristic things must be noticed in regard to this church. First, it became almost entirely Baptist and Methodist in faith; secondly, as a social institution it antedated by many decades the monogamic Negro home. From the very circumstances of its beginning, the church was confined to the plantation, and consisted primarily of a series of disconnected units; although, later on, some freedom of movement was allowed, still this geographical limitation was always important and was one cause of the spread of the decentralized and democratic Baptist faith among the slaves. At the same time, the visible rite of baptism appealed strongly to their mystic temperament. Today the Baptist Church is still largest in membership among Negroes, and has a million and a half communicants. Next in popularity came the churches organized in connection with the white neighboring churches, chiefly Baptist and Methodist, with a few Episcopalian and others. The Methodists still form the second greatest denomination, with nearly a million members. The faith of these two leading denominations was more suited to the slave church from the prominence they gave to religious feeling and fervor. The Negro membership in other denominations has always been small and relatively unimportant, although the Episcopalians and Presbyterians are gaining among the more intelligent classes today, and the Catholic Church is making headway in certain sections. After emancipation, and still earlier in the North, the Negro churches largely severed such affiliations as they had with the white churches, either by choice or by compulsion. The Baptist churches became independent, but the Methodists were compelled early to unite for purposes of episcopal government. This gave rise to the great African Methodist Church, the greatest Negro organization in the world, to the Zion Church and the Colored Methodist, and to the black conferences and churches in this and other denominations.

The second fact noted, namely, that the Negro church antedates the Negro home, leads to an explanation of much that is paradoxical in this communistic institution and in the morals of its members. But especially it leads us to regard this institution as peculiarly the expression of the inner ethical life of a people in a sense seldom true elsewhere. Let us turn then from the outer physical development of the church to the more important inner ethical life of the people who compose it. The Negro has already been pointed out many times as a religious animal—a being of that deep emotional nature which turns instinctively toward the supernatural. Endowed with a rich tropical imagination and a keen, delicate appreciation of Nature, the transplanted African lived in a world animate with gods and devils, elves and witches; full of strange influences—of Good to be implored, of Evil to be propitiated. Slavery, then, was to him the dark triumph of Evil over him. All the hateful powers of the Under-world were striving against him, and a spirit of revolt and revenge filled his heart. He called up all the resources of heathenism to aid,—exorcism and witchcraft, the mysterious Obi worship with its barbarous rites, spells and blood-sacrifice even, now and then, of human victims. Weird midnight orgies and mystic conjurations were invoked, the witch woman and the voodoo priest became the centre of Negro group life, and that vein of vague superstition which characterizes the unlettered Negro even today was deepened and strengthened.

In spite, however, of such success as that of the fierce Maroons, the Danish blacks and others, the spirit of revolt gradually died away under the untiring energy and superior strength of the slave masters. By the middle of the eighteenth century the black slave had sunk, with hushed murmurs, to his place at the bottom of a new economic system, and was unconsciously ripe for a new philosophy of life. Nothing suited his condition then better than the doctrines of passive submission embodied in the newly learned Christianity. Slave masters early realized this, and cheerfully aided religious propaganda within certain bounds. The long system of repression and degradation of the Negro tended to emphasize the elements in his character which made him a valuable chattel: courtesy became humility, moral strength degenerated into submission, and the exquisite native appreciation of the beautiful became an infinite capacity for dumb suffering. The Negro, losing the joy of this world, eagerly seized upon the offered conceptions of the next, the avenging Spirit of the Lord enjoining patience in this world, under sorrow and tribulation until the Great Day when He should lead His dark children home,—this became his comforting dream. His Preacher repeated the prophecy, and his bards sang:—

> Children, we all shall be free
> When the Lord shall appear!

This deep religious fatalism, painted so beautifully in Uncle Tom, came soon to breed, as all fatalistic faiths will, the sensualist side by side with the martyr. Under the lax moral life of the plantation, where marriage was a farce, laziness a virtue, and property a theft, a religion of resignation and submission degenerated easily, in less strenuous minds, into a philosophy of indulgence and crime. Many of the worst characteristics of the Negro masses of to day had their seed in this period of the slave's ethical growth. Here it was that the Home was ruined under the very shadow of the Church, white and black; here habits of shiftlessness took root, and sullen hopelessness replaced hopeful strife.

With the beginning of the abolition movement and the gradual growth of a class of free Negroes came a change. We often neglect the influence of the freedman before the war, because of the paucity of his numbers and the small weight he had in the history of the nation. But we must not forget that his chief influence was internal—was exerted on the black world, and that there he was the ethical and social leader. Huddled as he was in a few centres like Philadelphia, New York and New Orleans, his chief characteristic was intense earnestness and deep feeling on the slavery question. Freedom became to him a real thing and not a dream. His religion became darker and more intense, and into his ethics crept a note of revenge, into his songs a day of reckoning close at hand. The "Coming of the Lord" swept this side of Death, and came to be a thing to be hoped for in this day. Through fugitive slaves and irrepressible discussion this desire for freedom seized the black millions still in bondage, and became their one ideal of life. The black bards caught new notes, and sometimes even dared to sing:—

> Before I'll be a slave
> I'll be buried in my grave, And go home to my Jesus
> And be saved.

For fifty years Negro religion thus transformed itself and identified itself with the dream of Abolition until that which was a radical fad in the White North and an anarchistic plot in the White South had become a religion to the Black world. Thus, when Emancipation finally came, it seemed to the freedman a literal Coming of the Lord. His fervid imagination was stirred, as never before, by the tramp of armies, the blood and dust of battle and the wail and whirl of social upheaval. He stood dumb and motionless before the whirlwind—what had he to do with it? Was it not the Lord's doing and marvelous in his eyes? Joyed and bewildered with what came, he stood awaiting new wonders till the inevitable Age of Reaction swept over the nation and brought the crisis of today.

It is difficult to explain clearly the present critical stage of Negro religion. First, we must remember that living as the blacks do in close contact with a great modern nation and sharing, although imperfectly, the soul-life of that nation, they must necessarily be affected more or less directly by all the religious and ethical forces that are today moving the United States. These questions and movements are, however, overshadowed and dwarfed by the all-important question (to them) of their civil, political and economic status. They must perpetually discuss the "Negro Problem"—live, move, and have their being in it, and interpret all else in its light or darkness. With this come, too, peculiar problems of their inner life,—of the status of women, the maintenance of Home, the training of children, the accumulation of wealth and the prevention of crime. All this must mean a time of intense ethical ferment, of religious heart-searching and intellectual unrest. From the double life every American Negro must live, as a Negro and as an American, as swept on by the current of the nineteenth while yet struggling in the eddies of the fifteenth century,—from this must arise a painful self-consciousness, an almost morbid sense of personality and a moral hesitancy which is fatal to self-confidence. The worlds within and without the Veil of Color are changing, and changing rapidly, but not at the same rate, not in the same way, and this must produce a peculiar wrenching of the soul, a peculiar sense of doubt and bewilderment. Such a double life, with double thoughts, double duties and double social classes, must give rise to double words and double ideals, and tempt the mind to pretense or to revolt, to hypocrisy or to radicalism.

In some such doubtful words and phrases can one perhaps most clearly picture the peculiar ethical paradox that faces the Negro of today and is tingeing and changing his religious life. Feeling that his rights and his dearest ideals are being trampled upon, that the public conscience is even more deaf to his righteous appeal, and that all the reactionary forces of prejudice, greed and revenge are daily gaining new strength and fresh allies, the Negro faces no enviable dilemma. Conscious of his impotence, and pessimistic, he often becomes bitter and vindictive, and his religion, instead of a worship, is a complaint and a curse, a wail rather than a hope, a sneer rather than a faith. On the other hand, another type of mind, shrewder and keener and more tortuous too, sees in the very strength of the anti-Negro movement its patent weaknesses, and with Jesuitic casuistry is deterred by no ethical considerations in the endeavor to turn this weakness to the black man's strength. Thus we have two great and hardly reconcilable streams of thought and ethical strivings; the danger of the one lies in anarchy, that of the other in hypocrisy. The one type of Negro stands almost ready to curse God and, die, and the other is too often found a traitor to right and a coward before force; the one is wedded to ideals remote, whimsical, perhaps impossible of realization; the other for that life is more than meat and the body more than raiment. But, after all, is not all this simply the writhing of the age translated into black? The triumph of the Lie which today, with its false culture, faces the hideousness of the anarchist assassin?

Today the two groups of Negroes, the one in the North, the other in the South, represent these divergent ethical tendencies, the first tending toward radicalism, the other toward hypocritical compromise. It is no idle regret with which the white South mourns the loss of the old-time Negro—the frank, honest, simple old servant who stood for the earlier religious age of submission and humility. With all his laziness and lack of many elements of true manhood he was at least openhearted, faithful and sincere. Today he is gone, but who is to blame for his going? Is it not those very persons who mourn for him? Is it not the tendency born of Reconstruction and Reaction to found a society on lawlessness and deception, to tamper with the moral fibre of a naturally honest and straightforward people until the whites threaten to become ungovernable tyrants and the blacks criminals and hypocrites? Deception is the natural defense of the weak against the strong, and the South used it for many years against its conquerors; today it must be prepared to see its black proletariat turn that same two-edged weapon against itself. And how natural this is! The death of Nat Turner and John Brown proved long since to the Negro the present hopelessness of physical defense. Political defense is becoming less and less available, and economic defense is still only partially effective. But there is a patent defense at hand,—the defense of deception and flattery, of cajoling and lying. It is the same defense which the Jews of the Middle Age used and which left its stamp on their character for centuries. Today the young Negro of the South who would succeed cannot be frank and outspoken, honest and self-assertive; but rather he is daily tempted to be silent and wary, politic and sly; he must flatter and be pleasant, endure petty insults with a smile, shut his eyes to wrong; in too many cases he sees positive personal advantage in deception and lying. His real thoughts, his real aspirations must be guarded in whispers; he must not criticise, he must not complain. Patience, humility and adroitness must, in these growing black youth, replace impulse, manliness and courage. With this sacrifice there is an economic opening, and perhaps peace and some prosperity. Without this there is riot, migration or crime. Nor is this situation peculiar to the southern United States—is it not rather the only method, by which undeveloped races have gained the right to share modern culture? The price of culture is a Lie.

On the other hand, in the North the tendency is to emphasize the radicalism of the Negro. Driven from his birthright in the South by a situation at which every fibre of his more outspoken and assertive nature revolts, he finds himself in a land where he can scarcely earn a decent living amid the harsh competitions and the color discrimination. At the same time, through schools and periodicals, discussions and lectures, he is intellectually quickened and awakened. The soul, long pent up and dwarfed, suddenly expanded in new found freedom. What wonder that every tendency is to excess,—radical complaint, radical remedies, bitter denunciation or angry silence. Some sink, some rise. The criminal and the sensualist leave the church for the gambling hall and the bawdy-house, and fill the slums of Chicago and Baltimore; the better classes segregate themselves from the group-life of both white and black, and form an aristocracy, cultured but pessimistic, whose bitter criticism stings while it points out no way of escape. They despise the submission and subserviency of the Southern Negroes, but offer no other means by which a poor and oppressed minority can exist side by side with its masters. Feeling deeply and keenly the tendencies and opportunities of the age in which they live, their souls are bitter at the fate which drops the Veil between, and the very fact that this bitterness is natural and justifiable only serves to intensify it and make it more maddening.

Between the two extreme types of ethical attitude which I have thus sought to make clear, wavers the mass of the millions of Negroes North and South; and their religious life and activity partake of this social conflict within their ranks. Their churches are differentiating, now into groups of cold, fashionable devotees, in no way distinguishable from similar white groups save in color of skin, now into large social and business institutions catering to the desire for information and amusement of their members, warily avoiding unpleasant questions both within and without the black world and preaching in effect if not in word: Dum vivimus, vivamus.

But, back of this, still brood silently the deep religious feeling of the real Negro heart, the stirring, unguided might of powerful human souls who have lost the guiding star of the past and are seeking in the great night a new religious ideal. Some day the Awakening will come: when the pent-up vigor of ten million souls shall sweep irresistibly toward the Goal, out of the Valley Shadow of Death, where all that makes life worth living— Liberty, Justice and Right—is marked "For White People Only."

～ 13 ～

The Freedmen's Bureau

The problem of the twentieth century is the problem of the color line; the relation of the darker to the lighter races of men in Asia and Africa, in

America and the islands of the sea. It was a phase of this problem that caused the Civil War; and however much they who marched south and north in 1861 may have fixed on the technical points of union and local autonomy as a shibboleth, all nevertheless knew, as we know, that the question of Negro slavery was the deeper cause of the conflict. Curious it was, too, how this deeper question ever forced itself to the surface, despite effort and disclaimer. No sooner had Northern armies touched Southern soil than this old question, newly guised, sprang from the earth,—What shall be done with slaves? Peremptory military commands, this way and that, could not answer the query; the Emancipation Proclamation seemed but to broaden and intensify the difficulties; and so at last there arose in the South a government of men called the Freedmen's Bureau, which lasted, legally, from 1865 to 1872, but in a sense from 1861 to 1876, and which sought to settle the Negro problems in the United States of America.

It is the aim of this essay to study the Freedmen's Bureau,—the occasion of its rise, the character of its work, and its final success and failure,—not only as a part of American history, but above all as one of the most singular and interesting of the attempts made by a great nation to grapple with vast problems of race and social condition.

No sooner had the armies, east and west, penetrated Virginia and Tennessee, than fugitive slaves appeared within their lines. They came at night, when the flickering camp fires of the blue hosts shone like vast unsteady stars along the black horizon: old men, and thin, with gray and tufted hair; women with frightened eyes, dragging whimpering, hungry children; men and girls, stalwart and gaunt,—a horde of starving vagabonds, homeless, helpless, and pitiable in their dark distress. Two methods of treating these newcomers seemed equally logical to opposite sorts of minds. Said some, "We have nothing to do slaves." "Hereafter," commanded Halleck, "no slaves should be allowed to come into your lines at all; if any come without your knowledge, when owners call for them, deliver them." But others said, "We take grain and fowl; why not slaves?" Whereupon Fremont, as early as August, 1861, declared the slaves of Missouri rebels free. Such radical notion was quickly countermanded, but at the same time the opposite policy could not be enforced; some of the black refugees declared themselves freemen, others showed their masters had deserted them, and still others were captured with forts and plantations. Evidently, too, slaves were a source of strength to the Confederacy, and were being used as laborers and producers. "They constitute a military resource," wrote the Secretary of War, late in 1861; "and being such that they should not be turned over to the enemy is too plain to discuss." So the tone of the army chiefs changed, Congress forbade the rendition of fugitive and Butler's "contrabands" were welcomed as military laborers. This complicated rather than solved the problem for now the scattering fugitives became a steady stream, which flowed faster as the armies marched.

Then the long-headed man, with care-chiseled face, who sat in the White House, saw the inevitable, and emancipated the slaves of rebels on New Year's 1863. A month later Congress called earnestly for the Negro soldiers whom the act of July, 1862, had half grudgingly allowed to enlist. Thus the barriers were leveled, and the deed was done. The stream of fugitives swelled to a flood, and anxious officers kept inquiring: "What must be done with slaves arriving almost daily? Am I to find food and shelter for women and children?"

It was a Pierce of Boston who pointed out the way, and thus became in a sense the founder of the Freedmen's Bureau. Being specially detailed from the ranks to care for the freedmen at Fortress Monroe, he afterward founded the celebrated Port Royal experiment and started the Freedmen's Aid Societies. Thus, under the timid Treasury officials and bold army officers, Pierce's plan widened and developed. At first, the able bodied men were enlisted as soldiers or hired as laborers, the women and children were herded into central camps under guard, and "superintendents of contrabands" multiplied here and there. Centres of massed freedmen arose at Fortress Monroe, Va., Washington, D. C., Beaufort and Port Royal, S. C., New Orleans, La., Vicksburg and Corinth, Miss., Columbus, Ky., Cairo, Ill., and elsewhere, and the army chaplains found here new and fruitful fields.

Then came the Freedmen's Aid Societies, born of the touching appeals for relief and help from these centres of distress. There was the American Missionary Association, sprung from the Amistad, and now full grown for work, the various church organizations, the National Freedmen's Relief Association, the American Freedmen's Union, the Western Freedmen's Aid Commission,—in all fifty or more active organizations, which sent clothes, money, school books, and teachers southward. All they did was needed, for the destitution of the freedmen was often reported as "too appalling for belief," and the situation is growing daily worse rather than better.

And daily, too, it seemed more plain that this was no ordinary matter of temporary relief, but a national crisis; for here loomed a labor problem of vast dimensions. Masses of Negroes stood idle, or, if they worked spasmodically, were never sure of pay; and if perchance they received pay, squandered the new thing thoughtlessly. In these and in other ways were camp life and the new liberty demoralizing the freedmen. The broader economic organization thus clearly demanded sprang up here and there as accident and local conditions determined. Here again Pierce's Port Royal plan of leased plantations and guided workmen pointed out the rough way. In Washington, the military governor, at the urgent appeal of the superintendent, opened confiscated estates to the cultivation of the fugitives, and there in the shadow of the dome gathered black farm villages. General Dix gave over estates to the freedmen of Fortress Monroe, and so on through the South. The government and the benevolent societies furnished the means of cultivation, and the Negro turned again slowly to work. The systems of control, thus started, rapidly grew, here and there, into strange little governments, like that of General Banks in Louisiana, with its 90,000 black subjects, 50,000 guided laborers, and its annual budget of $100,000 and more. It made out 4000 pay rolls, registered all freedmen, inquired into grievances and redressed them, laid and collected taxes, and established a system of public schools. So too Colonel Eaton, the superintendent of Tennessee and Arkansas, ruled over 100,000, leased and cultivated 7000 acres of cotton land, and furnished food for 10,000 paupers. In South Carolina was General Saxton, with his deep interest in black folk. He succeeded Pierce and the Treasury officials, and sold forfeited estates, leased abandoned plantations, encouraged schools, and received from Sherman, after the terribly picturesque march to the sea, thousands of the wretched camp followers.

Three characteristic things one might have seen in Sherman's raid through Georgia, which threw the new situation in deep and shadowy relief: the Conqueror, the Conquered, and the Negro. Some see all significance in the grim front of the destroyer, and some in the bitter sufferers of the lost cause. But to me neither soldier nor fugitive speaks with so deep a meaning as that dark and human cloud that clung like remorse on the rear of those swift columns, swelling at times to half their size, almost engulfing and choking them. In vain were they ordered back, in vain were bridges hewn from beneath their feet; on they trudged and writhed and surged, until they rolled into Savannah, a starved and naked horde of tens of thousands. There too came the characteristic military remedy: "The islands from Charleston south, the abandoned ricefields along the rivers for thirty miles back from the sea, and the country bordering the St. John's River, Florida, are reserved and set apart for the settlement of Negroes now made free by act of war." So read the celebrated field order.

All these experiments, orders, and systems were bound to attract and perplex the government and the nation. Directly after the Emancipation Proclamation, Representative Eliot had introduced a bill creating a Bureau of Emancipation, but it was never reported. The following June, a committee of inquiry, appointed by the Secretary of War, reported in favor of a temporary bureau for the "improvement, protection, and employment of refugee freedmen," on much the same lines as were afterward followed. Petitions came in to President Lincoln from distinguished citizens and organizations, strongly urging a comprehensive and unified plan of dealing with the freedmen, under a bureau which should be "charged with the study of plans and execution of measures for easily guiding, and in every way judiciously and humanely aiding, time passage of our emancipated and yet to be emancipated blacks from the old condition of forced labor to their new state of voluntary industry."

Some half-hearted steps were early taken by the government to put both freedmen and abandoned estates under the supervision of the Treasury officials. Laws of 1863 and 1864 directed them to take charge of and lease abandoned lands for periods not exceeding twelve months, and to "provide in such leases or otherwise for the employment and general welfare" of the freedmen. Most of the army officers looked upon this as a welcome relief from perplexing "Negro affairs;" but the Treasury hesitated and blundered, and although it leased large quantities of land and employed many Negroes, especially along the Mississippi, yet it left the virtual control of the laborers and their relations to their neighbors in the hands of the army.

In March, 1864, Congress at last turned its attention to the subject, and the House passed a bill, by a majority of two, establishing a Bureau for Freedmen in the War Department. Senator Sumner, who had charge of the bill in the Senate, argued that freedmen and abandoned lands ought to be under the same department, and reported a substitute for the House bill, attaching the Bureau to the Treasury Department. This bill passed, but too late for action in the House. The debates wandered over the whole policy of the administration and the general question of slavery, without touching very closely the specific merits of the measure in hand.

Meantime the election took place, and the administration, returning from the country with a vote of renewed confidence, addressed itself to the matter more seriously. A conference between the houses agreed upon a carefully drawn measure which contained the chief provisions of Charles Sumner's bill, but made the proposed organization a department independent of both the War and Treasury officials. The bill was conservative, giving the new department general superintendence of all freedmen. It was to "establish regulations" for them, protect them, lease them lands, adjust their wages, and appear in civil and military courts as their "next friend." There were many limitations attached to the powers thus granted, and the organization was made permanent. Nevertheless, the Senate defeated the bill, and a new conference committee was appointed. This committee reported a new bill, February 28, which was whirled through just as the session closed, and which became the act of 1865 establishing in the War Department a "Bureau of Refugees, Freedmen, and Abandoned Lands." This last compromise was a hasty bit of legislation, vague and uncertain in outline. A Bureau was created, "to continue during the present War of Rebellion, and for one year thereafter," to which was given "the supervision and management of all abandoned lands, and the control of all subjects relating to refugees and freedmen," under "such rules and regulations as may be presented by the head of the Bureau and approved by the President." A commissioner, appointed by the President and Senate, was to control the Bureau, with an office force not exceeding ten clerks. The President might also appoint assistant commissioners in the seceded states, and to all these offices military officials might be detailed at regular pay.

The Secretary of War could issue rations, clothing, and fuel to the destitute, and all abandoned property was placed in the hands of the Bureau for eventual lease and sale to ex-slaves in forty-acre parcels.

Thus did the United States government definitely assume charge of the emancipated Negro as the ward of the nation. It was a tremendous undertaking. Here, at a stroke of the pen, was erected a government of millions of men,—and not ordinary men, either, but black men emasculated by a peculiarly complete system of slavery, centuries old; and now, suddenly, violently, they come into a new birthright, at a time of war and passion, in the midst of the stricken, embittered population of their former masters. Any man might well have hesitated to assume charge of such a work, with vast responsibilities, indefinite powers, and limited resources. Probably no one but a soldier would have answered such a call promptly; and indeed no one but a soldier could be called, for Congress had appropriated no money for salaries and expenses.

Less than a month after the weary emancipator passed to his rest, his successor assigned Major General Oliver O. Howard to duty as commissioner of the new Bureau. He was a Maine man, then only thirty-five years of age. He had marched with Sherman to the sea, had fought well at Gettysburg, and had but a year before been assigned to the command of the Department of Tennessee. An honest and sincere man, with rather too much faith in human nature, little aptitude for systematic business and intricate detail, he was nevertheless conservative, hard-working, and, above all, acquainted at first-hand with much of the work before him. And of that work it has been truly said, "No approximately correct history of civilization can ever be written which does not throw out in bold relief, as one of the great land marks of political and social progress, the organization and administration of the Freedmen's Bureau."

On May 12, 1865, Howard was appointed, and he assumed the duties of his office promptly on the 15th, and began examining the field of work. A curious mess he looked upon: little despotisms, communistic experiments, slavery, peonage, business speculations, organized charity, unorganized almsgiving,—all reeling on under the guise of helping the freedman, and all enshrined in the smoke and blood of war and the cursing and silence of angry men. On May 19 the new government—for a government it really was—issued its constitution; commissioners were to be appointed in each of the seceded states, who were to take charge of "all subjects relating to refugees and freedmen," and all relief and rations were to be given by their consent alone. The Bureau invited continued cooperation with benevolent societies, and declared, "It will be the object of all commissioners to introduce practicable systems of compensate labor," and to establish schools. Forthwith nine assistant commissioners were appointed. They were to hasten to their fields of work; seek gradually to close relief establishments, and make the destitute self-supporting; act as courts of law where there were no courts, or where Negroes were not recognized in them as free; establish the institution of marriage among ex-slaves, and keep records; see that freedmen were free to choose their employers, and help in making fair contracts for them; and finally, the circular said, "Simple good faith, for which we hope on all hands for those concerned in the passing away of slavery, will especially relieve the assistant commissioners in the discharge of their duties toward the freedmen, as well as promote the general welfare."

No sooner was the work thus started, and the general system and local organization in some measure begun, than two grave difficulties appeared which changed largely the theory and outcome of Bureau work. First, there were the abandoned lands of the South. It had long been the more or less definitely expressed theory of the North that all the chief problems of emancipation might be settled by establishing the slaves on the forfeited lands of their masters,—a sort of poetic justice, said some. But this poetry done into solemn prose meant either wholesale confiscation of private property in the South, or vast appropriations. Now Congress had not appropriated a cent, and no sooner did proclamations of general amnesty appear than the 800,000 acres of abandoned lands in the hands of the Freedmen's Bureau melted quickly away. The second difficulty lay in perfecting the local organization of the Bureau throughout the wide field of work. Making a new machine and sending out officials of ascertained fitness for a great work of social reform is no child's task; but this task was even harder, for a new central organization had to be fitted on a heterogeneous and confused but already existing system of relief and control of ex-slaves; and the agents available for this work must be sought for in an army still busy with war operations,—men in the very nature of the case ill fitted for delicate social work,—or among the questionable camp followers of an invading host. Thus, after a year's work, vigorously as it was pushed, the problem looked even more difficult to grasp and solve than at the beginning. Nevertheless, three things that year's work well worth the doing: it relieved a amount of physical suffering; it transported 7000 fugitives from congested centres back to the farm; and, best of all it inaugurated the crusade of the New England schoolma'am.

The annals of this Ninth Crusade yet to be written, the tale of a mission that seemed to our age far more quixotic than the quest of St. Louis seemed his. Behind the mists of ruin and rapine waved the calico dresses of women who dared, and after the hoarse mouthings of the field guns rang the rhythm of the alphabet. Rich and poor they were, serious and curious. Bereaved now of a father, now of a brother, now of more than these, they came seeking a life work in planting New England schoolhouses among the white and black of the South. They did their work well. In that first year they taught 100,000 souls and more.

Evidently, Congress must soon legislate again on the hastily organized Bureau, which had so quickly grown into wide significance and vast possibilities. An institution such as that was well-nigh as difficult to end as to begin. Early in 1866 Congress took up the matter, when Senator Trumbull, of Illinois, introduced a bill to extend the Bureau and enlarge its powers. This measure received, at the hands of Congress, far more thorough discussion and attention than its predecessor. The war cloud had thinned enough to allow a clearer conception of the work of emancipation. The champions of the bill argued that the strengthening of the Freedmen's Bureau was still a military necessity; that it was needed for the proper carrying out of the Thirteenth Amendment, and was a work of sheer justice to the ex-slave, at a trifling cost to the government. The opponents of the measure declared that the war was over, and the necessity for war measures past; that the Bureau, by reason of its extraordinary powers, was clearly unconstitutional in time of peace, and was destined to irritate the South and pauperize the freedmen, at a final cost of possibly hundreds of millions. Two of these arguments were unanswered, and indeed unanswerable: the one that the extraordinary powers of the Bureau threatened the civil rights of all citizens; and the other that the government must have power to do what manifestly must be done, and that present abandonment of the freedmen meant their practical re enslavement. The bill which finally passed enlarged and made permanent the Freedmen's Bureau. It was promptly vetoed by President Johnson, as "unconstitutional," "unnecessary," and "extrajudicial," and failed of passage over the veto. Meantime, however, the breach between Congress and the President began to broaden, and a modified form of the lost bill was finally passed over the President's second veto, July 16.

The act of 1866 gave the Freedmen's Bureau its final form,—the form by which it will be known to posterity and judged of men. It extended the existence of the Bureau to July, 1868; it authorized additional assistant commissioners, the retention of army officers mustered out of regular service, the sale of certain forfeited lands to freedmen on nominal terms, the sale of Confederate public property for Negro schools, and a wider field of judicial interpretation and cognizance. The government of the unreconstructed South was thus put very largely in the hands of the Freedmen's Bureau, especially as in many cases the departmental military commander was now made also assistant commissioner. It was thus that the Freedmen's Bureau became a full-fledged government of men. It made laws, executed them and interpreted them; it laid and collected taxes, defined and punished crime, maintained and used military force, and dictated such measures as it thought necessary and proper for the accomplishment of its varied ends. Naturally, all these powers were not exercised continuously nor to their fullest extent; and yet, as General Howard has said, "scarcely any subject that has to be legislated upon in civil society failed, at one time or another, to demand the action of this singular Bureau."

To understand and criticise intelligently so vast a work, one must not forget for an instant the drift of things in the later sixties. Lee had surrendered, Lincoln was dead, and Johnson and Congress were at loggerheads; the Thirteenth Amendment was adopted, the Fourteenth pending, and the Fifteenth declared in force in 1870. Guerrilla raiding, the ever present flickering after-flame of war, was spending its force against the Negroes, and all the Southern land was awakening as from some wild dream to poverty and social revolution. In a time of perfect calm, amid willing neighbors and streaming wealth, the social uplifting of 4,000,000 slaves to an assured and self-sustaining place in the body politic and economic would have been an herculean task; but when to the inherent difficulties of so delicate and nice a social operation were added the spite and hate of conflict, the Hell of War; when suspicion and cruelty were rife, and gaunt Hunger wept be side Bereavement,—in such a case, the work of any instrument of social regeneration was in large part foredoomed to failure. The very name of the Bureau stood for a thing in the South which for two centuries and better men had refused even to argue,—that life amid free Negroes was simply unthinkable, the maddest of experiments. The agents which the Bureau could command varied all the way from unselfish philanthropists to narrow-minded busybodies and thieves; and even though it be true that the average was far better than the worst, it was the one fly that helped to spoil the ointment. Then, amid all this crouched the freed slave, bewildered between friend and foe. He had emerged from slavery: not the worst slavery in the world, not a slavery that made all life unbearable,—rather, a slavery that had here and there much of kindliness, fidelity, and happiness,—but withal slavery, which, so far as human aspiration and desire were concerned, classed the black man and the ox together. And the Negro knew full well that, whatever their deeper convictions may have been, Southern men had fought with desperate energy to perpetuate this slavery, under which the black masses, with half-articulate thought, had writhed and shivered. They welcomed freedom with a cry. They fled to the friends that had freed them. They shrank from the master who still strove for their chains. So the cleft between the white and black South grew. Idle to say it never should have been; it was as inevitable as its results were pitiable. Curiously incongruous elements were left arrayed against each other: the North, the government, the carpetbagger, and the slave, hero; and there, all the South that was white, whether gentleman or vagabond, honest man or rascal, lawless murderer or martyr to duty.

Thus it is doubly difficult to write of this period calmly, so intense was the feeling, so mighty the human passions, that swayed and blinded men. Amid it all two figures ever stand to typify that day to coming men: the one a gray haired gentleman, whose fathers had quit themselves like men, whose sons lay in nameless graves; who bowed to the evil of slavery because its abolition boded untold ill to all; who stood at last, in the evening of life, a blighted, ruined form, with hate in his eyes. And the other, a form hovering dark and mother-like, her awful face black with the mists of centuries, had aforetime bent in love over her white master's cradle, rocked his sons and daughters to sleep, and closed in death the sunken eyes of his wife to the world; ay, too, had laid herself low to his lust and borne a tawny man child to the world, only to see her dark boy's limbs scattered to the winds by midnight marauders riding after Damned Niggers. These were the saddest sights of that woeful day; and no man clasped the hands of these two passing figures of the present-past; but hating they went to their long home, and hating children's children live today.

Here, then, was the field of work for the Freedmen's Bureau; and since, with some hesitation, it was continued by the act of 1868 till 1869, let us look upon four years of its work as a whole. There were, in 1868, 900 Bureau officials scattered from Washington to Texas, ruling, directly and indirectly, many million of men. And the deeds of these rulers fall mainly under seven heads,—the relief of physical suffering, the overseeing the beginnings of free labor, the buying and selling of land, the establishment of schools, the paying of bounties, the administration of justice, and the financier lag of all these activities. Up to June, 1869, over half a millions patients had been treated by Bureau physicians and surgeons, and sixty hospitals and asylums had been in operation. In fifty months of work 21,000,000 free rations were distributed at a cost of over $4,000,000,—beginning at the rate of 30,000 rations a day in 1865, and discontinuing in 1869. Next came the difficult question of labor. First, 30,000 black men were transported from the refuges and relief stations back to the farms, back to the critical trial of a new way of working. Plain, simple instructions went out from Washington,—the freedom of laborers to choose employers, no fixed rates of wages, no peonage or forced labor. So far so good; but where local agents differed *toto caelo* in capacity and character, where the personnel was continually changing, the outcome was varied. The largest element of success lay in the fact that the majority of the freedmen were willing, often eager, to work. So contracts were written,—50,000 in a single state,—laborers advised, wages guaranteed, and employers supplied. In truth, the organization became a vast labor bureau; not perfect, indeed,—notably defective here and there,—but on the whole, considering the situation, successful beyond the dreams of thoughtful men. The two great obstacles which confronted the officers at every turn were the tyrant and the idler: the slaveholder, who believed slavery was right, and was determined to perpetuate it under another name; and the freedman, who regarded freedom as perpetual rest. These were the Devil and the Deep Sea.

In the work of establishing the Negroes as peasant proprietors the Bureau was severely handicapped, as I have shown. Nevertheless, something was done. Abandoned lands were leased so long as they remained in the hands of the Bureau, and a total revenue of $400,000 derived from black tenants. Some other lands to which the nation had gained title were sold, and public lands were opened for the settlement of the few blacks who had tools and capital. The vision of landowning, however, the righteous and reasonable ambition for forty acres and a mule which filled the freedmen's dreams, was doomed in most cases to disappointment. And those men of marvelous hind-sight, who to day are seeking to preach the Negro back to the soil, know well, or ought to know, that it was here, in 1865, that the finest opportunity of binding the black peasant to the soil was lost. Yet, with help and striving, the Negro gained some land, and by 1874, in the one state of Georgia, owned near 350,000 acres.

The greatest success of the Freedmen's Bureau lay in the planting of the free school among Negroes, and the idea of free elementary education among all classes in the South. It not only called the schoolmistresses through the benevolent agencies, and built them school houses, but it helped discover and support such apostles of human development as Edmund Ware, Erastus Cravath, and Samuel Armstrong. State superintendents of education were appointed, and by 1870, 150,000 children were in school. The opposition to Negro education was bitter in the South, for the South believed an educated Negro to be a dangerous Negro. And the South was not wholly wrong; for education among all kinds of men always has had, and always will have, an element of danger and revolution, of dissatisfaction and discontent. Nevertheless, men strive to know. It was some inkling of this paradox, even in the unquiet days of the Bureau, that allayed an opposition to human training, which still to-day lies smouldering, but not flaming. Fisk, Atlanta, Howard, and Hampton were founded in these days, and nearly $6,000,000 was expended in five years for educational work, $750,000 of which came from the freedmen themselves.

Such contributions, together with the buying of land and various other enterprises, showed that the ex-slave was handling some free capital already. The chief initial source of this was labor in the army, and his pay and bounty as a soldier. Payments to Negro soldiers were at first complicated by the ignorance of the recipients, and the fact that the quotas of colored regiments from Northern states were largely filled by recruits from the South, unknown to their fellow soldiers. Consequently, payments were accompanied by such frauds that Congress, by joint resolution in 1867, put the whole matter in the hands of the Freedmen's Bureau. In two years $6,000,000 was thus distributed to 5000 claimants and in the end the sum exceeded $8,000,000. Even in this system fraud was frequent; but still the work put needed capital in the hands of practical paupers, and some, at least, was well spent.

The most perplexing and least successful part of the Bureau's work lay in the exercise of its judicial functions. In a distracted land where slavery had hardly fallen, to keep the strong from wanton abuse of the weak, and the weak from gloating insolently over the half-shorn strength of the strong, was a thankless, hopeless task. The former masters of the land were peremptorily ordered about, seized and imprisoned, and punished over and again, with scant courtesy from army officers. The former slaves were intimidated, beaten, raped, and butchered by angry and revengeful men. Bureau courts tended to become centres simply for punishing whites, while the regular civil courts tended to become solely institutions for perpetuating the slavery of blacks. Almost every law and method ingenuity could devise was employed by the legislatures to reduce the Negroes to serfdom,—to make them the slaves of the state, if not of individual owners; while the Bureau officials too often were found striving to put the "bottom rail on top," and give the freedmen a power and independence which they could not yet use. It is all well enough for us of another generation to wax wise with advice to those who bore the burden in the heat of the day. It is full easy now to see that the man who lost home, fortune, and family at a stroke, and saw his land ruled by "mules and niggers," was really benefited by the passing of slavery. It is not difficult now to say to the young freedman, cheated and cuffed about, who has seen his father's head beaten to a jelly and his own mother namelessly assaulted, that the meek shall inherit the earth. Above all, nothing is more convenient than to heap on the Freedmen's Bureau all the evils of that evil day, and damn it utterly for every mistake and blunder that was made.

All this is easy, but it is neither sensible nor just. Some one had blundered, but that was long before Oliver Howard was born; there was criminal aggression and heedless neglect, but without some system of control there would have been far more than there was. Had that control been from within, the Negro would have been reenslaved, to all intents and purposes. Coming as the control did from without, perfect men and methods would have bettered all things; and even with imperfect agents and questionable methods, the work accomplished was not undeserving of much commendation. The regular Bureau court consisted of one representative of the employer, one of the Negro and one of the Bureau. If the Bureau could have maintained a perfectly judicial attitude, this arrangement would have been ideal, and must in time have gained confidence; but the nature of its other activities and the character of its personnel prejudiced the Bureau in favor of the black litigants, and led without doubt to much injustice and annoyance. On the other hand, to leave the Negro in the hands of Southern courts was impossible.

What the Freedmen's Bureau cost the nation is difficult to determine accurately. Its methods of bookkeeping were not good, and the whole system of its work and records partook of the hurry and turmoil of the time. General Howard himself disbursed some $15,000,000 during his incumbency; but this includes the bounties paid colored soldiers, which perhaps should not be counted as an expense of the Bureau. In bounties, prize money, and all other expenses, the Bureau disbursed over $20,000,000 before all of its departments were finally closed. To this ought to be added the large expenses of the various departments of Negro affairs before 1865; but these are hardly extricable from war expenditures, nor can we estimate with any accuracy the contributions of benevolent societies during all these years.

Such was the work of the Freedmen's Bureau. To sum it up in brief, we may say: it set going a system of free labor; it established the black peasant proprietor; it secured the recognition of black freemen before courts of law; it founded the free public school in the South. On the other hand, it failed to establish good will between ex-masters and freed men; to guard its work wholly from paternalistic methods that discouraged self-reliance; to make Negroes landholders in any considerable numbers. Its successes were the result of hard work, supplemented by the aid of philanthropists and the eager striving of black men. Its failures were the result of bad local agents, inherent difficulties of the work, and national neglect. The Freedmen's Bureau expired by limitation in 1869, save its educational and bounty department. The educational work came to an end in 1872, and General Howard's connection with the Bureau ceased at that time. The work of paying bounties was transferred to the adjutant general's office, where it was continued three or four years longer.

Such an institution, from its wide powers, great responsibilities, large control of moneys, and generally conspicuous position, was naturally open to repeated and bitter attacks. It sustained a searching congressional investigation at the insistance of Fernando Wood in 1870. It was, with blunt discourtesy, transferred from Howard's control, in his absence, to the supervision of Secretary of War Belknap in 1872, on the Secretary's recommendation. Finally, in consequence of grave intimations of wrongdoing made by the Secretary and his subordinates, General Howard was court-martialed in 1874. In each of these trials, and in other attacks, the commissioner of the Freedmen's Bureau was exonerated from any willful misdoing, and his work heartily commended. Nevertheless, many unpleasant things were brought to light: the methods of transacting the business of the Bureau were faulty; several cases of defalcation among officials in the field were proven, and further frauds hinted at; there were some business transactions which savored of dangerous speculation, if not dishonesty; and, above all, the smirch of the Freedmen's Bank, which, while legally distinct from, was morally and practically a part of the Bureau, will ever blacken the record of this great institution. Not even ten additional years of slavery could have done as much to throttle the thrift of the freed men as the mismanagement and bankruptcy of the savings bank chartered by the nation for their especial aid. Yet it is but fair to say that the perfect honesty of purpose and unselfish devotion of General Howard have passed untarnished through the fire of criticism. Not so with all his subordinates, although in the case of the great majority of

these there were shown bravery and devotion to duty, even though sometimes linked to narrowness and incompetency.

The most bitter attacks on the Freedmen's Bureau were aimed not so
much at its conduct or policy under the law as at the necessity for any
such organization at all. Such attacks came naturally from the border
states and the South, and they were summed up by Senator Davis, of
Kentucky, when he moved to entitle the act of 1866 a bill "to promote
strife and conflict between the white and black races . . . by a grant of
unconstitutional power." The argument was of tremendous strength, but
its very strength was its weakness. For, argued the plain common sense of
the nation, if it is unconstitutional, unpracticable, and futile for the nation
to stand guardian over its helpless wards, then there is left but one alternative: to make those wards their own guardians by arming them with
the ballot. The alternative offered the nation then was not between full
and restricted Negro suffrage; else every sensible man, black and white,
would easily have chosen the latter. It was rather a choice between suffrage and slavery, after endless blood and gold had flowed to sweep
human bondage away. Not a single Southern legislature stood ready to
admit a Negro, under any conditions, to the polls; not a single Southern
legislature believed free Negro labor was possible without a system of
restrictions that took all its freedom away; there was scarcely a white man
in the South who did not honestly regard emancipation as a crime, and its
practical nullification as a duty. In such a situation, the granting of the ballot to the black man was a necessity, the very least a guilty nation could
grant a wronged race. Had the opposition to government guardianship of
Negroes been less bitter, and the attachment to the slave system less
strong, the social seer can well imagine a far better policy: a permanent
Freedmen's Bureau, with a national system of Negro schools; a carefully
supervised employment and labor office; a system of impartial protection
before the regular courts; and such institutions for social betterment as
savings banks, land and building associations, and social settlements. All
this vast expenditure of money and brains might have formed a great
school of prospective citizenship, and solved in a way we have not yet
solved the most perplexing and persistent of the Negro problems.

That such an institution was unthinkable in 1870 was due in part to certain acts of the Freedmen's Bureau itself. It came to regard its work as
merely temporary, and Negro suffrage as a final answer to all present per-
plexities. The political ambition of many of its agents and protégés led it
far afield into questionable activities, until the South, nursing its own
deep prejudices, came easily to ignore all the good deeds of the Bureau,
and hate its very name with perfect hatred. So the Freedmen's Bureau
died, and its child was the Fifteenth Amendment.

The passing of a great human institution before its work is done, like
the untimely passing of a single soul, but leaves a legacy of striving for

other men. The legacy of the Freedmen's Bureau is the heavy heritage of this generation. To day, when new and vaster problems are destined to strain every fibre of the national mind and soul, would it not be well to count this legacy honestly and carefully? For this much all men know: despite compromise, struggle, war, and struggle, the Negro is not free. In the backwoods of the Gulf states, for miles and miles, he may not leave the plantation of his birth; in well-nigh the whole rural South the black farmers are peons, bound by law and custom to an economic slavery, from which the only escape is death or the penitentiary. In the most cultured sections and cities of the South the Negroes are a segregated servile caste, with restricted rights and privileges. Before the courts, both in law and custom they stand on a different and peculiar basis. Taxation without representation is the rule of their political life. And the result of all this is, and in nature must have been, lawlessness and crime. That is the large legacy of the Freedmen's Bureau, the work it did not do because it could not.

I have seen a land right merry with the sun where children sing, and rolling hills lie like passioned women, wanton with harvest. And there in the King's Highway sat and sits a figure, veiled and bowed, by which the traveler's footsteps hasten as they go. On the tainted air broods fear. Three centuries' thought has been the raising and unveiling of that bowed human heart, and now, behold, my fellows, a century new for the duty and the deed. The problem of the twentieth century is the problem of the color line.

◡ 14 ◡

The Negro as He Really Is

Out of the North the train thundered, and we woke to see the crimson soil of Georgia stretching away bare and monotonous right and left. Here and there lay straggling unlovely villages; but we did not nod and weary of the scene for this is historic ground. Right across our track DeSoto wandered 360 years ago; here lies busy Atlanta, the City of the Poor White, and on to the southwest we passed into the land of Cherokees, the geographical centre of the Negro Problems—the centre of those 9,000,000 men who are the dark legacy of slavery. Georgia is not only thus in the middle of the black population of America, but in many other respects this race question has focused itself here. No other state can count as many as 850,000 Negroes in its population, and no other state fought so long and strenuously to gather this host of Africans.

On we rode. The bare red clay and pines of North Georgia began to disappear, and in their place came rich rolling soil, here and there well tilled. Then the land and the people grew darker, cotton fields and dilapidated buildings appeared, and we entered the Black Belt.

Two hundred miles south of Atlanta, two hundred miles west of the Atlantic, and one hundred miles north of the great Gulf lies Dougherty County. Its largest town, Albany, lies in the heart of the Black Belt, and is to-day a wide-stretched, placid, southern town, with broad street of stores and saloons flanked by row homes usually to the north and blacks to the south. Six days in the week the town looks decidedly too small for itself, and takes frequent and prolonged naps; but on Saturday suddenly the whole country disgorges itself upon this one spot, and a flood of black peasantry passes through the streets, fills the stores, blocks the side walks, chokes the thoroughfares, and takes full possession of the town. They are uncouth country folk, good-natured and simple, talkative to a degree, yet far more silent and brooding than the crowds of the Rhine-Pfalz, Naples, or Cracow. They drink a good deal of whiskey, but they do not get very drunk; they talk and laugh loudly at times, but they seldom quarrel or fight. They walk up and down the streets, meet and gossip with friends, stare at the shop-windows, buy coffee, cheap candy and clothes, and at dusk drive home.

Thus Albany is a real capital—a typical southern country town, the centre of the life of ten thousand souls; their point of contact with the outer world, their centre of news and gossip, their market for buying and selling, borrowing and lending, their fountain of justice and law.

We seldom study the condition of the Negro today honestly and care-fully. It is so much easier to assume that we know it all. And yet, how lit-tle we know of these millions—of their daily lives and longings, of their homely joys and sorrows, of their real short comings and the meaning of their crimes.

Dougherty County, Georgia, had, in 1890, ten thousand black folks and two thousand whites. Its growth in population* may thus be pictured:

This is the Cotton Kingdom, the shadow of a dream of slave empire which for a generation intoxicated a people. Yonder is the heir of its ruins— a black renter, fighting a failing battle with debt. A feeling of silent depres-sion falls on one as he gazes on this scarred and stricken land, with its silent mansions, deserted cabins and fallen fences. Here is a land rich in natural resources, yet poor; for despite the fact that few industries pay better divi-dends than cotton manufacture; despite the fact the modern dry-goods store with its mass of cotton-fabrics represents the high-water mark of retail store-keeping; despite all this, the truth remains that half the cotton-growers of the south are nearly bankrupt and the black laborer in the cotton fields is a serf.

The key-note of the Black Belt is debt. Not credit, in the commercial sense of the term, but debt in the sense of continued inability to make income cover expense. This is the direct heritage of the south from the wasteful economics of the slave regime, but it was emphasized and

---

*The boundaries of the county have frequently changed. It was a part of Early County first, then of Baker, and finally was laid out as Dougherty in 1853.

Year	Negroes	Whites	Totals
1820	225	551	776
1830	276	977	1,253
1840	1,779	2,447	4,226
1850	3,769	4,351	8,120
1860	6,088	2,207	8,295
1870	9,424	2,093	11,517
1880	10,670	1,952	12,622
1890	10,231	1,975	12,206
1899	9,000	—	—

brought to a crisis by the emancipation of the slaves. In 1860 Dougherty County had 6,079 slaves worth probably $2,500,000; its farms were estimated at $2,995,923. Here was $5,500,000 of property, the value of which depended largely on the slave system, and on the speculative demand for land once marvelously rich, but already devitalized by careless and exhaustive culture. The war then meant a financial crash; in place of the $5,500,000 of 1860, there remained in 1870 only farms valued at $1,739,470. With this came increased competition in cotton culture from the rich lands of Texas, a steady fall in the price of cotton followed from about fourteen cents a pound in 1860[†] until it reached four cents in 1893. Such a financial revolution was it that involved the owners of the cotton belt in debt. And if things went ill with the master, how fared it with the man?

The plantations of Dougherty in slavery days were not so imposing and aristocratic as those of Virginia. The Big House was smaller and usually one-storied, and set very near the slave cabins. The form and disposition of the laborers' cabins throughout the Black Belt, is today, the same as in slavery days. All are sprinkled in little groups over the face of the land centering about some dilapidated Big House where the head tenant or agent lives. There were reported in the county out side the corporate town of Albany 1,424 Negro families in 1899. Out of all these only a single one occupied a house of seven rooms; only fourteen have five-rooms or more. The mass live in one and two-room homes. The size and arrangements of a people's homes are a fair index to their condition. All over the face of the land is the one-room cabin; now standing in the shadow of the Big House, now staring at the dusty road, now rising dark and sombre amid the green of the cotton fields. It is nearly always old and bare, built of rough boards and neither plastered nor sealed. Light and ventilation are supplied by the single door and the square hole in the wall with its wooden shutter. Within is a fire-place, and smoky, and usually unsteady with age: A bed or two, a table, a wooden chest and a few chairs make up

[†]Omitting famine prices during the war.

the furniture, while a stray show-bill or a newspaper decorate the walls. We have come to associate crowding with homes in cities almost exclusively. Here in Dougherty County, in the open country, is crowding enough. The rooms in these cabins are seldom over twenty or twenty-five feet square, and frequently smaller; yet one family of eleven lives, eats and sleeps in one room, while thirty families of eight or more members live in such one-room dwellings.

To sum up, there are among these Negroes over twenty-five persons for every ten rooms of house accommodation. In the worst tenement abominations of New York and Boston there are in no case over twenty-two persons to each ten rooms, and usually not over ten. Of course, one small, close room in a city, without a yard, is in many respects worse than the larger single country room.

The one decided advantage the Negro has is a place to live outside his home—that is the open fields, where most of his life is spent.

Ninety-four per cent of these homes are rented and the question therefore arises, what in the industrial system of the Black Belt is responsible for these wretched tenements? There would seem to be four main causes. First, long custom, born in the time of slavery, has assigned this sort of a home to Negroes, until land owners seldom think of offering better houses. Should white labor be imported here, or the capital here invested be transferred to industries where whites are employed, the owners would not hesitate to erect cosy, decent homes, such as are often found near the new cotton factories. This explains why the substitution of white for black labor is often profitable—the laborer is far better paid and cared for. In the second place, the low standard of living among slaves is naturally inherited among freedmen and their sons; the mass of them do not demand better houses because they do not know what better houses are. Thirdly, the landlords as class have not yet come to realize that it is a good business investment to raise the standard of living among laborers by slow and judicious methods; that a Negro laborer who demands three rooms and fifty cents a day would give far more efficient work and leave a larger profit than a discouraged toiler herding his family in one room and working for thirty cents. Lastly, among such conditions of life there are few incentives to make the laborer become a better farmer. If he is ambitious, he moves to town or tries other kinds of labor; as a tenant farmer his outlook is almost hopeless, and following it as a makeshift he takes the house that is given him without protest.

That we may see more of the working out of these social forces, let us turn from the home to the family that lives in it. The Negroes in this country are noticeable both for large and small families; nearly a tenth of all the families are families of one—that is, lone persons living by themselves. Then, too, there is an unusual number of families of ten or more. The average family is not large, however, owing to the system of labor and the size of the homes, which tends to the separation of family groups. Then the large and continuous migration of young people to town brings down the average. So that one finds many families with hosts of babies, and many newly-married young couples, but comparatively few families with half-grown and grown children.

The families of one are interesting. Some of them—about a fifth—are old people. Away down at the edge of the woods will live some old grizzle-haired black man, digging wearily in the earth for his last bread.—Or yonder, near some prosperous Negro farmer, will sit alone a swarthy auntie, fat and good-humored, supported half in charity and half by odd jobs.

Probably the size of Negro families is decreasing, and that, too, from postponement of marriage, rather than from immorality or loss of physical stamina. Today in this county only two per cent of the boys and sixteen per cent of the girls under twenty are married. Most of the young men marry between the ages of twenty-five and thirty-five, and the girls between twenty and thirty—an advanced age for a rural people of low average culture.

The cause of this is without doubt economic stress—the difficulty of earning sufficient to rear a family. The result is the breaking of the marriage tie and sexual looseness. The number of separated persons is thirty-five per 1000—a, very large number. It would of course be unfair to compare this number of divorce statistics for many of these separated are in reality widowed, were the known, and in other cases the separation is not permanent. Nevertheless here lies the seat of greatest moral danger; there is little or no prostitution among these Negroes, and over four-fifths of the families, after house to house investigation, deserve to be classed as decent people with considerable regard for female chastity. The plague-spot in sexual relations is easy marriage and easy separation. This is no sudden development, nor the fruit of emancipation. It is a plain heritage from slavery. In those days Sam, with his master's consent, "took up" with Mary. No ceremony was necessary, and in the busy life of great plantations of the Black Belt it was usually dispensed with. If now the master needed Sam's work on another plantation or in another part of the same plantation, or if he took a notion to sell the slave, Sam's married life with Mary was usually unceremoniously broken, and then it was clearly to the master's interest to have both of them take new mates. This wide-spread custom of two centuries has not been eradicated in thirty years. Probably seventy-five per cent of the marriages now are performed by the pastors. Nevertheless, the evil is still deep seated and only a general raising of the standard of living will finally cure it.

The ignorance of the ex-slaves is far deeper than crude estimates indicate. It is ignorance of the world and its meaning, of modern economic organization, of the function of government, of individual worth and possibility—indeed, of all those things as to which it was for the interest of the slave system to keep the laboring class in profound darkness. Those very things then which a white boy absorbs from his earliest social atmosphere—starts with, so to speak, are the puzzling problems of the black boy's maturer years. And this, too, not by reason of dullness but for lack of opportunity.

It is hard for an individual mind to grasp and comprehend the real social condition of a mass of human beings without losing itself in details and forgetting that after all each unit studied is a throbbing soul. Ignorant it may be, and poverty-stricken, black and curious in limb and ways and thought; and yet it loves and hates, it toils and tires, it laughs and weeps its bitter tears, and looks in vague and awful longing at the grim horizon of its life—all this, even as you and I. These black thousands are not lazy; they are improvident and careless, they insist on breaking the monotony of toil with a glimpse at the great town-world on Saturday, they have their loafers and ne'er-do-weels, but the great masses of them work continuously and faithfully for a return and under circumstances that would call forth equal voluntary effort from few, if any, other modern laboring class. Over 88 per cent of them, men, women and children, are farmers. The rest are laborers on railroads, in the turpentine forests and elsewhere, teamsters and porters, artisans and servants. There are ten merchants, four teachers, and twenty-one who preach and farm.

Most of the children get their schooling after the "crops are laid by" and very few there are that stay in school after the spring work has commenced. Child-labor is found here in some of its worst phases, as fostering ignorance and stunting physical development.

Among this People there is no leisure class; ninety-six per cent of them are toiling—no one with leisure to turn the bare and cheerless cabin into a home, no old folks to sit beside the fire and hand down traditions of the past, little of careless, happy childhood and dreaming youth. The dull monotony of daily life is broken only by the Saturday trips to town.

The land is still fertile, despite long abuse. For nine and ten months in succession the crops will come if asked; garden vegetables in April, grain in May, melons in June and July, hay in August, sweet potatoes in September, and cotton from then to Christmas. And yet over two-thirds of the land there is but one crop and that leaves the toilers in debt. Why is this?

The merchant of the Black Belt is a curious institution—part banker, part landlord, part Contractor, and part despot. His store which used most frequently to stand at the cross roads and become the centre of a weekly village, has now moved to town and thither the Negro tenant follows him. The merchant keeps everything—clothes and shoes, coffee and sugar, pork and meal, canned and dried goods, wagons and plows, seed and, fertilizer—and what he has not in stock he can give you an order for the store across the way. Here, then, comes the tenant, Sam Scott, after he has contracted with some absent landlord's agent for hiring forty acres of land; he fingers his hat nervously until the merchant finishes his morning chat with Colonel Sanders, when he calls out "Well, Sam, what do you want?" Sam wants him to "furnish" him—i.e., to advance him food and clothing for the year, and perhaps seed and tools, until his crop is raised and sold. If Sam seems a favorable subject he and the merchant go to a lawyer and Sam executes a chattel mortgage on his mule and wagon in return for seed and a week's rations. As soon as the green cotton leaves appear above the ground another mortgage is given on the "crop." Every Saturday or at longer intervals Sam calls upon the merchant for his "rations;" a family of five usually gets about thirty pounds of fat sidepork and a couple of bushels of cornmeal a month. Beside this, clothing and shoes must be furnished. If Sam or his family is sick there are orders on the druggist and doctor. If the mule wants shoeing, an order on the blacksmith etc. If Sam is a hard worker and crops promise well, he is often encouraged to buy more—sugar, extra clothes, perhaps a buggy. But he is seldom encouraged to save. When cotton rose to ten cents last fall the shrewd merchants sold a thousand buggies in one season, mostly to black men.

The security offered for such transactions—a crop and chattel mortgage—may at first seem slight. And indeed, the merchants tell many a true tale of shiftlessness and cheating; of cotton picked at night, mules disappearing and tenants absconding. But on the whole the merchant of the Black Belt is the most prosperous man in the section. So skillfully and so closely has he drawn the bonds of the law and the tenant that the black man has often simply to choose between pauperism and crime; he "waives" all homestead exemptions in his contract; he cannot touch his own mortgaged crop, which the laws put almost in the full control of the landowner and of the merchant. When the crop is growing the merchant watches it like a hawk; as soon as it is ready for market he takes possession of it, sells it, pays the landowner his rent, subtracts his bill for supplies and if, as sometimes happens, there is anything left he hands it over to the black serf for his Christmas celebration.

The direct result of this system is an all-cotton scheme of agriculture and the continued bankruptcy of the tenant. The, currency of the Black Belt is cotton. It is a crop always salable for ready money, not usually subject to great yearly fluctuations in price, and one which the Negroes know how to raise. The landlord therefore demands his rent in cotton, and the merchant will accept mortgages on no other crop. There is no use asking the black tenant then to diversify his crops—he cannot under this system. Moreover, the system is bound to bankrupt the tenant. I remember once meeting a little one-mule wagon on the River road. A young black fellow sat in it driving listlessly, his elbows on his knees. His dark-faced wife sat beside him stolid, silent.

"Hello!" cried my driver—he has a most impudent way of addressing these people, though they seem used to it—"what have you got there?"

"Meat and meal," answered the man, stopping. The meat lay uncovered in the bottom of the wagon, a great thin side of fat pork covered with salt; the meal was in a white bushel bag.

"What did you pay for that meat?"

"Ten cents a pound." It could have been bought for six or seven cents cash.

"And the meal?"

"Two dollars." One dollar and ten cents is the cash price in town. So here was a man paying $5 for goods which he could have bought for $3 cash, and raised for $1 or $1.50.

Yet it is not wholly his fault. The Negro farmer started behind—started in debt. This was not his choosing, but the crime of this happy-go-lucky nation which goes blundering along with its Reconstruction tragedies, its Spanish war interludes and Philippine matinees, just as though God really were dead. Once in debt it is no easy matter for a whole race to emerge.

The other underlying causes of this situation are complicated but discernible. And one of the chief, outside the carelessness of the nation in letting the slave start with nothing, is the widespread opinion among the merchants and employers of the Black Belt that only by the slavery of debt can the Negro be kept at work. Behind this honest and widespread opinion, dishonesty and cheating of the ignorant laborers have a good chance to take refuge. And to all this must be added the obvious fact that a slave ancestry and a system of unrequited toil have not improved the efficiency or temper of the mass of black laborers. Nor is this peculiar to Sambo—it has in history been just as true of John and Hans, of Jacques and Pat, of all ground-down peasantries. Such is the situation of the mass of the Negroes in the Black Belt today, and they are thinking about it. Crime and a cheap, dangerous socialism are the inevitable results of this pondering. I see now that ragged black man sitting on a log, aimlessly whittling a stick. He mutters to me with the murmur of many ages when he says: "White man sit down whole year; Nigger work day and night and make crop; Nigger hardly gits bread and meat; white man sittin' down gits all. It's wrong."

A modern laboring class in most lands would find a remedy for this situation in migration. And so does the Negro, but his movement is restricted in many ways.

In considerable parts of all the gulf states, and especially in Mississippi, Louisiana and Arkansas, the Negroes on the plantations in the back country districts are still held at forced labor practically without wages. Especially is this true in districts where the farmers are composed of the more ignorant class of poor whites, and the Negroes are beyond the reach of schools and intercourse with their advancing fellows. If such a peon should run away, the sheriff, elected by white suffrage, can usually be depended on to catch the fugitive, return him and ask no questions. If he escapes to another county, a charge of petty thieving, easily true, can be depended on to secure his return. Even if some unduly officious person insist upon a trial, neighborly comity will probably make his conviction sure, and then the labor due the county can easily be bought by the master.

Such a system is unusual in the more civilized parts of the South, or near the large towns and cities; but in those vast stretches of land beyond the telegraph and newspaper the spirit of the Fourteenth Amendment is sadly broken. This represents the lowest economic depths of the black American peasant are in a study of the rise and condition of the Negro freeholder we must trace economic progress from this modern serfdom.

Even in the better ordered country districts of the south the free movement of agricultural laborers is hindered by the migration agent laws. The Associated Press informed the world not long since of the arrest of a young white man in south Georgia who represented the "Atlantic Naval Supplies Company," and who "was caught in the act of enticing hands from the turpentine farm of Mr. John Greer." The crime for which this young man was arrested is taxed $500 for each county in which the employment agent proposes to gather laborers for work outside the state. Thus the Negroes' ignorance of the labor market outside his own vicinity is increased rather than diminished by the laws of nearly every southern state.

Similar to such measures is the unwritten law of the back districts and small towns of the south, that the character of all Negroes unknown to the mass of the community must be vouched for by some white man. This is really a revival of the old Roman idea of the patron under whose protection the new-made freedman was put. In many instances this system has been of great good to the Negro, and very often, under the protection and guidance of the former master's family or other white friends, he progressed in wealth and morality. But the same system has in other cases resulted in the refusal of whole communities to recognize the right of a Negro to change his habitation and to be master of his own fortunes. A black stranger in Baker County, Georgia, for instance is liable to be stopped anywhere on the public highway and made to state his business to the satisfaction of any white interrogator. If he fails to give a suitable answer or seems too independent or "sassy" he may be arrested or summarily driven away.

As a result of such a situation arose, first, the Black Belt and, second, the Migration to Town. The Black Belt was not, as many assumed, a movement towards fields of labor under more genial climatic conditions; it was primarily a huddling together for self-protection; a massing of the black population for mutual defense in order to secure the peace and tranquility necessary to economic advance. This movement took place between emancipation and 1880 and only partially accomplished the desired results. The rush to town since 1880 is the counter movement of men disappointed in the economic opportunities of the Black Belt.

In Dougherty County, Georgia, one can see easily the results of this experiment in huddling for protection. Only ten per cent, of the adult population was born in the county, and yet the blacks outnumber the whites four or five to one. There is undoubtedly a security to the blacks in their very numbers—a personal freedom from arbitrary treatment, which makes hundreds of laborers cling to Dougherty in spite of low wages and economic distress. But a change is coming, and slowly but surely even here the agricultural laborers are drifting to town and leaving the broad acres behind. Why is this? Why do not the Negroes become landowners and build up the black landed peasantry, which has for a generation and more been the dream of philanthropist and statesman?

This is the question which this paper seeks to answer; it seeks to trace the rise of the black freeholder in one county of Georgia's Black Belt, and his struggle for survival, to picture present conditions and show why migration to town is the Negro's remedy. To the car-window sociologist, to the man who seeks to understand and know the south by devoting the few leisure hours of a holiday trip to unraveling the snarl of centuries—to such men very often the whole trouble with the black field-hand may be summed up by Aunt Ophelia's word: "Shiftless!" And yet they are not lazy, these men; they work hard when they do work, and they work willingly. They have no sordid selfish money-getting ways but a fine disdain for mere cash. They'll loaf before your face and work behind your back with good-natured honesty. Their great defect as laborers lies in their lack of incentive to work beyond the mere pleasure of physical exertion. They are careless because they have not found that it pays to be careful; they are improvident because the improvident ones of their acquaintance get on about as well as the provident. Above all they cannot see why they should take unusual pains to make the white man's land better or to take more care of his mule and corn.

On the other hand the white land-owner argues that any attempt to improve these laborers by increased responsibility or higher wages or better homes or land of their own would be sure to result in failure. He shows his northern visitor the scarred land, the ruined mansions, the worn-out soil and mortgaged acres and says, "This is Negro freedom!"

Now it happens that both master and man have just enough argument on their respective sides to make it difficult for them to understand each other. The Negro dimly personifies in the white man all his ills and misfortunes; if he is poor it is because the white man secures the fruits of his toil; if he is ignorant it is because the white man gives him neither time nor facilities to learn. And, indeed, if any misfortune happens to him it is because of some hidden machinations of "white folks." On the other hand the masters and the masters' sons have never been able to see why the Negroes, instead of settling down to be day laborers for bread and clothes, are infected with a silly desire to "rise" in the world, and are sulky, dissatisfied and careless where their fathers were happy and dumb and faithful. "Why! these niggers have an easier time than I do," said a puzzled Albany merchant to his black customer. "Yes," he replied "and so does yo' hogs."

Looking now at the county black population as a whole, we might attempt to divide it roughly into social classes. Forty-four families, all landowners, from their intelligence, property and home life would correspond to good middle class people anywhere. Seventy-six other families are honest working people of fair intelligence. One hundred and twenty-five families fall distinctly below the line of respectability and should be classed with the lewd, vicious and potentially criminal. This leaves the mass of the population, 1,229 families composed of the poor, the ignorant, the plodding toilers and shiftless workers—honest and well-meaning, with some, but not great, sexual looseness, handicapped by their history and present economic condition.

The class lines are by no means fixed and immutable. A bad harvest may ruin many of the best and increase the numbers of the worst.

The croppers are entirely without capital, even in the limited sense of food or money, to keep them from seed-time to harvest. All they furnish then is labor; the landowner furnishes land, stock, tools, seed and house, and at the end of the year the laborer gets from a third to a half of the crop. Out of his share, however, comes payment and interest for food and clothing advanced him during the year. Thus we have a laborer without capital and without wages, and an employer whose capital is largely his employees' wages. It is an unsatisfactory arrangement both to hirer and hired, and is usually in vogue on poor land with hard-pressed owners.

Above the croppers come the great mass of the black population who work the land on their own responsibility, paying rent in cotton and supported by the crop mortgage system. After the war this system was attractive to the freedmen on account of its larger freedom and its possibilities for making a surplus. But with the carrying out of the crop-lien system, the deterioration of the land and the slavery of debt, the position of the metayers has sunk to a dead level of practically unrewarded toil. Formerly all tenants had some capital, and often considerable, but absentee landlordism, rack-rent and falling cotton, have stripped them well nigh of all, and probably not over half of them in 1898 owned mules. The change from cropper to tenant was accomplished by fixing the rent. If, now, the rent fixed was reasonable, this was an incentive to the tenant to strive. On the other hand, if the rent was too high, or if the land deteriorated, the result was to discourage and check the efforts of the black peasantry. There is no doubt that the latter case is true; thus in Dougherty County every economic advantage of the price of cotton in the market and of the strivings of the tenant has been taken advantage of by the landlords and merchants, and swallowed up in rent and interest. If cotton rose in price, the rent rose even higher. If cotton fell the rent remained, or followed reluctantly. If a tenant worked hard and raised a large crop, his rent was raised the next year. If that year the crop failed, his corn was confiscated and his mule sold for debt. There were, of course, exceptions to this—cases of personal kindness and forbearance, but in the vast majority of cases the rule was to extract the uttermost farthing from the mass of the black farm laborers.

The result of such rack-rent can only be evil—abuse and neglect of the soil, deterioration in the character of the laborers, and a widespread sense of injustice. On this low plane half the black population of Dougherty County—perhaps more than half the black millions of this land—are today struggling.

A degree above these we may place those laborers who receive money for their work. Some receive a house with perhaps a garden spot, their supplies of food and clothing advanced and certain fixed wages at the end of the year varying from 30 to 60, out of which the supplies must be paid for with interest. About 18 per cent of the population belong to this class of semi-metayers, while 22 per cent are laborers paid by the month or year and either "furnished" by their own savings or perhaps more usually by some merchant who takes his chances of payment. Such laborers receive 35 cents to 40 cents a day during the working season. They are usually young unmarried persons, some being women, and when they marry they sink to the class of metayers, or, more seldom, be come renters.

The renters for fixed money rentals are the first of the emerging classes and form 4.6 per cent of the families. The sole advantage of this small class is their freedom to choose their crops, and the increased responsibility which comes through having money transactions. While some of the renters differ little in condition from the metayers, yet on the whole they are more intelligent and responsible persons and are the ones who eventually become landowners.

Landholding in this county by Negroes has steadily increased. They held nothing in 1870, but in 1880 they had 2,500 acres. By 1890 this had increased to 10,000 acres, and to 15,000 acres in 1898, owned by 81 families. Of the 185 Negro families who at one time or another have held land in this county during the last thirty years, 1 held his land 25 to 30 years; 4 held their land 20–25 years; 12 held their land 15–20 years; 12 held their land 10–15 years; 41 held their land 5–10 years, and 115 held their land 1–5 years. Most of those in the shorter period still hold their land, so that the record is not complete.

If all the black landowners who had ever held land here had kept it or left it in the hands of black men, the Negroes would have owned nearer 30,000 acres than the 15,000 they now hold. And yet these 15,000 acres are a creditable showing—a proof of no little weight of the worth and ability of the Negro people. If they had been given an economic start at emancipation, if they had been in an enlightened and rich community which really desired their best good, then we might per haps call such a result small or even insignificant. But for a few thousand ignorant field hands in the face of poverty, a falling market, and social stress to save and capitalize

$200,000 in a generation has meant a tremendous effort. The rise of a nation, the pressing forward of a social class, means a bitter struggle—a hard and soul-sickening battle with the world such as few of the more favored classes know or appreciate. Out of the hard economic conditions of this portion of the Black Belt only six per cent of the population have succeeded in emerging into peasant-proprietorship, and these are not all firmly fixed, but grow and shrink in number with the wavering of the cotton market. Fully 94 per cent have struggled for land and failed, and half of them sit in hopeless serfdom. For these there is one other avenue of escape toward which they have turned in increasing numbers, namely, migration to town. A glance at the distribution of land among the black owners curiously reveals this fact. In 1898 the holdings were as follows: Under 40 acres, 49 families; 40 to 250 acres, 17 families; 250 to 1,000 acres, 13 families; 1,000 or more acres, 2 families. Now in 1890 there were forty-four holdings, but only nine of these were under forty acres. The great increase of holdings then has come in the buying of small homesteads near town, where their owners really share in the town life. This then is a part of the rush to town. And for every landowner who has thus hurried away from the narrow life and hard conditions of country life how many field hands, how many tenants, how many ruined renters have joined that long procession? Is it not strange compensation? The sin of the country districts is visited on the town, and the social sores of city life today may, here in Dougherty County and perhaps in many places, near and far, look for their final healing without the city walls.

ᴄⁿ 15 ᴄⁿ

The Savings of Black Georgia

In a commonwealth as large as England and Wales live nearly a million black folk beside more than a million whites. Forty thousand of the fathers of these whites owned a half-million of the fathers and mothers of the blacks—owned them body and soul, bought them and sold them, and won wealth from their unpaid toil. Then, in a whirl of passion and blood, all this was changed, and angry, bankrupt masters looked askance upon 466,000 freedmen. The black people looked confidently northward for something in the line of mules and land. For one cannot live on bare freedom, and little else was in sight, save the grim old master. But the something did not come. To be sure, some marshy islands, half swallowed by the sea, were given to the freedmen, and part of them taken back again. Confiscated plantations were leased, but afterward had to be surrendered, so that by 1864 the freedmen had a bit of land, some bounty money, and their hands.

This story is to tell how the Georgia Negro, thus launched alone on turbulent seas, went to work to save something for himself and his children. In the first decade—1864 to 1874—he accumulated rapidly. A new enthusiasm burned in his soul; it seemed so strange a thing to call himself his own. The master was discouraged. He saw the end of an era, and mistook it for the end of the world. Some sold their land cheaply to the Negroes, others gave it away to favorite old slaves, in half-amused, half-bitter doubt. The Freedmen's Bureau helped and hindered. So in those first ten years Georgia Negroes secured 340,000 acres of land and over four million dollars worth of other property. Not that the land was of much account— it averaged but $4 an acre—or the rest of the property very desirable; still, it was a good beginning.

Then came stormy times. There was the Ku Klux Klan, the withdrawal of the Freedmen's Bureau, the panic of 1873, and the rise in the South of a new hatred of black men because of their blackness and because of the sins of others. A wise government left its wards defenseless before the tempest. What can picture the result better than this?

By 1880 conditions began to improve. Political troubles lessened, law and order prevailed to a larger extent, and, above all, economic forces were shaping themselves in this great undeveloped land. Cotton, which had been sinking steadily from the famine prices of war time to 10 cents a pound in the seventies, now rose suddenly again. The phrase "New South" crept into conversation, and the black laborers of Georgia spat on their hands and began to dig again. It was a wonderful spurt they made in saving in the following decade. Few peasantries can show a like record. In twelve years they increased their property in Georgia one hundred and sixty per cent, or from less than six to fifteen millions of dollars.

The thought of a commercial panic almost inevitably takes one's mind to Wall Street or Lombard. We have visions of stock exchanges, banks, millionaires. But this is but the froth of panics. The real storm, the real tragedy, is spread broadcast over the land. Away back in the country are the ruined homes, the mortgages foreclosed, the hopes of whole lives blighted. Down in the Black Belt of Georgia was felt the full flat force of the blow that struck honest industry in 1892 and 1893. To cap the disturbance in other industrial conditions, down fell the price of cotton: from 11 cents a pound in 1890 to 7-2/3 in 1892; then, with a moment of recovery, to 6 in 1895, and, after a temporary rise, to 5 in 1898 . . . The total property values of the State, Negro and white, felt the same heavy hand of financial depression. . . .

What followed? What must follow but irritation and disappointment, lawlessness and oppression, lynching and crime? Much has been written on the epidemic of barbarity that has recently disgraced the South. But in no case have I seen the panic of '93 given its true weight as a cause. Alone, without a delicate problem of race adjustment, crime was inevitable. In Georgia, in the South, there was added to the distress and vice of a struggling proletariat the dawning attempt of the New South to settle the status of black men. A series of new proscriptive laws were being passed which were peculiarly galling and insulting not to the worst but to the best of the Negroes. Disfranchisement and repression were in the air, and black Georgia grew discouraged. The poor and meaner whites along with their own distress became suddenly aware of the prosperity of their black neighbors and it made them jealous and angry. The Negroes in sudden misfortune became aware of the new slavery of debt—the crop-lien system—which, slowly and cunningly devised under the shadow of prejudice, now consists in carrying the mortgage system down till it includes not simply houses and lands, but vegetables, animals, and men, makes payment hard, interest enormous, and foreclosure easy. In the decade of prosperity a horde of rascals had sprung up to prey on the Negroes' industry and carelessness. There were unscrupulous Jews, grasping Yankees, sons of poor whites; they sold furniture on "installments," they founded tempting "insurance" schemes, they swindled with cheap clocks and organs, and, by the aid of careless laws and the silence of the silent South, they fleeced these black lambs shamelessly, and they are still fleecing.

Struggle, hesitation, and doubt has been the history of Georgia Negroes in the last decade. Often I have had them come to me, saying: "But what will be the end of it all? Is there any use striving? Will these white folks ever give the colored man a chance?"

Woe to the South when the Negro loses hope! In this crisis the tide has already turned, but it was dangerous sailing down there near the turning—how dangerous, few knew. In 1899 cotton rose with a jump to 8, then 10 cents a pound. In the whole land industrial conditions had already improved, and in the South the gospel of work outpreached the anathema of lawlessness. The black man today is saving again. Indeed, perhaps, rightly interpreted, that rise and fall of values in the nineties was but the passing of an abnormal wave, like that of the seventies.

Such have been the savings of Black Georgia. Considered in bulk and compared with the capitalization of the Steel Trust, they are modest, very modest. Yet in real value these fourteen millions mean something like $125 for each black family in Georgia—the accumulations of a generation starting with nothing. To appreciate rightly the whole meaning of this, one must consider the incomes. In the country where the crop-lien and contract-labor systems prevail, it is difficult to get at the real income. In 1898, when cotton was lowest, a group of two hundred and seventy-one black farm families, after twelve months' toil, came out at the end of the year as follows:

In debt, 165...............(3, bankrupt)

(61, $100 or more)

(54, $25–100)

(47, under $25)

Cleared nothing........(53)

Cleared somethin .....(53)

(27, under $25)

(21, $25–100)

(5, $100 and over)

In other words, the great mass of these people worked that year for their board and clothes. In more prosperous years they make more and spend more, for it savors of the gambler's risk and gain. In the cities and towns incomes are far better, but even here eighty per cent of the black families have incomes under $500 per year, and over forty per cent under $300. Expenses of living in the town are naturally higher. The incomes of those who earn less than $300 usually go like this:

Rent = 12%

Food = 45%

Clothes = 21%

Taxes = 2%

Misc. = 20%

Those who have from $300 to $500 income spend it this way:

Rent = 9%

Food = 40%

Clothes = 18%

Taxes = 2%

Misc. = 30%

The savings made from these families are distributed in bits here and there, and not concentrated in a few hands. The average size of the Negro land-holdings, outside of towns, is sixty-three acres. Nearly a third of the farms are under ten acres, a little over a fourth from ten to forty acres, and less than a fourth forty to one hundred acres. Half the farms are worth less than $100, and only ten per cent are assessed $500. The towns with something over one-tenth of the total Negro population own one-third of the total property—a fact that shows that some beside the vagabonds are hastening to town.

Outside land and homes there is little investment of savings. Two and a half millions are in mules, cattle, and stock for the farms; a half-million in farming tools and a million and a half in household furniture; $73,000 is invested in merchandise.

Thus has the Georgia freedman saved. It is but a beginning, but a beginning to be proud of and to be encouraged. There is no one Negro problem and consequently no one solution. The day is dawning when this will be more widely recognized, and the man with the panacea will be publicly stamped as a quack. Among other Negro problems, here is one problem of encouraging savings among men whom the Nation for centuries taught to be shiftless. A movement for penny savings banks and land and building associations is needed throughout the South, to atone for the shameful disgrace of the Freedman's Bank, and to make thrift worth while.

In the beautiful new business block built by the Prudential Insurance Company in Atlanta, Ga., is a great marble corridor. Within this are two passenger elevators and a freight elevator. On the latter is this sign: *"For Negroes and other large Packages."* A people who in the midst of public insult and private wrong have saved fourteen millions in a generation deserve encouragement. Their blackness certainly means something—it means Pluck.

∼ 16 ∼

The Spawn of Slavery: The Convict-Lease System in the South

A modified form of slavery survives wherever prison labor is sold to private persons for their pecuniary profit.

—Wines

Two systems of controlling human labor which still flourish in the South are the direct children of slavery, and to all intents and purposes are slavery itself. These are the crop-lien system and the convict-lease system. The crop-lien system is an arrangement of chattel mortgages so fixed that the housing, labor, kind of agriculture and, to some extent, the personal liberty of the free black laborer is put into the hands of the landowner and merchant. It is absentee landlordism and the "company-store" systems united and carried out to the furthest possible degree. The convict-lease system is the slavery in private hands of persons convicted of crimes and misdemeanors in the courts. The object of the present paper is to study the rise and development of the convict-lease system, and the efforts to modify and abolish it.

Before the Civil War the system of punishment for criminals was practically the same as in the North. Except in a few cities, however, crime was less prevalent than in the North, and the system of slavery naturally modified the situation. The slaves could become criminals in the eyes of the law only in exceptional cases. The punishment and trial of nearly all ordinary misdemeanors and crimes lay in the hands of the masters. Consequently so far as the state was concerned, there was no crime of any consequence among Negroes. The system of criminal jurisprudence had to do, therefore, with whites almost exclusively, and as is usual in a land of scattered population and aristocratic tendencies, the law was lenient in theory and lax in execution.

On the other hand, the private well-ordering and control of slaves called for careful cooperation among masters. The fear of insurrection was ever before the South, and the ominous uprising of Cato, Gabriel, Vesey, Turner, and Toussaint made this fear an ever-present nightmare. The result was a system of rural police, mounted and on duty chiefly at night, whose work it was to stop the nocturnal wandering and meeting of slaves. It was usually an effective organization, which terrorized the slaves, and to which all white men belonged, and were liable to active detailed duty at regular intervals.

Upon this system war and emancipation struck like a thunderbolt. Law and order among the whites, already loosely enforced, became still weaker through the inevitable influence of conflict and social revolution. The freedman was especially in an anomalous situation. The power of the slave police supplemented and depended upon that of the private masters. When the masters' power was broken the patrol was easily transmuted into a lawless and illegal mob known to history as the Ku Klux Klan. Then came the first, and probably the most disastrous, of that succession of political expedients by which the South sought to evade the consequences of emancipation. It will always be a nice question of ethics as to how far a conquered people can be expected to submit to the dictates of a victorious foe. Certainly the world must to a degree sympathize with resistance under such circumstances. The mistake of the South, however, was to adopt a kind of resistance which in the long run weakened her moral fiber, destroyed respect for law and order, and enabled gradually her worse elements to secure an unfortunate ascendency. The South believed in slave labor, and was thoroughly convinced that free Negroes would not work steadily or effectively. The whites were determined after the war, therefore, to restore slavery in everything but in name. Elaborate and ingenious apprentice and vagrancy laws were passed, designed to make the freedmen and their children work for their former masters at practically no wages. Some justification for these laws was found in the inevitable tendency of many of the ex-slaves to loaf when the fear of the lash was taken away. The new laws, however, went far beyond such justification, totally igniting that large class of freedmen eager to work and earn property of their own, stopping all competition between employers, and confiscating the labor and liberty of children. In fact, the new laws of this period recognized the Emancipation Proclamation and the Thirteenth Amendment simply as abolishing the slave-trade.

The interference of Congress in the plans for reconstruction stopped the full carrying out of these schemes, and the Freedmen's Bureau consolidated and sought to develop the various plans for employing and guiding the freedmen already adopted in different places under the protection of the Union army. This government guardianship established a free wage system of labor by the help of the army, the striving of the best of the blacks, and the cooperation of some of the whites. In the matter of adjusting legal relationships, however the Bureau failed. It had, to be sure, Bureau courts, with one representative of the ex-master, one of the freedman, and one of the Bureau itself, but they never gained the confidence of the community. As the regular state courts gradually regained power, it was necessary for them to fix by their decisions the new status of the freedmen. It was perhaps as natural as it was unfortunate that amid this chaos the courts sought to do by judicial decisions what the legislatures had formerly sought to do by specific law—namely, reduce the freedmen to serfdom. As a result, the small peccadilloes of a careless, untrained class were made the excuse for severe sentences. The courts and jails became filled with the careless and ignorant, with those who sought to emphasize their new-found freedom, and too often with innocent victims of oppression. The testimony of a Negro counted for little or nothing in court, while the accusation of white witnesses was usually decisive. The result of this was a sudden large increase in the apparent criminal population of the Southern states—an increase so large that there was no way for the state to house it or watch it even had the state wished to. And the state did not wish to. Throughout the South laws were immediately passed authorizing public officials to lease the labor of convicts to the highest bidder. The lessee then took charge of the convicts—worked them as he wished under the nominal control of the state. Thus a new slavery and slave-trade was established.

THE EVIL INFLUENCES

The abuses of this system have often been dwelt upon. It had the worst aspects of slavery without any of its redeeming features. The innocent, the guilty, and the depraved were herded together, children and adults, men and women, given into the complete control of practically irresponsible men, whose sole object was to make the most money possible. The innocent were made bad, the bad worse; women were outraged and children tainted; whipping and torture were in vogue, and the death rate from cruelty, exposure, and overwork rose to large percentages. The actual bosses over such leased prisoners were usually selected from the lowest classes of whites, and the camps were often far from settlements or public roads. The prisoners often had scarcely any clothing, they were fed on a scanty diet of corn bread and fat meat, and worked twelve or more hours a day.

After work each must do his own cooking. There was insufficient shelter; in one Georgia camp, as late as 1895, sixty-one men slept in one room, seventeen by nineteen feet, and seven feet high. Sanitary conditions were wretched, there was little or no medical attendance, and almost no care of the sick. Women were mingled indiscriminately with the men, both in working and sleeping, and dressed often in men's clothes. A young girl at Camp Hardmont, Georgia, in 1895, was repeatedly outraged by several of her guards, and finally died in childbirth while in camp.

Such facts illustrate the system at its worst—as it used to exist in nearly every Southern state, and as it still exists in parts of Georgia, Mississippi, Louisiana, and other states. It is difficult to say whether the effect of such a system is worse on the whites or on the Negroes. So far as the whites are concerned, the convict-lease system lowered the respect for courts, increased lawlessness, and put the states into the clutches of penitentiary "rings." The courts were brought into politics, judgeships became elective for shorter and shorter terms, and there grew up a public sentiment which would not consent to considering the desert of a criminal apart from his color. If the criminal were white, public opinion refused to permit him to enter the chain gang save in the most extreme cases. The result is that even today it is very difficult to enforce the laws in the South against whites, and red-handed criminals go scot-free. On the other hand, so customary had it become to convict any Negro upon a mere accusation, that public opinion was loathe to allow a fair trial to black suspects, and was too often tempted to take the law into their own hands. Finally the state became a dealer in crime, profited by it so as to derive a net annual income for her prisoners. The lessees of the convicts made large profits also. Under such circumstances, it was almost impossible to remove the clutches of this vicious system from the state. Even as late as 1890 the Southern states were the only section of the Union where the income from prisons and reformatories exceeded the expense.[‡] Moreover, these figures do not include the county gangs where the lease system is today most prevalent and the net income the largest.

The effect of the convict-lease system on the Negroes was deplorable. First it linked crime and slavery indissolubly in their minds as simply forms of the white man's oppression. Punishment, consequently, lost the most effective of its deterrent effects, and the criminal gained pity instead of disdain. The Negroes lost faith in the integrity of courts and the fairness of juries. Worse than all, the chain gangs became schools of crime which hastened the appearance of the confirmed Negro criminal upon the scene. That some crime and vagrancy should follow emancipation was inevitable. A nation cannot systematically degrade labor without in some degree debauching the laborer. But there can be no doubt but that the

[‡]Bulletin No. 8, Library of State of New York. All figures in this article are from this source.

Income and Expense of State Prisons and Reformatories, 1890

	Earnings	Expense	Profit
New England	$299,735	$1,204,029	. . . .
Middle States	71,252	1,850,452	. . . .
Border States	597,898	962,411	. . . .
Southern States*	938,406	890,432	$47,974
Central States	624,161	1,971,795	. . . .
Western States	378,036	1,572,316	. . . .

*South Carolina, Georgia, Alabama, Mississippi, Louisiana, Texas and Arkansas.

indiscriminate careless and unjust method by which Southern courts dealt with the freedmen after the war increased crime and vagabondage to an enormous extent. There are no reliable statistics to which one can safely appeal to measure exactly the growth of crime among the emancipated slaves. About seventy per cent of all prisoners in the South are black; this however, is in part explained by the fact that accused Negroes are still easily convicted and get long sentences, while whites still continue to escape the penalty of many crimes even among themselves. And yet allowing for all this, there can be no reasonable doubt but that there has arisen in the South since the war a class of black criminals, loafers, and ne'er-do-weels who are a menace to their fellows, both black and white.

The appearance of the real Negro criminal stirred the South deeply. The whites, despite their long use of the criminal court for putting Negroes to work, were used to little more than petty thieving and loafing on their part, and not to crimes of boldness, violence, or cunning. When, after periods of stress or financial depression, as in 1892, such crimes increased in frequency, the wrath of a people unschooled in the modern methods of dealing with crime broke all bounds and reached strange depths of barbaric vengeance and torture. Such acts, instead of drawing the best opinion of these states and of the nation toward a consideration of Negro crime and criminals, discouraged and alienated the best classes of Negroes, horrified the civilized world, and made the best white Southerners ashamed of their land.

WHAT HAS BEEN DONE

Nevertheless, in the midst of all this a leaven of better things had been working, and tile had effects of the epidemic of lynching quickened it. The great difficulty to be overcome in the South was the false theory of work and of punishment of wrong-doers inherited from slavery. The inevitable result of a slave system is for a master class to consider that the slave exists for his benefit alone—that the slave has no rights which the master is bound to respect. Inevitably this idea persisted after emancipation. The black workman existed for the comfort and profit of white people, and the interests of white people were the only ones to be seriously considered. Consequently, for a lessee to work convicts for his profit was a most natural thing. Then, too, these convicts were to be punished, and the slave theory of punishment as pain and intimidation. Given these ideas, and the convict-lease system was inevitable. But other ideas were also prevalent in the South; there were in slave times plantations where the well-being of the slaves was considered, and where punishment meant the correction of the fault rather than brute discomfort. After the chaos of war and reconstruction passed, there came from the better conscience of the South a growing demand for reform in the treatment of crime. The worst horrors of the convict-lease system were attacked persistently in nearly every Southern state. Back in the eighties George W. Cable, a Southern man, published a strong attack on the system. The following decade Governor Atkinson, of Georgia, instituted a searching investigation, which startled the state by its revelation of existing conditions. Still more recently Florida, Arkansas, and other states have had reports and agitation for reform. The result has been marked improvement in conditions during the last decade. This is shown in part by the statistics of 1895; in that year the prisons and reformatories of the far South cost the states $204,483 more than they earned, while before this they had nearly always yielded an income. This is still the smallest expenditure of a section, and looks strangely small beside New England's $1,190,564. At the same time, a movement in the right direction is clear. The laws are being framed more and more so as to prevent the placing of convicts altogether in private control. They are not, to be sure, always enforced, Georgia having several hundreds of convicts so controlled in 1895 despite the law. In nearly all the Gulf states the convict-lease system still has a strong hold, still debauches public sentiment and breeds criminals.

The next step after the lease system was to keep the prisoners under state control, or, at least, regular state inspection, but to lease their labor to contractors, or to employ it in some remunerative labor for the state. It is this stage that the South is slowly reaching today so far as the criminals are concerned who are dealt with directly by the states. Those whom the state still unfortunately leaves in the hands of county officials are usually leased to irresponsible parties. Without doubt, work, and work worth the doing—i.e., profitable work—is best for prisoners. Yet there lurks in this system a dangerous temptation. The correct theory is that the work is for the benefit of the criminal—for his correction, if possible. At the same time, his work should not be allowed to come into unfair competition with that of honest laborers, and it should never be an object of traffic for pure financial gain. Whenever the profit derived from the work becomes the object of employing prisoners, then evil must result. In the South today it is natural that in the slow turning from the totally indefensible private lease system, some of its wrong ideas should persist. Prominent among these persisting ideas is this: that the most successful dealing with criminals is that which costs the state least in actual outlay. This idea still dominates most of the Southern states. Georgia spent $2.38 per capita on her 2,938 prisoners in 1890, while Massachusetts spent $62.96 per capita on her 5,227 prisoners. Moreover, by selling the labor of her prisoners to the highest bidders, Georgia not only got all her money back, but made a total clear profit of $6.12 on each prisoner. Massachusetts spent about $100,000 more than was returned to her by prisoners' labor. Now it is extremely difficult, under such circumstances, to prove to a state that Georgia is making a worse business investment than Massachusetts. It will take another generation to prove to the South that an apparently profitable traffic in crime is very dangerous business for a state; that prevention of crime and the reformation of criminals is the one legitimate object of all dealing with depraved natures, and that apparent profit arising from other methods is in the end worse than dead loss. Bad public schools and profit from crime explain much of the Southern social problem. Georgia, Florida and Louisiana, as late as 1895, were spending annually only $20,799 on their state prisoners, and receiving $80,493 from the hire of their labor.

Moreover, in the desire to make the labor of criminals pay, little heed is taken of the competition of convict and free laborers, unless the free laborers are white and have a vote. Black laborers are continually displaced in such industries as brick-making, mining, road-building, grading, quarrying, and the like, by convicts hired at $3, or thereabouts, a month.

The second mischievous idea that survives from slavery and the convict-lease system is the lack of all intelligent discrimination in dealing with prisoners. The most conspicuous and fatal example of this is the indiscriminate herding of juvenile and adult criminals. It need hardly be said that such methods manufacture criminals more quickly than all other methods can reform them. In 1891, of all the Southern states, only Texas, Tennessee, Kentucky, Maryland, and West Virginia made any state appropriations for juvenile reformatories. In 1895 Delaware was added to these, but Kentucky was missing. We have, therefore:

	1890	1895
New England	$632,634	$851,581
Border States	233,020	174,781
Southern States	10,498	33,910

And this in face of the fact that the South had in 1890 over four thousand prisoners under twenty years of age. In some of the Southern states—notably, Virginia—there are private associations for juvenile reform, acting in cooperation with the state. These have, in some cases, recently received state aid, I believe. In other states, like Georgia, there is permissive legislation for the establishment of local reformatories. Little has resulted as yet from this legislation, but it is promising.

I have sought in this paper to trace roughly the attitude of the South toward crime. There is in that attitude much to condemn, but also something to praise. The tendencies are today certainly in the right direction, but there is a long battle to be fought with prejudice and inertia before the South will realize that a black criminal is a human being, to be punished firmly but humanely, it is the sole object of making him a safe member of society, and that a white criminal at large is a menace and a danger. The greatest difficulty today in the way of reform is this race question. The movement for juvenile reformatories in Georgia would have succeeded some years ago, in all probability, had not the argument been used: it is chiefly for the benefit of Negroes. Until the public opinion of the ruling masses of the South can see that the prevention of crime among Negroes is just as necessary, just as profitable, for the whites themselves, as prevention among whites, all true betterment in courts and prisons will be hindered. Above all, we must remember that crime is not normal; that the appearance of crime among Southern Negroes is a symptom of wrong social conditions—of a stress of life greater than a large part of the community can bear. The Negro is not naturally criminal; he is usually patient and law-abiding. If slavery, the convict-lease system, the traffic in criminal labor, the lack of juvenile reformatories, together with the unfortunate discrimination and prejudice in other walks of life, have led to that sort of social protest and revolt which we call crime, then we must look for remedy in the sane reform of these wrong social conditions, and not in intimidation, savagery, or the legalized slavery of men.

～ 17 ～

Of the Training of Black Men

From the shimmering swirl of waters where many, many thoughts ago the slave-ship first saw the square tower of Jamestown have flowed down to our day three streams of thinking: one from the larger world here and over-seas, saying, the multiplying of human wants in cultured lands calls for the world-wide cooperation of men in satisfying them. Hence arises a new human unity, pulling the ends of earth nearer, and all men, black, yellow, and white. The larger humanity strives to feel in this contact of living nations and sleeping hordes a thrill of new life in the world, crying, If the contact of Life and Sleep be Death, shame on such

Life. To be sure, behind this thought lurks the afterthought of force and dominion—the making of brown men to delve when the temptation of beads and red calico cloys.

The second thought streaming from the death-ship and the curving river is the thought of the older South: the sincere and passionate belief that somewhere between men and cattle God created a *tertium quid*, and called it a Negro,—a clownish, simple creature, at times even lovable within its limitation, but straitly foreordained to walk within the Veil. To be sure, behind the thought lurks the afterthought,—some of them with favoring chance might become men, but in sheer self-defense we dare not let them, and build about them walls so high, and hang between them and the light a veil so thick that they shall not even think of breaking through.

And last of all there trickles down that third and darker thought, the thought of the things themselves, the confused half-conscious mutter of men who are black and whitened, crying Liberty, Freedom, Opportunity— vouchsafe to us, O boastful World, the chance of living men! To be sure, behind the thought lurks the afterthought: suppose, after all, the World is right and we are less than men? Suppose this mad impulse within is all wrong, Some mock mirage from the untrue?

So here we stand among thoughts of human unity, even through conquest and slavery; the inferiority of black men, even if forced by fraud; a shriek in the night for the freedom of men who themselves are not yet sure of their right to demand it. This is the tangle of thought and afterthought wherein we are called to solve the problem of training men for life.

Behind all its curiousness, so attractive alike to sage and dilettante, lie its dim dangers, throwing across its shadows at once grotesque and awful. Plain it is to us that what the world seeks through desert and wild we have within our threshold,—a stalwart laboring force, suited to the semi-tropics; if, deaf to the voice of the Zeitgeist, we refuse to use and develop these men, we risk poverty and loss. If, on the other hand, seized by the brutal after thought, we debauch the race thus caught in our talons, selfishly sucking their blood and brains in the future as in the past, what shall save us from national decadence? Only that saner selfishness which, Education teaches men, can find the rights of all in the whirl of work.

Again, we may decry the color prejudice of the South, yet it remains a heavy fact. Such curious kinks of the human mind exist and must be reckoned with soberly. They cannot be laughed away, nor always successfully stormed at, nor easily abolished by act of legislature. And yet they cannot be encouraged by being let alone. They must be recognized as facts, but unpleasant facts; things that stand in the way of civilization and religion and common decency. They can be met in but one way: by the breadth and broadening of human reason, by catholicity of taste and culture. And so, too, the native ambition and aspiration of men, even though they be black, backward, and ungraceful, must not lightly be dealt with.

To stimulate wildly weak and untrained minds is to play with mighty fires; to flout their striving idly is to welcome a harvest of brutish crime and shameless lethargy in our very laps. The guiding of thought and the deft coordination of deed is at once the path of honor and humanity.

And so, in this great question of reconciling three vast and partially contradictory streams of thought, the one panacea of Education leaps to the lips of all: such human training as will best use the labor of all men without enslaving or brutalizing; such training as will give us poise to encourage the prejudices that bulwark society, and stamp out those that in sheer barbarity deafen us to the wail of prisoned souls within the Veil, and the mounting fury of shackled men.

But when we have vaguely said Education will set this tangle straight, what have we uttered but a truism? Training for life teaches living; but what training for the profitable living together of black men and white? Two hundred years ago our task would have seemed easier. Then Dr. Johnson blandly assured us that education was needful solely for the embellishments of life, and was useless for ordinary vermin. Today we have climbed to heights where we would open at least the outer courts of knowledge to all, display its treasures to many, and select the few to whom its mystery of Truth is revealed, not wholly by truth or the accidents of the stock market, but at least in part according to deftness and aim, talent and character. This programme, however, we are sorely puzzled in carrying out through that part of the land where the blight of slavery fell hardest, and where we are dealing with two backward peoples. To make here in human education that ever necessary combination of the permanent and the contingent—of the ideal and the practical in workable equilibrium—has been there, as it ever must in every age and place, a matter of infinite experiment and frequent mistakes.

In rough approximation we may point out four varying decades of work in Southern education since the Civil War. From the close of the war until 1816 was the period of uncertain groping and temporary relief. There were army schools, mission schools, and schools of the Freedman's Bureau in chaotic disarrangement, seeking system and cooperation. Then followed ten years of constructive definite effort toward the building of complete school systems in the South. Normal schools and colleges were founded for the freedmen, and teachers trained there to man the public schools. There was the inevitable tendency of war to underestimate the prejudices of the master and the ignorance of the slave, and all seemed clear sailing out of the wreckage of the storm. Meantime, starting in this decade yet especially developing from 1885 to 1895, began the industrial revolution of the South. The land saw glimpses of a new destiny and the stirring of new ideals. The educational system striving to complete itself saw new obstacles and a field of work ever broader and deeper. The Negro colleges, hurriedly founded, were inadequately equipped, illogically distributed, and of varying efficiency and grade; the normal and high schools were doing little more than common school work, and the common schools were training but a third of the children who ought to be in them, and training these too often poorly. At the same time the white South, by reason of its sudden conversion from the slavery ideal, by so much the more became set and strengthened in its racial prejudice, and crystallized it into harsh law and harsher custom; while the marvelous pushing forward of the poor white daily threatened to take even bread and butter from the mouths of the heavily handicapped sons of the freedmen. In the midst, then, of the larger problem of Negro education sprang up the more practical question of work, the inevitable economic quandary that faces a people in the transition from slavery to freedom, and especially those who make that change amid hate and prejudice, lawlessness and ruthless competition.

The industrial school springing to notice in this decade, but coming to full recognition in the decade beginning with 1895, was the proffered answer to this combined educational and economic crisis, and an answer of singular wisdom and timeliness. From the very first in nearly all the schools some attention had been given to training in handiwork, but now was this training first raised to a dignity that brought it in direct touch with the South's magnificent industrial development, and given an emphasis which reminded black folk that before the Temple of Knowledge swing the Gates of Toil.

Yet after all they are but gates, and when turning our eyes from the temporary and the contingent in the Negro problem to the broader question of the permanent uplifting and civilization of black men in America, we have a right to inquire, as this enthusiasm for material advancement mounts to its height, if after all the industrial school is the final and sufficient answer in the training of the Negro race; and to ask gently, but in all sincerity, the ever recurring query of the ages, Is not life more than meat, and the body more than meat? And men ask this today all the more eagerly because of sinister signs in recent educational movements. The tendency is here, born of slavery and quickened to renewed life by the crazy imperialism of the day, to regard human beings as among the material resources of a land to be trained with an eye single to future dividends. Race prejudices, which keep brown and black men in their "places," we are coming to regard as useful allies with such a theory, no matter how much they may dull the ambition and sicken the hearts of struggling human beings. And above all, we daily hear that an education that encourages aspiration, that sets the loftiest of ideals and seeks as an end culture and character rather than bread-winning, is the privilege of white men and the danger and delusion of black.

Especially has criticism been directed against the former educational efforts to aid the Negro. In the four periods I have mentioned, we find first, boundless, planless enthusiasm and sacrifice then the preparation of teachers for a vast public school system; then the launching and expansion of that school system amid increasing difficulties; and finally the training of workmen for the new and growing industries. This development has been sharply ridiculed as a logical anomaly and flat reversal of nature. Soothly we have been told that first industrial and manual training should have taught the Negro to work, then simple schools should have taught him to read and write, and finally, after years, high and normal schools could have completed the system, as intelligence and wealth demanded.

That a system logically so complete was historically impossible, it needs but a little thought to prove. Progress in human affairs is more often a pull than a push, surging forward of the exceptional man, and the lifting of his duller brethren slowly and painfully to his vantage ground. Thus it was no accident that gave birth to universities centuries before the common schools, that made fair Harvard the first flower of our wilderness. Son in the South: the mass of the freedmen at the end of the war lacked the intelligence so necessary to modern workingmen. They must first have the common school to teach them to read, write, and cipher. The white teachers who flocked South went to establish such a common school system. They had no idea of founding colleges; they themselves at first would have laughed at the idea. But they faced, as all men since them have faced, that central paradox of the south, the social separation of the races. Then it was the sudden volcanic rupture of nearly all relations between black and white, in work and government and family life. Since then a new adjustment of relations in economic and political affairs has grown up—an adjustment subtle and difficult to grasp, yet singularly ingenious, which leaves still that frightful chasm at the color line across which men pass at their peril. Thus, then and now, there stand in the South two separate worlds; and separate not simply in the higher realms of social intercourse, but also in church and school, on railway and streetcar, in hotels and theatres, in streets and city sections, in books and newspapers, in asylums and jails, in hospitals and graveyards. There is still enough of contact for large economic and group cooperation, but the separation is so thorough and deep that it absolutely precludes for the present between the races anything like that sympathetic and effective group training and leadership of the one by the other, such as the American Negro and all backward peoples must have for effectual progress.

This the missionaries of '68 soon saw; and if effective industrial and trade schools were impractical before the establishment of a common school system, just as certainly no adequate common schools could be founded until there were teachers to teach them. Southern whites would not teach them; Northern whites in sufficient numbers could not be had. If the Negro was to learn, he must teach himself, and the most effective help that could be given him was the establishment of schools to train

Negro teachers. This conclusion was slowly but surely reached by every student of the situation until simultaneously, in widely separated regions, without consultation or systematic plan, there arose a series of institutions designed to furnish teachers for the untaught. Above the sneers of critics at the obvious defects of this procedure must ever stand its one crushing rejoinder: in a single generation they put thirty thousand black teachers in the South; they wiped out the illiteracy of the majority of the black people of the land, and they made Tuskegee possible.

Such higher training schools tended naturally to deepen broader development: at first they were common and grammar schools, then some became high schools. And finally, by 1900, some thirty-four had one year or more of studies of college grade. This development was reached with different degrees of speed in different institutions: Hampton is still a high school, while Fisk University started her college in 1871, and Spelman Seminary about 1896. In all cases the aim was identical: to maintain the standards of the lower training by giving teachers and leaders the best practicable training and above all to furnish the black world with adequate standards of human culture and lofty ideals of life. It was not enough that the teachers of teachers should be trained in technical normal methods; they must also, so far as possible, be broad-minded, cultured men and women, to scatter civilization among a people whose ignorance was not simply of letters, but of life itself.

It can thus be seen that the work of education in the South began with higher Institutions of training, which threw off as their foliage common schools, and later industrial schools, and at the same time strove to shoot their roots ever deeper toward college and university training. That this was an inevitable and necessary development, sooner or later, goes without saying; but there has been, and still is, a question in many minds if the natural growth was not force and if the higher training was not either overdone or done with cheap and unsound methods. Among white Southerners this feeling is widespread and positive. A prominent Southern journal voiced this in a recent editorial:

"The experiment that has been made to give the colored students classical training has not been satisfactory. Even though many were able to pursue the course, most of them did so in a parrot-like way, learning what was taught, but not seeming to appropriate the truth and import of their instruction, and gradually without sensible aim or valuable occupation for their future. The whole scheme has proved a waste of time, efforts, and the money of the state."

While most fair-minded men would recognize this as extreme and over-drawn, still without doubt many are asking, Are there a sufficient number of Negroes ready for college training to warrant the undertaking? Are not too many students prematurely forced into this work? Does it not have the effect of dissatisfying the young Negro with his environment?

And do these graduates succeed in real life? Such natural questions cannot be evaded, nor on the other hand must a nation naturally skeptical as to Negro ability assume an unfavorable answer without careful inquiry and patient openness to conviction. We must not forget that most Americans answer all queries regarding the Negro a priori, and that the least that human courtesy can do is to listen to evidence.

The advocates of the higher education of the Negro would be the last to deny the incompleteness and glaring defects of the present system: too many institutions have attempted to do college work, the work in some cases has not been thoroughly done, timid quantity rather than quality has sometimes been sought. But all this can be said of higher education throughout the land; it is the almost inevitable incident of educational growth, and leaves the deeper question of the legitimate demand for the higher training of Negroes untouched. And this latter question can be settled in but one way—by a first hand study of the facts. If we leave out of view all institutions which have not actually graduated students from a course higher than that of a New England high school, even though they be called colleges; if then we take the thirty-four remaining institutions, we may clear up many misapprehensions by asking searchingly, What kind of institutions are they, what do they teach, and what sort of men do they graduate?

And first we may say that this type of college, including Atlanta, Fisk and Howard, Wilberforce and Lincoln, Biddle, Shaw, and the rest, is peculiar, almost unique. Through the shining trees that whisper before me as I write, I catch glimpses of a boulder of New England granite, covering a grave, which graduates of Atlanta University have placed there:—

in greateful memory of their
former teacher and friend
and of the unselfish life he
lived, and the noble work he
wrought; that they, their
children, and the children's
children might be blessed.

This was the gift of New England to the freed Negro: not alms, but a friend; not cash, but character. It was not and is not money these seething millions want, but love and sympathy, the pulse of hearts beating with red blood; a gift which today only their own kindred and race can bring to the masses, but which once saintly souls brought to their favored children in the crusade of the sixties, that finest thing in American history, and one of the few things untainted by sordid greed and cheap vainglory. The teachers in these institutions came not to keep the Negroes in their place, but to raise them out of their places where the filth of slavery had wallowed them. The colleges they founded were social settlements; homes where the best of the sons of the freedmen came in close and sympathetic touch with the best traditions of New England. They lived and ate together, studied and worked, hoped and harkened in the dawning light. In actual formal content their curriculum was doubtless old-fashioned, but in educational power it was supreme, for it was the contact of living souls.

From such schools about two thousand Negroes have gone forth with the bachelor's degree. The number in itself is enough to attest the argument that too large a proportion of Negroes are receiving higher training. If the ratio to population of all Negro students throughout the land, in both college and secondary training, be countered, Commissioner Harris assures us "it must be increased to five times its present average" to equal the average of the land.

Fifty years ago the ability of Negro students in any appreciable numbers to master a modern college course would have been difficult to prove. Today it is proved by the fact that four hundred Negroes, many of whom have been reported as brilliant students, have received the bachelor's degree from Harvard, Yale, Oberlin, and seventy other leading colleges. Here we have, then, nearly twenty-five hundred Negro graduates, of whom the crucial query must be made, How far did their training fit them for life? It is of course extremely difficult to collect satisfactory data on such a point,—difficult to reach the men, to get trustworthy testimony, and to gauge that testimony by any generally acceptable criterion of success. In 1900, the Conference at Atlanta University undertook to study these graduates, and published the results. First they sought to know what these graduates were doing, and succeeded in getting answers from nearly two-thirds of the living. The direct testimony was in almost all cases corroborated by the reports of the colleges where they graduated, so that in the main the reports were worthy of credence. Fifty-three per cent of these graduates were teachers,—presidents of institutions, heads of normal schools, principals of city school systems, and the like. Seventeen per cent were clergymen; another seventeen per cent were in the professions, chiefly as physicians. Over six per cent were merchants, farmers, and artisans, and four per cent were in the government civil service. Granting even that a considerable proportion of the third unheard from are unsuccessful, this is a record of usefulness. Personally I know many hundreds of these graduates, and have corresponded with more than a thousand; through others I have followed carefully the life-work of scores; I have taught some of them and some of the pupils whom they have taught lived in homes which they have builded, and looked at life through their eyes. Comparing them as a class with my fellow students in New England and in Europe, I cannot hesitate in saying that nowhere have I met men and women with a broader spirit of helpfulness, with deeper devotion to their life-work, or with more consecrated determination to succeed in the face of bitter difficulties than among Negro college-bred men. They have, to be sure, their proportion of ne'er-do-weels, their pedants and lettered fools, but they have a surprisingly small proportion of them; they have not that culture of manner which we instinctively associate with university men, forgetting that in reality it is the heritage from cultured homes, and that no people a generation removed from slavery can escape a certain unpleasant rawness and *gaucherie*, despite the best of training.

With all their larger vision and deeper sensibility, these men have usually been conservative, careful leaders. They have seldom been agitators, have withstood the temptation to head the mob, and have worked steadily and faithfully in a thousand communities in the South. As teachers they have given the South a commendable system of city schools and large numbers of private normal schools and academies. Colored college-bred men have worked side by side with white college graduates at Hampton; almost from the beginning the backbone of Tuskegee's teaching force has been formed of graduates from Fisk and Atlanta. And today the institute is filled with college graduates, from the energetic wife of the principal down to the teacher of agriculture, including nearly half of the executive council and a majority of the heads of departments. In the professions, college men are slowly but surely leavening the Negro church, are healing and preventing the devastations of disease, and beginning to furnish legal protection for the liberty and property of tired toiling masses. All this is needful work. Who would do it if Negroes did not? How could Negroes do it if they were not trained carefully for it? If white people need colleges to furnish teachers, ministers, lawyers, and doctors, do black people need nothing of the sort?

If it be true that there are an appreciable number of Negro youth in the land capable by character and talent to receive that higher training, the end of which is culture, and if the two and a half thousand who have had something of this training in the past have in the main proved themselves useful to their race and generation, the question then comes, What place in the future development of the South ought the Negro college and college-bred man to occupy? That the present social separation and acute race sensitiveness must eventually yield to the influences of culture as the South grows civilized is clear. But such transformation calls for singular wisdom and patience. If, while the healing of this vast sore is progressing, the races are to live for many years side by side, united in economic effort, obeying a common government, sensitive to mutual thought and feeling, yet subtly and silently separate in many matters of deeper human intimacy if this unusual and dangerous development is to progress amid peace and order, mutual respect and growing intelligence, it will call for social surgery at once the delicatest and nicest in modern history. It will demand broad-minded, upright men both white and black, and in its final accomplishment American civilization will triumph. So far as white men are concerned, this fact is today being recognized in the South, and a happy renaissance of university education seems imminent. But the very voices that cry hail to this good work are, strange to relate, largely silent or antagonistic to the higher education of the Negro.

Strange to relate for this is certain, no secure civilization can be built in the South with the Negro as ignorant, turbulent proletariat. Suppose we seek to remedy this by making them laborers and nothing more: they are not fools, they have tasted of the Tree of Life, and they will not cease to think, will not cease attempting to read the riddle of the world. By taking away their best equipped teachers and leaders, by slamming the door of opportunity in the faces of their bolder and brighter minds, will you make them satisfied with their lot? or will you not rather transfer their leading from the hands of men taught to think to the hands of untrained demagogues? We ought not to forget that despite the pressure of poverty, and despite the active discouragement and even ridicule of friends, the demand for higher training steadily increases among Negro youth: there were, in the years from 1875 to 1890, twenty-two negro graduates from northern colleges; from 1885 to 1890 there were forty-three, and from 1895 to 1900, nearly 100 graduates. From Southern negro colleges there were, in the same three periods, 143, 413, and over 500 graduates. Here, then, is the plain thirst for training; by refusing to this Talented Tenth the key to knowledge can any sane man imagine that they will lightly lay aside their yearning and contentedly become hewers of wood and drawers of water?

No. The dangerously clear logic of the Negro's position will more and more loudly assert itself in that day when increasing wealth and more intricate social organization preclude the South from being, as it so largely is, simply an armed camp for intimidating black folk. Such waste of energy cannot be spared if the South is to catch up with civilization. And as the black third of the land grows in thrift and skill, unless skillfully guided in its larger philosophy, it must more and more brood over the red past and the creeping, crooked present, until it grasps a gospel of revolt and revenge and throws its new-found energies athwart the current of advance. Even today the masses of the Negroes see all too clearly the anomalies of their position and the moral crookedness of yours. You may marshal strong indictments against them, but their counter-cries, lacking though they be in formal logic, have burning truths within them which you may not wholly ignore, O Southern Gentlemen if you deplore their presence here, they ask, Who brought us? When you shriek, Deliver us from the vision of intermarriage, they answer, that legal marriage is infinitely better than systematic concubinage and prostitution. And if in just fury you accuse their vagabonds of violating women, they also in fury quite as just may wail: the rape which your gentlemen have done against helpless black women in defiance of your own laws is written on the foreheads of two millions of mulattoes, and written in effaceable blood. And finally, when you fasten crime upon this race as its peculiar trait, they may answer that slavery was the arch-crime, and lynching and lawlessness its twin abortion; that color and race are not crimes, and yet they it is which in this land receive most unceasing condemnation, North, East, South, and West.

I will not say such arguments are wholly justified—I will not insist that there is no other side to the shield; but I do say that of the nine millions of Negroes in this nation, there is scarcely one out of the cradle to whom these arguments do not daily present themselves in the guise of terrible truth. I insist that the question of the future is how best to keep these millions from brooding over the wrongs of the past and the difficulties of the present, so that all their energies may be bent toward a cheerful striving and cooperation with their white neighbors toward a larger, juster, and fuller future. That one wise method of doing this lies in the closer knitting of the Negro to the great industrial possibilities of the South is a great truth. And this the common schools and the manual training and trade schools are working to accomplish. But these alone are not enough. The foundations of knowledge in this race, as in others, must be sunk deep in the college and university if we would build a solid, permanent structure. Internal problems of social advance must inevitably come, problems of work and wages, of families and homes, of morals and the true valuing of the things of life; and all these and other inevitable problems of civilization the Negro must meet and solve largely for himself, by reason of his isolation; and can there be any possible solution other than by study and thought and an appeal to the rich experience of the past? Is there not, with such a group and in such a crisis, infinitely more danger to be apprehended from half-trained minds and shallow thinking than from over-education and over-refinement? Surely we have wit enough to found a Negro college so manned and equipped as to steer successfully between the dilettante and the fool. We shall hardly induce black men to believe that if their bellies be full it matters little about their brains. They already dimly perceive that the paths of peace winding between honest toil and dignified manhood call for the guidance of skilled thinkers, the loving, reverent comradeship between the black lowly and black men emancipated by training and culture.

The function of the Negro college then is clear: it must maintain the standards of popular education, it must seek the social regeneration of the Negro, and it must help in the solution of problems of race contact and cooperation. And finally, beyond all this, it must develop men. Above our modern socialism, and out of the worship of the mass, must persist and evolve that higher individualism which the centres of culture protect; there must come a loftier respect for the sovereign human soul that seeks to know itself and the world about it; that seeks a freedom for expansion and self-development; that will love and hate and labor in its own way, untrammeled alike by old and new. Such souls aforetime have inspired and guided worlds, and if we be not wholly bewitched by our Rhine-gold, they shall again. Herein the longing of black men must have respect: the rich and bitter depth of their experience, the unknown treasures of their inner life, the strange rendings of nature they have seen, may give the world new points of view and make their loving, living, and doing precious to all human hearts. And to themselves in these the days that try their souls the chance to soar in the dim blue air above the smoke is to their finer spirits boon and guerdon for what they lose on earth by being black.

I sit with Shakespeare and he winces not. Across the color line I move arm in arm with Balzac and Dumas, where smiling men and welcoming women glide in gilded halls. From out the caves of Evening that swing between the strong limbed earth amid the tracery of the stars, I summon Aristotle and Aurelius and what soul I will, and they come all graciously with no scorn nor condescension. So, wed with Truth, I dwell above the Veil. Is this the life you grudge us, O knightly America? Is this the life you long to change into the dull red hideousness of Georgia? Are you so afraid lest peering from this high Pisgah, between Philistine and Amalekite, we sight the Promised Land?

～ 18 ～

Hopeful Signs for the Negro

It has often been said that it takes a deeper philosopher to interpret the Present than to read the Past or predict the Future. The whirling web of infinitely intricate thoughts and forces which make the modern world renders problems like those affecting the American Negro peculiarly liable to misapprehension and misinterpretation. Paradoxical as the statement may seem, this is especially apt to be the case when efforts for social betterment and reform are wide-spread and earnest; for reform must begin with a search for truth, with the laying bare of wrongs and weaknesses, and with agitation and complaint. All this is puzzling and distracting, and thus while a growing and acute sense of injury, evil, and bewilderment are in themselves by no means proof of Good, they are the almost inevitable accompaniments of a strife toward the Better. They are signs of the Divine discontent with the Imperfect.

From the failures of others to appreciate these facts, some students of the Negro problems—myself included—are continually accused of pessimism when they point out wrongs, and complain of injustice when in reality their very course shows in most cases an optimistic belief in possible betterment.

The belief that the Negro is steadily improving, and that consequently the problems affecting him are, despite some untoward signs, becoming less hopeless and unsolvable, is widespread among careful students of the situation, and it is based upon the evidences of progress and the changes in public opinion. It is not, to be sure, easy to say precisely what the Negro has accomplished in his single generation of freedom: between boasting and detraction, and praise and blame, the casual reader still stands in considerable doubt. And yet that the Negroes are better off as freemen than as slaves practically everyone admits, and a careful sifting of the reliable evidence would seem to establish the following particular lines of betterment:

In forty years the Negro has—

1. Established the monogamic home;
2. Earned a living as a free laborer;
3. Learned to read and write;
4. Saved some of his earnings;
5. Begun to develop the Exceptional Man—the group leader.

To realize these facts one must ever keep in mind the great saying of Frederick Douglass: "Judge me not from the heights I have attained, but from the depths whence I came." The work of the free Negro has been and long will be that of catching up with civilization.

Take, for instance the matter of home life: to the Negro falls the task, not of restoring a home life, but of building one anew out of the poor material of the past; aboriginal polygamy and plantation concubinage and promiscuity. It goes without saying that under such conditions no perfect reform could be accomplished in a single generation. Sexual looseness, marital infidelity, and desertion are the natural fruit of slavery, and they still persist largely among Negroes. The encouraging feature of the situation is the undeniable progress made since the war. The number of pure, well-conducted Negro homes has increased a thousand fold, the ideal of home life has broadened, the standard of womanly honor has been raised, and there can be found today a large and growing percentage of Negro homes which compare favorably with the average of the nation.

Emancipation means and always has meant crime and vagabondage. These are the natural replies of nature to sudden, violent change. That the change of 1863 was accomplished with so little social revolt as it was, is marvelous. In part this was due to severe repression and co-ercion on the part of the ex-masters; mainly, it was due to the willingness of the free Negro to work, and his eagerness to rise. Thus in a generation the critical transition from a patriarchal communism with forced unpaid labor, to an individualistic free labor system has been largely accomplished, and the whole center of the Negro problem is shifted a step nearer the great labor problem of the common country. Traces of the old system still remain—in laziness and theft, in starvation wages and peonage; but the crisis is past, and the mass of Negroes are earning their living by the sweat of their faces.

In general intelligence the advance of the Negro has been so rapid and marked that the only refuge of doubters is to decry intelligence in itself as a decisive proof of progress. Yet to most people it is highly significant and hopeful to reflect that while in 1870 80 per cent of the Negroes of the country, and 85 per cent of the Negroes of the South could neither read nor write, today nearly three-fifths of the colored people read and write, and over 50 per cent of the black voters can read their ballots. Equally surprising is the fact that the mass of the race has been taught by an army of nearly thirty thousand Negro teachers, and that some of these teachers in turn have been educated by the 2,500 college-bred Negroes which southern and northern colleges have graduated. In addition to these, there have been a number of professional men trained—hundreds of physicians, a considerable per cent of the thousands of clergymen, and a few lawyers.

Slaves can know nothing of thrift. All their training and instruction preclude habits of foresight and saving, and encourage shirking and thoughtless squandering. To-day we see the fruit of this training among Negroes. In no other line is effort more needed than in teaching the Negro how to spend his earnings to the best advantage. Even here, however, the signs of progress are numerous and inspiring. The Negroes of Georgia owned property assessed at five millions of dollars in 1875. Today they have accumulated fifteen and a half million representing something between thirty and forty millions in real value. The Negroes of Virginia own about one-sixth of the land of the state, and pay $50,000 a year in direct taxes on property assessed at sixteen millions. The Negroes of North Carolina are assessed at more than ten millions, and a recent census bulletin shows that the farm property alone of Arkansas Negroes is worth about thirty millions. Probably, therefore, the statement sometimes seen that the colored people of the United States own two hundred million dollars worth of property is an understatement rather than an exaggeration. The same number of thrifty Yankees, starting with nothing would have saved far more than this; still, considering the circumstances, this is a decidedly better result than anyone had a right to expect. Even today there is little to encourage thrift, among the thriftless in the South, and there is crying need of penny savings banks and similar institutions.

Finally, men of Negro blood are beginning to be conspicuous for their deeds and deserts. "Who's Who in America" contains the names of a dozen or more Negroes—some because they are prominent Negroes, but most of them because they are prominent men. Douglass and Crummell, Tanner and Washington, Dunbar and Chesnutt are distinguished and epoch-making figures, judged by any standard. The Negro race is no longer dumb, and whatever one's opinion may be of its average ability and destiny, clearly it has already produced men who fully measure up to the best standards of modern civilization. For many years it was an unanswerable argument when men asked: What has a Negro ever done? Who ever looked at a Negro's picture? or read a black poet's verses? or heard of a Negro's book? And yet all these impossible things have come to pass. At one time no one thought of inviting the Negro to discuss his own situation in conferences on the race problem, any more than a forest commission would invite the trees. Today if he is absent from such discussion his absence must be apologized for. These changes have come silently, almost imperceptibly, and yet, looking backward, we can all see and feel them. Through words and deeds, here and there, now and then in the newspapers and magazines, and in a hundred struggling newspapers of its own, this race is awakening to articulate speech and concerted action.

The second class of signs of progress is the changes of public opinion toward the Negro. One can easily see this by noting the tone of public discussion. Twenty years ago the favorite theme was the Negro's place in the Human Family, and the two camps of opponents were those who insisted from the evidence of the convolutions of his brain and the protruding of his heel that he was a sort of anthropoid ape, and those who maintained that he was a man and a brother and sought to explain away the Curse of Canaan. Today there are still belated pilgrims arguing these same recondite theses; but most persons to-day agree that the Negro is a member of the Human Family, with corresponding rights and duties. To be sure many still think his place is toward the foot of the table, and yet all admit that he may rise and improve in time—how far he may rise and how much he may improve is still a matter of dispute.

Again public opinion today, for the first time, is coming to recognize classes among Negroes, and to suspect any discussion that the colored civil service clerks of Washington and the plantation peons of Mississippi under one head. Men are beginning to see that there are Negroes representing all degrees of training, ability and wealth, and that the differentiation is rapidly progressing.

The place for argument today, then, is not so much the existence of a Better among black folk, as it is the ability of the Worst to follow their footsteps.

Even a [George] Fitzhugh today would hesitate to entitle his pamphlet "Cannibals all! Or Slaves without Masters." Of course Hayti is still available as a bogey, and yet most men admit that Negroes as a race will work and work willingly. They do not always work intelligently or effectively but they are not the lazy vagabonds which the opponents of emancipation predicted they would be.

In the matter of Negro education there have been great changes in public opinion from the time when a Louisiana legislator stopped stock still at the sight of a Negro school and said, "A school for niggers? this is the height of absurdities." Today even the South admits that some degree of education is necessary for Negroes and the country at large insists upon good elementary and industrial training. The ground of discussion now is not whether or not the Negro shall have schools, but rather what kind of schools he shall have. Even those who oppose the higher training of the Negroes in secondary schools and colleges have ceased to argue against the ability of black boys to take such courses—this has been proven in nearly every college of the land—but rather against the present expediency of such training considering the economic and social condition of the race.

Above all the Negro race is gaining respect. There was a time when all allusions to Negroes in the public press were chiefly confined to ridicule, caricature, gross invective, or maudlin pity. This has not wholly passed away, especially in the South and in the dispatches of the Associated Press. And yet there is more evident a disposition to take the Negro seriously; listen to him with respect, and to demand the opinion of experts on –his condition rather than the mouthings of fanatics. Even in the present disfranchising movement, when the nation is perpetrating a monstrous wrong upon a helpless minority, none but fellows like [Benjamin] Tillman presume to base their argument simply on the color-line. In practice they disfranchise black men alone, but in theory they attack only ignorance and poverty. Such action in deference to public opinion is a vast gain in thirty years.

Considering, then, what the Negro may fairly be said to have accomplished, and considering how far an unwilling public opinion has been constrained to recognize this progress, there is ample ground for the belief that right and justice will ultimately prevail in this land, and men will be judged not by their color but by their desert. And the strongest element in this belief is the persistent striving of the Negro. A weaker race would have succumbed; a less daring race would have surrendered in despair. But the American Negro doggedly persists in his demands, and persistently struggles to deserve all that he asks. He never has abated, and never will abate one jot or tittle from his determination to attain in this land perfect equality before the law with his fellow citizens. And in this unwearied struggle lies his greatest hope, for nations as well as men usually get what they earnestly ask for.

～ 19 ～

Possibilities of the Negro: The Advance Guard of the Race

It is usually considered that Negroes are today contributing practically nothing of importance to American civilization; that only one or two individuals of Negro blood have so risen above the average of the nation as rightly to be judged men of mark. Nor is this assumption to be wondered at, for in the world of work men are not labeled by color. When, then, the average American rushes to his telephone there is nothing in the look of the transmitter to tell him that it is part product of a Negro brain; when the whizz of the engine weaves cloth, drags trains, and does other deeds of magic, it does not tell the public that the oil which smooths its turning is the composition of a black man; if the medical student reads in DaCosta of the skilled surgeon who recently sewed up a hole in a living man's heart he will not read that the surgeon was colored; the wanderer amid the beauties of the Luxemburg is not apt to know from the dark hues of the "Raising of Lazarus" the still darker hues of its painter; and it was a Texas girl who naïvely remarked: "I used to read Dunbar a good deal until I found out that he was a nigger."

Such ignorance of the work of black men is natural. A man works with his hands and not with his complexion, with his brains and not with his facial angle; and the result of his work is human achievement and not necessarily a "social problem." Thus his work becomes gathered up and lost in the sum of American deeds, and men know little of the individual. Consequently the average American, accustomed to regarding black men as the outer edge of humanity, not only easily misses seeing the colored men who have accomplished something in the world common to both races, but also misses entirely the work of the men who are developing the dark and isolated world of the black man.

So here I am seeking to bring to mind something of what men of African blood are today doing in America, by selecting as types ten living Negroes who in ability and quite regardless of their black blood have raised themselves to a place distinctively above the average of mankind. Just how far they have risen I am not attempting to say, for human accomplishment is a thing difficult to judge; and particularly difficult in the case of people whose ability and worth is a matter of hot questioning between friends who exaggerate and foes who persistently belittle. I do not say, then, how much of genius or transcendent ability these men have; I do say that measured by any fair standard of human accomplishment they are distinctively men of mark, and that they all have enough black blood in their veins to disfranchise them in Alabama.

Of the fields of endeavor conspicuously open to Americans there are four chief groups: the field of commerce and industry, in which this land has gained world-wide preeminence; the field of political life, in the governing of a continent and seventy millions under republican forms; the field of the learned professions, law, medicine, preaching, and teaching; and, finally, the paths of literature and art, as expressive of the mighty life of a new world. In these four lines of striving the men I notice work.

In commerce and industry the Negro started as the dumb-driven tobacco-hand and cotton raiser—the bottom of the system, without apparent initiative or mechanical ingenuity. Yet today partial records of the United States Patent Office show that 357 patents are known to have been granted Negroes, covering all fields of mechanical contrivances. Foremost among living Negro inventors are Woods and [Elijah] McCoy. The latter is the pioneer in the matter of machinery lubricators; the former is a skilled electrician. Granville I. Woods has patented thirty-five devices; they began with a steam boiler furnace in 1884, and include four kinds of telegraphing apparatus, four electric railway improvements, two electric brakes, a telephone system, a battery, and a tunnel construction for electric roads. His telephone transmitter was assigned to the Bell Telephone Company, and is in use by them. Many of his other inventions have found wide currency, as for instance, the electrical controller system used on the Manhattan Elevated Railway. Mr. Woods was born forty-four years ago, and although he had his difficulties, yet a man with so rare a gift of mechanical ingenuity could hardly be kept back by the handicap of color.

On the other hand, in the world of commerce and business, where men work elbow to elbow and come in close personal touch, there is room for the very effective bar of race prejudice, especially on account of the large part conscious selection plays. A business man may be looking for talent, but he does not look for it in his black office boy or porter; and even if signs of it appear, he is usually certain that he must be deceived—that it is the "imitative" gift only. Consequently the Negro, being a small consumer, is almost shut out of the white business system, and can only enter the business field among his own people, and then in the face of ruthless and skilled competition. For such reasons the Negro business man has developed slowly, and has only reached conspicuous success in cases where special circumstances gave him a chance to stand against competition. The skill of the Philadelphia and New York caterers gave them a chance before the war, but the large capitalism of post-bellum times drove them out of business and gave their sons no opportunity to enter the new system save as menials. Today it is the small retail business and cooperative enterprise of various kinds that is opening new fields which the Negro is entering.

In 1881 a Virginia Negro organized a mutual benefit insurance society in Richmond, with a capital of $150 and one hundred members. Today the "True Reformers," under the presidency of Mr. W. I. Taylor, the successor of the originator, has 50,000 members and $223,500 in real estate; it has paid $2,000,000 in insurance claims, and has established, besides its main business, a bank, a real estate department, a weekly newspaper, an Old Folks' Home, five grocery and general merchandise stores, and a hotel. Such a phenomenal growth, when one considers the material and the opportunity, means unusual ability of management; and it seems fair to rate the president and chief director of this remarkable business as a person of more than average ability according to any standard. To be sure, the organization has undoubtedly stormy times ahead, and yet it is already over twenty years of age, and weathered with conspicuous success the storm of 1893. The savings bank department was opened in 1889 with $4000 capital. Today the bank has 10,000 depositors, and had done a business up to December, 1900, of $7,426,450.92. The real estate department was established in 1882. It now owns fifteen halls, three farms, two dwellings, and one hotel, and holds fourteen halls on lease. The *Reformer*, which is their weekly paper, has a circulation of 8000 copies. A farm for the Old Folks' Home has been bought for $14,000, and a small town laid out. The latest department is the mercantile and industrial association; this association conducts stores in Richmond, Washington, Manchester, Portsmouth, and Roanoke, and these stores did a combined business of $75,000 in 1901. They are rated as "O.K." by the mercantile agencies, and are on a strictly cash basis.

Turning now to the field of political and social activity we may note a long line of Negroes conspicuous in the past, beginning with Toussaint L'Ouverture, American by influence if not by birth, and going past Alexander Hamilton, whose drop of African fire quite recently sent Mrs. Gertrude Atherton into hysterics, down to Purvis, Nell, Douglass and Bruce. All these are dead, and today, strange as the assertion may seem, the leading Negro political leader is Booker T. Washington. Mr. Washington is not a teacher: he has spent little time in the classroom; he is not the originator or chief exponent of the educational system which he so fervently defends. He is primarily the political leader of the New Commercial South, and the greatest of such leaders since Appomattox. His ability has been show is not so much in his educational campaign, nor in his moral earnestness, as in the marvelous facility by which he has so manipulated the forces of a strained political and social situation as to bring about among the factors the greatest consensus of opinion in this country since the Missouri Compromise. He has done this by applying American political and business methods to an attempted solution of the Negro problem. Realizing the great truth that the solution of this vexed question demands above all that somehow, sometime, the southern whites and blacks must agree and sympathize with each other, Mr. Washington started to advertise broadly his proposed basis of agreement so that men might understand it. With this justification, he advertised with a thoroughness that astonished the nation. At the same time he kept his hand on the pulse of North and South, advancing with every sign of good will and generosity, and skillfully retreating to silence or shrewd disclaimer at any sign of impatience or turmoil. The playing of this game has been simply wonderful, the success phenomenal. To be sure not all men like the outcome, not all men fail to see the terrible dangers of this effort at compromise. Some have felt it their duty to speak strongly against Mr. Washington's narrow educational program, and against the danger of his apparent surrender of certain manhood rights which seem to be absolutely essential to race development and national weal; and above all, against his failure to speak a strong, true note for justice and right; but all this is beside the object of this paper. Of Mr. Washington's great ability as a politic leader of men there can scarce be two opinions. He is manifestly one of the greatest living southerners, and one of the most remarkable of Americans.

It must not be thought that with this new political leadership the old political activity has stopped. The Negro is not eliminated from politics and never will be; he is simply passing through a new phase of the exercise of his political power. Here and there in the legislation of the land his work and influence may still be felt. It has been said several times in various places that the keenest and, in many respects, the most able member of the last Illinois legislature was a Negro lawyer, Edward H. Morris. Mr. Morris represented the richest legislative district in Illinois, the First; on some occasions he presided over the deliberations of the House; he was chairman of the important committee on elections, member of five or six of the other leading committees, and also a member of the steering committee of the Republican party. Born in Kentucky forty-five years ago, he was admitted to the bar at the age of twenty-one, and since then, in the severe competition of a great city, handicapped by color, he has become one of the strong members of the western bar, with a practice of at least $20,000 a year. Many people will qualify their admiration for the unquestionable ability of Mr. Morris by a wish that he was less closely identified with the Chicago political machine, or that his great skill as a lawyer had not been used to free tax-collector Gunning from the toils of the law, or to draw up that marvel of ingenuity, the Illinois municipal ownership bill. On the other hand, Mr. Morris may point with real satisfaction to his defence of the civil-rights legislation, his winning of the suit between Cook County and the city of Chicago, and also of the test case over the taxation of the net receipts on insurance companies.

Continuing in the field of the learned professions it should be noted that no single sign of Negro progress has been of such marked significance as the rise of the Negro physician in the last ten years. The really striking fact about the recent post-office case at Indianola was the driving out of a successful Negro physician, who was crowding the white physicians to the wall, at the same time with the postmistress. It was but a short time ago that a Negro led his class at the Harvard Medical School, and another one in Philadelphia passed the best medical examination in many years under the State authorities. By far the most conspicuous of Negro physicians, for his skill as a surgeon and his unique contributions to science, is Dr. Daniel H. Williams, of Chicago. Dr. Williams, born in Pennsylvania in 1858, is attending surgeon to the Cook County and Provident hospitals in Chicago, and was formerly at the head of the Freedman's Hospital in Washington. In 1893 Dr. Williams operated upon

a stab wound of the heart which had pierced the pericardium; the operation was successful, and the patient was known to be alive three years
afterward.

> Official records do not give a single title descriptive of suture of the peri-
> cardium or heart in the human subject. This being the fact, this case is the
> first successful or unsuccessful case of suture ever recorded.

So said the *Medical Record*, of March 27, 1897. The case attracted the attention of the medical world, as have several other cases of Dr. Williams. It
was only last summer that the Charlotte *Medical Journal* of North Carolina
published a violent article against Negro physicians, stating that the for-
mation of the Negro head was such that they could never hope to gain
efficiency in such a profession. About the same time the editors, Doctors
Register and Montgomery, were writing the following letter to Dr.
Williams in blissful ignorance of his race:

> We have just read a paper of yours entitled "A Report of Two Cases of
> Cesarean section under Positive Indications with Termination in
> Recovering" that was recently published in *Obstetrics*. You are an attractive
> writer. Is it possible for us to get you to do a little editorial writing for us?

Turning now to the professions of teaching and preaching we must
expect here a limited development in certain directions: for the Negro
teacher is almost invariably confined in his work to Negro schools where
the pay is small, the tasks excessive and the grades low. No matter how
much promise a Negro student may show, the path of scholarship is closed
to him in most cases: he can practically never be made assistant or tutor
with time for study and research. Thus a man like Kelly Miller can only by
dint of extraordinary exertion rise above the average of teachers. He was
born two years after the Emancipation Proclamation, and early showed
even in the wretched country schools of South Carolina a mathematical
mind of unusual keenness; but few careers are open to a Negro in mathematics, be he ever so skillful. To be sure, he studied at the Naval
Observatory and in the post-graduate school of Johns Hopkins—politely
unwelcomed. Eventually he became a professor in Howard University—at
a small salary, with much work, and in a position where prospective revenue from students did not attract text-publishers to his really good work
in mathematics. Despite all this he rose slowly, steadily—as a writer on
mathematical subjects, as a student of race problems, as a social leader of
that group of 90,000 black folk at the nation's capital, who are in many
respects the advance guard of nine millions. His subtle, forceful articles
have been read in the *Forum*, the *Outlook*, and the *Dial*; his voice and peculiar power of argument and expression have been heard before many noted
clubs and gatherings, and his recent monograph for the United States
Bureau of Education is of exceptional value. Far beyond, however, this
record of tangible work stands the forceful personality of a clean-hearted,

clear-witted man—an inspirer of youth, a leader of his people, and one who is coming slowly to be recognized as a notable American.

The Negro in this land has produced many ministers of religion of considerable power, from Richard Allen and James Varick to Lemuel Haynes and [Henry] Highland Garnet. But I have chosen as typifying the Negro minister, not one of its forceful orators and organizers—one of that peculiar dynasty of the socio-religious Negro church who have built up this powerful organization—but rather a moral regenerator, an inspirer of ideal Christian living, such as the world, even in its most callous days, has ever recognized and honored. Of such sort were Daniel Payne, the Little Father of a million African Methodists, and Alexander Crummell, the master Christian. These have passed, and their mantle of moral earnestness and impeccable character falls worthily on Francis J. Grimké. In Washington there stands a small red church on Fifteenth Street, well worth your visiting. It was one of the earliest tangible protests of the better part of the Negro world against noise and emotionalism in religion. The children of its founders and their children's children have worshiped here until it has grown to be in a special sense the moral center of black Washington. Here, if you sit of a Sunday morning, you will see immediately the perfect earnestness and moral fervor of the tall, thin preacher whose stern, carved lineaments are so impressive; and you will hear a simple, clear-cut sermon with fearless conclusions. It will be easy for you to see the influence for goodness and truth and purity that now for full twenty-one years has gone forth from these lips and out from these low doors; perhaps some time in life you may learn how the influence of this one man, and of her whom God joined to him, has in the course of half a century of life, through the medium of a pure home, a righteous church, and unquestioned personal integrity, so built itself into the lives and hearts of a myriad of men and women as to make the world visibly better for their living.

The late Dr. [James] McCosh considered Mr. Grimké, when studying at Princeton, "as able and promising a student as any we had," and the same kind of testimony has followed his life work as pastor, as school commissioner of the District of Columbia, as trustee of Howard University, and as preacher at Hampton and Tuskegee.

> I do not really know whether I have done anything worth mentioning or not. . . . I have thought of but one thing—the work, in which I have been deeply, profoundly interested. I have longed with all my heart to be of service to our poor, struggling race, and have labored as best I could to help it in the effort which it is making to rise. No one has felt more keenly than I have the wrongs that have been perpetrated upon us and are still being perpetrated upon us in this country. In spite of all the tremendous odds against us, I am not disposed, however, to become despondent. I have faith in God; faith in the race; and faith in the ultimate triumph of right.

Be Strong!
It matters not how deep entrenched the wrong, How hard the battle goes, the day,
how long. Faint not, fight On! Tomorrow comes the song.

It is in this faith that I am living and moving and working. I have not the
faintest doubt as to the outcome, if we will trust in God and do our level best.

So are the souls who will yet make the Negro race the salt of this poor
earth.

Thus we have striven in the world of work. But the Negro, as the world
has yet to learn, is a child of the spirit, tropical in birth and imagination,
and deeply sensitive to all the joy and sorrow and beauty of life. His message to the world, when it comes in fullness of speech and conscious
poster, will be the message of the artist, not that of the politician or shopkeeper. Already now, and in the past, have flashed faint forerunners, half-
conscious of the message in them, choked at times by its very fervor:
[Phyllis] Wheatley, the crude singer, [Ira] Aldridge, the actor, [William]
Burleigh, and [J.] Rosamond Johnson. Over the sea the masters have
appeared—Pushkin and Dumas and Coleridge Taylor—aye, and Robert
Browning, of whose black blood the world but whispers. Here in America
three artists have risen to places of recognized importance—[Henry
Ossawa] Tanner, the painter; [Paul Laurence] Dunbar, the poet; and
[Charles Wadell] Chesnutt, the novelist.

Widely different are these men in origin and method. Dunbar sprang
from slave parents and poverty; Chesnutt from free parents and thrift;
while Tanner was a bishop's son. To each came his peculiar temptation—
to Dunbar the blight of poverty and sordid surroundings; to Tanner the
active discouragement of men who smiled at the idea of a Negro wanting
to paint pictures instead of fences; and to Chesnutt the temptation of
money making—why leave some thousands of dollars a year for scrib-
bling about black folk? Of the dozens of colored men who, if encouraged,
might have thought and painted and sung, these three alone pressed on,
refusing lightly to be turned aside.

So out of the heart of Dunbar bubbled the lyrics of lowly life—in inimitable rhythm and beauty, with here and there a tinge of the sorrow songs.
Tanner painted slowly, carefully, with infinite pains and alluring color,
deeply original and never sensational, until his pictures hang in many of
the world's best galleries. Chesnutt wrote powerfully, but with great
reserve and suggestiveness, touching a new realm in the borderland
between the races and making the world listen with one short story.

These are the men. But already you are impatient with a question,
"How much Negro blood have they?" The attitude of the American mind
toward the mulatto is infinitely funny. Mixture of blood is dire damnation, cry the men who did the mixing, and then if a prophet arise within
the Veil or a man of any talent—"That is due to his mixed blood," cry the

same men. If, however, we study cases of ability and goodness and talent among the American Negroes, we shall have difficulty in laying down any clear thesis as to the effect of amalgamation. As a matter of historic fact the colored people of America have produced as many remarkable black men as mulattoes. Of the men I have named, three are black, two are brown, two are half white, and three are three-fourths white. Many of those with white blood had one or two generations' start of the others, because their parents or grandparents were natural children of rich Southerners, who sent them North and educated them while the black men toiled in the fields. Then, too, the mulatto is peculiarly the child of the city; probably two-thirds of the city colored people are of mixed blood; and it is the city that inspires and educates the lowly and opens the doors of opportunity. If we choose among these men the two of keenest intellect, one is black and the other is brown; if we choose the three of strongest character, two are yellow and one is black. If we choose three according to their esthetic sensibility, one is black, one is yellow, and one is three-fourths white. And so on. Let wise men decide from such cases the exact effect of race mixture, for I cannot.

But what has this to do with the main point? The fact remains that these men, all of them, are representatives of the American Negroes, and whether they represent the five million black, or the four million brown, yellow, and white hosts of this group, they all equally represent those who suffer from caste proscription, from political disability, and wanton narrowing of opportunity. And against this injustice their lives make eloquent and ringing protest.

⌁ 20 ⌁

The Problem of Work

"In the sweat of thy face shall thou eat bread" was the legend of the Hebrew fathers, and from primitive times to this, perhaps no other single idea has so dominated the thoughts of men and influenced their lives. The idea of work is one of those simple concepts which become vast by their very simplicity. For after all, in their larger and more universal aspects, slavery, emancipation and the present Negro problems are merely problems of work, and we can perhaps approach them in no clearer way than by considering them as phenomena of that mangled mass of effort whereby men seek to live.

We all remember Browning's picture of the morning sunlight pouring over Italian hills, and the bursting cry of the watchers

O Day, if I squander a wavelet of thee
A mite of my twelve-hours' treasure
The least of thy gazes or glances
(Be they grants thou art bound to or gifts above measure)
One of thy choices or one of thy chances
(Be they tasks God imposed thee or freaks at thy pleasure)
—My Day, if I squander such labor or leisure, Then shame fall as Azolo,
mischief on me!

This wild impulse to be up and doing, the impatience to be about our father's business, we all have felt. It is seen in the restless leaping of the hound as well as in the whirl of the world city. Not only in the world of men is this impulse to effort so ordered and organized as to be called distinctly work. So true is this that one may early measure civilization by noting the world of work—the organization for toil in which a race or nation lives. Nature is prodigal with her gifts to men and yet her gifts are not wholly free—and the toll must ever be paid; harvest will not come save after planting and tending, fleece will not clothe till it be shorn and woven and the very ripened fruit must be gathered to be eaten. Moreover even the child soon learns that some self-denial today means greater enjoyment to-morrow—that the fruit saved today may return a hundred fold in the spring and this continuous labor long unrewarded reaps extravagant returns after years.

The meaning of work in the world then is clear save for the satisfaction of certain primitive impulses and by moving and doing it is not in itself the end of life, but the means of larger living the threshold at the entrance of life whereat one must answer the questions: What we shall eat and what we shall drink and where withal we shall be clothed? And afterwards it comes to be a flight of ever ascending steps—the labor of love and learning, the toil of prophet and seer, sweeping above and beyond both time and dreaming.

And so, as I have said, if we turn to the world of men we may everywhere measure in a way their status by their attitude toward work. The state of savagery is essentially that of idleness and indolence, of unbridled indulgence, and unforeseeing and spasmodic toil. Such groups ever linger on the edge of extermination and are the playthings of chance and luck; their types survive in more highly organized groups, for society does not raise itself bodily from beneath but stretches upward, so that the most cultivated of nations have always their sub-strata of savages.

A group or tribe of men cannot long remain in simple savagery; a mass of men who work only when they are hungry and desist when their bellies are filled—who think only of present wants and give neither thought nor labor to the future—such groups must later change their mode of life or slowly die away. In history both have happened—the destruction of human life through laziness and lack of ordinary foresight has been and is vast, while on the other hand the stress of want—hunger, thirst and cold—have been the most potent factors in starting men toward civilization.

The essential characteristic of barbarism, that first step above savagery, is its economic organization. The tribe is no longer a fortuitous mass of men, but each member has assigned him, by chance or choice, certain duties toward his fellows and they toward him. These duties are primarily economic and designed to ward off hunger and the destruction of nature and men. The first division of toil is between men and women. The work of hunting and defence—of facing the wild beasts of the fields and breasting the blows of fiercer human enemies has always fallen to the lot of men, while the labor of tending the fields and flocks and rearing of children is given to the women. Within each class again arise differences of duties—the men lead and follow in military hierarchy, they fill the various offices of governments, and among the women we have the beginnings of barter and trade.

Now the ultimate destiny of such barbarous tribes depends largely upon the faithfulness with which these various duties of co-operation are performed and upon the surrounding incentives to struggle—the rocks and seas, the beasts and warriors, the rain and shine. Up in Western Europe where the bleak winds sweep the cold sea sands and the tall silent pines stand sorrowful, with hunger the wandering skin-clad tribes had a grim battle with death and starvation. Some of them became stunted dwarfs and died slowly in the caves and haunted wood, and some became fierce marauding warriors and wandered south toward the wealth and civilization of Italy. In Northern Africa the land teemed with plenty and floods of sunshine poured itself over the lofty central plateau. Tall black warriors wandered down the dark valley of the Nile, met and mingled with the invading Semites of the North and founded Egypt. Other bands moved southward and the noise of battle echoed in the still thick forests, and after the conquest life was easy for the earth was wanton with her fruit.

These cases illustrate certain characteristics of barbarous peoples—they wander on the face of the earth seeking food and change and in their wanderings they meet new peoples and learn new things. Vast influence these may have upon their future. Strange beautiful lands unfold themselves suddenly before them; standing on the foothills of the Alps the Germans looked into Italy—great smiling plains, rolling hills, and nestling lakes lay there in the sunshine and above all tall stately towns, built from shining rock and all unlike the caves and mud huts of their homes. It is thus this civilization is handed on thro' the meeting of diverse peoples—thro' the knowledge gained and treasured and carefully used.

Thereupon nomadic tribes gradually cease their restless wandering and settle themselves, and again arrange and distribute the work before them in accordance with the ideas of dawning civilization.

In a primitive civilization the work of men is laid out in greater detail and nicer precision. There are the priests, the warriors, the merchants, the artisans and the slaves; the wives, the concubines and the servants. The task is not simply to ward off the enemy and prevent hunger and keep out the cold, but to conquer and subdue neighbors and bend them to the common weal, to provide luxury for the palate and live in comfort. But no sooner is this larger and more intricate task of organization and co-operation undertaken than certain new problems of human will and adaptability—of internal arrangement—arise. Differences in the ability of men and in their wants and desires are manifest and above all increased difficulty arises in distributing among the members of the community the work they must each do and the share of common goods they can each receive. The careless communism of barbarism slips away and increasing and varied wants entail increased toil. The hard, grim drudgery of life, the digging and delivering, hauling and lifting become terrifying tasks as the wants of men increased in number intensity and regularity: and three devices were adopted to help the toilers—tools, beasts of burden and slaves; they took the shape of ploughs and wagons, horses and cattle, and above all, the bought and captured men of other nations; and thus within the group grew up distinctions which had scarcely existed before. On the other hand, when the corn was harvested and the cloth woven, when places of honor and profit were to be distributed, there arose again curious difficulties over the way in which individuals must share in the common income, difficulties not settled even in our day in accordance with any easily recognizable rule of logic or entire justice, and in these earlier days settled rather by might and chance and the ultimate survival of certain varying standards of fitness.

So variations and difference of condition rose within the group, some being poor and some rich, a few cultured and a few savage, some honored and some despised, some free and some enslaved, and thus in Athens and Cairo, in Peking and in Rome, the civilization of the world crept on.

I have dwelt on this sketch of the evolution of work among men in order to emphasize the supreme importance of organized toil in any colored civilized nation! The work our hands must find to do, can never be a matter of mere individual will or caprice—it must always be group service, the work of each for all, of all for each, whether the vast design be conscious or unconscious. And the better the work is done, the less there is of friction and suffering—the larger measure of energy and strength is left for making life more than meat and the body more than raiment.

It is peculiarly fitting then that we should recollect such facts because we stand as members—albeit wavering members—yet members of a strangely important nation. There have been upon earth in the great past many groups of people more highly cultured than the Americans of this nation—there have been nations of greater imperial splendor, finer monuments, greater literatures and deeper thought; but never before in the fulness of time have so large a mass of people solved so thoroughly and startlingly the economic problem of furnishing themselves with shelter, victuals and drink as those of this nation, and so deep have these economic foundations been laid that given the necessary access of mental strength and moral purpose. It is quite conceivable that there may rise on the valley of the Mississippi a nation as cultured to-morrow as it is rich today.

With the history of this peculiar nation our connection has been at once interesting and fateful, and especially has it had to do with this same stupendous industrial development. The slavery in America was not that slavery of barbarous and semi civilized times of which I have spoken—a slavery at once defensible as an economic instrument and an humane alternative. But American slavery was the child of that wonderful fifteenth century—the century of the Renaissance, of the awakening of feudal empire to new economic possibilities.

In the vale of the Arno the new age was born—there where the golden river winds and sings beneath the spirit of Michelangelo, Dante and Lorenzo the Magnificent. The age of perpetual warfare was passing; it was possible for the civilized world to heat some of its swords into plowshares and devote a portion of that energy which had budded the new Latin-Germanic nations into furnishing them with better bread and meat, clothing and houses. Foreign trade offered the easiest method of accomplishing this and with one voice Europe called to the sea. On the edge of the world sat Prince Henry of Portugal, whose sailors cautiously crept across the line and seized in 1442 black slaves in the oases below the Sahara. The deep meaning of this did not flash upon the world until the discovery of America. Then the sudden appearance beyond the waters of a great fertile continent presented new and puzzling problems to Europe. They sought first to call it India—for India was a land where deft hands had already fashioned wealth into cunning forms and were ready to sell their wares to the pale foreigners from beyond the world. But in America everything lay raw and unmoulded save the pittance of gold which the Spaniards snatched and for a moment the world hesitated, for here was digging and delving to be done, harsh toil and sweat, before the rich and miserly earth would yield her increase. The toilers of Europe, however, were bound to the soil. They could not move; the feudal system had made them part and parcel of a mighty chain—above the king, by the grace of God, then a nobility proud of its deeds and privileges, then the merchant-artisans bound to their cities and the guilds, and finally over the broad land the bent forms of toiling peasants bound to the soil. Where was the labor for the development of new lands and climes? The nobles were venturesome and sailed the seas, conquering and thirsty for gold, but they would not work by reason of their nobility and could not work by reason of their training. The merchant-artisans had the commerce of Europe to develop with their skill and were of little use as yet in a land where commerce was still unborn. Last came the peasants with the hard hands and great knotted muscles. They had the brawn for the work, and the brain and the daring would gradually come, under the influence of better wages and freer conditions. Clearly then the new-found American was a call to the laborers of Europe and slowly, half fearfully, they started to respond.

Then came the crime that set civilization back 500 years. There were not enough laborers to fill the wallets of the noble adventurers quickly enough; the laborers were strangely selfish and thought of their own interests before those of their masters, and so first the Spanish in their Haytian gold mines, and then the thrifty Dutch and finally the brutal English turned to stealing men to make them work in America and enrich Europe. The wonderful chance to raise the peasantry of Europe by means of the riches of America was pushed back hundreds of years. The internal development of Africa was arrested, the dark races brought in sudden premature contact with all that is worst in European culture, and the problem of work in America was solved in a manner befitting the Dark Age rather than the Age of Enlightenment.

Now the danger of a system of slavery is not so much the inherent cruelty of the system as it is the difficulty it puts in the way of growth and change. In the world of work the problem is continually one of the nicest co-operation among all members of society in doing work which must be done—any mal-adjustment, waste of energy, is not only a dead loss in the present but prophesies disaster for the future. Now in any but a very primitive form of society slavery is a waste of human energy and a mal-adjustment of society. If the slaves are men they are bound in time to become dissatisfied and bitter with their toil, to perform it carelessly and inefficiently and consequently to demand such oversight and repression from the other members of society as to cripple seriously the whole scheme of co-operative toil. A slave society must, therefore, be a sort of military feudalism and every tendency to grow—to give more attention to industry rather than fighting, to doing rather than stopping, to making rather than unmaking, is crushed out by fear and incapacity. So one of two things must happen: Either such a society must retrograde, or it must get rid of slavery. In the United States both things happened side by side; in the North slavery died early and a free labor system replaced it; in the South retrogression set in, altho' the prosperity of the rest of the world kept the flame flickering with artificial brightness, but at last it flared itself out in 1863.

Then came the real crisis, the sudden turning of millions of men to find their places in the modern world of labor—men who had for centuries been trained in the labor system of primitive times. This is the crisis which today is upon us and which we must face consciously and bravely. First of all we must recognize the meaning and working of the modern world-industry.

There sit in the world today four cities which typify modern civilization—Rome, its growth; Paris, its beauty; New York, its energy, and London, its world wide unity. I remember once creeping across the plains of the Campagna to where in the moonlight lay the dim walls of Rome, guarded by the great dome of St. Peter. There rests the Rome of the Republic—scattered bits of stone crushed and hidden lay in the dying splendors of the Rome of Augustus. There sits the Rome of the Popes with the memory of Hildebrand and Leo and above all the Rome of Unification, of Victor Emmanuel and Cavour. One cannot look upon this city, so blended with the memory of saint and Caesar, without realizing with what infinite cost the thread of civilization has been handed on to men from that dim past when the puny city struggled with the wild beasts, to the day when Garibaldi struggled with mightier and wilder forces. The first lesson then that a people new as we are must learn is the slow and painful growth of the civilization we seek to share and the care we must exercise that this delicate plant receives no mortal hurt at our hands.

I remember standing in Paris, there where the mighty avenue sweeps from the palace of the Tuileries to the Arc de Triomphe—from the memory of the 14th Louis to the smoke of Austerlitz. At few other places on earth can one catch so brilliant a glimpse of the possibilities of civilization—the wealth and daintiness, the taste and decorum, the delicate blending of toil and pleasure into a whole, whose beauty is wonderful—all this gives the toilers beyond the seas a glimpse of life above the practical and material into the realm of the world beautiful.

All of us know New York—its bustle and hurry, its seeming maze of effort and rush, and yet above it the wonderful system of work that blends and co-ordinates millions of hands and brains, and helps them feed and clothe and shelter the world. But even here one does not catch so true a glimpse of the bewildering complexity of the mighty machinery that holds the world-industry as one sees in London. A dark, grim city, stolid and crowded, not beautiful but reverent, striking the beholder with a certain awe when he realizes that here the industry of the world centres—that this is that central venous ganglion, sensitive to every movement of the world market—in San Francisco and Calcutta, in Valparaiso and Moscow, in Havana and Hong Kong. It is difficult to grasp so wide a field of work and yet we must gain some faint idea of it if we would understand the world about us.

A grain of wheat sprouts in Minnesota—a hungry child cries in Spain. In the age of Pericles the child might have died of starvation and the wheat rotted in teeming abundance, but today the Spaniard has but to stretch forth his hand to buy cheap bread made from the fruit of these wheat fields. It seems a simple accomplishment but in reality it has taken infinite thought, ingenuity, toil and patience to accomplish this result. The farmer raises his wheat—toils in planting and tending, reaping and grinding. He raises far more wheat than he needs, far more than his neighbors need, and yet he has a strange faith that it will be sold. And he toils on. Up in the dark forests of Michigan a woodman is felling trees. He does not need trees—he has not use for them—no reverence for their beauty and splendor—he cuts them because he knows a man who will buy them from him. Down in the mines of Pennsylvania a crouching man, begrimed and weary, picks away at the ore. He has no use for it—it is sickening toil, but he and his family must live, and men pay him to dig ore. In a small office in Chicago sits a man who deals in lumber. He pays the workmen in the forests, he pays the planers in the mills and then the ship builders and the car builders pay him; across the hall sits the dealer in iron ore, who pays the miners and is paid by the steel makers and iron manufacturers. Beneath the rolling smoke dusky buildings dot the shores of the lake and the glare of furnaces show us the Nibelugen's conjuring wheels and cars; a thousand miles away the rhythmic ring of hammers echo on the building ships and hoarse-voiced engines shriek in the still night. Then the farmer sells his wheat and the cars whirl it across the land and ships carry it over the sea and it lies in the baker's pantry of Madrid. But many is the vicissitude it has escaped: if the farmer raises too much wheat it will be useless and perish with his unpaid toil; if the woodman cut too many trees they will rot, and the lumbermen losing money must cut the woodmen's wages; if the miner digs too much ore it lies as a drug on the market and all summer the miner lies out of work.

But if this be the Scylla of toil there is also the Charybdis; if there is too little food raised, speculation and fear rage, and men starve; if too little wood and iron are ready there are no cars to carry the gold grain; if the ships are not done in time, the grain rots in the elevators and there is poverty and bankruptcy. Nor is this all; such work over vast areas, along myriads of men and at all times and seasons, cannot be done at random, carelessly, but must entail infinite forethought and calculation; how much grain here, how much iron there, how much wages here; when goods must be delivered: what prices must be asked and offered. It takes a year to plant and reap and therefore a year ahead men must calculate; it takes ten years to build and plan a railroad and therefore ten years ahead men must plan and arrange; it takes a century to build a great centre of industry and therefore 100 years ahead human brains must prophesy. Failure and accident must be met, the dangers of over confidence, the disaster of panic—all this from one infinitely small point of view is the world of modern industry and into this world it is that we and our boys and girls must enter.

Now to enter such a world—to become part of the massive and delicate machinery that today binds men in mutual labor—is no light task, especially for those who having long been perforce at the very bottom of usefulness seek to raise themselves to more responsible and delicate tasks and thereby reap richer reward. First of all we must note that the American Negroes already in the mass form some part of the machinery—in the raising of the staple products of Southern agriculture: Cotton, tobacco, sugar and rice—they are of prime importance, and in domestic service they form a large and numerous class. These were the two occupations of slavery times and have naturally descended to the freedmen's sons. If, however, we compare the occupations of blacks and whites in America we find some striking contrasts: Agriculture, mining and domestic service occupy nearly nine-tenths of the Negroes and but three-fifths of the native whites; the great avenues of trade and manufacturing, where the wealth of the country is made, occupy over a third of the native whites and only a tenth of the Negroes. The demand for labor rising from so large a proportion of manufactures has been filled by the incoming foreign immigrants, so that these occupations form almost a direct complement to that of the Negroes; while 60 per cent of the Negroes are farmers and miners, only 25 per cent of the foreign whites are in these industries. While 10 per cent of the Negroes are in trade and manufacturing, nearly half of the foreigners are so engaged. Only in domestic service, where each furnish 30 per cent of their numbers, do these two classes meet in competition.

Now the most significant economic change among Negroes in the last ten or twenty years has been their influx into Northern cities; today New York has three-fourths as many Negroes as New Orleans, Philadelphia has nearly twice as many as Atlanta, Chicago has more than Savannah, and Detroit nearly as many as Austin, Texas. In general the Negro in Northern cities has become a problem. The center of that problem is the question of occupations—the problem of work.

It is manifest that improvement in the Negro's condition can come in two ways; by increased efficiency in present occupations and by entering new occupations. It cannot be said that as a class the Negroes are good farmers or good servants. And this is quite natural—natural because their training was not such as would tend to make self-reliant, business-like farmers nor intelligent, careful servants; and natural again because the best of the younger generation do not willingly share either of these vocations. While, however, this is natural, it is nevertheless dangerous, for we must remember that the condition of survival today in modern industrial civilization is finding an assured place in the great co-operative machine which binds the world in human toil. Slavery gave us a place as farm laborers and servants, and freedom still leaves us that place to a degree. This is our chance, and today the chance of one out of every ten of us to earn our bread and butter. Not only this, but the chance of our rising out of the dead past up into the higher things of the future depends upon our being careful not to surrender the great economic advantage we have here until we have gained foothold in loftier places. On the other hand it would be cruel nonsense, utter blindness for us to check the natural ambition of our children to be more than hewers of wood and drawers of water. During the present century if the advance of the Negro people is normal and satisfactory the number of Negro farmers ought to decrease about ten per cent, the number of servants about one-half, while merchants and manufacturers should be three times as numerous as now among us, and there should be at least twice as many professional men.

Such a change, however, involves tremendous social strain; it means careful selection, extreme faithfulness, and unusual efficiency, and it will be like marshalling and maneuvering a body of skirmishers in the very teeth of the armed hosts of the enemy. The change, too, must come gradually, generation by generation. It is idle to suppose that grown men and women can casually change from farmers to lawyers, or from servants to ministers. We have had quite enough of that sort of idiotic nonsense. The real permanent change will come when the children of farmers are trained carefully to be farmers, merchants and physicians and the children of servants to be servants, blacksmiths and carpenters.

Thus the problem of work, the question of occupation, of earning an honest and honorable living, becomes for us, in its broader and more permanent aspect, a problem of the family—a matter of the intelligent training of children for such careers as can be opened or may now be open to them.

It is this point that I wish this paper especially to emphasize. Our family life is not strong, and, considering its history, the wonder is that it is not far weaker. And yet the centre of our family problem—the point of most serious attention—is changing. Yesterday it was a sheer question of marriage morals—today it is the right training of children; yesterday it had to do with the fearful shadow of concubinage, thrown in our face by the black death of slavery—today it deals with the serious problem of training boys and girls into men and women—souls big with the promise of usefulness and girded with truth.

In the very start we err and err sadly along with our fellow Americans in the giving of our children in marriage. We make it a matter of chance and joke, of haphazard infatuation which we dignify under the name of falling in love. We choose our wives when they are dressed for parade and not when they are girded for housework—when they are at play and not when they are at work—ever in the gayety of laughter and never in the depths of sorrow and care; and when we have chosen them we seek in them smirks, tricks and diversion, rather than strong counsel and common sense. We choose our husbands for their looks and stature, their clothes and carriage, rather than for their ability, pluck and intelligence. We are not singular in this—it is the national crime of America, where parents have so strangely abdicated their God-given right and duty as matchmakers, and the result of it is daily seen in the grim grist of the divorce courts. This is not our excuse, it is rather our warning, to teach us so to launch our children on the sea of matrimony that at least some time may be given to the sailing and not all the energy taken in keeping peace among the passengers.

Our attitude toward our children is too much like our attitude towards storms and accidents in general. We greet them with a gasp of surprise, we never know how to provide for them until provision is no longer necessary, and we seldom consider that we have in our hands infinite human spirits which we may make and mould, not, to be sure, as we will, but into many useful and mighty forms. These are endless problems of childhood and youth—the training of mind and heart, the strengthening of the body, the planting of ideas and ideals. But one thing which I emphasize and the thing we are far too laggard in teaching, is that this is a world of work— a world where men must toil and delve—where in weariness we must eat, in sweat we must struggle, and that the true glory of living is the glory of work well done.

That even above the common light of day into the realms where Art and Science sit singing, even there

> To the heights by great men gained and kept
> Were not attained by sudden flight,
> But they while their companions slept
> Were toiling upward in the night.

There is no lesson that Negro boys and girls so need to master, so need to have unceasingly inculcated as that of the necessity of work—of the hell of idleness—they must be made to know that there is no labor so menial as not to be infinitely above doing nothing, and the mother and father who deliberately allow children to daudle and loaf at home because they cannot find work suited to their dainty hands, deserves the harvest of crime and worthlessness which those children will surely bring upon them—work, tho' it be humble and ill paid, work tho' it be in sorrow and humility, work in the face of obstacle and adversity, is the school that makes men, women and angels.

But the training of the child must not stop here. To say that the lowest work is better than idleness is not saying that we should rear our children to be nothing but servants. On the contrary, with the larger vision of life vouchsafed to us, with the wider knowledge that we have of the world's wants and ways, we, as parents, must continually consider toward what especial field of work the demand of the times and the especial bent of the child incline it. Infinite mistakes are made here which sensible people must avoid. Sickly sentimentality puts the idealist into business, and the mathematician into the church; the dull plodder into the lawyer's chair and the nimble wit on the farm.

Small wonder that we see so many misfits and failures—such continually turning and trying of this and that vocation. It is, to be sure, no easy task to foresee the kind of man the child will make, but is certainly more fruitful to look forward than to look back—to plan for the future than to let the child drift aimlessly into an unknown world.

Now there are great difficulties today in starting any child upon a career—greater than in other ages, because the careers are greater the industrial machine is larger, requiring the extreme of deftness and ability and at the same time leaving less room for executive individuality or original inventiveness. Slowly but surely the accidents of industry are beginning to be eliminated, the waste of mind and matter to be reduced to a minimum. We call part of this movement the growth of trusts and recognizing the tremendous power for good and evil rightly fear to leave it unlimited in the hands of selfish men, and yet the movement is inevitable—the day of wasteful individualistic competition is going, and the day of consolidation, long ago foretold by socialists, is dawning. Its dawning, however, increases, as I have said, the difficulties of young men. The Jack-of-all-trades is not wanted—there is little time for wavering and choosing, and the small savings of ordinary men will scarcely today capitalize the most modest of businesses.

Notwithstanding this the demand for trained men, for men who know some one thing and know it well, the demand for reliable men who can be depended on to shoulder and carry well the vast responsibility of some part of this human industrial machine, the demand for women who can do more than look pretty—the demand for such persons far outstrips the supply, and the families that can furnish such workers will find enviable careers open to their children.

And what richer legacy can a parent leave to a child than the opportunity to labor at the work he is fitted for, to toil at the toil he loves. The father may give him wealth and the mother love, but the gift of God is work.

High on the dark still waters of the northern lakes there rose in the dim and misty past the solemn grandeur of Thunder Cape guarding the gateways of the north, knitting its mighty brows above the forests and the fitful waste of purple waters. The red man shot 'round it, whirling in his birch canoe, singing to the hills the last song of Hiawatha as he passed

> To the islands of the Blessed,
> To the kingdom of Ponemah,
> To the Land of the Hereafter.
> But the mountain sat all silently and the wastes were dumb.

Out of the bosom of the rising sun came the Frenchmen—the cowled and girded priest, the splendid warrior fresh from the kingliest court in Europe. The wolves howled in the forests and the deer trembled; the mountain echoed but spoke not, and still the wilderness lay sad and silent.

And then out of the south, over the hills rock-ribbed and ancient as the sun, came a cry and behind the cry came the Englishmen. They came and threw themselves athwart the bosom of the land and sucked the dew and grovelled in the earth. They called our black fathers and our fathers' fathers over the sad seas with their great arms and dogged strength. The sun cursed the toilers and yet they toiled on; the north wind swept over them—the icy breath of the Seven Seas—and yet they toiled on—toiled till the sea laughed and the wilderness blushed and burst with golden grain, 'till the furnace glowed and the engine screamed and on the forehead of the mountain flashed the glory of a new civilization—the Revelation of St. Work the Divine.

Not with the French baptism of fire shall we conquer. O sons of my fathers, nor yet with the Indian song of many waters, but chastened and ennobled by the baptism of toil—wrought wrongly upon us by the English, but also wrought bravely by themselves—by this baptism of toil we stoop among the toiling nations of the earth and stoop to conquer.

Awake then, put on thy strength O Zion, despise not the day of little things, the behest of humble service.

> All service ranks the same with God,
> If now as formerly he trod
> Paradise, his presence fills
> Our earth—each only as God wills
> Can work—God's puppets, best and worst
> Are we.
> There is no last, nor first.

✎ **21** ✎

The Training of Negroes for Social Power

The responsibility for their own social regeneration ought to be placed largely upon the shoulders of the Negro people. But such responsibility must carry with it a grant of power; responsibility without power is a mockery and a farce. If, therefore, the American people are sincerely anxious that the Negro shall put forth his best efforts to help himself, they must see to it that he is not deprived of the freedom and power to strive. The responsibility for dispelling their own ignorance implies that the power to overcome ignorance is to be placed in black men's hands; the lessening of poverty calls for the power of effective work; and the responsibility for lessening crime calls for control over social forces which produce crime.

Such social power means, assuredly, the growth of initiative among Negroes, the spread of independent thought, the expanding consciousness of manhood; and these things today are looked upon by many with apprehension and distrust, and there is systematic and determined effort to avoid this inevitable corollary of the fixing of social responsibility. Men openly declare their design to train these millions as a subject caste, as men to be thought for, but not to think; to be led, but not to lead themselves.

Those who advocate these things forget that such a solution flings them squarely on the other horn of the dilemma: such a subject child-race could never be held accountable for its own misdeeds and shortcomings; its ignorance would be part of the Nation's design, its poverty would arise partly from the direct oppression of the strong and partly from thriftlessness which such oppression breeds; and, above all, its crime would be the legitimate child of that lack of self-respect which caste systems engender. Such a solution of the Negro problem is not one which the saner sense of the Nation for a moment contemplates; it is utterly foreign to American institutions, and is unthinkable as a future for any self-respecting race of men. The sound afterthought of the American people must come to realize that the responsibility for dispelling ignorance and poverty and uprooting crime among Negroes cannot be put upon their own shoulders unless they are given such independent leadership in intelligence, skill, and morality as will inevitably lead to an independent manhood which cannot and will not rest in bonds.

Let me illustrate my meaning particularly in the matter of educating Negro youth.

The Negro problem it has often been said, is largely a problem of ignorance—not simply of illiteracy, but a deeper ignorance of the world and its ways, of the possibilities of human souls. This can be gotten rid of only by training; and primarily such training must take the form of that sort of social leadership which we call education. To apply such leadership to themselves, and to profit by it, means that Negroes would have among themselves men of careful training and broad culture, as teachers and teachers of teachers. There are always periods of educational evolution when it is deemed quite proper for pupils in the fourth reader to teach those in the third. But such a method, wasteful and ineffective at all times, is peculiarly dangerous when ignorance is widespread and when there are few homes and public institutions to supplement the work of the school. It is, therefore, of crying necessity among Negroes that the heads of their educational system—the teachers in the normal schools, the heads of high schools, the principals of public systems, should be unusually well trained men; men trained not simply in common-school branches, not simply in the technique of school management and normal methods, but trained beyond this, broadly and carefully, into the meaning of the age whose civilization it is their peculiar duty to interpret to the youth of a new race, to the minds of untrained people. Such educational leaders should be prepared by long and rigorous courses of study similar to those which the world over have been designed to strengthen the intellectual powers, fortify character, and facilitate the transmission from age to age of the stores of the world's knowledge.

Not all men—indeed, not the majority of men, only the exceptional few among American Negroes or among any other people—are adapted to this higher training, as, indeed, only the exceptional few are adapted to higher training in any line; but the significance of such men is not to be measured by their numbers, but rather by the numbers of their pupils and followers who are destined to see the world through their eyes, hear it through their trained ears, and speak to it through the music of their words.

Such men, teachers of teachers and leaders of the untaught, Atlanta University and similar colleges seek to train. We seek to do our work thoroughly and carefully. We have no predilections or prejudices as to particular studies or methods, but we do cling to those time-honored sorts of discipline which the experience of the world has long since proven to be of especial value. We sift as carefully as possible the student material which offers itself, and we try by every conscientious method to give to students who have character and ability such years of discipline as shall make them stronger, keener, and better for their peculiar mission. The history of civilization seems to prove that no group or nation which seeks advancement and true development can despise or neglect the power of well-trained minds; and this power of intellectual leadership must be given to the talented tenth among American Negroes before this race can seriously be asked to assume the responsibility of dispelling its own ignorance. Upon the foundation-stone of a few well equipped Negro colleges of high and honest standards can be built a proper system of free common schools in the South for the masses of the Negro people; any attempt to found a system of public schools on anything less than this—on narrow ideals, limited or merely technical training—is to call blind leaders for the blind.

The very first step toward the settlement of the Negro problem is the spread of intelligence. The first step toward wider intelligence is a free public-school system; and the first and most important step toward a public-school system is the equipment and adequate support of a sufficient number of Negro colleges. These are first steps, and they involve great movements: first, the best of the existent colleges must not be abandoned to slow atrophy and death, as the tendency is today; secondly, systematic attempt must be made to organize secondary education. Below the colleges and connected with them must come the normal and high schools, judiciously distributed and carefully manned. In no essential particular should this system of common and secondary schools differ from educational systems the world over. Their chief function is the quickening and training of human intelligence; they can do much in the teaching of morals and manners incidentally, but they cannot and ought not to replace the home as the chief moral teacher; they can teach valuable lessons as to the meaning of work in the world, but they cannot replace technical schools and apprenticeship in actual life, which are the real schools of work. Manual training can and ought to be used in these schools, but as a means and not as an end—to quicken intelligence and self-knowledge and not to teach carpentry; just as arithmetic is used to train minds and not skilled accountants.

Whence, now, is the money coming for this educational system? For the common schools the support should come from local communities, the State governments, and the United States Government; for secondary education, support should come from local and State governments and private philanthropy; for the colleges, from private philanthropy and the United States Government. I make no apology for bringing the United States Government in thus conspicuously. The General Government must give aid to Southern education if illiteracy and ignorance are to cease threatening the very foundations of civilization within any reasonable time. Aid to common-school education could be appropriated to the different States on the basis of illiteracy. The fund could be administered by State officials, and the results and needs reported upon by United States educational inspectors under the Bureau of Education. The States could easily distribute the funds so as to encourage local taxation and enterprise and not result in pauperizing the communities. As to higher training, it must be remembered that the cost of a single battle-ship like the *Massachusetts* would endow all the distinctive college work necessary for Negroes during the next half-century; and it is without doubt true that the unpaid balance from bounties withheld from Negroes in the Civil War would, with interest, easily supply this sum.

But spread of intelligence alone will not solve the Negro problem. If this problem is largely a question of ignorance, it is also scarcely less a problem of poverty. If Negroes are to assume the responsibility of raising the standards of living among themselves, the power of intelligent work and leadership toward proper industrial ideals must be placed in their hands. Economic efficiency depends on intelligence, skill, and thrift. The public-school system is designed to furnish the necessary intelligence for the ordinary worker, the secondary school for the more gifted workers, and the college for the exceptional few. Technical knowledge and manual dexterity in learning branches of the world's work are taught by industrial and trade schools, and such schools are of prime importance in the training of colored children. Trade-teaching cannot be effectively combined with the work of the common schools because the primary curriculum is already too crowded, and thorough common-school training should precede trade-teaching. It is, however, quite possible to combine some of the work of the secondary schools with purely technical training, the necessary limitations being matters of time and cost: the question whether the boy can afford to stay in school long enough to add parts of a high-school course to the trade course, and particularly the question whether the school can afford or ought to afford to give trade-training to high-school students who do not intend to become artisans. A system of trade-schools, therefore, supported by State and private aid, should be added to the secondary school system.

An industrial school, however, does not merely teach technique. It is also a school—a center of moral influence and of mental discipline. As such it has peculiar problems in securing the proper teaching force. It demands broadly trained men: the teacher of carpentry must be more than a carpenter, and the teacher of the domestic arts more than a cook; for such teachers must instruct, not simply in manual dexterity, but in mental quickness and moral habits. In other words, they must be teachers as well as artisans. It thus happens that college-bred men and men from other higher schools have always been in demand in technical schools, and it has been the high privilege of Atlanta University to furnish during the thirty-six years of its existence a part of the teaching force of nearly every Negro industrial school in the United States, and today our graduates are teaching in more than twenty such institutions. The same might be said of Fisk University and other higher schools. If the college graduates were today withdrawn from the teaching force of the chief Negro industrial schools, nearly every one of them would have to close its doors. These facts are forgotten by such advocates of industrial training as oppose the higher schools. Strong as the argument for industrial schools is—and its strength is undeniable—its cogency simply increases the urgency of the plea for higher training-schools and colleges to furnish broadly educated teachers.

But intelligence and skill alone will not solve the Southern problem of poverty. With these must go that combination of homely habits and virtues which we may loosely call thrift. Something of thrift may be taught in school, more must be taught at home; but both these agencies are helpless when organized economic society denies to workers the just rewards of thrift and efficiency. And this has been true of black laborers in the South from the time of slavery down through the scandal of the Freedmen's Bank to the peonage and crop-lien system of today. If the Southern Negro is shiftless, it is primarily because over large areas a shiftless Negro can get on in the world about as well as an industrious black man. This is not universally true in the South, but it is true to so large an extent as to discourage striving in precisely that class of Negroes who most need encouragement. What is the remedy? Intelligence—not simply the ability to read and write or to sew—but the intelligence of a society permeated by that larger vision of life and broader tolerance which are fostered by the college and university. Not that all men must be college-bred, but that some men, black and white, must be, to leaven the ideals of the lump. Can any serious student of the economic South doubt that this today is her crying need?

Ignorance and poverty are the vastest of the Negro problems. But to these later years have added a third—the problem of Negro crime. That a great problem of social morality must have become eventually the central problem of emancipation is as clear as day to any student of history. In its grosser form as a problem of serious crime it is already upon us. Of course it is false and silly to represent that white women in the South are in daily danger of black assaulters. On the contrary, white womanhood in the South is absolutely safe in the hands of ninety-nine per cent of the black men—ten times safer than black womanhood is in the hands of white men. Nevertheless, there is a large and dangerous class of Negro criminals, paupers, and outcasts. The existence and growth of such a class, far from causing surprise, should be recognized as the natural result of that social disease called the Negro problem; nearly every untoward circumstance known to human experience has united to increase Negro crime: the slavery of the past, the sudden emancipation, the narrowing of economic opportunity, the lawless environment of wide regions, the stifling of natural ambition, the curtailment of political privilege, the disregard of the sanctity of black men's homes, and, above all, a system of treatment for criminals calculated to breed crime far faster than all other available agencies could repress it. Such a combination of circumstances is as sure to increase the numbers of the vicious and outcast as the rain is to wet the earth. The phenomenon calls for no delicately drawn theories of race differences; it is a plain case of cause and effect.

But, plain as the causes may be, the results are just as deplorable, and repeatedly today the criticism is made that Negroes do not recognize sufficiently their responsibility in this matter. Such critics forget how little power today Negroes have over their own lower classes. Before the black murderer who strikes his victim today, the average black man stands far more helpless than the average white, and, too, suffers ten times more from the effects of the deed. The white man has political power, accumulated wealth, and knowledge of social forces; the black man is practically disfranchised, poor, and unable to discriminate between the criminal and the martyr. The Negro needs the defense of the ballot, the conserving power of property, and, above all, the ability to cope intelligently with such vast questions of social regeneration and moral reform as confront him. If social reform among Negroes be without organization or trained leadership from within, if the administration of law is always for the avenging of the white victim and seldom for the reformation of the black criminal, if ignorant black men misunderstand the functions of government because they have had no decent instruction, and intelligent black men are denied a voice in government because they are black—under such circumstances to hold Negroes responsible for the suppression of crime among themselves is the cruelest of mockeries.

On the other hand, a sincere desire among the American people to help the Negroes undertake their own social regeneration means, first, that the Negro be given the ballot on the same terms as other men, to protect him against injustice and to safeguard his interests in the administration of law; secondly, that through education and social organization he be trained to work, and save, and earn a decent living. But these are not all: wealth is not the only thing worth accumulating; experience and knowledge can be accumulated and handed down, and no people can be truly rich without them. Can the Negro do without these? Can this training in work and thrift be truly effective without the guidance of trained intelligence and deep knowledge—without that same efficiency which has enabled modern peoples to grapple so successfully with the problems of the Submerged Tenth? There must surely be among Negro leaders the philanthropic impulse, the uprightness of character and strength of purpose, but there must be more than these. Philanthropy and purpose among blacks as well as among whites must be guided and curbed by knowledge and mental discipline—knowledge of the forces of civilization that make for survival, ability to organize and guide those forces, and realization of the true meaning of those broader ideals of human betterment which may in time bring heaven and earth a little nearer. This is social power—it is gotten in many ways by experience, by social contact, by what we loosely call the chances of life. But the systematic method of acquiring and imparting it is by the training of youth to thought, power, and knowledge in the school and college. And that group of people whose mental grasp is by heredity weakest, and whose knowledge of the past is for historic reasons most imperfect, that group is the very one which needs above all, for the talented of its youth, this severe and careful course of training; especially if they are expected to take immediate part in modern competitive life, if they are to hasten the slower courses of human development, and if the responsibility for this is to be in their own hands.

Three things American slavery gave the Negro—the habit of work, the English language, and the Christian religion; but one priceless thing it debauched, destroyed, and took from him, and that was the organized home. For the sake of intelligence and thrift, for the sake of work and morality, this home-life must be restored and regenerated with newer ideals. How? The normal method would be by actual contact with a higher home-life among his neighbors, but this method the social separation of white and black precludes. A proposed method is by schools of domestic arts, but, valuable as these are, they are but subsidiary aids to the establishment of homes; for real homes are primarily centers of ideals and teaching and only incidentally centers of cooking. The restoration and raising of home ideals must, then, come from social life among Negroes themselves; and does that social life need no leadership? It needs the best possible leadership of pure hearts and trained heads, the highest leadership of carefully trained men.

Such are the arguments for the Negro college, and such is the work that Atlanta University and a few similar institutions seek to do. We believe that a rationally arranged college course of study for men and women able to pursue it is the best and only method of putting into the world Negroes with the ability to use the social forces of their race so as to stamp out crime, strengthen the home, eliminate degenerates, and inspire and encourage the higher tendencies of the race not only in thought and aspiration but in every-day toil. And we believe this, not simply because we have argued that such training ought to have these effects, or merely because we hope for such results in some dim future, but because already for years we have seen in the work of our graduates precisely such results as I have mentioned: successful teachers of teachers, intelligent and upright ministers, skilled physicians, principals of industrial schools, business men, and, above all, makers of model homes and leaders of social groups, out from which radiate subtle but tangible forces of uplift and inspiration. The proof of this lies scattered in every State of the South, and, above all, in the half-unwilling testimony of men disposed to decry our work.

Between the Negro college and industrial school there are the strongest grounds for co-operation and unity. It is not a matter of mere emphasis, for we would be glad to see ten industrial schools to every college. It is not a fact that there are today too few Negro colleges, but rather that there are too many institutions attempting to do college work. But the danger lies in the fact that the best of the Negro colleges are poorly equipped and are today losing support and countenance, and that, unless the Nation awakens to its duty, ten years will see the annihilation of higher Negro training in the South. We need a few strong, well-equipped Negro colleges, and we need them now, not tomorrow; unless we can have them and have them decently supported, Negro education in the South, both common-school and industrial, is doomed to failure, and the forces of social regeneration will be fatally weakened, for the college today among Negroes is, just as truly as it was yesterday among whites, the beginning and not the end of human training, the foundation and not the capstone of popular education.

Strange, is it not, my brothers, how often in America those great watchwords of human energy—"Be strong!" "Know thyself!" "Hitch your wagon to a star!"—how often these die away into dim whispers when we face these seething millions of black men? And yet do they not belong to them? Are they not their heritage as well as yours? Can they bear burdens without strength, know without learning, and aspire without ideals? Are you afraid to let them try? Fear rather, in this our common fatherland, lest we live to lose those great watchwords of Liberty and Opportunity which yonder in the eternal hills their fathers fought with your fathers to preserve.

~ **22** ~

The Development of a People

In the realm of physical health the teachings of Nature, with its stern mercy and merciful punishment, are showing men gradually to avoid the mistake of unhealthful homes, and to clear fever and malaria away from parts of earth otherwise so beautiful. Death that arises from foul sewage, bad plumbing or vitiated air we no longer attribute to "Acts of God," but to "Misdeeds of Man," and so work to correct this loss. But if we have escaped Mediaevalism to some extent in the care of physical health, we certainly have not in the higher realm of the economic and spiritual development of people. Here the world rests, and is largely contented to rest, in a strange fatalism. Nations and groups and social classes are born and reared, reel sick unto death, or tear forward in frenzied striving. We sit and watch and moralize, and judge our neighbors or ourselves foredoomed to failure or success, not because we know or have studied the causes of a peoples' advance, but rather because we instinctively dislike certain races, and instinctively like our own.

This attitude cannot long prevail. The solidarity of human interests in a world which is daily becoming physically smaller, cannot afford to grope in darkness as to the causes and incentives to human advance when the advance of all depends increasingly on the advance of each. Nor is it enough here to have simply the philanthropic impulse—simply a rather blind and aimless desire to do good.

If then we would grapple intelligently with the greater problem of human development in society, we must sit and study and learn even when the mad impulse of aimless philanthropy is striving within, and we find it easier to labor blindly rather than to wait intelligently.

In no single set of human problems is this striving after intelligence, after real facts and clear thinking, more important than in answering the many questions that concern the American Negro. And especially is this true since the basic axiom upon which all intelligent and decent men, North and South, white and black, must agree, is that the best interests of every single American demand that *every Negro make the best of himself.*

But what is good and better and best in the measure of human advance? and how shall we compare the present with the past, nation with nation, and group with group, so as to gain real intelligent insight into conditions and needs, and enlightened guidance? Now this is extremely difficult in matters of human development, because we are so ignorant of the ordinary facts relating to conditions of life, and because, above all, criteria of life and the objects of living are so diverse.

And yet the desire for clear judgment and rational advance, even in so intricate a problem as that of the races in the United States, is not hopeless. First of all, the most hopeful thing about the race problem today is, that people are beginning to recognize its intricacy and be justly suspicious of any person who insists that the race problem is simply this or simply that—realizing that it is not simply anything. It is as complex as human nature, and you do well to distrust the judgment of any man who thinks, however honestly, that any one simple remedy will cure evils that arise from the whirling wants and longings and passions of writhing human souls.

Not only do we today recognize the Negro problems as intricate, but we are beginning to see that they are pressing—asking, demanding solution; not to be put off by half measures, not answered by being handed down in thinly disguised yet even larger form to our children. With these intricate and pressing problems before us, we ask searchingly and often for the light; and here again we are baffled. An honest gentleman from the South informs us that there are fully as many illiterate Negroes today in the South as there were at Emancipation. We gasp with astonishment, and as we are asking "Where then is all our money and effort gone?" another gentleman from the South, apparently just as honest, tells us that whereas nine-tenths of the Negroes in 1870 could not read and write, today fully three-fifths of them can; or, again, the Negroes themselves exult over the ownership of three hundred million dollars worth of real estate, while the critic points out that the Negroes are a burden to the South, since forming a third of the population they own but one-twenty-fifth of the property.

Such seemingly contradictory propositions and others even more glaring, we hear every day, and it is small wonder that persons without leisure to weigh the evidence find themselves curiously in the dark at times and anxious for reliable interpretation of the real facts.

Much of this befogging of the situation is apparent rather than real. As a matter of fact, the statements referred to are not at all contradictory. There are today more illiterate Negroes than in 1870, but there are six times as many who can read and write. The real underlying problem is dynamic, not static. Is the educational movement in the right direction, and is it as rapid as it is safe? or, in other words, What is satisfactory advance in education? Ought a people to learn to read and write in one generation or in a hundred years? How far can we hasten the growth of intelligence, avoiding stagnation on the one hand, and abnormal forcing on the other? Or take the question of property ownership; it is probably true that only a twenty-fifth of the total property of the South belongs to the Negro, and that the Negro property of the land exceeds three hundred million. Here, again, brute figures mean little, and the comparison between black and white is misleading. The basic question is, How soon after a social revolution like emancipation ought one reasonably to expect the appearance of habits of thrift and the accumulation of property? Moreover, how far is the accumulating of wealth indicative of general advance in moral habits and sound character, or how far is it independent of them or in spite of them?

In other words, if we are to judge intelligently or clearly of the development of a people, we must allow ourselves neither to be dazzled by figures nor misled by inapt comparisons, but we must seek to know what human advancement historically considered has meant and what it means today, and from such criteria we may then judge the condition, development and needs of the group before us. I want then to mention briefly the steps which groups of men have usually taken in their forward struggling, and to ask which of these steps the Negroes of the United States have taken and how far they have gone. In such comparisons we cannot, unfortunately, have the aid of exact statistics, for actual measurement of social phenomena is peculiar to the Nineteenth century—that is, to an age when the cultured Nations were full-grown, and we can only roughly indicate conditions in the days of their youth. A certain youth and childhood is common to all men in their mingled striving. Every where, glancing across the seas of human history, we note it. The average American community of today has grown by a slow, intricate and hesitating advance through four overlapping eras. First, there is the struggle for sheer physical existence—a struggle still waging among the submerged tenth, but settled for a majority of the community long years ago. Above this comes the accumulation for future subsistence—the saving and striving and transmuting of goods for use in days to come—a stage reached today tentatively for the middle classes and to an astounding degree by a few. Then in every community there goes on from the first, but with larger and larger emphasis as the years fly, some essay to train the young into the tradition of the fathers—their religion, thought and tricks of doing. And, finally, as the group meets other groups and comes into larger spiritual contact with nations, there is that transference and sifting and accumulation of the elements of human culture which makes for wider civilization and higher development. These four steps of subsistence, accumulation, education and culture-contact are not disconnected, discreet stages. No nation ever settles its problems of poverty and then turns to educating children; or first accumulates its wealth and then its culture. On the contrary, in every stage of a nation's growing all these efforts are present, and we designate any particular age of a people's development as (for instance) a struggle for existence, because, their conscious effort is more largely expended in this direction than in others; but despite this we all know, or ought to know, that no growing nation can spend its whole effort on today's food lest accumulation and training of children and learning of their neighbors—lest all these things so vitally necessary to advance be neglected, and the people, full-bellied though they be, stagnate and die because in one mighty struggle to live they forget the weightier objects of life.

We all know these very obvious truths, and yet despite ourselves certain mechanical conceptions of society creep into our everyday thought. We think of growing men as cogs in some vast factory—we would stop these wheels and set these others going, hasten that department and retard this; but this conception applied to struggling men is mischievously wrong. You cannot stop the education of children in order to feed their fathers; the children continue to grow—something they are bound to learn. What then shall it be: truth, or half-truth, good or bad? So, too, a people may be engaged in the pressing work of accumulating and saving for future needs—storing grain and cotton, building houses, leveling land; but all the time they are learning something from inevitable contact with men and nations and thoughts—you cannot stop this learning; you cannot postpone it. What then shall this learning—this contact with culture—be? a lesson of fact or fable? of growth or debauchery? the inspiration of the schools or the degradation of the slums? Some thing it must be, but what? The growth of society is an ever-living, many-sided, bundle of activities, some of which are emphasized at different ages, none of which—can be neglected without peril, all of which demand guidance and direction. As they receive this, the nation grows; as they do not, it stagnates and dies.

Whence now must the guidance and direction come? It can come only from four great sources: the precepts of parents, the sight of Seers, the opinion of the majority, and the tradition of the grandfathers; or, in other words, a nation or group of people can be taught the things it must learn in its family circles, at the feet of teachers and preachers, by contact with surrounding society, by reverence for the dead Hand—for that mighty accumulation of customs and traditions handed down generation after generation.

And thus I come to the center of my theme. How far do these great means of growth operate among American Negroes and influence their development in the main lines of human advancement?

Let me take you journeying across mountains and meadows, threading the hills of Maryland, gliding over the broad fields of Virginia, climbing the blue ridge of Carolina and seating ourselves in the cotton kingdom. I would not like you to spend a day or a month here in this little town; I should much rather you would spend ten years, if you are really studying the problem; for casual visitors get casual ideas, and the problems here are the growth of centuries.

From the depot and the cluster of doubtful houses that form the town, pale crimson fields with tell-tale gullies stretch desolately away. The whole horizon looks shabby, and there is a certain awful leisure in the air that makes a westerner wonder when work begins. A neglected and uncertain road wanders up from the depot, past several little stores and a post-office, and then stops hesitatingly and melts away into crooked paths across the washed-out cotton fields. But I do not want you to see so much of the physical as of the spiritual town, and first you must see the color line. It stands at the depot with "waiting room for white people" and "waiting room for colored people," and then the uninitiated might lose sight of it; but it is there, there and curiously wandering, but continuous and never ending. And in that little town, as in a thousand others, they have an eleventh commandment, and it reads "Thou shalt not Cross the Line." Men may at times break the sixth commandment and the seventh, and it makes but little stir. But when the eleventh is broken, the world heaves. And yet you must not think the town inhabited by anything inhuman. Simple, good hearted folks are there—generosity and hospitality, politeness and charity, dim strivings and hard efforts—a human world, aye, even lovable at times; and one cannot argue about that strange line—it is simply so.

Were you there in person I could not take you easily across the line into the world I want to study. But in spirit let me lead you across. In one part of the town are sure to be clustered the majority of the Negro cabins; there is no strict physical separation; on some streets whites and blacks are neighbors, and yet the general clustering by color is plain. I want to take you among the houses of the colored people, and I start not with the best, but with the worst: a little one-room box with a family of eight. The cabin is dirty, ill-smelling and cheerless; the furniture is scant, old and worn. The man works when he has no whiskey to drink, which is comparatively seldom. The woman washes and squanders and squanders and washes. I am not sure that the couple were ever married formally, but still they'll stick together in all probability for life, despite their quarreling. There are five children, and the nameless child of the eldest daughter makes the last member of the family. Three of the children can spell and read a bit, but there's little need of it. The rest of the family are in ignorance, dark and dense. Here is a problem of home and family. One shudders at it almost hopelessly, or flares in anger and says: why do these people live like animals? Why don't they work and strive to do? If the stranger be from the North he looks suspiciously at the color line and shakes his head. If he be from the South he looks at it thankfully and stamps his foot. And these two attitudes are in some respects typical. We look around for the forces keeping this family down, or with fatalistic resignation conclude that nothing better is to be expected of black people. Exactly the same attitude with which the man of a century or so ago fought disease: looked about for the witch, or wondered at the chastening of the Lord; but withal continued to live in the swamps. There are forces in the little town to keep Negroes down, but they do not wholly explain the condition of this family. There are differences in human capabilities, but that they are not based on color can be seen in a dozen Negro homes up the street. What we have in degraded homes like this is a plain survival from the past.

What was slavery and the slave trade? Turn again with me even at the risk of hearing a twice-told tale and, as we have journeyed in space to this little southern town, so journey again in time, back through that curious crooked way along which civilization has wandered looking for the light. There was the nineteenth century—a century of material prosperity, of systematic catering to human wants, that men might eat, drink, be clothed and transported through space. And with this came the physical freeing of the soul through the wonders of science and the spread of democracy. Such a century was a legitimate offspring of the eighteenth century, of the years from 1700 to 1800, when our grandfathers' grandfathers lived—that era of revolution and heart searching that gave the world George Washington and the French Revolution. Behind the eighteenth century looms the age of Louis XIV of France, an age of mighty leaders: Richelieu, Gustavus Adolphus, and Oliver Cromwell. Thus we come back on the world's way, through three centuries of imperialism, revolution and commercial democracy, to two great centuries which prepared Europe for the years from 1600 to 1900—the century of the Protestant Reformation and the century of the Renaissance. The African Slave trade was the child of the Renaissance. We do not realize this; we think of the slave trade as a thing apart, the incident of a decade or a century, and yet let us never forget that from the year 1442, when Antonio Gonzales first looked upon the river of Gold, until 1807, when Great Britain first checked the slave trade, for three hundred and sixty-five years Africa was surrendered wholly to the cruelty and rapacity of the Christian man-dealer, and for full five hundred years and more this frightful heart disease of the Dark Continent destroyed the beginnings of Negro civilization, overturned governments, murdered men, disrupted families and poisoned the civilized world. Do you want an explanation of the degradation of this pitiful little nest perched in the crimson soil of Georgia? Ask your fathers and your fathers' fathers, for they know. Nay, you need not go back even to their memories.

In 1880 a traveler crossed Africa from Lake Nyassa to Lake Tanganyika. He saw the southern end of the lake peopled with large and prosperous villages. The next traveler who followed in 1890 found not a solitary human being—nothing but burned homes and bleaching skeletons—he tells us that the Wa-Nkonde tribe to which these people belonged, was, until this event, one of the most prosperous tribes in East Central Africa. Their people occupied a country of exceptional fertility and beauty. Three rivers, which never failed in the severest drought, ran through their territory, and their crops were the richest and most varied in the country. They possessed herds of cattle and goats; they fished in the lake with nets; they wrought iron into many-patterned spear-heads with exceptional ingenuity and skill; and that even artistic taste had begun to develop among them was evident from the ornamental work of their huts, which were unique for clever construction and beauty of design. This people, in short, by their own inherent ability and the natural resources of their country, were on the high road to civilization. Then came the overthrow. Arab traders mingled with them, settled peacefully among them, obeyed their laws, and gained their confidence. The number of the traders slowly increased; the power of the chief was slowly undermined, until, at last, with superior weapons and reinforcements, every vestige of the tribe was swept away and their lands laid in red ruins. Fourteen villages they razed from the ground and, finally, seizing more slaves than they could transport, drove the rest into the tall dry grass and set it on fire; and in the black forest was silence.

This took place in the nineteenth century during your lives, in the midst of modern missionary effort. But worse was the tale of the eighteenth century and the seventeenth century and the sixteenth century, and this whole dark crime against a human race began in 1442 when the historic thirty Negroes landed in Lisbon.

Systematic man-hunting was known in ancient times, but it subsided as civilization advanced, until the Mohammedan fanatics swept across Africa. Arabian slavery, however, had its mitigations. It was patriarchal house service; the slave might hope to rise and, once admitted to the household of faith, he became in fact, and not merely in theory, a man and a brother. The domestic slavery of the African tribes represented that first triumph of humanity that leads the savage to spare his foe's life and use his labor. Such slaves could and did rise to freedom and preferment; they became parts of the new tribe. It was left to Christian slavery to improve on all this—to make slavers a rigid unending caste by adding to bondage the prejudice of race and color. Marauding bands traversed the forests, fell upon native villages, slew the old and young and drove the rest in herds to the slave market; tribe was incited against tribe, and nation against nation. As Mr. Stanley tells us,

> While a people were thus subject to capture and expatriation, it was clearly impossible that any intellectual or moral progress could be made. The greater number of those accessible from the coast were compelled to study the best methods of avoiding the slaver and escaping his force and his wiles; the rest only thought of the arts of kidnapping their innocent and unsuspecting fellow creatures. Yet, contradictory as it may appear to us, there were not wanting at the same time zealous men who devoted themselves to Christianity. In Angola, Congo and Mozambique, and far up the Zambesi, missionaries erected churches and cathedrals, appointed bishops and priests who converted and baptized; while at the mouth of the Congo, the Niger and the Zambesi their countrymen built slave barracoons, and anchored their murderous slave ships. Europeans legalized and sanctioned the slave trade; the public conscience of the period approved it; the mitred heads of the church blessed the slave gangs as they marched to the shore, and the tax-collector received the levy per head as lawful revenue.§

The development of the trade depended largely upon the commercial nations, and, as they put more and more ruthless enterprise into the traffic, it grew and flourished. First came the Portuguese as the world's slave trader, secured in their monopoly by the Bull of Demarcation issued by Pope Alexander VI. Beginning in 1442 they traded a hundred and fifty years, until Portugal was reduced to a province of Spain in 1580 and her African settlements neglected. Immediately the thrifty Dutch began to monopolize the trade, and held it for a century, until Oliver Cromwell deprived them of it. The celebrated Dutch West India Company intrigued with native states and gained a monopoly of the trade in Negroes from 1630 to 1668. They whirled a stream of cargoes over the great seas, filled the West Indies, skirted the coasts of America and, sailing up the curving river to Jamestown, planted the Negro problems in Virginia in 1619. Then the English scented gain and bestirred themselves mightily.

Two English slave ships sailed from Plymouth in the middle of the sixteenth century, but the great founder of the English slave trade was Sir John Hawkins. Queen Elizabeth had some scruples at the trade in human beings, and made Hawkins promise to seize only those who were willing to go with him—a thing which he easily promised and easily forgot. This Sir John Hawkins was a strange product of his times. Brave, ruthless, cruel and religious: a pirate, a man-stealer and a patriot. He sailed to Africa in the middle of the sixteenth century, and immediately saw profits for English gain. He burned villages, murdered the natives and stole slaves, and then, urging his crew to love one another and serve God daily, he sailed merrily westward to the Spanish West Indies in the good ship called the "Jesus," and compelled the Spaniards to buy slaves at the muzzle of his guns.

Thus the English slave trade began under Queen Elizabeth, was encouraged under James I, who had made the translation of our Bible, and renewed by Oliver Cromwell, the great Puritan, who fought for it and seized the island of Jamaica as a slave market. So kings, queens and countries encouraged the trade, and the English soon became the world's greatest slave traders. New manufactures suitable to the trade were introduced into England, and the trade brought so much gold to Great Britain that they named the pieces "guineas" after the slave coast. Four million dollars a year went from England, in the eighteenth century, to buy slaves. Liverpool, the city where the trade centered, had, in 1783, nine hundred slave ships in the trade, and in eleven years they carried $76,000,000 worth of slaves to America, and they did this on a clear profit of $60,000,000.

These vast returns seduced the conscience of Europe. [Samuel] Boswell, the biographer of Dr. Johnson, called the slave trade "an

§This is from Henry M. Stanley, *Slavery and the Slave Trade* (New York: Harper & Brothers, 1893), p. 5.

important necessary branch of commerce," and probably the best people of England were of this opinion, and were surprised and indignant when [Thomas] Clarkson and [William] Wilberforce began their campaign.

Gradually aroused by repeated and seemingly hopeless assaults, the conscience of England awoke and forbade the trade, in 1807, after having guided and cherished it for one hundred and fifty years. She called for aid from America, and America apparently responded in the statutes of 1808. But, true to her reputation as the most lawless nation on earth, America made no attempt to enforce the law in her own territory for a generation, and, after that, refused repeatedly and doggedly to prevent the slave trade of the world from sailing peacefully under the American flag for fifty years—up until the very outbreak of the Civil War. Thus, from 1442 to 1860, nearly half a millennium, the Christian world fattened on the stealing of human souls.

Nor was there any pretence of charity in the methods of their doing. The capture of the slaves was organized deceit, murder and force; the shipping of them was far worse than the modern shipping of horses and cattle. Of this middle passage across the sea in slow sailing ships, with brutal sailors and little to eat, it has often been said "that never in the world before was so much wretchedness condensed in so little room." The Negroes, naked and in irons, were chained to each other hand and foot, and stowed so close that they were not allowed more than a foot and a half each. Thus, crammed together like herrings in a barrel, they contracted putrid and fatal disorders, so that those who came to inspect them in the morning had frequently to pick dead slaves out of their rows and unchain their corpses from the bodies of their wretched mates. Blood and filth covered the floors, the hot air reeked with contagion, and the death rate among the slaves often reached fifty per cent, not to speak of the decimation when once they reached the West Indian plantations.

The world will never know the exact number of slaves transported to America. Several thousand came in the fifteenth century, tens of thousands in the sixteenth, and hundreds of thousands in the seventeenth. In the eighteenth century more than two and one-half millions of slaves were transported, and in 1790 Negroes were crossing the ocean at the rate of sixty thousand a year. Dunbar thinks that nearly fifteen millions were transported in all.

Such was the traffic that revolutionized Africa. Instead of man-hunting being an incident of tribal wars, war became the incident of man-hunting. From the Senegal to St. Paul de Loanda winding, beaten tracks converged to the sea from every corner of the Dark Continent, covered with the blood of the foot-sore, lined with the bleaching bones of the dead, and echoing with the wails of the conquered, the bereaved and the dying. The coast stood bristling with forts and prisons to receive the human cattle. Across the blue waters of the Atlantic two hundred and fifty ships a year hurried to the west, with their crowded, half-suffocated cargoes. And during all this time Martin Luther had lived and died, Calvin had preached, Raphael had painted and Shakespeare and Milton sung; and yet for four hundred years the coasts of Africa and America were strewn with the dying and the dead, four hundred years the sharks followed the scurrying ships, four hundred years Ethiopia stretched forth her hands unto God. All this you know, all this you have read many a time. I tell it again, lest you forget.

What was slavery to the slave trade? Not simply forced labor, else we are all in bondage. Not simply toil without pay, even that is not unknown in America. No, the dark damnation of slavery in America was the destruction of the African family and of all just ideals of family life. No one pretends that the family life of African tribes had reached modern standards—barbarous nations have barbarous ideals. But this does not mean that they have no ideals at all. The patriarchal clan-life of the Africans, with its polygamy protected by custom, tradition and legal penalty, was infinitely superior to the shameless promiscuity of the West Indian plantation, the unhallowed concubinage of Virginia or the prostitution of Louisiana. And these ideals slavery broke and scattered and flitted to the winds and left ignorance and degradation in their train.

When the good New England clergyman thought it a shame that slaves should herd like animals, without a legal marriage bond, he devised a quaint ceremony for them in which Sally promised Bob to cleave to him. For life? Oh no. As long as "God in his providence" kept them on the same plantation. This was in New England where there was a good deal more conscience than in Georgia. What ideal of family life could one reasonably expect Bob and Sally to have? The modern American family (considering the shame of divorce) has not reached perfection; yet it is the result of long training and carefully fostered ideals and persistent purging of the socially unfit.

As I study this family in the little southern town, in all its degradation and uncleanness, I cannot but see a plain case of cause and effect. If you degrade people the result is degradation and you have no right to be surprised at it. Nor am I called upon to apologize for these people, or to make fun of their dumb misery. For their condition there is an apology due, witness High Heaven; but not from me.

Upon the town we have visited, upon the state, upon this section, the awful incubus of the past broods like a writhing sorrow, and when we turn our faces from that past, we turn it not to forget but to remember; viewing degradation with fear and not contempt, with awe and not criticism, bowing our head and straining willing ears to the iron voice

. . . of Nature merciful and stern.
I teach by killing, let others learn.

But the Negroes of the South are not all upon this low level. From this Nadir they stretch slowly, resolutely upward, by infinite gradation, helped now by the hand of a kindly master or a master's son, now by the sacrifice of friends; always by the ceaseless energy of a people who will never submit to burial alive.

Look across the street of your little southern town: here is a better house—a mother and father, two sons and a girl. They are hard-working people and good people. They read and write a little and, though they are slow and good natured, they are seldom idle. And yet they are unskilled, without foresight, always in debt and living from hand to mouth. Hard pressed they may sink into crime; encouraged they may rise to comfort, but never to wealth. Why? Because they and their fathers have been trained this way. What does a slave know of saving? What can he know of forethought? What could he learn even of skill, save in exceptional cases? In other words, slavery must of necessity send into the world of work a mass of unskilled laborers who have no idea of what thrift means; who have been a part of a great economic organization but had nothing to do with its organizing; and so when they are suddenly called to take a place in a greater organization, in which free individual initiative is a potent factor, they cannot, for they do not know how; they lack skill and, more than that, they lack ideals!

And so we might go on: past problems of work and wages, of legal protection, of civil rights and of education, up to this jaunty, little yellow house on a cross street with a flower-bed struggling sturdily with the clay, with vines and creepers and a gleam of white curtains and a decorous parlor. If you enter this house you may not find it altogether up to your ideals. A Dutch housekeeper would find undiscovered corners, and a fastidious person might object to the general scheme of decoration. And yet, compared with the homes in the town, white or black, the house is among the best. It may be the home of a Negro butcher who serves both sides of the color line, or of a small grocer, a carpenter, a school teacher or a preacher. Whatever this man may be, he is a leader in a peculiar sense—the ideal-maker in his group of people. The white world is there, but it is the other side of the color line; it is seen distinctly and from afar. Of white and black there is no mingling in church and school, in general gatherings. The black world is isolated and alone; it gets its ideals, its larger thoughts, its notions of life, from these local leaders; they set the tone to that all-powerful spiritual world that surrounds and envelopes the souls of men; their standards of living, their interpretation of sunshine and rain and human hearts, their thoughts of love and labor, their aspirations and dim imaginings—all that makes *life*.

Not only does this group leader guide a mass of men isolated in space, but also isolated in time. For we must remember that not only did slavery overthrow the Negro family and teach few lessons of thrift and foresight;

it also totally broke a nation from all its traditions of the past in every realm of life. I fear I cannot impress upon you the full meaning of such a revolution. A nation that breaks suddenly with its past is almost fatally crippled. No matter how crude or imperfect that past may be, with all its defects, it is the foundation upon which generations to come must build. Beauty and finish and architectural detail are not required of it, but the massive weight of centuries of customs and traditions it must have. The slave trade, a new climate, a new economic regime, a new language and a new religion separated the American Negro as completely from his fatherland as it is possible for human agencies to do. The result is curious. There is a certain swaying in the air, a tilting and a crumbling, a vast difficulty of adjustment—of making the new ideas of work and wealth, of authority and right, fit in and hitch themselves to something gone; to the authority of the fathers, the customs of the past in a nation without grandfathers. So, then, the Negro group leader not only sets present standards, but he supplies in a measure the lack of past standards, and his leading is doubly difficult, since with Emancipation there came a second partial breaking with the past. The leader of the masses must discriminate between the good and bad in the past; he must keep the lesson of work and reject the lesson of concubinage; he must add more lessons of moral rectitude to the old religious fervor; he must, in fine, stand to this group in the light of the interpreter of the civilization of the twentieth century to the minds and hearts of people who, from sheer necessity, can but dimly comprehend it. And this man—I care not what his vocation may be—preacher, teacher, physician, or artisan, this person is going to solve the Negro problem; for that problem is at bottom the clash of two different standards of culture, and this priest it is who interprets the one to the other.

Let me for a moment recapitulate. In the life of advancing peoples there must go on simultaneously a struggle for existence, accumulation of wealth, education of the young, and a development in culture and the higher things of life. The more backward the nation the larger sum of effort goes into the struggle for existence; the more forward the nation the larger and broader is the life of the spirit. For guidance, in taking these steps in civilization, the nation looks to four sources: the precepts of parents, the sight of seers, the opinion of the majority and the traditions of the past.

Here, then, is a group of people in which every one of these great sources of inspiration is partially crippled: the family group is struggling to recover from the debauchery of slavery; and the number of the enlightened leaders must necessarily be small; the surrounding and more civilized white majority is cut off from its natural influence by the color line; and the traditions of the past are either lost, or largely traditions of evil and wrong.

Any one looking the problem squarely in the face might conclude that it was unjust to expect progress, or the signs of progress, until many generations had gone by. Indeed, we must not forget that those people who claimed to know the Negro best, freely and confidently predicted during the abolition controversy—

1. That free Negroes would not, and could not, work effectively.
2. That the freedman who did work, would not save.
3. That it was impossible to educate Negroes.
4. That no members of the race gave signs of ability and leadership.
5. That the race was morally degenerate.

Not only was this said, it was sincerely and passionately believed, by honorable men who, with their forefathers, had lived with the Negro three hundred years. And yet today the Negro in one generation forms the chief laboring force of the most rapidly developing part of the land. He owns twelve million acres of land, two hundred and fifty million dollars worth of farm property, and controls—as owner or renter five hundred millions. Nearly three-fifths of the Negroes have learned to read and write. An increasing number have given evidence of ability and thoughtfulness—not, to be sure, of transcendent genius, but of integrity, large knowledge and common-sense. And finally there can be today no reasonable dispute but that the number of efficient, law-abiding and morally upright black people in this land is far larger than it ever was before, and is daily growing. Now these obvious and patent facts do not by any means indicate the full solution of the problem. There are still hosts of idle and unreliable Negro laborers; the race still, as a whole, has not learned the lesson of thrift and saving; fully seventy-five per cent are still fairly designated as ignorant. The number of group leaders of ability and character is far behind the demand, and the development of a trustworthy upper class has, as is usually true, been accompanied by the differentiation of a dangerous class of criminals.

What the figures of Negro advancement mean is, that the development has been distinctly and markedly in the right direction, and that, given justice and help, no honest man can doubt the outcome. The giving of justice means the recognition of desert wherever it appears; the right to vote on exactly the same terms as other people vote; the right to the equal use of public conveniences and the educating of youth in the public schools. On these points, important as they are, I will not dwell. I am more interested here in asking how these struggling people may be actually helped. I conceive that such help may take any one of four forms:—

1. Among a people deprived of guiding traditions, they may be furnished trained guidance in matters of civilization and ideals of living.
2. A people whose family life is not strongly established must have put before them and brought home to them the morals of sane and sanitary living.
3. The mass of Negro children must have the keys of knowledge put into their hands by good elementary schools.

4. The Negro youth must have the opportunity to learn the technical skill of modern industry.

All these forms of help are important. No one of them can be neglected without danger of increasing complications as time flies, and each one of them are lines of endeavor in which the Negro cannot be reasonably expected to help himself without aid from others. For instance, it cannot be seriously expected that a race of freedmen would have the skill necessary for modern industry. They cannot teach themselves what they themselves do not know, and consequently a legitimate and crying need of the south is the establishment of industrial schools. The public school system is one of the foundation stones of free republican government. Negro children, as well as other children, have a right to ask of the nation knowledge of reading, writing and the rules of number, together with some conception of the world in time and space. Not one Negro child in three is today receiving any such training or has any chance to receive it, and a decent public school system in the South, aided by the National government, is something that must come in the near future, if you expect the race problem to be settled.

Here then are two great needs: public schools and industrial schools. How are schools of any sort established? By furnishing teachers. Given properly equipped teachers and your schools are a foregone success; without them, I care not how much you spend on buildings and equipment, the schools are a failure. It is here that Negro colleges, like Atlanta University, show their first usefulness.

But, in my list of ways in which the Negro may legitimately be helped to help himself, I named two other avenues of aid, and I named them first because to my mind they are even of more importance than popular education. I mean the moral uplift of a people. Now moral uplift comes not primarily from schools, but from strong home life and high social ideals. I have spoken of the Negroes' deficiency in these lines and the reason of that deficiency. Here, then, is a chance for help, but how? Not by direct teaching, because that is often ineffective and it is precluded in the South by the color line. It can be done, to my mind, only by group leadership; by planting in every community of Negroes black men with ideals of life and thrift and civilization, such as must in time filter through the masses and set examples of moral living and correct thinking to the great masses of Negroes who spend but little of their life in schools. After all the education of men comes but in small degree from schools; it comes mostly from the fireside, from companionships, from your social set, from the opinion of each individual's little world. This is even more true of the Negro. His world is smaller. He is shut in to himself by prejudice; he has, by reason of his poverty, little time for school. If he is to learn, he must learn from his group leaders, his daily companions, his social surroundings, his own dark world of striving, longing and dreaming. Here, then, you must plant the seed of civilization. Here you must place men educated, not merely in the technique of teaching or skill of hand, but above and beyond that into a thorough understanding of their age and the demands and meaning of modern culture. In so far as the college of today stands for the transmission from age to age of all that is best in the world's deeds, thoughts and traditions, in so far it is a crying necessity that a race, ruthlessly torn from its traditions and trained for centuries awry, should receive back through the higher culture of its gifted children some of the riches of the great system of culture into which it has been thrust. If the meaning of modern life cannot be taught at Negro hearthsides because the parents themselves are untaught, then its ideals can be forced into the centres of Negro life only by the teaching of higher institutions of learning and the agency of thoroughly educated men.

⌁ 23 ⌁

The Negro Problem from the Negro Point of View: The Parting of the Ways

The points upon which American Negroes differ as to their course of action are the following: First, the scope of education; second, the necessity of the right of suffrage: third, the importance of civil rights; fourth, the conciliation of the South; fifth, the future of the race in this country.

The older opinion as built up under the leadership of our great dead, Payne, Crummell, Forten and Douglass, was that the broadest field of education should be opened to black children; that no free citizen of a republic could exist in peace and prosperity without the ballot; that self-respect and proper development of character can only take place under a system of equal civil rights; that every effort should be made to live in peace and harmony with all men, but that even for this great boon no people must willingly or passively surrender their essential rights of manhood; that in future the Negro is destined to become an American citizen with full political and civil rights, and that he must never rest contented until he has achieved this.

Since the death of the leaders of the past there have come mighty changes in the nation. The gospel of money has risen triumphant in church and state and university. The great question which Americans ask today is, "What is he worth?" or "What is it worth?" The ideals of human rights are obscured, and the nation has begun to swagger about the world in its useless battleships looking for helpless peoples whom it can force to buy its goods at high prices. This wave of materialism is temporary; it will pass and leave us all ashamed and surprised; but while it is here it strangely maddens and blinds us. Religious periodicals are found in the van yelling for war; peaceful ministers of Christ are leading lynchers: great universities are stuffing their pockets with greenbacks and kicking the little souls of students to make them "move faster" through the courses of study, the end of which is ever *"Etwas schaffen"* and seldom *"Etwas sein."* Yet there are signs of change. Souls long cramped and starved are stretching toward the light. Men are beginning to murmur against the lower tendencies and the sound of the Zeitgeist strikes sensitive ears with that harrowing discord which prefigures richer harmony to come.

Meantime an awakening race, seeing American civilization as it is, is strongly moved and naturally misled. They whisper: What is the greatness of the country? is it not money? Well then, the one end of our education and striving should be moneymaking. The trimmings of life, smatterings of Latin and music and such stuff—let that wait till we are rich. Then as to voting, what is the good of it after all? Politics does not pay as well as the grocery business, and breeds trouble. Therefore get out of politics and let the ballot go. When we are rich we can dabble in politics along with the president of Yale. Then, again the thought arises: What is personal humiliation and the denial of ordinary civil rights compared with a chance to earn a living? Why quarrel with your bread and butter simply because of filthy Jim Crow cars? Earn a living; get rich, and all these things shall be added unto you. Moreover, conciliate your neighbors, because they are more powerful and wealthier, and the price you must pay to earn a living in America is that of humiliation and inferiority.

No one, of course, has voiced this argument quite so flatly and bluntly as I have indicated. It has been expressed rather by the emphasis given industrial and trade teaching, the decrying of suffrage as a manhood right or even necessity, the insistence on great advance among Negroes before there is any recognition of their aspirations, and a tendency to minimize the shortcomings of the South and to emphasize the mistakes and failures of black men. Now, in this there has been just that degree of truth and right which serves to make men forget its untruths. That the shiftless and poor need thrift and skill, that ignorance can not vote intelligently, that duties and rights go hand in hand, and that sympathy and understanding among neighbors is prerequisite to peace and concord, all this is true. Who has ever denied it, or ever will? But from all this does it follow that Negro colleges are not needed, that the right of suffrage is not essential for black men, that equality of civil rights is not the first of rights and that no self-respecting man can agree with the person who insists that he is a dog? Certainly not, all answer.

Yet the plain result of the attitude of mind of those who, in their advocacy of industrial schools, the unimportance of suffrage and civil rights and conciliation, have been significantly silent or evasive as to higher training and the great principle of free self-respecting manhood for black folk—the plain result of this propaganda has been to help the cutting down of educational opportunity for Negro children, the legal disfranchisement of nearly

5,000,000 of Negroes and a state of public opinion which apologizes for lynching, listens complacently to any insult or detraction directed against an eighth of the population of the land, and silently allows a new slavery to rise and clutch the South and paralyze the moral sense of a great nation.

What do Negroes say to this? I speak advisedly when I say that the overwhelming majority of them declare that the tendencies today are wrong and that the propaganda that encouraged them was wrong. They say that industrial and trade teaching is needed among Negroes, sadly needed; but they unhesitatingly affirm that it is not needed as much as thorough common school training and the careful education of the gifted in higher institutions; that only in this way can a people rise by intelligence and social leadership to a plane of permanent efficiency and morality. To be sure, there are shorter and quicker methods of making paying workingmen out of a people. Slavery under another name may increase the output of the Transvaal mines, and a caste system coupled with manual training may relieve the South from the domination of labor unions. But has the nation counted the cost of this? Has the Negro agreed to the price, and ought he to agree? Economic efficiency is a means and not an end; this every nation that cares for its salvation must remember.

Moreover, notwithstanding speeches and the editorials of a subsidized Negro press, black men in this land know that when they lose the ballot they lose all. They are no fools. They know it is impossible for free workingmen without a ballot to compete with free workingmen who have the ballot; they know there is no set of people so good and true as to be worth trusting with the political destiny of their fellows, and they know that it is just as true today as it was a century and a quarter ago that "Taxation without representation is tyranny."

Finally, the Negro knows perfectly what freedom and equality mean— opportunity to make the best of oneself, unhandicapped by wanton restraint and unreasoning prejudice. For this the most of us propose to strive. We will not, by word or deed, for a moment admit the right of any man to discriminate against us simply on account of race or color. Whenever we submit to humiliation and oppression it is because of superior brute force; and even when bending to the inevitable we bend with unabated protest and declare flatly and unswervingly that any man or section or nation who wantonly shuts the doors of opportunity and self defense in the faces of the weak is a coward and knave. We refuse to kiss the hands that smite us, but rather insist on striving by all civilized methods to keep wide educational opportunity, to keep the right to vote, to insist on equal civil rights and to gain every right and privilege open to a free American citizen.

But, answer some, you cannot accomplish this. America will never spell opportunity for black men; it spelled slavery for them in 1619 and it will spell the same thing in other letters in 1919. To this I answer simply: I do not believe it. I believe that black men will become free American citizens if they have the courage and persistence to demand the rights and treatment of men, and cease to toady and apologize and belittle themselves. The rights of humanity are worth fighting for. Those that deserve them in the long run get them. The way for black men today to make these rights the heritage of their children is to struggle for them unceasingly, and if they fail, die trying.

～ 24 ～

To Solve the Negro Problem

So far as the presence of ten million men of African descent in this country forms a "Negro" problem it can only be settled in one way—by treating every individual according to his deserts with absolute impartiality: If he is a seer, heed him; if he is a poet, listen to him; if he is an artisan, work with him; if he is a criminal, reform him. Treat these men with unwavering justice, neither wheedle nor curse them, open the doors of opportunity and cheer them through, giving them sympathy, encouragement, punishment, correction, and inspiration as they need. Justice then will settle the problem of race and caste today as it did in the world's yesterday.

So far as the presence of ten million freedmen and their children in this land forms a problem of ignorance, idleness, and crime, apply to these social diseases the very remedies which the world is using on all submerged classes. What is ignorance? It is a wrong and narrow estimate of life and its possibilities, and its cure is the public school, which puts the keys to knowledge into the hands of all. What is idleness and shiftlessness and inefficiency? It is ignorance of the satisfaction of work and doing, and it is cured by strong, pure home life and by the training of head and hand. What is crime? It is the careless or vicious deed of the unsocial creature who refuses to bow to the common good. We cure it by all the ways in which goodness and beauty and truth creep into the human heart—by inspiration, by the letting in of the light.

So these black men must be lifted: they must have common schools; today not one in three of their children have them. They must have thrift and skill which come from industrial training in home and school and life. But above all they must have inspiration: the uplift from above, the voices of preachers and leaders, the guiding hands of teachers and writers, the light that streams from such human institutions as men have invented to conserve and increase and hand down the civilization of the present and past call them what you will: churches, libraries, social settlements, colleges—these are what men need who are climbing heights they have not known before. They that walk in darkness need the light. Light is justice. Justice will cure caste.

～ 25 ～

What Intellectual Training Is Doing for the Negro

How easily one generation forgets the problems of its fathers! We call it still the Negro problem, and yet it has changed its form in every decade. Our fathers asked, Can the Negro be educated? We are asking, How shall the Negro be educated? The very asking of this latter question shows that the former has been answered. We still differ as to the objects and extent of the training that ought to be given to the Negroes, but no sane man today questions of their ability to be educated. Indeed, how can it be questioned? Compare the statistics of illiteracy. They are crude measurements of knowledge, and yet they have their value. In 1870, just after emancipation, four-fifths of the Negroes ten years old and over could not read and write. Ten years later this was reduced to seven-tenths, in 1890 to 57 per cent, and in 1900 to 44.5 per cent. If we had not been so busy discussing Mr. Roosevelt's dinner list in recent years, we would have hailed the educational returns of the twelfth census with a chorus of generous approval for colored people, for today, for the first time in history, the majority of American Negroes can read and write. The exact figures particularly for the South are of great interest:

Illiterate Colored Persons over Nine Years Old

States	1870	1880	1890	1900
District of Columbia	70.5	48.4	35.0	24.2
Missouri	72.7	53.9	41.7	28.0
West Virginia	74.4	55.0	44.4	32.3
Florida	84.1	70.7	50.6	38.5
Maryland	69.5	59.6	50.1	35.2
Delaware	71.3	57.5	49.5	38.1
Arkansas	81.2	75.0	53.5	43.0
Texas	88.7	75.4	52.5	38.2
Tennessee	82.4	71.7	54.2	41.6
Kentucky	83.8	70.4	55.9	40.1
Virginia	88.9	73.2	52.7	44.6
North Carolina	84.8	77.4	60.1	47.6
Mississippi	87.0	75.2	60.9	49.1
South Carolina	81.1	78.5	64.1	52.8
Georgia	92.1	81.6	67.3	52.3
Alabama	88.1	80.6	69.1	57.4
Louisiana	85.9	79.1	72.1	61.1
United States	79.9	70.0	57.1	44.5

Nor is this solely the result of the nation's generosity to the freedmen. In the first place, the nation did all it could to keep Negroes ignorant in the earlier years, and, in the second place, the public-school system of the South is the child of those very Negro governments which it is the fashion now to damn. The tale is not too old to tell:

Alabama, in 1832, fined any one teaching Negroes to "spell, read, or write," $250 to $500.

Georgia, in 1770, fined such persons $20, and in 1829 declared:

> If any slave, negro, or free person of color, or any white person, shall teach any other slave, negro, or free person of color to read or write either written or printed characters, the same free person of color or slave shall be punished by fine and whipping, or fine or whipping, at the discretion of the court; and if a white person so offend, he, she, or they shall be punished with a fine not exceeding $500 and imprisonment in the common jail, at the discretion of the court.

Louisiana, in 1830, provided imprisonment from one to twelve months for such malefactors.

Missouri, in 1847, passed an act saying that "No person shall keep or teach any school for the instruction of Negroes or mulattoes in reading or writing in this State."

North Carolina prohibited Negro schools in 1835, and South Carolina did the same by her acts of 1740, 1800, and 1833.

Virginia prohibited all teaching of Negroes in 1831.

The Northern States, too, either impeded or gave no encouragement to the teaching of Negroes in the early half of the nineteenth century.

Thus untrained, and suddenly, violently, thrust into freedom and responsibility, what did these black men do? Many things, without doubt, extravagant and wrong. But some things they did do well, as Albion W. Tourgee has so clearly shown:

> They instituted a public-school system in a region where public schools had been unknown. They opened the ballot-box and jury-box to thousands of white men who had been debarred from them by a lack of earthly possessions. They introduced home rule into the South. They abolished the whipping-post, the branding-iron, the stocks, and other barbarous forms of punishment which had up to that time prevailed. They reduced capital felonies from about twenty to two or three. In an age of extravagance, they were extravagant in the sums appropriated for public works. In all that time no man's rights of person were invaded under the forms of law.

Thomas E. Miller, a Negro member of the late Constitutional convention of South Carolina, said:

> The gentleman from Edgefield (Mr. Tillman) speaks of the piling up of the State debt, of jobbery and speculation during the period between 1869 and 1873 in South Carolina; but he has not found voice eloquent enough, nor

pen exact enough, to mention those imperishable gifts bestowed upon South Carolina between 1873 and 1876 by Negro legislators—the laws relative to finance, the building of penal and charitable institutions, and, greatest of all, the establishment of the public-school system. Starting as infants in legislation in 1869, many wise measures were not thought of, many injudicious acts were passed. But in the administration of affairs for the next four years, having learned by experience the results of bad acts, we immediately passed reformatory laws touching every department of State, county, municipal, and town governments. These enactments are today upon the statute-books of South Carolina. They stand as living witnesses of the Negro's fitness to vote and legislate upon the rights of mankind.

Although recent researches have shown in the South some germs of a public-school system before the war, there can be no reasonable doubt but what common school instruction in the South, in the modern sense of the term, was founded by the Freedman's Bureau and missionary societies, and that the State public-school systems were formed mainly by Negro reconstruction governments.

But a public-school system without teachers is a body without a head. Whence were the teachers coming for the Negro schools? Not from the white North, for, try as they might, they could send but a few; not from the white South. Negroes themselves must teach themselves. "Could they?" asked the nation. The Negro answered with thirty thousand black teachers in charge of two million school children a single generation after emancipation. Not only is this true, but the Negro contributed largely to the support of their own schools. Their schools in the South cost about five millions in 1899; of this they contributed in direct and indirect taxes nearly four millions, if we may trust the estimates of the Sixth Atlanta Conference.

The cost of white and Negro schools in the Southern States may be summarized as follows:

Total whites, 5–20 years of age	7,065,115
Total Negroes, 5–20 years of age	3,263,016
Percentage of whites, 5–20 years of age	68.40
Percentage of Negroes, 5–20 years of age	31.60
Cost of white schools	$31,755,320 (87.20%)
Cost of Negro schools	4,675,504 (12.80%)
If the Negro schools were equal to white schools, they would cost	$14,670,586
Net deficiency of Negro schools	9,995,085
Total actual cost of white and Negro schools, 1899	36,430,825
Total cost of schools if Negro schools equaled white schools	46,425,906

If white and Negro schools were equal to
  Massachusetts schools, they would cost,
  approximately   150,000,000
Net annual deficiency which the United States
  government might contribute to, in part,
  approximately   100,000,000

For higher training Negroes have something less than two hundred fifty high and normal schools, and about ten small colleges, doing effective work. Nor is this more than is needed. The United States Commissioner of Educations says:

> While the number in colored high schools and colleges had increased some-what faster than the population, it had not kept pace with the general average of the whole country, for it had fallen from 30 per cent to 25 per cent of the average quota. Of all colored pupils one (1) in one hundred was engaged in secondary and higher work and that ratio had continued substantially for the past twelve years. If the ratio of colored population in secondary and higher education is to be equal to the average for the whole country, it must be increased to five times its present average.

If this be true of the secondary and higher education, it is safe to say that the Negro has not one-tenth his quota in college studies. How baseless, therefore, is the charge of too much higher training! We need Negro teachers for the Negro common schools, and we need first-class normal schools and colleges to train them. This is the work of higher Negro education, and it must be done.

Besides these facilities, we have an increasing number of manual training and trade schools; about one hundred institutions give some such training, out of which five or six are thoroughly equipped, and have sent out over a thousand trained artisans.

What has been the result of all this education? It has increased the intelligence and efficiency of Negro workmen, it has led to the buying of twelve million acres of land and at least $300,000,000 worth of property, and it has developed a class of aspiring young colored men and women who are striving for the full enjoyment of American citizenship, and have become the group leaders and ideal makers of their people. On the other hand, education has not settled the Negro problems; it has merely changed them. It has, however, more and more focused national thought upon the real kernel of these problems—*viz.*, Shall black men be treated as men? So long as it could be answered, They are not men and never will be; they can not be educated; they will not work voluntarily and save—so long as this could be said, the real question was clouded. But today American Negroes are as intelligent as most European peasants, a large and growing class is as intelligent and moral as the average of the nation, and a select few compare with the very best of the white race. The crucial Negro problem is the treatment and rights of these emerging classes. Will education settle these newer Negro problems? No; it will aggravate them. What, then shall we do? Give up the training of black men, or cheapen it, or train them simply as "hands"? No; let us be honest and straightforward, and realize that if making men better, wiser, and more ambitious brings "problems," then let the problems come, and let good men try to solve them righteously rather than to avoid them.

∾ 26 ∾

The Negro Ideals of Life

The first thought of one glancing over the program is that, after all, the ideals of living cannot vary essentially because of a person's vocation or sex or race, but that all of us living in the same world, struggling with the same problems, and facing the mystery of the same death, must and do discover in the maze of fact and thought essentially the same great landmarks to guide and cherish men.

But no sooner do we come to this realization than there arises almost immediately the question, Who are men? Who compose the group, the nation, or the race whose common experiences are like to mine, who stand bound to me in common aspiration and sympathy, in common ideal? And here it is, in answer to this question, that there must rise warning voices, the voices of those who cry, It is not simply the capitalists who are men. And today we add, It is not simply the laborer, it is not simply men who are men, but men's mothers and daughters, too, and finally that the world of men holds men of many colors and races, and that it is not white men alone who aspire to life's higher ideal, and demand the possibility of their realization.

All this is so easy to say and so easy to applaud that we forget and are even eager to forget the cruelty of the world's past answers to the question, Who are men? They are members of my tribe, said the world in its childhood: my fellow-tribesmen may ask of me peace and courtesy and help. In their upward struggles they may grasp my hand; for the ideals toward which they grope are man's, and we are brothers. This for my tribesmen; but for the men of other tribes there is eternal enmity, blood feud, war and death. They are less than I am, less than we are, inferior, undeveloped child-folk. This was in the world's childhood; but its spirit persists all through the world's history, and it lingers today here in America and in Atlantic City.

In later days, when the world was half grown and walled within dotted busy cities, came again the pressure of the world-old query, "Who are men?" The answer was larger than the answer of the past, and yet the conception of common humanity stretched but grudgingly beyond the city walls and never beyond the curling sea. Even when the organized living of men broadened with nations, the natural narrowness of human beings struggled to segregate men into different classes with differing destinies and ideals. And if, in the day of the reign of the privileged class, men had asked men of the ideals of life, what more natural counter-question than this, Whose lives?

In the boast of having risen far above the narrowness of this class conception no land has equalled or approached ours. And yet of all great modern nations not a single one has more resolutely or doggedly persisted in denying the attribute of manhood to a large proportion of its inhabitants, and persisted in making for these pariahs ideals of living and aspiration far different from those of the rest of their fellow-men.

Not only has this been true in the past, but today with reiterated emphasis we are being told that, in allowing certain men to be men in the same sense that other men are men, lurks dire danger to the republic, to civilization, and to religion, particularly of the Presbyterian type. And so persistently is this dogma being repeated that, not simply is the mass of unthinking men receiving it as true gospel, but men and women like you, men whose fathers fought for a wider humanity, women whose mothers dreamed of a real human unity, such people are beginning to apologize and temporize and to ask hesitatingly and sweetly, Would you not better give up your right to vote willingly? Would you not better ask the proprietors of public places to discriminate against you and insult you? Would it not be politic to allow labor unions without a protest to deny your right to work? Would it not be nobler to allow white men to propose concubinage and prostitution to your women so as to avoid all danger of your proposing marriage to theirs? In fact, a class of educated and conscientious Americans is today bluntly and soberly proposing to ten millions of their darker fellows that they consent to be half men because so furious an opposition will not yet let them be men.

Under the tremendous pressure of this voiced and un-voiced demand, is it curious, my hearers, that some of us black men have fallen before the temptation, have learned all too well the language of cheapened ideals, and have flung them wide among our people amid the thunders of your applause and the dulcet rattle of your gold?

This popular philosophy of the American Negro and his destiny would, if it spoke here this morning, have little part in those ideals of living held before the larger world. What have Negroes to do with science? They should hoe. The only literature they need is cook-books. Their labor movement consists in making themselves so cheap to their employers that the color line is worth 20 per cent to him, and the vision of their women is, and ought to be, the vision of keeping somebody's kitchen clean.

This we are tempted and urged and almost forced to say. And yet this there are those of us who will never declare. There are those of us so true to the birthright of all American citizens, of all dwellers in the light of the twentieth century, that we will not consent that any human being, white or black, shall be excluded arbitrarily from the pursuit of any human ideals for which he is fit.

And right here comes the confusion of tongues. The same men that cry, Throw back the doors of opportunity to all men, cry, too, less loudly, but more insistently, These black men are unfit. And then to you as listeners comes the vision. You remember the black maid who was so slovenly; you remember the loafers at those Southern depots; you remember the funny efforts of some black and half-trained lawyer; you remember—oh, one remembers so many things when one wants to remember. And yet not one of these implied criticisms of the black race touches the real righteousness of the case. When stars of life swing high, and the gates lift up their heads, surely it is not necessary to remind men that few can find the narrow way to these ideals; but what hinders? Not stature, not their beauty, not their race, not their color, but their fitness. If, then, any man be unfit to realize the higher ideals of living, that unfitness bars him from the path. We have no cause to worry lest ignorant men become scientists or unskilled men lead modern business, but we have cause to worry when the way of life is closed to men not because of their unfitness, but because of their race.

Why is it that a great nation should persist in stooping to such senseless discrimination? The reason is not far to seek. We have not learned the true lesson of democracy. Few people are proof against the delicate flattery of being considered a little better than their neighbors. It touches the fatal weakness of any race to find itself in position to look down upon another race. Hold themselves as they will, and argue as they may, there is something so peculiarly reasonable in the thought "I am worthier than he" that, far from arguing the matter, we start with this as the axiom and end in the unblushing murder of human ambition. The very ease of this descent to Avernus is its fatal danger. You will, I am sure, pardon the allusion, but, I think if ever on an American program I came elsewhere than at the end, I should be quite unable to speak from sheer surprise, and this from no conscious design, but by half-unconscious reasoning. Can the interests of men who are slaves and the sons of slaves, and still enslaved, be placed before the interests of science, or next to the interests of women or beside the representation of that organized railway labor which in nearly all cases excludes black men by constitutional provision from membership in their unions?

And yet out of this slough into which America has for so long blindly blundered it takes but the clear hearted vision of the righteous to point the unerring way they are men who act as men. They may aspire who do aspire. The ideals of life may freely lead all those who will be led, and any effort at any time or place to choke and darken a human life, to chill ambition, to limit accomplishment, to narrow opportunity for any reason save the one clear and self-proving reason of unfitness is barbarism,—the same despicable savagery that leads one clansman to murder another simply because he belongs to another clan, that leads one nation to hate and fight all other nations, that strove for centuries to make the world and its opportunities the exclusive perquisites of certain men's sons.

I trust I have not spoken too strongly for your ears on this matter. It is today of singular interest, of fearful importance. The world has fought and staggered through blood and dust to the conception of a broader and broader humanity, a free and freer human soul. The African slave trade precipitated the final battle of this fight here in America and here in America it must be fought out. To give up now is moral death and religious cowardice. We must take and hold these everlasting heights that men are not men because of their color but that men are men in spite of it.

If now once this great ground principle is fixed, that Negroes are men,—an indivisible part of that great humanity which works and aspires,—then what are the ideals of life that interest them in common with other men? Ask that question is to answer it. They are the same. They, with all men, strive to know and to do, to organize and to dream, to fight in that great battle of the west in the glow of the setting sun.

They have, however, by reason of their history, their peculiar paths to peace. Their problem of ignorance differs not in kind, but in degree from problems of ignorance the world over, but in degree it differs as 5 per cent of illiteracy differs from 50 per cent. Their problem of thrift and thriftlessness is peculiarly human, but it is intensified for two hundred years of forced labor. Their problem of sexual chastity is not greater than the same problem among the English a century ago, but it is great enough to be menacing, and the reason of its menace lies in the crimes which men have perpetrated and do perpetrate against a helpless people.

With such a program of social reform facing him, the young Negro American is called to high ideals of work and sacrifice. He of all men is called to sink his individuality in the larger personality of the vast group of his fellows, to forget his own life that others may live, to sacrifice his personal ease and pleasure in order that some of the meaning of life may trickle down to the dark and unmoved masses.

Not only this. This would be his program of life if all the gates of opportunity were open, if all the way of life lay clear and beckoning to all men despite their color. But this is not so. Upon all the burden of uplifting his fellows this class of Americans must feel in every thought and motion the hindrance and contempt of their fellows, the sneer of the critic, the wavering of the friend, the vindictive hatred of the enemy. To hold his balance, then, in this whirling chaos and keep his head from swimming, to combine at once keen insight into the faults of his own people and unsparing criticism of the aggressions of others, to be hopeful in the face of hopeless meanness, and righteously hopeless when they who see the tendencies of the day persist in calling all of them hopeful, to work on in hot, ceaseless energy, while others neutralize his efforts by cold contempt,—this program of life calls for men; and, when you see it daily being carried out, see the decrease of black ignorance by tremendous strides, the increase of Negro property holding by leaps and bounds, the strengthening of family life, and the persistent, unceasing refusal to be satisfied with anything but the highest and best, such a struggle of men ought to call on you for sympathy, aid, and the unwavering support of their ideals.

The battle, then, for a humanity as broad as the dwellings of men, a struggle for human uplift through work and sacrifice, a refusal to let that work be stopped by the enmity, contempt, and prejudice of their fellows, and a persistent clinging to the broadest ideals in the face of the narrowest opportunities,—this is the fight that black men of America are today waging in that far-flung battle line that ever beats against the stars.

❧ 27 ❧

The Future of the Negro Race in America

There are, as it seems to me, four ways in which the American Negro may develop: first, his present condition of serfdom may be perpetuated; secondly, his race may die out and become extinct in this land; thirdly, he may migrate to some foreign land; and fourthly, he may become an American citizen.

In all history slavery has usually been succeeded by a period of semi-slavery or serfdom. Just how far this is necessary, and how far it is the result of imperfect emancipation, it is difficult to determine. There was a disposition in the United States, for a few years following the Civil War, to insure the complete emancipation of the Negro slave. This was a tremendously difficult undertaking, but not necessarily impossible. The nation, however, quickly tired of the task, and the present state of serfdom ensued. Throughout the United States the mass of the Negro population is curtailed in personal liberty, is insecure in life and property, has peculiar difficulty in earning a decent living, has almost no voice in its own government, does not enjoy adequate educational facilities, and suffers, no matter what its ability or desert, discount, impertinence and contempt, by reason of race and color. To be more specific, it is clear that Negroes are usually unable to enjoy fully the ordinary rights of domicile or of travel, the use of public conveniences, and of many facilities for instruction and entertainment. The black man is in continual danger of mob violence in New York as in New Orleans, in the West as in the South; his economic condition is especially unfortunate; he was emancipated suddenly, without land, capital, or tools, or skill, and generously bidden to go to work, be sober, and save money. He did go to work, he did work faithfully, and he did save some money. And yet his most frantic efforts, under the circumstances, could not save him from sinking into an economic serfdom which, at its best, is organized and systematic pauperism. To turn astray in modern competitive industry a mass of ignorant, unguided working men, whose employers despise them, and for whom the rest of the nation evinces only spasmodic concern, is to invite oppression. The result is oppression. On the plantations of the southern backwoods the Negro is a peon bound to the soil without wages or rights; throughout the rural South cunningly devised labor laws—laws to contract and lien, vagrancy, and employer and servant—are so applied to black men as to reduce them to the level of fourteenth-century serfs. In the cities of the South and in the North the color line is so drawn as to increase competition against the Negro, restrict his chances of employment, and lower his labor price, and while agencies for his degradation welcome and invite him, those for his uplifting are closed or coldly tolerant.

In a day when political power is, for weal or woe, so intimately bound up with economic success and efficiency, the Negro is being systematically and quickly disfranchised. Taxation without representation is the rule of his life. In the South he is taxed for libraries which he may not use, for public high schools and colleges which he may not attend, and for public parks where he cannot sit. The fear of political consequences or of labor strikes never deters an employer from discharging his Negro hands or reducing their wages, while that same fear may keep out Negro laborers or lead to the substitution of whites even at an economic disadvantage.

In regard to the present educational facilities of the land only one Negro child in three receives regular instruction, and that for only a few months in the year, under teachers often poorly equipped and sometimes not equipped at all. It is fair to say that less than 20 per cent of the Negro children in the United States today are getting good elementary school training. There are a number of poorly furnished high schools for training teachers, and a few institutions doing college work. The only branch of education that today can command large and ungrudging support is manual and industrial training, the importance of which, great as it certainly is, is being obviously exaggerated and unduly emphasized at present. If those at the higher schools for Negroes' training should turn their class-rooms into blacksmiths' shops and make wagons instead of making men, they would get far more enthusiastic support. They have not all seen fit to do this—not that for a moment they fail to recognize the importance of wagons or fail to honor the artisan. They simply maintain that there is a place in the world for training men as such, and until the public comes to agree with them they must close their doors.

In this plain statement I am not seeking to minimize the vast efforts put forth for Negro education in the United States; I am simply pointing out that, great as those efforts have been, they are strikingly inadequate, and that under present conditions the majority of Negro children are growing up in ignorance, and without the proper moral and intellectual leadership of adequately trained teachers, ministers, and heads of families.

And finally the whole social atmosphere in which the Negro lives and works, the intangible and powerful spiritual environment of the race, is such as to foster more and more either a false humility or hypocrisy, or an unreasoning radicalism and despair.

This is a condition of serfdom. Its symptoms vary, of course, in time and place; localities might easily be found where certain phases of the condition are better then I have indicated, and others where they are worse. The picture I have painted is perhaps an average one.

Now, I have said that *the first possible future of the American Negro* is the perpetuation and perfection of this present serfdom. This would involve the strengthening of present proscriptive laws, the further disfranchisement of black men, and the legal recognition of customary caste distinctions. This has been the distinct tendency of the South in the last decade, and this program has gained respectful hearing and acquiescence in influential parts of the North.

The question then is: What does such a policy involve so far as the Negro is concerned? If along with the repression and proscription there could be expected cheerful acquiescence in inferiority and faithful work, then this solution would have much in its favor. It is, however, difficult to see how under the long continuance of the present system anything but degeneration into hopelessness, immorality, and crime could ensue. Under modern conditions of life and social and economic organization, a permanent and successful caste system is impossible. The essence of modern democracy is the placing in the hand of the individual the power and responsibility for maintaining his right and liberty; and even in the larger social democracy which we see in the future the cornerstone must be that no social group is to be placed at the mercy of, or in entire dependence upon, the sense of justice of another group. Today and to-morrow the reduction of a mass of men to permanent or long-continued economic and political inferiority means the deliberate reduction of their chances of survival, and the deliberate encouragement of degeneration among them.

In any social group, however prosperous, degenerative tendencies may always be disclosed. The situation becomes critical and fatal when such tendencies are more than those of upbuilding and progress. Among American Negroes the tendencies to degeneration, while not yet in the ascendency, have undoubtedly been encouraged and fostered by the history of the last two decades. Today men criticize American Negroes and say that they are not trustworthy—they cannot bear responsibility; they seem lacking in self-respect and personal dignity and in courage; and they have even lost something of the tact and courtesy of their fathers. Now a careful consideration of these defects will clearly show that they are the children, and the legitimate children, of a caste system. What is it that slavery and serfdom has been most assiduous in teaching the Negro if it be not timidity, lack of a sense of personal worth, and inability to bear responsibility, and must not such teaching eventually engender carelessness and lack of courtesy? These men must be ever hesitant as to their rights and duties; in the face of continued disappointment their courage must waver; it is hard to maintain one's self-respect when all the world, even to the urchins on the street, regard you with evident contempt; and self-reliance and persistency must be fed by reasonable hope of success if it is to become characteristic of a people.

On the other hand, those qualities of character which, by four hundred years of persistent artificial selection, have been partially educated out of the Negro are the very qualities upon which the civilized world is putting an exaggerated emphasis today. A people without pluck that borders on brazenness and courage akin to brutality is ruthlessly thrust aside, euphoniously designated as "lesser breeds without the law," and is robbed, routed, and raped by every civilized agency from the battleship to the Christian Church.

From such considerations it seems inevitable that the present policy of the nation toward the Negro must eventually result in increasing hopelessness, immorality, and crime. Indeed, it is one of the most curious developments of the present to witness the widespread and touching surprise of the people of the United States at the spread of crime among Negroes. Men shake their heads and say, "How surprising! And such a docile and sweet-tempered race!" And yet is it surprising? If you enslave and oppress a people, ravish and degrade their women, emancipate them into poverty, helplessness, and ignorance, systematically teach them humility in a braggart age—would you expect to develop angels or devils? The Negro criminal has appeared, and Negro crime is spreading. Is this phenomenon a new and peculiar race characteristic, or simply the logical effect of known causes?

Suppose, now, that these tendencies to degenerate among the Negroes gain the ascendency over the persistent struggles of the Negro to rise; suppose that crime and immorality gain such a headway as to check and choke the accumulation of wealth and the education of children—what then?

There seems to be a fatuous and curious notion among some Americans that such a consummation is devoutly to be wished; they discover with evident glee any indication that a wholesale process of degeneration has finally mastered the Negro. But has America no interest—no merely self-ish interest—in such an outcome? If men fear with a mighty fear an epidemic of smallpox, or are urged to extraordinary exertions to stamp out yellow fever, can they look with equanimity and lack-lustre eye upon the infection of ten million neighbors with a far more deadly virus? Can anyone but a fool think it is to his interest to make every ninth man in his country a pauper and a criminal, in addition to the growing load of his own degenerates? Not even a rich and healthy land like America could, without imminent and lasting peril, stand the moral and physical shock, the frightful contagion which must accompany the slow degradation and social murder of ten million human souls. Every selfish interest of this land—and I hesitate to appeal to higher motives—every selfish interest of this land demands that if the Negro is to remain there he be raised and raised rapidly to the level of the best culture of the day.

The second possible future of the American Negro arises from the possibility hinted at that the Negro is not destined to remain long in this land. It is the expectation of many Americans, and Americans too of honesty and integrity, that gradually but inevitably the Negro will die out before degeneration sets in to such an extent as to make him a menace to the land. These are the portion of Americans who cannot conceive how the Negro can ever become an integral part of this republic; for the sake of the land, therefore, and the interests of the many, and from no especial dislike or prejudice against the Negro, they hope that the race will either die out or migrate from the land. This is the practical and unemotional way in which the Darwinian doctrine of survival is applied in America to the Negro problem. And I presume it is fair to say that a very large proportion, if not the majority, of the thinking people of America have adopted this attitude.

The question of race and survival which is thus touched upon is of so deep a significance today, when European civilization is coming in contact with nearly all the world's great races, that it is of the utmost importance that sane and correct ideas on the subject should be current among the mass of citizens. Today this is not the case. On the contrary, there is unfortunately widespread ignorance of the doctrines of race survival and human efficiency current even among people who ought to think more clearly. And this ignorance is helped on by the marvellous ignorance of human history permissible among people called intelligent, among Jingo writers, and the readers of Kipling's doggerel.

In such way we have come to a more or less clearly conceived public opinion which considers the present civilization of Europe and America as by far the greatest the world has seen; which gives the credit of this culture to the white Germanic peoples, and considers that these races have a divine right to rule the world in such way as they think best. This, I take it, is the creed of most Englishmen and Americans today. That such a creed is dangerous and needs the most careful scrutiny and revision is clear from the extraordinary deeds that have been committed under its guidance. The red-handed crimes that today may be laid at the door of men who have honestly and sincerely sought to work in accordance with this scheme of survival are enough to cause heart-searching among decent people, not to mention Christians and Christian Churches.

I need cite here but a single case. There lies to the westward of America, in the summer seas, a cluster of islands bursting with beauty and fragrance, with men and women and children neither better nor worse than the average of primitive folk. Some of the grandfathers and grandmothers of present Americans wandered over there with the Bible in their hands and the golden rule of Christ on their lips. They told these children of the sea of Christian civilization founded on Justice and Truth and Right, and then they invited their fellow-citizens to come over and finish the tale. And they came, and with them came land-grabbers, swindlers, and whoremongers, who began the work of robbery and debauchery until finally they suddenly discovered that the God of the Americans never intended islands so sweet and rich for weak-minded immoral Hawaiians, so they stole the soil from beneath the converts' feet, sent their queen wandering on the face of the earth, and gave the booty to America, and America took it. You may dress this tale of Hawaii in the most gracious clothing you can command. You may emphasize the degradation of the nation, the guileless altruism of the Americans, and the present prosperity of the sugar-planters; and yet if there sits beyond the stars a God of Justice who metes out to men their reward for murder and theft and adultery, then the blood of this helpless people will rest on America and on its children's children.

This is but one of the many tales of nineteenth-century enterprise in civilizing the heathen, and arranging for the survival of the fittest: West Africa, South Africa, Uganda, the Congo Free State, China, Cuba, and the Philippines are similar chapters. Making all due allowance for different ways of interpreting facts, it must be confessed by all honest men that a theory of human civilization which stands sponsor for the enormities committed by European civilization on native races is an outrage and a lie.

But do the theories of Darwin and Spencer, properly interpreted, support any crude views of justice and right and the spread of civilization as those current today? It may be safely answered they do not. Ignorant and selfish interpretation of great longer be allowed to obscure and degrade those laws.

First of all, the man of true learning and breadth of views is less sanguine of the overmastering completeness of our present culture, of its incomparable superiority over civilizations of the past. He sees its strength and its weaknesses, and above all he realizes that the one conspicuous triumph of modern culture—namely, the diffusion of its benefits among the lower strata of society—is an accomplishment which is, logically, a flat contradiction to the theory of the natural aristocracy of races. He knows that the world has staggered and struggled up to the idea that if national welfare is not simply the welfare of a privileged few, and he consequently has serious doubts of a theory of races which assumes that white-faced men must inherit the earth simply because they have bigger guns and morals, and which forestalls the writhings of other races by branding them as inferior and then sitting on them.

Such a course is not simply arrogant, it is at once dangerous and unreasonable. Why is it that, while European races are at present leading civilization, most African races are in barbarism? This is a question that cannot be satisfactorily and definitely answered. A Greek of the age of Pericles might have put just as puzzling and unanswerable a query to the ancestors of the present Europeans who were crawling about the forests of Germany half-naked and periodically drunk. And the ancient Egyptians in the day of their glory might have put equally uncomfortable queries to the ancestors of the Greeks. Why at certain times in the world's history civilizations have flashed up here and there, have smoldered and died, smoldered and burned anew, while the rest of the world lay still in common darkness, is a mystery which true intelligence frankly acknowledges to be such.

But the failure of complete knowledge here is not denial or disparagement of the great light thrown upon race development by the theories of evolution and by sociological research. It has become clearer to us that races and nations as well as men may be healthy and vigorous, may contract diseases and waste away, may commit sin and pay the penalty. It may easily happen too that circumstances and surroundings which favor one race may be fatal to another. And it is here that those who look for the extinction of the Negro in America may legitimately take their stand. If, for instance, under conditions of civilized life as favorable as ordinary justice can make them, a race of people have not the sheer physical stamina to survive, then, however pitiable the spectacle, there is little that surrounding civilization can do. And it certainly cannot jeopardize the lives and prospects of the great mass of people by efforts to save a doomed remnant. While this is certainly true, it is by no means certain that such a case often occurs. Nearly all the instances of native races fading away on the advent of civilization have been instances where the fading away was easily explicable. If all authority is stripped from a people, their customs interfered with, their religion laughed at, their children corrupted, and ruin, gambling, and prostitution forced upon them—such a proceeding will undoubtedly kill them off and kill them quickly. But that is not the survival of the fittest—it is murder.

Turning, then, to the second possible future of the Negro in America— namely, that he may die out—must be candidly acknowledged that this is quite possible. If the Negro is given no voice in his own government and welfare, if he continues increasingly to be shut out of employment, if his wages become lower and lower, and his chances of justice and consideration less; if, in consequence of this, he loses hope and lets himself sink deeper and deeper into carelessness, incompetence and crime; if instead of educating his brains, we get increasing pleasure and profit in making him simply a useful instrument of labor—a mere hand—if his common school system continues to be neglected, if his family life has no respect in custom and little, in law, it is quite possible—I might say probable—that that the Negro will dwindle away and die from starvation and excess. This will simply add a few million more murders to the account of civilization; it would, of course, prove nothing as to the stamina and capabilities of the Negro race.

Such a course of action is to-day impossible, however. The chances are that, along with the repressive, discouraging, and debauching influences, philanthropic and educational agencies will continue their work and in some degree counteract them. In such event everything depends on the ability of the Negroes to keep up their courage and hope. If they succeed in this, the chances of their dying out are exceedingly small. A people that have withstood the horrors of the African slave trade, American slavery, reconstruction, disfranchisement, the disruption of the family, unhealthy homes, famine, pestilence, and disease, and, above all, the studied, ingenious, and bitter prejudice and contempt of their fellow-citizens, and yet, in a single century, with practically no additions from without, have increased from one to ten million souls, are, to say the least, in no immediate danger of extinction. If extinction comes, it will be a long and tedious process covering many decades, accompanied by widespread crime and disease, and caused by unusual race bitterness and proscription. And during such a process we must always face the possibility of revolt and insurrection on the part of the oppressed.

I was sitting in the Philadelphia depot not long ago with the editor of an influential paper. We spoke of a late riot against Negroes, and he turned to me after several minutes of general talk and said point-blank, "Why didn't the Negroes fight?" I answered, "Because they are hopeful." The Negro knows that in a trial of brute strength the odds are infinitely against him. He still believes, however, that he can in other ways gain success at some time. So long as that hope remains general, there is little chance of widespread degeneration or extinction. But when that hope goes, and in its place comes blank despair when the desperation of disappointed striving and the mockery of effort seize the millions of black people in this land, no man can answer for the consequences. That seventy-two millions can eventually overpower nine millions goes without saying. But it will cost something.

Suppose, then, that we acknowledge that present conditions cannot continue, that the doctrine of the survival of the fittest races is incapable of advancement, or likely with an ordinary chance of living to become extinct in America, there are then left two possible alternatives—the migration of the Negro or his raising himself to full citizenship.

It is the irony of fate that the solution of the Negro problem which would seem in some respects most simple is made complex and improbable by the very theory that most warmly supports it—viz., the theory of race incompatibility and relative inferiority. I mean this, the present tendency among civilized nations towards landgrabbing and overawing weaker nations and races makes the possibility of any permanent settlement by American Negroes being left in peace extremely small. Nay, more, the absorption has already gone so far that nowhere is there left in the world a foothold for a new nation; certainly not in Africa, where every inch of soil is claimed, and where the Negro immigrant would only exchange the tyranny of America for the tyranny of Europe, with the additional disadvantage of being further from the ear of the sovereign power.

Moreover, modern methods make it impossible to hold a rich or even moderately rich country without capital to exploit it. Yet the Negro immigrants from the United States must be comparatively poor. Let a gold mine appear in their midst, or an iron mine, or even good crops of potatoes, and immediately some one would hear the voice of God calling him to rescue this beautiful land from the lazy blacks—at a profit of seventy per cent.

If there were a land where Negro immigrants would be welcomed, and reasonably secure of their rights and liberties and of a chance to earn a living, it might and undoubtedly would attract a large proportion of American Negroes. It would, however, attract the very class that America could best afford to keep—the intelligent, the thrifty, those who had some capital and those who had self-respect. In other words, you would skim the cream from the mass, and leave perhaps a worse problem than before.

The hope that an asylum beyond the sea would attract all the Negro population, or that they could be under any circumstances removed en masse, is, of course, chimerical. Five hundred Negro children are being born every twenty-four hours in America. To carry these alone out of the country would call for a fleet of a dozen or score of ships plying constantly between America and the African coast. No such stupendous transplanting of a nation has ever been successfully attempted in human history. Six million Negroes were brought to Brazil, but it took three hundred years and cost perhaps ten million human lives. Unless the transportation is to be sheer butchery, the property of Negroes must be bought from them, and those with no property must be furnished with tools and food; transportation across the United States must be given and subsistence while in transport; indeed, it is safe to say that the cost of such an enterprise would exceed the cost of the Civil War even taking it for granted that the Negro wished to go and he does not wish to do so. He has sense enough not to jump from the frying pan into the fire, not to give up a fighting chance in

America for a hopeless struggle against the combined civilized world. A helpless child may be ill-treated and abused in its own home, but that is little excuse for midnight wandering amid the marauders of the street.

There is left the last alternative—the raising of the Negro in America to full rights and citizenship. And I mean by this no half-way measures; I mean full and fair equality. That is, the chance to obtain work regardless of color to aspire to position and preferment on the basis of desert alone, to have the right to use public conveniences to enter public places of amusement on the same terms as other people, and to be received socially by such persons as might wish to receive them. These are not extravagant demands, and yet their granting means the abolition of the color line. The question is: Can American Negroes hope to attain to this result? The answer to this is by no means simple. To use mathematical terms, the problem is a dynamic one, with two dependent and two independent variables. Let us consider first the dependent variables: they are the social condition of the Negro on the one hand, and public opinion or social environment on the other. These are dependent variables in the sense that, as the social condition of the Negro improves, public opinion toward him is more tolerant, and vice versa, as public opinion is more sympathetic, it is easier for him to improve his social condition. Now, thinkers unacquainted with the problem often see here an easy solution. One says: "Let the Negroes improve in morality, gain wealth and education, and the battle is won." The other says: "Let public opinion change toward the Negro, give him work and encouragement, treat him fairly and justly, and he will rapidly rise in the world." Here are two propositions which contain a subtle logical contradiction, and yet practically all of the solutions of the Negro problem outside the radical ones I have mentioned have been based on the emphasis of one of these propositions. From 1860–1880 the United States insisted on the duty of liberalizing the public conscience; from 1880 to 1900 they have insisted on social progress among the Negroes. The difficulty with these propositions is that each one is a half-truth which may under certain circumstances become a flat mockery. I saw once in the Black Belt a tall sad-faced young fellow with a new wife and baby; he had married in the spring and started up in the world with a mule and cabin furniture. But the season was bad, cotton fell in price, and at harvest time the landlord took the cotton and took the mule, and stripped the cabin of bed and chairs and bureau, and left the little family naked to the world. Shall I tell that man that the way to gain the world's respect and help is to rise in the world and become wealthier and wiser? On the other hand, a New York merchant hires a Negro servant: he finds her incompetent, untrustworthy and slovenly; his meals are late and not worth eating when they come; his servant is unaccommodating and sour-faced, and leaves without notice. Is there anything to be gained in telling this man that a more liberal attitude and broader appreciation towards the colored race will make them more careful and deserving? And yet, while taken apart these phrases are half true, if not at times untrue, yet taken together they certainly express a truth—viz., that, given a continuous employment in social conditions, there will follow increased respect and consideration, and given liberal intelligent public interest, there will be stimulated in any class a desire to be richer, truer, and better. The difficulty is, with the problem stated thus dynamically, to get the double movement started; social condition may greatly improve before public opinion realizes it. Public opinion may grow liberal before men are aware of the new chances opening. And, above all, the continual tendency in such dynamic problems is to a stable equilibrium—where public opinion becomes fixed and immovable, and social condition merely holds its own. That has been the continual tendency with the Negro problem; for a few brief years after the war a whirling revolution of public opinion was accompanied by a phenomenal rush and striving upward. Then the public conscience grew cold, the cement of the new nation hardened, and while in a few brief years we had turned slaves into serfs, we left them mainly serfs, nothing more. In fine there is a great and important truth in the often-spoken-of interdependence of condition and environment in the rise of a social group; but it is no simple thing—it is rather a matter of peculiar subtlety and complexity.

There is a further point: when I said that public opinion and social condition were dependent variables, and varied inversely to each other, it must have occurred to many that sometimes this variable failed to respond proportionately; that an improving people, sometimes far from reaping approbation, reap additional hate and difficulty, and increasing liberality in the national conscience is sometimes repaid by degradation and degeneration. In plainer terms, there is, without doubt, an independent element in these variable social quantities which is above all rule and reason. And in the matter of social condition and the independent variable is the question of the real capability of the Negro race; and deep down beyond all questions of public prejudice. Radical partisans usually place themselves upon these arguments. The radical American Southerner says that back of all questions of social conditions lies the ineradicable question of race, and that varieties of the human species so utterly different as the white and black races can never live together on a basis of equality; either subordination or extermination must ensue when they come in contact. The radical Negro, on the other hand, resents warmly any intimation that the Negro race is deficient in ability and capacity compared with other races; he points out that for such differences as exist today good and sufficient cause may be found in the slave trade and slavery reconstruction; he insists that every generation in this land has seen Negroes of more than ordinary ability from Phillis Wheatley and [Benjamin] Banneker to Douglass and Dunbar. He thinks that in the history of the modern world Negro genius has shown itself in Pushkin, Toussaint L'Ouverture, and Alexander Dumas, not to mention men whose

Negro blood was seldom acknowledged from the time of the Pharaohs to that of Robert Browning.

There are a good many exaggerations and contradictions in the statements made in regard to the accomplishments of the Negro race since emancipation, but it is clear beyond dispute that the Negro has done five things. He has (1) restored home, (2) earned a living, (3) learned to read and write, (4) saved money and bought some twelve million acres of land, (5) begun to furnish his own group leaders.

There is no way of denying that these comparatively simple things are really extraordinary accomplishments. The Negro home is not thoroughly pure or self-protecting or comfortable, but it is a home created by main strength out of a system of concubinage and amid discouragement and mockery. The living earned has been a poor one, and yet without hesitation, lawlessness, or wholesale pauperism the Negroes have changed themselves from dumb driven cattle to laborers bearing the responsibility of their own support.

From enforced ignorance so great that over 90 per cent of the colored people could not read and write at the close of the war, they have brought themselves to the place where 56 per cent can read and write. Starting a generation ago, without a cent or the ownership of their own bodies, they have saved property to the value of not less than 300,000,000 dollars, besides supporting themselves; and finally they have begun to evolve among themselves men who know their situation and needs.

All this does not prove that the future is bright and clear, or that there is no question of race antipathy or Negro capacity; but it is distinctly and emphatically hopeful, and in the light of history and human development it puts the burden of proof rather on those who deny the capabilities of the Negro than on those who assume that they are not essentially different from those of other members of the great human family.

If such a hopeful attitude toward the race problem in America is to prevail, then the attitude of the cultured classes of England and Europe can do much to aid its triumph. Hitherto English sympathy and opinion has been largely cast on the side of slavery and retrogression. Can we not hope for a change? Better than that, may we not look for an example of large-hearted tolerance and far-seeing philanthropy in the treatment of our brothers in South Africa that may shame the sons of English men in the United States?

～ 28 ～

St. Francis of Assisi

You have all been recently talking and thinking of San Francisco, that opulent, busy city which one day faced the shining western waters and the next fell into poverty, death and ruin because beneath its feet the earth trembled. Such strange catastrophe gives the whole world pause; it is not new, it is old, so old, and yet ever and again, we need to be reminded that back of the hurrying throbbing life of every city and every day lie the world-old things—birth and death, joy and sorrow, human love and human hate— that these and these alone make life; and with these each life must deal.

We remember this all the more keenly in the case of San Francisco because of the magic spell of the city's golden history and because of the life of the man after whom this stricken metropolis was named: He stands forth in the world's annals as one of those saints and prophets who sought to read life's riddle and tell the world its true unraveling. San Francisco is the Spanish form of the name of St. Francis of Assisi and it is to his life and life teaching that I want to call your attention:

The fullness of his young manhood and his riper years lay in the 13th century, that last great cyclone of the Middle Age, 700 long years ago. It is hard to picture the life of other years and other centuries and yet remember that there lived boys and girls then, throbbing with life as you are, listening and waiting for the call. It was the day of Dante and Philip the Fair; the day when Venice and Genoa were in the first flush of their glory, and the German Hansa towns were building their quaint and beautiful guild halls. All through the world ran the thrill of that restless striving and awakening; then it was that a boy was born in the sweet Italian city of Assisi, in Umbria, perhaps a hundred miles north of Rome. His father, Pietro Bernadone, was a rich merchant trading to France, and while the mother would piously name the boy John, the father proudly called him Francis after his rich and beloved France, and showered his wealth upon him. Wealth then meant even more than wealth means now, and now it means much. Think of a handsome, red-blooded boy, born in the beautiful hills of a beautiful land, surrounded by luxury, pampered by his parents and flattered and bowed down to by all his little world. Accompanied by a crowd of gay young fellows he spent a glorious, roystering youth—fishing for trout and sturgeon in the mountain streams, dancing in the merry Springtime, drinking the clear white wine in Summer and feasting in the red Autumnal days.

Was not this a glorious life? Suppose that before you tonight stretched this golden vista of wealth and laughter and gay abandon—would you not be perfectly happy? Probably you would. Probably for a time life would be simply singing as it was for a time with Francis of Assisi.

After that, however—if you were honest and unselfish, if you opened your clear eyes and looked upon the real world there would come to you as there came to this gay Italian 700 years ago a sense of vague discomfort, of unfilled destiny, of wasted power. There would rise a dim realization of the misery and sorrow of the world on which your strident gayety would fall almost as mockery, as blasphemy.

Not that it would seem wrong to be joyful but rather that your joy alone would not suffice—not that it would be wrong to laugh, but that laughter would not cure all the world's ills, and that the world has ills. Something would be lacking—a great dark void of crying want stretching forth out of the shadowy valley and up the tremulous sides of the great wide hills, crying, till souls must listen, even in their laughter—your soul and mine, the soul of Socrates and Jesus Christ, and the soul of St. Francis of Assisi.

This time of listening—of pausing, of sudden assumption of responsibility, we call Commencement—the Beginning of Life. To some of you it comes to-night—to others it has come earlier than this formal celebration and still to others it will not come till many years have passed with their messages of warning and enlightenment. To Francis of Assisi it came just in his budding manhood and he paused in astonishment to ask these questions—old and ever new:

What am I? And what is this world about me? And this world and I—how shall we live together in laughter and work?

So the youth sat him down in the sunshine and pondered—hearing the shouting of his companions afar, dreaming over the faint echo of music and seeing new meaning in the sun and river. What thought came to him? The thought of every awakening young soul. Is life joy? Yes and no—*yes*, because it is right to be happy and yet—*no*, because I cannot be happy in the midst of a world full of misery. Is life wealth? Yes and no—*yes*, because wealth is but that stored and garnered work which ministers to men's wants, and yet—*no*, because there are human wants and aspirations that no heaped treasure can satisfy. Is life glory and fame—yes and no—*yes*, for fame is the right reward of work well done and yet—*no*, for much of the world's greatest applause is given for work ill-done and undone.

So the boy pondered as all boys ponder—not consciously and clearly, but subtly and half doubtingly. When he faced the gift of joy he threw himself into the mad vortex of delight and then slowly withdrew and looked on the pain and sorrow about him; when he faced the gift of wealth, he tossed away the gold lightly, spending like a prince, wearing his silken hose and velvet doublet, drinking and feasting until he noticed men starving by the roadside. He threw them alms; they seized them and were hungry again and in their dull eyes he saw a greater, deeper hunger—"*not alms but a friend!*" it cried. Then he faced the luring glory of fame, and what was fame in the Middle Age but war? He donned the warrior's flashing uniform—he heard the martial music swelling on the olive crowned hills of Urobria—he listened to the tramping of a hundred horsemen as they cried "Long live Assisi—down with Perugia!" Among the singing waters they thundered, drunk with the mad wine of conquest in that great yellow Italian morning—but at evening they came wandering back. There was blood upon their garments, and the horror of murder in their souls. The damp sharp wind beat mercilessly on the naked misery of a soldier, dying in a way-side ditch, and Francis of Assisi paused and undid the chased and silver buckle of his velvet cloak and lay it gently across the wretched man. And then all silently he rode into the night.

And that night he turned suddenly, swiftly, as all men turn at the turning points of life, crying "Not by wealth nor by violence but by my spirit, saith the Lord." And he meant by this that the joy of the world was not to be gained by selfishness nor by force but by the broad bonds of human sympathy. And what was true seven hundred years ago—is it not true tonight?

Quaintly and cheerfully he began his life work. "Poverty shall be my bride," he said—poverty and beggary would he wed, and wandering human charity would be his life calling. He gathered a little band about him and thus St. Francis of Assisi became the little brother of the poor, a beggar and an outcast among men, a listener to birds and little children. Nor does all this sound as strange today as it did in the year of our Lord, 1208. We Americans have a certain contempt for the poor and unfortunate, but our attitude toward human misfortune is angelic beside the disdain of the 13th century. Then it was only the wealthy and well-born who were people. Beneath the knot of privileged aristocrats festered the mass of neglected and despised poor beggars and unfortunates, poor working men, cripples, feebleminded and insane, all too far below the world, the good rich world, for the world to notice. When Francis turned from his idle playing and spending of wealth and his work of war and faced the bitter misery of the world; when he said: The greatest evil of Italy is Poverty, and I will make the Lady, Poverty, my bride—his proud father Pietro threw up his hands in horror and disgust. "Fool," he cried, "to give up wealth, position and fame for a crazy cause—you are no son of mine." But Francis crossed his breast and cried: "Pietro, Pietro Bernadone until now I have called you father but hence forth I can truly say with these 'Our Father who art in heaven,' for he is my wealth and hope." Out in the world then he wandered alone. His friends wagged their heads and laughed, as some friends will, but his mother waited. And then, not suddenly and triumphantly; but slowly in weary years and sickening strife, after defeat and ridicule, persecution and doubt, came the new deep revelation. Along the dusty Italian roads moved rough clad silent men, gentle of speech, preaching Peace and Patience, tending the wounded, relieving the distressed and reclaiming the erring. It was the first great mediaeval effort at social reform, at organized charity, at the work of the visiting nurse. It was the first great recognition in the Middle Age of the abject misery of the masses of men, the first listening to the wretched cry of outcast humanity.

The pebble thrown widened in ever circling waves of good until the beggar of 1208 stood at the head of the vast movement which swept the Christian world, dashed its spray on the strongholds of Mohammed, and has lived even to our day. So St. Francis grew to busy, blameless, gentle life, the friend of birds and living things, the helper of the poor and needy, a homeless wanderer yet standing before kings and the mighty of the earth; until after less than 50 years of life he found eternal rest on the Vine-clad bosom of the Appenines, and the marks of the sorrows of God rested on his hands and heart.

Why have I brought you this old fashioned tale of the life of a mediae-val saint? Century after century has rolled by since his dust crumbled and floated in the mists that hover on the head waters of the Arno and the Tiber. The world has changed into a hastening, hurrying hungry whirl of weal and woe—Why should we look backward rather than forward for our guiding star?

I have brought this life back to your memory to fix in your minds a certain attitude toward wealth and distinction, and the need and place of human training to emphasize this attitude. The lesson of the life of St. Francis of Assisi is not, as some hastily infer, the renunciation of wealth, and the deification of poverty. It is on the contrary simply this great truth: The work of the world is to satisfy the world's great wants. Now the world wants material wealth, such as food and clothing and shelter, but this is not all, nor even the greater part of its need. It wants human service and human sympathy, it wants knowledge and inspiration, it wants hope and truth and beauty, and so great are these greater wants that often their satisfaction demands in some St. Francis of Assisi an utter renunciation of much of the material good of the world, that its spiritual starvation may be satisfied. In the 13th century this was peculiarly true. So poverty stricken was the world in simple human goodness that it actually needed this more than it needed food and clothes, and to this need a brave, unselfish man addressed himself. Today, in the 20th century the world is rich in material resources and richer too than ever before in spiritual content. And yet even today we are not so wealthy in human sympathy that we can turn our attention wholly to material wealth and neglect the greater wants of the world—soul. On the contrary, our very excess of material accumulation and deftness of process is additional reason for increased attention toward making men more intelligent, more unselfish and more broadly human.

Thus is it not clear that with all the change in time and circumstances there remains the same old questions of attitude toward life? What am I, and what is the world, and this world and I, how shall we laugh and work together?

Ever in this questioning the old human drama is acted again and again on the hard grey bosom of the earth. Ever the joyous youth arises in the great dim morning of life and sees the golden lure of endless joy and wealth beckoning on the horizon.

Ever the blood of the growing man hears the wild trumpet blast of deeds and fame, and ever then in life's commencement comes the still small voice of wisdom: "Not by wealth nor violence but by my spirit saith the Lord." This was the history of St. Francis of Assisi and this will be your history, my young friends. And for this reason I am asking you to pause tonight and listen to the old story and learn the life lesson it contains.

It would be full easy, let me repeat, to misinterpret such a history; to tell you that joy has no part in life, that wealth is merely temptation, that fame is mockery and that only by total renunciation can come the real good of living. Yet this would be wrong—this is untrue, and least of all does the life of St. Francis teach this contradiction of life. Rather his life emphasizes the beauty and joy of living, but not simply for ourselves, rather for all men, his life emphasizes the need and use of work and wealth but it also emphasizes the fact that material wealth satisfies only a part of life's want and that it may be necessary to sacrifice a part or even the larger part of material well-being for the advancement of science and humanity. Indeed at all times human life must be a balancing of limited means against infinite ends, and while all these life objects are desirable yet some are more desirable than others, and the poverty of human energies and resources forces us always to choose the more weighty and important and let the others wait. In St. Francis's day this choosing left him in direst physical poverty. In our day this is not necessary and yet the choosing of the greater needs of life today by any individual and any nation precludes all thought of great individual wealth, for material wealth is not man's sole aim but rather wealth of mind and soul as well as of body should be his ambition; and finally the life of St. Francis shows that true fame—the only fame worth having and striving for is the "Well done" of that master who knows the sweat of the toil and the worth of the service.

Such is the lesson which in a thousand lives and a thousand places the world is seeking to teach its children, and this is the true object of the public school system whose fruition and celebration you and the throng of your friends represent tonight.

Put this in terse and concrete meaning, what does the 20th century demand of the youth who, standing at the threshold and commencement of life, wish to do for their world something of the work that St. Francis did for his?

It demands, I take it, four great things:

Ambition	or	Force
Ideal	or	Object
Renunciation	or	Unselfishness
Technique	or	Work.

First of all it demands ambition—the striving within your souls of every latent power of doing, of all the slumbering fire,—the quickening of muscle and stretching of sinew, and the burning, scintillating flash of brain—the whole massed might of this wonderful human machine, alert, panting instinct with holy zeal to hurl itself into the world's work. That was the thing with which Francis of Assisi started the fiery impulse, the joyous enthusiasm, the unshaken determination to make life tell for its utmost in spite of the contempt and mocking of men or the machinations of the devil—that is the spirit that must animate you, young men and women, as you step forth into the world tonight. I mean, too, by ambition not the mere desire for success—not the mere following up of *successful* endeavor. Any fool can have that. But I mean grim grit—tenacious bull-dog courage to face defeat and disappointment and still aspire. That defiant attitude toward the ills of life that [W.E.] Henley sang of when he cried:

> Out of the night that covers me
> Black as the pit from pole to pole,
> I thank what ever gods may be
> For my unconquerable soul.
> In the fell clutch of circumstance
> I have not winced or cried aloud,
> Under the bludgeonings of chance
> My head is bloody but unbowed.
> It matters not how straight the gate.
> How charged with punishment the scroll,
> I am the master of my fate,
> I am the captain of my soul.

This dynamic power is the first demand of modern life, but alone this power is dangerous. It is the bridled charger stamping at the portcullis and chafing his bit—it is the armoured warrior gleaming in the morning sun, twisting and twirling his spear but at the sight, the world trembles and cries whither—to murder or rescue, to good or bad, to life or death?

So tremulous with balanced possibilities of good and evil is ambitious youth at this life crisis that many good people at times half cry out against ambition, half preferring lifeless, nerveless, unawakened mediocrity to the stirrings of such infinite power as may, to be sure, knock at the gate of Heaven and may just as surely rattle the doorposts of hell. These days of commencement, my children, are the days when you may begin the greater life, and they are days when you may start in the paths that lead to crime and debauchery and the neverending throng of unsorrowed dead. This is the reason that in these later years we hear so little said to Negro youth of ambition, power, unconquerable resolve. Men fear you and some fear lest, with the might of power of manhood you may fail, and some, I shame to say, fear lest you may succeed. But I do not fear you because I know you. I know that being but human some of you must needs fail and the very force of your young energy drive you downward, but I know too that most of you will not fail but will triumph with the triumph of ten millions.

The great efficient cause of this triumph when it comes will be your education. Life is not learned at a leap. This world is too old and complicated to be known by sudden inspiration. For this reason we educate children; for this reason, the state seeks to give its future citizens the knowledge of the Tree of Life, lest in the evening they see the flaming of the sword of death.

But what does this education teach or essay to teach? It seeks to teach the other three of the four things mentioned:

1. The ideals toward which civilization strives.
2. The good which can today be done.
3. The technical method by which each one can help do this work.

Or as I have said: IDEAL—that "one far off divine event toward which the whole creation moves"; renunciation, which but means the choice of the best possible good for all out of the infinite desirable; and finally the best actual method of doing your share. Thus stated the work of an educational system seems easy and clear and it would be if the ideal were fixed and unchangeable, the duty of renunciation clear and undoubted, and the technique of life always the same. But this is far from true. Life is flux and change. Ideals rise, expand and grow; the choice of the better among the good is the most baffling of life's dark problems and with every changing want, invention, and discovery, the technique of industry and work changes.

Thus the educational system has within itself eternal conflict. It can never be final, it can only continually hold clear its vast aim to teach children the greater goals toward which men are striving, to teach them what of these are at present attainable, and then to give to mind and hand such training as shall make them efficient helpers in the world's work of attaining these goods.

In the working out of the details there must ever be thought, controversy and often dispute.

I doubt not that many of my younger hearers and not a few of the older ones have been as sorely puzzled in these later days as to the true aim and method as were Pietro the father, and Francis the son, 700 years ago. On the one hand come those educators and seers crying "Hitch your wagon to a star" and on the other hand come the business men and artisans saying "learn by doing—earn a living." Now it does not settle the real conflict of thought and aim here expressed by assuming that these are but two sides of the same advice. They may be and they may not be. Given a St. Francis with a holy zeal to relieve the wretchedness of outcast humanity and it were the essence of wisdom to cry in his ear: Learn by doing—succor the first beggar that crosses your path, systematize your work, so that your followers may live and earn their living at this work. On the other hand given a Francis, son of Pietro, whose ideal of life was selfishly to display his wealth and fight and carouse—to tell him to learn by doing and earn that sort of living would be to send him to the devil as fast as money could pay the bills. So today given young black men with the dynamic of ambition and add to this an education which on the one hand gives them ideals of human service and manly renunciations and on the other teaches them the world's experience and the technique of modern industry—given these things and you have a perfect system of training. But given young boys and girls of your age starting out with the idea that the chief object of living is to gain as much cash and personal applause as can be gotten without serious infraction of the criminal code—to add an ever so thorough knowledge of the technique of modern industry to such low and perverted ideals is to disgrace the righteous ambition of a people and ruin the hope of the Negro race.

So long as the world consists of the fortunate and unfortunate, the weaker and the stronger, the rich and the poor, true human service will involve ideal and renunciation. If you really have at heart the good of the world you simply cannot give your whole time and energy to the selfish seeking of your own personal good. If you wish the Negro Race to become honest, intelligent and rich, you cannot make the accumulation of wealth for yourself the sole object of your education and life. The object of St. Francis of Assisi was not to make the world poorer by his poverty but richer. No doctrine of universal selfishness will ever reform society and lift men to the highest plane, simply because the world is too full of careless unfortunates, incompetent and vicious souls. While you are confining yourself to the work of selfishly raising yourself, these forces are dragging down a dozen of your neighbors and children. You must be your brother's keeper as well as your own, or your brother will drag you and yours down to his ruin.

The life of St. Francis teaches us then that renunciation is the inevitable first payment for healthy social uplift; not renunciation to poverty such as the 13th century demanded for the 20th century is plainly physical poverty in the back ground but certainly today among us a renunciation of dreams of great wealth and instead contentment with humble means, along with deep unselfish devotion to a splendid cause. This is the equipment which is needed today as sadly and pressingly as in any century of the Middle Age.

On the other hand the further the world goes on its journey of civilization the greater the need of specialization and technique—men must know how to do the world's work. They must have the specialized skill, knowledge and insight to do a practical piece of the labor well. The skilled artisan approaches today the inspired artist and both in common strive and sweat and toil. For what? For so much a day? No, for the glory of their handicraft, for the good their work does the human beings whose welfare is their welfare. Their bride is not Poverty but Carpentry or

Painting or Weariness or Pain, and their reward is the reward of St. Francis, a better, truer, richer world.

Thus the work of the public school is not on the one hand to fire aimless ambition without sound ideals, not to inspire human hearts with a vision of the true, the good and the beautiful, without pointing the practical way of realizing some of these dreams here and now in their own lives; not to imagine on the one hand that Desire and Knowledge alone will lift a race out of poverty and weakness, nor dream on the other hand that infinite skill with hammer or hoe will ever lead a man to do that which his native ambition and educated aspiration do not inspire him to do, remembering in the colored schools particularly that great as is the need of a new race for technical skill and efficiency, there is even greater need for the lifting and training of the racial consciousness in knowledge and inspiration, renunciation and ideal.

I trust then, young men and women, that the years of training which these public schools have given you freely, with vast expenditure of treasure and human energy; have placed you tonight on that great vantage ground where the burning ambition of your youth has been, on the one hand inspired by ideals as broad and human as those that inspired St. Francis of Assisi, and has on the other hand taught you something of the actual technique of living and earning a living. If this is true then it remains for me only to greet you and cry God speed.

Two years ago it was to have been my pleasure to greet others of your schoolmates on such a day as this. I cannot tell you how much sorrow my misfortune in not being here then, has caused me since; it cannot be atoned for in words but its hurt is helped by the pleasure of greeting you tonight and of greeting them through you. So doubtless it will be in your lives; the careers you enter will be builded of interlaced joy and sorrow, shade and shine, and although shadow-hands from other worlds will join in that building yet in your hands will the major part of the making of your lives lie. Build well. Build stubbornly and doggedly, build carefully and painfully with skilled technique but above all build by some large and worthy plan. Face defeat as cheerfully as triumph. Face success as coolly as defeat. Face anything that comes and then not only here tonight but there in the mists of God's great morning, when his darker children bring their hard-won triumphs up from the Gates of Despair and the Valley of the Shadow of death, lay your laurels not on your own heads but at the feet of those mothers and fathers who have nurtured you and toiled for you and smoothed the way of your life is with their own grey hairs and tears—with their own life-blood.

As it was the great object of St. Francis of Assisi to bring peace and succor to the down trodden of his day—let it be your highest ambition to be able one day to say to this heart-hurt and weary mother race of ours:

Thy sun shall no more go down,
Neither shall thy moon withdraw itself;
For the Lord shall be thine everlasting light,
And the days of thy mourning shall be ended.

ᏹ **29** ᏹ

The Negro in the Large Cities

The problem of the city is one that belongs to modern civilization and is not peculiar to any race or to any nation. Its essential is the concentration of people in certain great centers so that they can work and cooperate and think together. Now, any class of people who belong to modern civilization, or who are trying to belong, must feel this impulse, this trend toward the great centers of culture and work. The American Negro has felt this, and when, therefore, we think of him as connected with the great modern city problems, we must remember that that connection is not peculiar to his case. He would not belong to modern civilization if he was not drawn toward the city.

But there are certain peculiarities in the strength of the motives that draw him from the country to the Southern cities. The new South is an urban South; the old South was a rural South. The result is that we have today in Southern cities a great change and impulse toward better things, while in the country we have conditions not very far removed from the time of slavery. Visitors to the South, casual tourists and car-window sociologists forget this. They see the cities, Atlanta, Savannah, New Orleans and possibly some centers like Charlotte, and Columbus, and Anniston, but they do not see the great bare stretch of plantations which make the real "Black Belt." Consequently, the contrast between country and city in the South is much greater than that in the North.

It is not simply a contrast in means of entertainment, in companionship and chances for diversified industries, but it is a far greater difference in methods of work, conceptions of human relationships, accessibility to the ordinary decencies of life. Emancipation, therefore, to the freedman and his sons came not when the document was signed or a law was promulgated, but at a time, in most cases, when they could leave the plantation and its surroundings, and go to town or to city.

In the South there has been developed a caste system succeeding the slavery of other days. Into this caste system every Negro, no matter what his ability or aspirations may be, is thrust; on the other hand, there lie to northward a large number of great centers where the possibility of escaping caste in its most aggravating personal features is offered; consequently, the Northern city has for nearly a generation been a place of escape for those persons in the South who could not endure the grinding and humiliating conditions of caste there.

BLACK PROBLEM ANOMALIES

Now, these things explain certain anomalies in the race problems which careless and superficial theorists are apt to forget—it is said for instance: Why do Negroes stand the treatment they get in the South? Why don't they stick together and defend themselves? The answer is very clear: The least docile of the Southern Negroes have a chance to escape North; so long as that chance is open freely, this docility will, to a certain extent, mark the Southern Negro.

Again, persons wonder at crime among Negroes in the North. They say we can explain crime in the South as a natural result of emancipation and different social conditions, but how about the large percentage of crime among Negroes in Chicago and New York and Boston? The answer to that is equally clear. The criminal is the most migratory of all social classes, both by his own instinct and by the policy of police forces. So the Northern criminals, in 75 per cent of the cases, are not products of Northern conditions, but perfectly logical results of Southern conditions.

In the third place, how is it, people say, that there should be a problem of work among Northern Negroes, in particular, when they can get plenty of work to do if they stay South, and when even in the North you have to beg to get good servants or "workingmen of various kinds." The answer here is that these workingmen have been dissatisfied with the social conditions in the South, for which you have no right to blame them. When, now, they come to the North, they stand in the place of immigrants, and untrained immigrants at that, ignorant of the city's ways, not versed in its demands and open to all the allurement of idleness and vice and crime.

Considering then that the trend cityward is a natural social force at the present time, and that it is accentuated in the case of the Negro by the contrast between the country and city in the South and the refuge offered in the North, we may ask what is the duty of a great Northern city like New York toward this problem, and toward these people.

We may look upon that duty from three points of view. In the first place, New York has a duty not simply to itself but to the whole country, because it is the greatest single center of modern civilization in America. It cannot escape the vast responsibility of such a civilization. It must seek not simply to settle its Negro problem, or its Jewish problem, or its city problem, or its civic problem from its own selfish point of view, but for the sake of the South with its race problem, and for the sake of the North and its economic problem. New York must attack and solve the phases of these problems which come to it and must bring to bear great wealth of intelligence and stamina which the whole land has poured into this island.

WHAT NEW YORK CAN DO

New York can see that its citizens have decent homes, that the physical surroundings of the New York family shall be made such that it will not be impossible to bring children up decently. This problem the New York public is attacking, but it is not doing what it should so far as its Negro population is concerned. Now, when it is asked to do for this Negro population what it is doing for the white workmen, the demand is not made on the score of charity but as a matter of self-defence and far-sighted policy so far as the city is concerned.

It is a dangerous thing for New York to have any class of people poorly and viciously housed, and dangerous not so much to the people thus housed as to the better class of the community. Today in New York it is a matter of very great difficulty for a decent, self-respecting, hard-working Negro family to hire a house in a respectable community at a reasonable price, or at a price which other persons of similar social class would be asked to pay.

In the second place, New York should see that its children receive good common school training. Here again, the city is remiss so far as its Negro children are concerned. There are too many schools in this city where Negro children receive such outrageous treatment from teachers as to be thoroughly discouraged in their search of training.

In the third place—and this perhaps is the greatest problem—New York should see to it, first, that every colored man who wants to work gets a chance to work; that not only does he get a chance, but that he is encouraged to try to do the very best work that he is capable of doing, and that his work is rewarded as well as that of other persons. This may be asking for colored men more than what is done for whites, and in a certain sense it is. It is to be expected that a race with the training that we have had should have tendencies toward idleness, toward lack of self-respect and indifferent ambition, and that these tendencies should be accentuated by every bit of prejudice and discrimination. A city like this, therefore, that needs workers, that is a center of work, should make a special effort to overcome these tendencies among colored people by giving them unusual chances.

ENCOURAGEMENT NEEDED

In the fourth place, the city should see to it that the various avenues of uplift, of enlightenment and encouragement which it is furnishing for its citizens should be open freely to its colored citizens, and that they should be encouraged especially to take advantage of them. Perhaps in no other respect do Northern cities fail more in their duty than in this. Every great city has its playgrounds, its libraries, its evening schools, its trade schools, its lecture courses, etc., but only in exceptional cases are Negroes expected to take advantage of these. Usually the appearance of a Negro for admission to any one of these raises an amount of discussion and advice which is exceedingly painful to any self-respecting applicant. The result is that in most cases the Negro simply avoids these things.

If a city like New York should attempt to furnish decent people with decent homes at reasonable prices, regardless of color; should see that the schools are open to all alike; should see that opportunities for work and promotion are opened to all, and particularly to colored people, and should see that the opportunities for uplift and development given the public are, so far as Negroes are concerned, not confined to the baldest forms of charity; if New York should do this, what would be the result? Would it not encourage more Negroes to come to New York? It certainly would.

A liberal policy in home, school, work and culture will bring to New York a far different class of Negroes. More than that, if you are interested in the South and its problems, if you want to help settle them according to justice and decency, your first step should be to clear your own skirts. So long as you are unjust, so long as I find difficulty in getting a simple meal of victuals in New York, you can hardly cavil at Atlanta.

ᔕᔕ 30 ᔕᔕ

Georgia Negroes and Their Fifty Millions of Savings

One state in the Union has kept a series of economic measurements of the freedman and his sons for a period of thirty-five consecutive years. Two other states have recent partial records, but Georgia alone has an account of Negro property from Reconstruction times to the present. To the facts and meaning of these figures I want to call attention.

Emancipation had its legal, educational, economic, and moral phases. Legal emancipation came in 1863. Educational emancipation is coming more slowly, as the record of Georgia shows.

There is a larger amount of illiteracy in Georgia today than there was in 1870, which shows how poorly public-school facilities have kept pace with population. But the illiterates of today have a body of educated black men to lead them, who have been trained chiefly in the private schools supported by philanthropy.

It is, however, in the economic phase of emancipating black men that the nation is most deeply interested today, because slavery was largely, if not primarily, an economic problem. And since the economic development of the United States is its greatest and most absorbing world-triumph, we are, naturally, especially attracted to the economic phases of all its social problems.

The slave was practically penniless when freed. The 3,500 free Negroes of Georgia, and the semi-free, city artisans hiring their time, may have had as much as $50,000 worth of property throughout the state in 1863, but this is doubtful. Probably they did not have half that much. Emancipation, therefore, spelled poverty, complete, and dire poverty, to the black men who for the first time were left on their own resources.

The Government gave temporary outdoor relief and, by hiring large numbers of black soldiers and laborers, distributed a fund of ready cash. Only one attempt at permanently solving the problem of poverty was made in Georgia. This was a distribution among the fugitives of semi-swamp lands in the south-east part of the state. Much of this land was subsequently taken back, but some was sold at nominal prices for back taxes and the titles of many of the black occupiers were thus confirmed. But this merely touched the outskirts of a larger problem of land for the landless. Still the nation hesitated and finally withdrew, leaving the freed-man in economic slavery.

Then the struggle began and lasts to our day—the struggle of the black man to earn a living, maintain a home, and lay aside savings for the future. These official figures of the State of Georgia give an indication of the progress that has been made.

From the almost nothing of 1863, the Georgia Negro had come to the place, in 1907, where he was assessed at twenty-five millions of dollars. This does not include untaxed church and school property, and, as the assessments in Georgia are very low, this amount probably is not more than 50 per cent of the market value of all property. So that we may hazard the estimate that Georgia Negroes have saved about fifty million dollars.

Turning now to the details of this saving, one is especially interested in the land. The Negroes of Georgia own today a twenty-fourth part of the soil of the state and nearly one-twentieth of the cultivated land. Their holdings amount to 1,420,888 acres, or 2,220 square miles—a tract of land larger than Delaware (2,050 square miles). It is assessed at $7,149,225, but it is worth nearly $15,000,000, which was the price the United States paid for the Louisiana Purchase.

THE INCREASE OF LAND HELD
BY NEGROES IN GEORGIA

The chart which pictures the buying of this land shows that the accumulation has been steady from the start. This, however, does not mean that all who have bought land have held it. On the contrary, the losses have been large and continuous. Probably for every acre owned by a black man today in Georgia an acre has been lost by some other. But so all-pervasive is the land-hunger that, as the failures dropped out, the ranks have been more than filled, and the amount of land held by Negroes has increased steadily. The rise of the land values shows more variation. At first, Negroes bought waste land, the average assessed value of which was a little more than $3. This went on for the first ten years, and when the old land became more valuable, and higher-priced, new land was bought until the average assessed value per acre rose to $4 in 1895, and to $5.03 in 1905. The farm land held by Negroes in 1907 was assessed at $5.49 per acre, which was higher than the average value of the farm land of the state ($5.28).

More totals, however, teach but little; for a half-dozen large owners, rich by good luck, may raise the average and give a false appearance of prosperity to a poverty-stricken mass. A careful examination of typical counties indicates the following approximate division of land throughout the state.

A little less than a third of the owners have small garden spots or house lots outside the city limits, comprising about a sixtieth of the total land owned. Another portion of the population, slightly less than a third, have the traditional 40 acres, comprising an eighth of the land owned. A sixth of the owners hold a little over a sixth of the land in parcels between 50 and 100 acres, while something less than a fifth hold nearly half the land in tracts of from 100 to 300 acres. The remaining quarter of the land is held by that thirtieth part of the Negro owners who are the large landlords of the race. Comparing this with the condition seven years earlier, we find the smaller holdings growing larger, but no growth in the relative proportion of large landlords.

The number whose land holdings are worth less than $100 have decreased from nearly a half to a little more than a third in seven years, while the proportion of land of that low value has decreased nearly one-half. The land holdings worth from $100 to $300 are still in the hands of a third of the owners, but they have decreased relatively to the higher values. Holdings worth $500 or more have increased in proportion, constituting now nearly 60 per cent of the total value and held by one-sixth of the owners.

We see, then, a wide distribution of small holdings among a mass of people with little apparent tendency to concentration, but evidences of a general advance in prosperity among them all. Perhaps a more intimate glance at one county will make this phase of the situation still clearer. Liberty County is covered with sand and swamps. It is perhaps the most interesting black county in Georgia. In 1695, a Harvard graduate led a colony of New England Puritans from Dorchester, Mass., to South Carolina. The place selected, however, proved unhealthy and, attracted by Oglethorpe's Georgia, they secured a grant of 32,000 acres of land on the present site of Liberty County and removed there in 1752. They already owned slaves, and thus there came to the colony 280 whites and 536 Negroes. During the Revolution, in spite of the number of its slaves, the town of Darien adopted strong resolutions against slavery. The slaves were well treated, were received in equal fellowship in the church, their family life carefully protected so that to this day mulattoes are rare in the county, and often asylum was offered here for fugitive slaves. Liberty

County voted solidly against secession. After the Civil War, the land there was largely thrown on the market. At Woodville, Ogeechee, and Belmont, colonies of Negroes united and bought land, and they now own 56,000 acres.

The increase in the value of stock shows great variations, due in part to the custom among landlords of selling mules to their tenants subject to a chattel mortgage. The foreclosing of these mortgages after a bad season, or the rapid buying of mortgaged stock after a good season, makes the increase a fluctuating line. While a considerable proportion is still mortgaged, this proportion is certainly decreasing. The tools used on Negro farms are still few and simple, consisting mainly of the plow and hoe, with some more complicated machinery like cotton-planters, although in recent years there has been a notable increase in the use of better tools.

When we turn now to the methods of farming, we find two great economic movements in Georgia and throughout the South. One is the progressive breaking up of the great plantations of slavery time. This movement has been accelerated by the land-hunger of the Negro peasant. The other movement is the concentration of the ownership of these small farms in a few hands. Three hundred Georgia landlords own twenty or more farms each, comprising more than 600,000 acres in all.

The large farmer, facing a labor famine, lets out his farm on shares or to rent and, when tenants fail, he has recourse to vagrant laws and to encouraging immigration. Immigrant labor is, however, more difficult to "hold" than Negro labor, is more land-hungry, and knows more of modern enterprise. Thus the peasantry are pressing the landlords hard. Amid it all, farm land is growing more and more valuable over-topping today its value before the war, when it included the bodies of men.

Negroes more and more dislike the plantation methods of controlling labor and farmers facing a labor famine are particularly incensed at the numbers of Negro idlers, loafers, and criminals in cities, and make regular efforts by means of drastic vagrant laws to force them to work. From this attitude and its wide-spread discussion has arisen the idea that the city Negro is typified by the shiftless, idle class which is usually in evidence on the streets. Statistics throw much light on this point.

One of the phenomena of emancipation was the migration of Negroes from country to city. The city had nameless attractions for the field hand, and a great wave of immigrants rushed cityward on the first appearance of the Northern armies. Then came a subsidence, when many disappointed sightseers and idlers returned to work in the field. This was followed by a second, steadier wave of migration, which increased Georgia's Negro town population from 40,000 in 1870 to 160,000 in 1900. Nearly 85 per cent of the Georgia Negroes still live in the country, and it is often represented that only the idle and vicious come to town to escape honest toil. This is not borne out by the figures of the increase of city real estate, nor by the fact that the town

Negroes, representing a little more than 5 per cent of the population, own nearly 25 per cent of the property. The individuals of the city group surpass the countrymen in individual wealth, but here again property is pretty evenly divided and the well-to-do are few in proportion. The contrast between 1906 and 1899 is more striking in the city group, showing that, in 1899, a small number of the richer Negroes owned more than a fifth of all the property, while more than 25 per cent of the poorer ones had but 4 per cent in sums under $100. Today the distribution is much more equitable.

The property of the Georgia Negroes has been accumulated with difficulty. There are few encouragements or inducements for the poor to save in Georgia. Wages are low, the race problem tends to lower self-respect, happenings like the Atlanta riot decrease confidence, and the laws do not adequately protect the poor against cheating and fraud. Despite this, saving is possible. First, there is the soil, abused but still rich; and then there is the sheer physical fact of the presence of a laboring force of a million human beings. The races have increased evenly in Georgia, almost step by step.

Until 1863, 99 per cent of the blacks were slaves. Still it is not correct to say that the white Georgians owned them, since two-thirds of the whites held no slaves at all, but were themselves the economic victims of the system and, as is so humanly characteristic, hated and despised the Negroes as tools and supplanters. The large slaveholders formed but 20 per cent of the population and held 90 per cent of the slaves.

This explains much post-bellum history. To the non-slaveholding whites the Negro was a contemptible interloper, supplanting him in his natural right to earn a living and held over him by the fostering arm of the slaveholder. The slave, on the other hand, looked on the non-slaveholder with his master's eyes. When freedom came, the poorer whites still regarded the Negroes as their economic rival and proceeded to use political power against them and their masters. The control of political power came into the hands of the large number of whites who had had little power before. It did not, however, extend to the Negroes. The Negro was partially crushed beneath the new political heel and beneath the new economic power. Yet, Negro labor was needed and, despite sentiment and rivalry, the Negro could earn a living. His occupations were menial; preferment in all lines was slow, and in many lines impossible; his wages were low, and his avenues of expenditure limited. Nevertheless, he is making a living and even saving something. How is he doing it?

If we look at the Negro bread winners in 1900, we find that 41 per cent are still farm laborers, that is, economically nearest to slavery. Some still occupy old slave cabins, many live on the same plantations, and tens of thousands in the immediate neighborhood where their fathers served. They form a great, ignorant, largely unawakened mass of serfs. Next above them are the 34 per cent of laborers and servants: They are Negroes who have left the plantation to work on railroads, in lumber camps, and as servants and laborers in cities and towns. They are better paid, freer, and more intelligent, and are in part successors of the old house-servant class, the best trained of the slaves. Only in part, however, do they represent this class, for the sons of the house servants have largely gone to higher economic levels, leaving only a tradition of house service to guide the rising field hands—a fact that Southern housewives forget. These laborers and servants can be roughly divided into two classes—one a class of steady workers, good-natured, obliging, and fairly efficient, with here and there numbers of highly efficient, semi-skilled, and trusted men. Such Negroes are saving money and, with the other higher economic classes, have an assured economic foothold. Part of this class of laborers and servants, however, are less satisfactory. They have progressed far enough to revolt against being dumb, driven cattle, but not far enough to see a clear way to escape. They form an inefficient group of casual workers, having little heart or interest in their work, spending carelessly, and saving little or nothing. From their lower ranks come crime, and the progress of the Negro is, by the casual onlooker, measured by the emergence of this class, which is largely in evidence on city streets and in average kitchens. The next step brings us to the independent farmer. Here, again, there are obvious divisions. In 1900, the Negro farmers in Georgia were divided in this way: landowners, 14 per cent; renters, 42 per cent; share tenants, 44 per cent.

The share tenants are often but a degree better off than farm laborers, and it is only the better part of the renters and the owners that are independent farmers in the modern sense. Above the farmers come classes of assured economic footing—the 20,000 artisans, the 5,000 ministers, teachers, and physicians, and the 3,000 merchants. Some of the artisans and seamstresses are poorly trained and paid, but other artisans are masters; the ministers as a class receive far more than their mental and moral equipment deserves; but physicians and teachers are well trained; and the merchants are unusually successful in a field far removed from slavery and its teaching.

The merchant is one of the most interesting figures among the new Negroes. Slavery trained farmers, servants, laborers, and a few artisans, but no merchants. Of all vocations, then, this has been hardest for the Negro to learn. Figures of stocks carried by Negro merchants, although undoubtedly very incomplete, show that they have increased in value from about $50,000 in 1889 to more than $200,000 in 1907, although the increase has not been at all steady.

One thing needs to be said in concluding. These figures are absolute proof of nothing, but they are certainly hopeful. If they teach anything, they teach that the tendency to save, here manifest, should be encouraged. It is not being encouraged today. An old washerwoman came to me last fall when, apparently because of a land speculation in Cuba, the Neal Bank of Atlanta had failed. This bank had thousands of dollars of Negroes' small savings, which its president had solicited. This woman had lost her all in the failure—$200—which stood between her and the poverty of old age. But she had lost more than $200—she had lost hope—hope which even the slow repayment of 40 per cent of her loss has not restored. Three times the chief Negro depositories of savings have failed in Atlanta. In the country there are no savings-banks. The savings of black Georgia in country districts have been made in spite of the absence of the most primitive facilities for saving. Usually, the only dependence of these poor peasants is the personal honesty of some white landlord. Much of this accumulated wealth is a monument to the honesty of such men. But alas! there is no corresponding record of the loss of money and courage through systematic cheating and chicanery. What the Negro needs, and what the South needs, are postal savings-banks.

⌁ 31 ⌁

Negro Property

There are a great many Americans who would not willingly class themselves either as friends or enemies of the Negro race. They want to know the facts of the case; they say that, theoretically, human aspirations of various sorts may be commendable, but that the aspiration that counts and must be reckoned with, is that which expresses itself in deeds. When, therefore, Negroes ask political rights, this class of people are inclined to answer: Is not this race, in the main, too careless and lazy to be trusted with the responsibilities of citizenship? This charge of laziness has long been reiterated against Negroes, so long, in fact, that few ask for its proof.

Today it happens that proof is accumulating rapidly which shows that lack of thrift is not characteristic of the Negro-American. This proof lies in the accumulated property of black folk, and more especially in the increasing rate of accumulation.

To be sure, the possession of property today in America is by no means so infallible a result of work and thrift as it was a century ago. The organization of industry is such throughout the land that larger and larger numbers of hard working and careful laborers are unable to accumulate property. Particularly in the South, among farm laborers, who form over half the workers, a system of deliberate exploitation is so widespread that the man who accumulates property must be exceptional in many ways.

Accumulated property, then, among Negroes in the United States is even a greater indication of labor and thrift than among whites, since their economic opportunities are fewer, the inherited wealth far less.

The data upon which a study of Negro wealth can be based is unfortunately very incomplete; it consists of the returns as to the ownership of homes and farms in the censuses of 1890 and 1900; the value of farms in the census of 1900, and the assessed value of Negro property in three states—North Carolina since 1900; Virginia, since 1891, and Georgia, since 1874.

In 1890, out of 1,410,769 Negro heads of families, 264,288 owned their farms or homes, or 18.7 per cent. In 1900, of 1,707,690 homes, 372,444 were owned or 21.8 per cent, a gain of 3.1 per cent. The census of 1900 showed that there were 187,799 farms in the United States owned by Negroes, containing about 12,000,000 acres. These farms constituted a little over one-fourth of all the Negro farms, while one-fifth of all Negro homes were owned. Negro farmers increased about 37 per cent between 1890 and 1900, but the number of farm owners increased over 57 per cent. These Negro farm owners had, in 1900, over $175,000,000 worth of farm property, and raised in 1899 more than $50,000,000 worth of products.

Colored tenants rent 25,000,000 acres, worth $360,000,000, and raise $200,000,000 worth of products. Owners and tenants together, that is, all Negro farmers, controlled 746,717 farms, with an acreage about the size of New England, valued at a half-billion dollars. They raise $255,741,145 worth of products each year.

On the basis of the returns of the census of 1900, a committee of the American Economic Association reported that: "The evidence in hand leads your committee to the conclusion that the accumulated wealth of the Negro race in the United States in 1900 was approximately $350,000,000 and probably neither less than $250,000,000 nor more than $350,000,000.

Since 1900 we have the figures from three states to guide us: In North Carolina, the assessed value of Negro property has risen from $9,478,399, in 1900 to $21,253,581 in 1908, an increase of 124.2 per cent. In Virginia, Negro property increased from $12,089,965 in 1891, to $15,856,570 in 1900, or 31.1 per cent. In 1908 it had risen to $25,628,336, an increase of 61.6 per cent over 1900, and of 111.9 per cent over 1891. In Georgia, the assessed property of Negroes, starting at $6,157,798 in 1874, increased to $12,322,003 in 1890, or 100.1 per cent. In 1900 it had increased to $14,118,720, or 14.6 per cent over 1890, and 129.2 per cent over 1874. In 1908 it was $27,042,672, or 91.5 per cent over 1900, and 119.4 per cent over 1890.

In 1890, Negro church property was reported as valued at $26,626,448. In 1906 it was valued at $56,636,159, an increase of 112.7 per cent in sixteen years. We find, then, the following percentages of increase in Negro property:

Homes and farms owned between 1890 and 1900	40.9
Property in North Carolina owned between 1900 and 1908	124.2
Property in Virginia owned between 1900 and 1908	61.6
Property in Georgia owned between 1900 and 1908	91.5
Negro church property owned between 1890 and 1906	112.7

From this it seems fair to conclude that the rate of property accumulation among Negroes is accelerating very rapidly, and that if the figures above hold good for the whole country, which is conjectural, but probable, then, to use the phraseology of the American Economic Association Committee, the accumulated wealth of the Negro race in the United States in 1907 may be approximately $550,000,000, and probably neither less than $550,000,000 nor more than $600,000,000.

PERIODICAL WRITINGS APPEARING IN *CRISIS MAGAZINE: A RECORD OF THE DARKER RACES,* 1910–1934

INTRODUCTION

Reform Writing and Periodical-based Leadership within Crisis Magazine: A Record of the Darker Races, *1910–1934*

When considering Du Bois's *Crisis* writings, David Levering Lewis makes a peculiar observation, noting that the magazine was "infused with a mystical fervor that bordered on the religious."[1] While Lewis doesn't explain why *Crisis* contained a near-religious tone, perhaps he—along with many other *Crisis* commentators—never fully considered Du Bois's unremitting efforts to construct a utilitarian periodical that would help supply African American leadership through a reform rhetoric. All the same, some commentaries have come close to describing how Du Bois might have positioned *Crisis* in this unique endeavor. Raymond Wolters suggests in *Du Bois and His Rivals* (2002), "In the annals of leadership, Du Bois is unusual because he rose by dint of editing a magazine."[2] In his *W. E. B. Du Bois and American Political Thought* (1997), Adolph Reed wrote, "Specifically he emphasized the need for a type of reform education comparable to 'missionary' work whose purpose would be to educate the public to 'facts' . . . Du Bois's emphasis on education and information as the principal tools of social activism tied his views on science and progress to his ideas about leadership for uplift. The uplift mission was from the outset an integral element of his approach to knowledge and education."[3] Roland E. Wolseley wrote in *The Black Press, USA* (1990), "Journalism to Du Bois, it is true, was only a tool to advance his sociological studies of the black race or to aid him in his plans to help the race."[4] And finally, Henry Moon, who became editor of *Crisis* and the NAACP's director of public relations in 1966, stated in "History of the *Crisis*": "Dr. Du Bois recognized that the magazine had been established as the official organ of the NAACP, an arrangement which he never basically challenged. Yet the *Crisis* was a singularly personal journal."[5]

While each of these descriptions equally offers arresting suppositions about Du Bois's schemes for periodical authorship, Elliott Rudwick's *W. E. B. Du Bois: A Study in Minority Group Leadership* (1960) offers the best explanation about Du Bois's plans for a utilitarian periodical when he proposed its founding to NAACP executive committee members in 1910, for Rudwick's conclusion situates Du Bois's idea for the periodical within his longstanding ideals about scholarly leadership in reform matters along with the NAACP's latent ambitions to reform African American social behavior:

> He was still imprisoned by his old conception—the *Crisis*, rather than serving the NAACP as its interpreter to the public, was the pre-eminent division. The organization was just piddling along but in his estimation the *Crisis* would make the NAACP possible. The journal was the grand mentor of the race—it alone could teach Negroes not only how to protest *but how to live*. After colored Americans had received sufficient indoctrination from the *Crisis* "branch," they would be better able to fit into the NAACP branch.[6]

Rudwick's passage points to a remarkable interplay in which both Du Bois's and the NAACP's interests were mutually served through *Crisis*. Du Bois used the magazine to employ his rhetorical eloquence and expertise on behalf of the organization's overarching protest aims (which he undoubtedly shared), but just as clearly, Du Bois used *Crisis* "to bring the Negro movement into the main current of humanitarian reform," thereby positioning the NAACP—and himself—as the African American community's foremost leader in this endeavor.[7] For this reason, it was important for *Crisis* to address more pressing concerns than simply racial discrimination to gain serious consideration from African American readers, who were already calcified from such unceasing assaults. Relying upon a remarkable breadth of academic training, Du Bois addressed social problems arising from within the African American community, and his reform suggestions were directed toward improper moral and ethical behavior; thus, *Crisis*—to some extent—became the mouthpiece for a newfangled reform rhetoric that would set forth periodical-based leadership in reform matters that ran counter to the traditional reform discourses found in Negro churches.

On June 8, 1910, William English Walling—a wealthy white southerner, writer, settlement house worker, and socialist, as well as the NAACP's earliest founder—asked Du Bois to come work full-time in an unnamed capacity for the newly formed organization. Du Bois would not immediately abandon his Atlanta University position until a final offer had been made that might allow him—at least to some extent—to continue his research and reform work through social science. In his reply to Walling's letter, Du Bois wrote, "In looking over your budget it occurs to me that no provision is made for research work, unless something is included under postage."[8] After negotiations were finalized, the unnamed full-time position quickly evolved into an all-purpose named one, giving him first the title of executive committee member, then director of publications and research, and, soon thereafter, founder and editor of *Crisis*. Du Bois described the curious nexus between the titles in his 1968 autobiography:

I accepted the offer of the NAACP in 1910 to join their new organization in New York as Director of Publications and Research. My new title showed that I had modified my program of research but by no means abandoned it . . . This new field of endeavor represented a distinct break from my previous purely scientific program. While "research" was still among my duties, there were in fact no funds for such work. My chief efforts were devoted to editing and publishing The *Crisis*, which I founded on my own responsibility and over the protest of many of my associates. With the *Crisis* I essayed a new role of interpreting to the world the hindrances and aspirations of American Negroes.[9]

Although the NAACP's final offer did not include funding for a research program similar to the one he headed up at Atlanta University, it became evident that Du Bois had finally found an institution that could satisfactorily sponsor a periodical for reforming behavior in the African American community, as well as protest. In this regard, the unique alliance was surprisingly beneficial to the organization's plans as well. In addition to the fact that NAACP leaders could find no one better qualified than Du Bois to oversee field research and writings about racial injustices and atrocities perpetrated against American Negroes, his selection also helped facilitate the organization's latent concerns to *advance* the Negro race by "fitting these people" for successful participation in American society.[10]

To be sure, protecting Negroes from lynching, discrimination, and injustice was the organization's chief intention throughout its institutional history.[11] The newly formed 1909 National Negro Committee—the NAACP's former designation—made it unmistakably clear that its efforts were to be directed against persons or groups who participated in or indirectly supported a systematic practice of racial oppression directed toward the American Negro. In its initial 1909 platform, the committee declared that its primary objective would be to "denounce the ever-growing oppression of our 10,000 colored fellow citizens as the greatest menace that threatens the country."[12] In spite of this, a closer examination of the committee's initial 1909 purpose statement also suggests that their goals were not merely confined to eliminating Negro oppression; they would also be interested in advancing and aiding Negroes as well. The 1909 document went on to assert: "the nearest hope lies in the immediate and patiently continued enlightenment of the people who have been inveigled in a campaign of oppression." Thus, although the NAACP's protest efforts against racist institutional practices in American society are a well-known backdrop for Du Bois's more vituperative protest writings appearing in *Crisis*, the group's 1909 declaration actually represents a two-tiered approach for solving African American social problems. The first tier demanded a cessation of racial persecution against blacks, while the second tier included reformatory efforts within the African American community.

Similar to American Negro Academy founders, NAACP organizers understood that their work on behalf of African Americans had to address significant social problems stemming from moral and ethical shortcomings. Immediately after its founding, the group received initial support from organizations that were mainly interested in the NAACP's aims to *enlighten* African Americans through reform efforts. For instance, the National Federation of Religious Liberals, a collection of religious persons and organizations, unanimously adopted a resolution supporting the NAACP's founding at their conference held in Philadelphia on May 11, 1910. The first paragraph of the federation's resolution read:

> We would place on record our deep sympathy with the efforts made by our colored fellow-citizens, or in their behalf, to improve their material condition, to acquire a better industrial and professional education, to attain to higher standards of domestic and social living, to safeguard their constitutional and political rights, and to elevate their race in accord with the ideals of American citizenship and human brotherhood.[13]

While the document also cautiously endorsed the more radical parts of the NAACP's governing aims, the resolution's crux suggests that the federation's support was based upon the NAACP's efforts to help Negroes "to attain to higher standards of domestic and social living." This sentiment echoed the rhetoric of religious personages such as Celia Wooley, a prominent Unitarian minister and founder of Chicago's Frederick Douglass Center, whose support for the NAACP was also rooted in reforming African American social problems. Although the NAACP would receive support from religious persons and organizations, its reform ideals would be significantly different from what religious affiliates might have anticipated. It would be education and social science, not religious dogma, that would inform the association's position in all reform matters inside the African American community. Joel Spingarn, chairman of the NAACP's executive board, summed it up best when he suggested later that the organization would "make a studied effort to work with Negro churches."[14]

In addition to the NAACP's executive leadership, leading scientists who were affiliated with America's most prestigious universities, as well as trained social workers "who knew the Negro problem," played crucial roles in shaping the association's seminal reform interests in the African American community.[15] Among them were Livingston Farand, an anthropologist from Columbia University; Burt G. Wilder, a neurologist and zoologist from Cornell University; another Columbia professor, Edwin R. A. Seligman; Franz Boaz, an internationally renowned anthropologist whose work was applied by African American intellectuals such as Zora Neale Hurston to African American culture; Henry Moskowitz, a social worker among New York immigrants; Mary White Ovington, a wealthy and educated social worker and reformer who published several important works about African American social issues (she was also the most active NAACP executive member in reform efforts within the African American community during the period Du Bois edited and wrote for *Crisis*); and the distinguished social philosopher and educator John Dewey. The foundational contributions of these reformers and scientists to the association would primarily come in the form of presentations offering "scientific refutation of erroneous popular beliefs about the Negro."[16] These persons would play a critical role in dispelling notions about the powerlessness of reform efforts to overcome the deep-rooted social depravity found in early-twentieth-century African American communities.

While the NAACP would largely yield its organizational interests in reforming the African American community to the National Urban League, individual executive board members such as Arthur Spingarn, Mary White Ovington, James Weldon Johnson, and Du Bois would from time to time lend their names to various campaigns devoted to reforming African American social behavior.[17] For instance, Arthur Spingarn, who would later publish *Laws Relating to Sex Morality in New York City* (1926), initiated the founding of the Circle of Negro Relief in November 1917. Executive board members James Weldon Johnson and Du Bois also played a role in the group's founding and were listed as part of an original board of directors that included such prominent African American leaders as Tuskegee's new president, Robert Russa Moton, Mary McLeod Bethune, and J. Rosamond Johnson, who was a distinguished Negro songwriter and coauthor of "Lift Every Voice and Sing," the Negro national anthem. During their brief association with the group— Spingarn, Johnson, and Du Bois would sever ties with the organization in 1921—these NAACP executive leaders worked closely with the Social Hygiene Association to form a definite health program designed to combat serious concerns arising from sexual immorality in the New York and national African American communities. Although the Circle for Negro Relief would change the tenor of its work to wartime Negro relief due to the unanticipated advent of World War I, the organization retained its original slogan for a number of years: "All moral reform programs grow out of the people who suffer and stand in need of them."[18] In the end, however, Du Bois's *Crisis* writings, including those solicited expressly for the magazine, would become the organization's primary mouthpiece for reform in the African American community.

NOTES

1. David Levering Lewis, *W. E. B. Du Bois: Biography of a Race (1868–1919)* (New York: Henry Holt, 1993), 417.

2. Raymond Wolters, *Du Bois and His Rivals* (Columbia: University of Missouri Press, 2002), 78.

3. Adolph Reed, *W. E. B. Du Bois and American Political Thought* (Oxford: Oxford University Press, 1997), 49–50.

4. Roland E. Wolseley, *The Black Press, USA* (Ames: Iowa State University Press, 1990), 58.

5. Henry Moon, "History of the *Crisis*," *Crisis*, vol. 78 (November 1970): 21.

6. Elliott M. Rudwick, *A Study in Minority Group Leadership* (Philadelphia: University of Pennsylvania Press, 1960), 170.

7. Charles Flint Kellogg, *NAACP: A History of the National Association for the Advancement of Colored People, Vol. 1 (1909–1920)* (Baltimore: Johns Hopkins University Press, 1976), 53.

8. William English Walling, "To Dr. Du Bois," 8 June 1910, *The Correspondence of W. E. B. Du Bois: Volume I (Selections, 1877–1934)*, ed. and comp. Herbert Aptheker (Amherst: University of Massachusetts Press, 1973), 169–70; Du Bois, "To William English Walling," *The Correspondence of W. E. B. Du Bois: Volume I (Selections, 1877–1934)*, 170–71. For a more comprehensive history on the founding of the National Association for the Advancement of Colored People, see Flint Kellogg, *NAACP*; Warren St. James, *The National Association for the Advancement of Colored People: A Case Study in Pressure Groups* (New York: Exposition Press, 1958); Robert Jack, *History of the National Association for the Advancement of Colored People* (Boston: Meador, 1943); Carolyn Wedlin, *Inheritors of the Spirit: Mary White Ovington and the Founding of the NAACP* (New York: John Wiley and Sons, 1998); Mary White Ovington, *The Walls Came Tumbling Down* (New York: Arno Press, 1969); Ovington, *Black and White Sat Down Together* (New York: Feminist Press, 1995); Walter White, *A Man Called White* (New York: Arno Press, 1969); B. Joyce Ross, *J.E. Spingarn and the Rise of the NAACP, 1911–1939* (New York: Athenaeum, 1972).

9. Du Bois, *The Autobiography of W. E. B. Du Bois* (New York: International Publishing, 1968), 155–56.

10. Du Bois, "A Memorandum to the Board of Directors of the National Association for the Advancement of Colored People," *Pamphlets and Leaflets by W. E. B. Du Bois*, ed. and comp. Herbert Aptheker (White Plains, N.Y.: Kraus-Thomson, 1986), 116.

11. "Platform Adopted by the National Negro Committee, 1909," Container A-1, The National Association for the Advancement of Colored People Papers, Manuscript Division, Library of Congress, Washington, D.C.

12. "Platform Adopted by the National Negro Committee, 1909," Container A-1, The National Association for the Advancement of Colored People Papers, Manuscript Division, Library of Congress, Washington, D.C.

13. "Conference Minutes of the National Federation of Religious Liberals," Container A-8, The National Association for the Advancement of Colored People Papers, Manuscript Division, Library of Congress, Washington, D.C.

14. "1915 Annual Report," Container A-1, The National Association for the Advancement of Colored People Papers, Manuscript Division, Library of Congress, Washington, D.C.

15. Du Bois, *Autobiography*, 254.

16. Kellogg, 58.

17. See Ovington, *The Walls Came Tumbling Down*, 112. Ovington describes the decision to curtail much of the NAACP's reform program:

> Most fortunately, about six months after we began, the Urban League was formed. George Haynes, sociologist from Fisk University, came into our office one morning with plans to form a national organization in the fields of employment and philanthropy. Elizabeth Walton and Hollingsworth Wood were in back of him. Some of us gasped at having so large a field of "advancement" taken out of our program, but nothing could have been more fortunate. We could not have raised money for "philanthropy" as successfully as an organization with a less militant program and securing employment is a business in itself. So the two national organizations divided the field, working together from time to time as action demanded.

18. "Circle for Negro Relief," Container 1-3, Reel #1, The Papers of Arthur B. Spingarn, Manuscript Division, Library of Congress, Washington, D.C.

⌁ **32** ⌁

Business and Philanthropy

The talented, systematic, hardheaded youth of our nation are put into business. We tell them that the object of business is to make money. Our dull, soft-headed, unsystematic youth we let stray into philanthropy to work for the good of men. Then we wonder at our inability to stop stealing. This is the great American paradox.

Small wonder that we see in our world two armies: one large and successful, well dressed and prosperous. They say bluntly: "We are not in business for our health—business pays!" The other army is seedy and diffident and usually apologetic. It says: "There are things that ought to be done, and we are trying to do them—philanthropy begs." Between the business men, pure and simple, and the professional philanthropists waver the world's hosts—physicians, lawyers, teachers, and servants, some regarding their work as philanthropy, most of them looking at it as business and testing its success by its pay.

Business pays.

Philanthropy begs.

Business is reality, philanthropy is dream: business first, philanthropy afterward—is this true? No, it is not. It is the foundation falsehood of our perverted social order.

In reality it is business enterprise that continually tends to defeat its own ability to pay and it is philanthropy that works to preserve a social order that will make the larger and broader and better business enterprises pay.

What is meant when we say a business pays? Simply this: that for the service rendered or the thing given, the public will today pay valued equivalent in services or goods. Men do this because of their present wants. Given a people wanting certain things and corresponding business enterprises follow. Will the demand continue? That depends: the satisfaction of these wants minister to the real health and happiness of the community, the demand will continue and grow; if not, eventually either the business or the nation will die. The fact then that a business pays today is no criterion for future. The liquor traffic pays and so does the publishing of school books; houses of prostitution pay and so do homes for renting purposes and yet alcoholism and prostitution mean death while education and homes mean life to this land.

The amount then that a business pays is no test of its social value. It may pay and yet gradually destroy the larger part of all business enterprise. Here enters philanthropy. Its object is to do for men not what they want done, but that which, for their own health, they ought to want done. Will such service pay? Possibly will: possibly the people will want the service as soon as they learn of it and lo! "Philanthropy and five per cent" appears. More often, however, the people do not recognize the value of the new thing—do not want it; will not use baths or have anything to do with coffee rooms. Will they pay, then? If they perform a service necessary to human welfare and the people are gradually learning what is really for their good, then sometimes such philanthropy pays. If it does not pay then the service offered was really unnecessary or the people to whom it was offered has ceased to advance toward betterment and are in danger of death.

The test, then, of business is philanthropy; that is, the question as to how far business enterprise is doing for men the things they ought to have done for them, when we consider not simply their present desires, but their future welfare. Just here it is that past civilizations have failed. Their economic organization catered to fatal wants and persisted in doing so, and refused to let philanthropy guide them. Just so today. When ever a community seats itself helplessly before a dangerous public desire, or an ingrained prejudice, recognizing clearly its evil, but saying, "We must cater to it simply because it exists," it is final; change is impossible. Beware; the epitaph of that people is being written.

It is just as contemptible for a man to go into the grocery business for personal gain as it is for a man to go into the ministry for the sake of the salary.

There is not a particle of ethical difference in the two callings. The legitimate object of both men is social service. The service of one is advice, inspiration and personal sympathy; the service of the other is fresh eggs and prompt delivery. Thus "from the blackening of boots to the whitening of souls" there stretches a chain of services to be done for the comfort and salvation of men.

Those who are doing these things are doing holy work, and the *work done*, not the *pay received*, is the test of the working. Pay is simply the indication of present human appreciation of the work, but most of the world's best work has been, and is being done, unappreciated.

"Ah, yes," says the cynic, "but do you expect men will work for the sake of working?" Yes, I do. That's the reason most men work. Men want work. They love work. Only give them the work they love and they will ask no pay but their own soul's "Well done!" True it is that it is difficult to assign to each of the world's workers the work he loves; true it is that much of the world's drudgery will ever be disagreeable; but pay will never destroy inherent distaste, nor (above the starvation line) will it form a greater incentive than social service, if we were but trained to think so.

These things are true, fellow-Americans; therefore, let us, with one accord, attack the bottom lie that supports graft and greed and selfishness and race prejudice: namely, that any decent man has at any time any right to adopt any calling or profession for the sole end of personal gain.

"Surely," gasp the thrifty, "the first duty of man is to earn a living!" This means that a man must at least do the world a service such as men, constituted as they are today, will requite with the necessities of life. This is true for some men always; perhaps for most men today. We pray for some sweet morning when it will be true for all men. But it was not true for Socrates, nor for Jesus Christ.

~ 33 ~

Education

The fifteenth annual Conference for Education in the South was held in Nashville on April 3, 4 and 5. As usual, the colored people were not represented, save on the opening night, when, *mirabile dictu*, a delegation from Fisk University occupied seats on the floor of the great convention hall, the gallery of which was crowded by at least 1,500 white students of the various educational institutions located in Nashville. This admission of Fisk in itself was a step forward, but no colored orator had an opportunity to plead for his race, and the Middle Tennessee Colored Teachers' Association met in the city simultaneously without a single representative of the conference appearing before these colored men and women.

But while the conference did not permit a representative of thirty per cent of the people in whose behalf it is laboring to appear before it—there was considerable ill-feeling among the colored people in Nashville prior to the convention when this became known—it is undeniable that there was greater freedom of speech allowed at this conference than at any other. The plea for universal education for all children, black or white, was heard at almost every session, and there were two very interesting subconferences on the education of the Negro, presided over by Dr. James H. Dillard, the executive secretary of the Slater Fund and Jeanes Foundation, whose work on behalf of the Negro deserves the highest praise. He stated, among other things, that while it was the fashion in the South, and rightly so, to praise the old-time Negro mammy, he thought that the splendid devotion of the colored women now working in the schools for their race was still more worthy of recognition and praise.

The national association was represented at this conference by its executive chairman and Dr. Dillard agreed to co-operate with the association and other agencies' in compiling a list of the worthy, and also another of one of the unworthy, schools for the Negro in the South of the college or industrial type.

It was interesting to note the eagerness to discuss the question of Negro education by the Southern white men and women who participated. One of the ablest of the latter made a plea that if an organization for the supervision the Negro schools were established colored men should have equal participation with the white. For, she said, being herself disfranchised and belonging to a sex whose interests in public matters such as schooling had heretofore been administered by men who did not represent her sex, she could sympathize with any colored man who felt that he ought to have a hearing where the interests of his race were being discussed and managed.

One of the most significant addresses of the main conference was delivered on the last evening by Mr. W. D. Weatherford, of the national committee of the Y. M. C. A., on the education of the Negro in the South. It is so admirable a statement of the case that the national association expects to reprint it as one of its leaflets. His statement that young college men in the South in increasing numbers are devoting themselves to work among the colored people was most encouraging to hear. Indeed, the whole tone and nature of the conference, despite the exclusion of Negro delegates, showed that in the South, progress is being made in the right direction. Ten years ago nobody dared advocate universal Negro education without apologizing for it. Any Southerner who advocated educating the Negro had to apologize for doing so. Nobody thought of apologizing at Nashville, and fifteen years hence, we trust, it will seem perfectly natural to have colored men speaking for their race at all these gatherings.

⌁ 34 ⌁

Education

Consider this argument: Education is the training of men for life. The best training is experience, but if we depended entirely upon this each generation would begin where the last began and civilization could not advance.

We must then depend largely on oral and written tradition and on such bits of typical experience as we can arrange for the child's guidance to life.

More than that, children must be trained in the technique of earning a living and doing their part of the world's work.

But no training in technique must forget that the object of education is the child and not the things he makes.

Moreover, a training simply in technique will not do because general intelligence is needed for any trade, and the technique of trades changes.

Indeed, by the careful training of intelligence and ability, civilization is continually getting rid of the hardest and most exhausting toil, and giving it over to machines, leaving human beings freer for higher pursuits and self development.

Hence, colored people in educating their children should be careful:

First: To conserve and select ability, giving to their best minds higher college training.

Second: They should endeavor to give all their children the largest possible amount of general training and intelligence before teaching them the technique of a particular trade, remembering that the object of all true education is not to make men carpenters, but to make carpenters men.

Is not this reasoning sound? Could you imagine an educator of any experience who would take material exception to it? Would you call it revolutionary or in the nature of a "personal" attack?

Certainly not.

Yet this very argument, with illustrations and emphasis delivered to some seven hundred apparently well-pleased folk in Indianapolis, has had the most astounding results. The *Indianapolis Star* in a leading editorial denounced it as "dangerous!"

A leading white philanthropist of abolition forbears considered it not only "misleading" and "mischievous" but a covert and damaging personal attack!

The supervisor of the colored schools of Indianapolis wrote to express regret that the lecture had seemed to attack his school curriculum and ideals, and the assistant superintendent of schools in the District of Columbia hastens to give advice!

Yet where is the flaw in the argument?

There is no flaw, but there are serious flaws in the thinking of some of these critics.

The first flaw is the naive assumption that the paraphernalia of a school shows the education it is imparting. If some people see a Greek book and a cap and gown, they conclude that the boy between them is receiving higher education. But is he? That depends. If other people see a hammer, a saw and a cook book, they conclude that the boy who uses them is being trained in intelligence, ability and the earning of a living. But is he? That depends.

When the proud principal of a school shows workshop and kitchen, table and pie, one may be interested, but one is no more convinced than when another shows an array of Greek roots and rounded phrases. One must merely remark: The end of education is neither the table nor the phrase—it is the boy; what kind of boys are you training here? Are they boys quickened in intelligence, with some knowledge of the world they live in? Are they trained in such ways as to discover their true bent and ability, and to be intelligently guided to the choice of a life work? Then your system is right. Otherwise it is wrong, and not all the gingham dresses in Indiana will justify it.

The second flaw is the more or less conscious determination of certain folk to use the American public-school system for the production of laborers who will do the work they want done. To them Indianapolis exists for the sake of its factories and not the factories for the sake of Indianapolis. They want dinners, chairs and motor cars, and they want them cheap; therefore use the public schools to train servants, carpenters and mechanics. It does not occur to them to think of workingmen as existing for their own sakes. What with impudent maids, and half-trained workingmen, they are tired of democracy; they want caste; a place for everybody and everybody in his father's place with themselves on top, and "Niggers" at the bottom where they belong. To such folk the problem of education is strikingly simple. To teach the masses to work; show them how to do things; increase their output; give them intelligence, of course; but this as a means, not as an end, and be careful of too much of it. Of course, if a meteoric genius bursts his birth's invidious bar, let him escape but keep up the bars, and as most men are fools, treat them and train them as such.

It was such darkened counsels as these that brought the French Revolution. It is such mad logic as this that is at the bottom of the social unrest today.

The lecturer came to Indianapolis not to criticise, but to warn—not to attack, but to make straight the way of the Lord. He is no despiser of common humble toil; God forbid! He and his fathers before him have worked with their hands at the lowliest occupations and he honors any honest toilers at any task; but he makes no mistake here. It is the toilers that he honors, not the task—the man and not the Thing. The Thing may or may not be honorable—the man always is.

Yet the despising of men is growing and the caste spirit is rampant in the land; it is laying hold of the public schools and it has the colored public schools by the throat, North, East, South and West. Beware of it, my brothers and dark sisters; educate your children. Give them the broadest and highest education possible; train them to the limit of their ability, if you work your hands to the bone in doing it. See that your child gets, not the highest task, but the task best fitted to his ability, whether it be digging dirt or painting landscapes; remembering that our recognition as common folk by the world depends on the number of men of ability we produce—not great geniuses, but efficient thinkers and doers in all lines. Never forget that if we ever compel the world's respect, it will be by virtue of our heads and not our heels.

~ 35 ~

The Black Mother

The people of America, and especially the people of the Southern States, have felt so keen an appreciation of the qualities of motherhood in the Negro that they have proposed erecting a statue in the National Capital to the black mammy. The black nurse of slavery days may receive the tribute of enduring bronze from the master class.

But this appreciation of the black mammy is always of the foster mammy, not of the mother in her home, attending to her own babies. And as the colored mother has retreated to her own home, the master class has cried out against her. "She is thriftless and stupid," the white mother says, "when she refuses to nurse my baby and stays with her own. She is bringing her daughter up beyond her station when she trains her to be a teacher instead of sending her into my home to act as nursemaid to my little boy and girl. I will never enter her street, heaven forbid. A colored street is taboo and she no longer deserves my approval when she refuses to leave her home and enter mine."

Let us hope that the black mammy, for whom so many sentimental tears have been shed, has disappeared from American life. She existed under a false social system that deprived her of husband and child. Thomas Nelson Page, after—with wet eyelids—recounting the virtues of his mammy, declares petulantly that she did not care for her own children. Doubtless, this was true. How could it have been otherwise? But just so far as it was true it was a perversion of motherhood.

Let the present-day mammies suckle their own children. Let them walk in the sunshine with their own toddling boys and girls and put their own sleepy little brothers and sisters to bed. As their girls grow to womanhood, let them see to it that, if possible, they do not enter domestic service in those homes where they are unprotected and where their womanhood is not treated with respect. It the midst of immense difficulties, surrounded by caste, and hemmed in by restricted economic opportunity, let the colored mother of today build her own statue, and let it be the four walls of her own unsullied home.

～ 36 ～

The Ostrich

Some folks are mental ostriches. We are not referring to their intellectual digestions, although there we realize is room for a whole editorial. We are referring now to the method of mind that is able to persuade itself that the unseen is non-existent. An astounding number of people rushing through earth's deserts escape the evil that haunts them by sticking their heads in a hole in the ground and saying insistingly: "I don't believe it, and even if it is true I won't regard it."

Now the World is without doubt full of things, incidents, thoughts, men that are best disregarded; that are, best unheard, unseen, ignored. But make no mistake, friend of the unseeing eye, for there is evil in the world which may not be ignored and that cannot be escaped by sticking our head in the ground and closing our eyes.

The race situation today is not beautiful; although the reasons for hope and encouragement far outweigh the evil, yet he is a fool who ignores that evil or tries to forget its threatening aspect. The first step toward the righting of wrongs is knowledge—illumination.

Face the race problem like men, frankly and carefully, but none the less determinedly. Let your children face it. Don't seek to sneak away from the evil and forget the poor suffering brothers and sisters who cannot escape, who must work and writhe and fight. Remember that bad as the truth is, it is a little better than the apprehension; and Devilish as the situation in certain parts of the South is it is just a little better than the Negro in the North pictures it—particularly in that part of the North which wishes to hide its head.

There is absolutely nothing in the race problem today which is insoluble by peaceful human endeavor. The world has cured worse ill than it faces today, and the Negro race has triumphantly survived worse oppression than that which it suffers here and now. Why then hide our discouraged heads? Why seek to escape that which true manhood must know, if it will fight intelligently? All things are bad? Very well; let's first know just how bad they are, and then let's make them better. Social reform without knowledge is futile. Knowledge without attempted betterment is criminal. The complacency of the donkey is annoying, but the cowardice of the ostrich is dangerous.

⌁ **37** ⌁

The Immediate Program of the American Negro

The immediate program of the American Negro means nothing unless it is mediate to his great ideal and the ultimate ends of his development. We need not waste time by seeking to deceive our enemies into thinking that we are going to be content with a half loaf, or by being willing to lull our friends into a false sense of our indifference and present satisfaction.

The American Negro demands equality—political equality, industrial equality and social equality; and he is never going to rest satisfied with anything less. He demands this in no spirit of braggadocio and with no obsequious envy of others, but as an absolute measure of self-defense and the only one that will assure to the darker races their ultimate survival on earth.

Only in a demand and a persistent demand for essential equality in the modern realm of human culture can any people show a real pride of race and a decent self-respect. For any group, nation or race to admit for a moment the present monstrous demand of the white race to be the inheritors of the earth, the arbiters of mankind and the sole owners of a heritage of culture which they did not create, nor even improve to any greater extent than the other great division of men—to admit such pretense for a moment is for the race to write itself down immediately as indisputably inferior in judgment, knowledge and common sense.

The equality in political, industrial and social life which modern men must have in order to live, is not to be founded with sameness. On the contrary, in our case, it is rather insistent upon the right of diversity;—upon the right of a human being to be a man even if he does not wear the same cut of vest, the same curl of hair or the same color of skin. Human equality does not even entail, as is sometimes said, absolute equality of opportunity; for certainly natural inequalities of inherent genius and varying gift make this a dubious phrase. But there is a more and more clearly recognized minimum of opportunity and maximum of freedom to be, to move and to think, which the modern world denies to no being which it recognizes as a real man.

These involve both negative and positive sides. They call for freedom on the one hand and power on the other. The Negro must have political freedom; taxation without representation is tyranny. American Negroes of today are ruled by tyrants who take what they please in taxes and give what they please in law and administration, in justice and in injustice; and the great mass of black people must stand helpless and voiceless before a condition which has time and time again caused other peoples to fight and die.

The Negro must have industrial freedom. Between the peonage of the rural South, the oppression of shrewd capitalists and the jealousy of certain trade unions, the Negro laborer is the most exploited class in the country, giving more hard toil for less money than any other American, and have less voice in the conditions of his labor.

In social intercourse every effort is being made today from the President of the United States and the so-called Church of Christ down to saloons and boot-blacks to segregate, strangle and spiritually starve Negroes so as to give them the least possible chance to know and share civilization.

These shackles must go. But that is but the beginning. The Negro must have power; the power of men, the right to do, to know, to feel and to express that knowledge, action and spiritual gift. He must not simply be free from the political tyranny of white folk, he must have the right to vote and to rule over the citizens, white and black, to the extent of his proven foresight and ability. He must have a voice in the new industrial democracy which is building and the power to see to it that his children are not in the next generation trained to be the mudsills of society. He must have the right to social intercourse with his fellows. There was a time in the atomic individualistic group when "social intercourse" meant merely calls and tea-parties; today social intercourse means theatres, lectures, organizations, churches, clubs, excursions, travel, hotels,—it means in short Life; to bar a group from such methods of thinking, living and doing is to bar them from the world and bid them create a new world;—a task to which no single group is today equal; it is to crucify them and taunt them with not being able to live.

What now are the practical steps which must be taken to accomplish these ends?

First of all before taking steps the wise man knows the object and end of his journey. There are those who would advise the black man to pay little or no attention to where he is going so long as he keeps moving. They assume that God or his vice-gerent the White Man will attend to the steering. This is arrant nonsense. The feet of those that aimlessly wander land as often in hell as in heaven. Conscious self-realization and self-direction is the watchword of modern man, and the first article in the program of any group that will survive must be the great aim, equality and power among men.

The practical steps to this are clear. First we must fight obstructions; by continual and increasing effort we must first make American courts either build up a body of decisions which will protect the plain legal rights of American citizens or else make them tear down the civil and political rights of all citizens in order to oppress a few. Either result will bring justice in the end. It is lots of fun and most ingenious just now for courts to twist law so as to say I shall not live here or vote there, or marry the woman who wishes to marry me. But when to-morrow these decisions throttle all freedom and overthrow the foundation of democracy and decency, there is going to be some judicial house cleaning.

We must *secondly* seek in legislature and congress remedial legislation; national aid to public school education, the removal of all legal discriminations based simply on race and color, and those marriage laws passed to make the seduction of black girls easy and with out legal penalty.

Third the human contact of human beings must be increased; the policy which brings into sympathetic touch and understanding, men and women, rich and poor, capitalist and laborer, Asiatic and European, must bring into closer contact and mutual knowledge the white and black people of this land. It is the most frightful indictment of a country which dares to call itself civilized that it has allowed itself to drift into a state of ignorance where ten million people are coming to believe that all white people are liars and thieves, and the whites in turn to believe that the chief industry of Negroes is raping white women.

Fourth only the publication of the truth repeatedly and incisively and uncompromisingly can secure that change in public opinion which will correct these awful lies. THE CRISIS, our record of the darker races, must have a circulation not of 35,000 chiefly among colored folk but of at least 250,000 among all men who believe in men. It must not be a namby-pamby box of salve, but a voice that thunders fact and is more anxious to be true than pleasing. There should be a campaign of tract distribution—short well written facts and arguments—rained over this land by millions of copies, particularly in the South, where the white people know less about the Negro than in any other part of the civilized world. The press should be utilized—the 400 Negro weeklies, the great dailies and eventually the magazines, when we get magazine editors who will lead public opinion instead of following afar with resonant brays. Lectures, lantern-slides and moving pictures, co-operating with a bureau of information and eventually becoming a Negro encyclopedia, all these are efforts along the line of making human beings realize that Negroes are human.

Such is the program of work against obstructions. Let us now turn to constructive effort. This may be summed up under (1) economic co-operation (2) a revival of art and literature (3) political action (4) education and (5) organization.

Under economic co-operation we must strive to spread the idea among colored people that the accumulation of wealth is for social rather than individual ends. We must avoid, in the advancement of the Negro race, the mistakes of ruthless exploitation which have marked modern economic history. To this end we must seek not simply home ownership, small landholding and saving accounts, but also all forms of co-operation, both in production and distribution, profit sharing, building and loan associations, systematic charity for definite, practical ends, systematic migration from mob rule and robbery, to freedom and enfranchisement, the emancipation of women and the abolition of child labor.

In art and literature we should try to loose the tremendous emotional wealth of the Negro and the dramatic strength of his problems through writing, the stage, pageantry and other forms of art. We should resurrect forgotten ancient Negro art and history, and we should set the black man before the world as both a creative artist and a strong subject for artistic treatment.

In political action we should organize the votes of Negroes in such congressional districts as have any number of Negro voters. We should systematically interrogate candidates on matters vital to Negro freedom and uplift. We should train colored voters to reject the bribe of office and to accept only decent legal enactments both for their own uplift and for the uplift of laboring classes of all races and both sexes.

In education we must seek to give colored children free public school training. We must watch with grave suspicion the attempt of those who, under the guise of vocational training, would fasten ignorance and menial service on the Negro for another generation. Our children must not in large numbers, be forced into the servant class; for menial service is still, in the main, little more than an antiquated survival of impossible conditions. It has always been as statistics show, a main cause of bastardy and prostitution and despite its many marvelous exceptions it will never come to the light of decency and honor until the house servant becomes the Servant in the House. It is our duty then, not drastically but persistently, to seek out colored children of ability and genius, to open up to them broader, industrial opportunity and above all, to find that Talented Tenth and encourage it by the best and most exhaustive training in order to supply the Negro race and the world with leaders, thinkers and artists.

For the accomplishment of all these ends we must organize. Organization among us already has gone far but it must go much further and higher. Organization is sacrifice. It is sacrifice of opinions, of time, of work and of money, but it is, after all, the cheapest way of buying the most priceless of gifts—freedom and efficiency. I thank God that most of the money that supports the National Association for the Advancement of Colored People comes from black hands: a still larger proportion must so come, and we must not only support but control this and similar organizations and hold them unwaveringly to our objects, our aims and our ideals.

~ **38** ~

Discipline

Our children are soon returning to school and it may be well to warn parents and teachers, especially of colored private schools and colleges in the South, of certain dangers ahead.

I have before me as I write a catalog of a small and undoubtedly deserving colored school in South Carolina. I am particularly struck by the extraordinary character of the regulations: Girls are forbidden to wear jewelry; students are allowed to write to their parents on Saturday and their letters are subject to inspection; students must attend all religious exercises; a school conference is held in the interest of student and teacher and attendance is obligatory; students must not loan each other money or clothing; they must attend all meals promptly and punctually; they must not dispute with teachers; their rooms must be open for inspection at 7 A.M., etc. All this indicates a prison-like discipline, an insistence on the letter of the law at variance with our modern conception of education.

In the same sort of way the larger southern colleges are insisting upon a discipline which is growing more and more irksome to their students. Outbreaks have occurred at several large institutions. We may talk as we will of students "running" an institution and the necessity of obedience and all that kind of thing, but we must, nevertheless, remember that it is not the business of the school to break the student's will, to reduce him to an automaton, or to "make" him do things. On the contrary, a real school wishes to turn out a self-disciplined man; self-reliance, self-respect and initiative are the things to be emphasized and our schools will forestall trouble and approach nearer the ideal of education if they would do away with some of these medieval rules and look upon their students as embryonic men and women rather than as babes or imbeciles.

⌁ **39** ⌁

Hampton

The death of Hollis Burke Frissell, principal of Hampton Institute, brings that institution and its work prominently before the public. It is, therefore, peculiarly fitting that the following correspondence should be made public:

Dear Dr. Du Bois:

In preparation for the Fiftieth Anniversary of Hampton Institute, efforts are being made to collect the necessary material for the history of the school. It is a matter of history that for many years the colored people were opposed to the type of education offered them at Hampton and were consequently also opposed to the school itself. For the sake of learning the facts in regard to this matter I am writing to you and to a number of other prominent colored men to ask for statements in regard to the facts in the case.

I shall be very grateful if you will send me a statement in regard to the attitude (with reasons) of the colored people who were opposed to industrial education during the early days of Hampton and who are still in some cases opposed to it.

Will you kindly say in this connection whether you will object to the use of your name, if that is thought desirable? * * *

(MISS) J. E. DAVIS.

Dear Miss Davis:

I have a wide acquaintance with educated colored folk. My interpretation of their attitude is that they do not oppose and never have opposed Hampton Institute because it teaches industries. On the contrary they recognize Hampton as probably the best center of trade for Negroes in the United States.

It is true, however, that educated Negroes in the past and at present hold Hampton and some of her methods in grave distrust. They recognize the worth of her work—the fine spirit of many of her teachers, past and present, and the splendid character of her graduates, but at the same time, they cannot forget three important facts:

1. The course of study at Hampton is so arranged that it cannot be made to fit in with the higher courses of education, as adopted by the leading educational institutions of the United States. Granted that Hampton is and ought to be the finishing school for nine-tenths of her students, the fact remains that Hampton deliberately makes it impossible for her most promising and brilliant students to receive college training or higher technical and professional training, save at great disadvantage and a wellnigh fatal loss of time. Friends of Hampton have defended this action by asserting (a) that the Negro does not need college training and (b) that if the colleges do not fit the Hampton course of study, they are wrong and not Hampton. Both these assertions educated Negroes regard as preposterous. There are hundreds of Hampton men who deserve and could efficiently use longer and more thorough courses of training than Hampton gives, but who find themselves at the age of nineteen or twenty in an educational blind alley, with further progress barred. They must go out as half-educated, partially-trained men, when they might be developed to full efficiency. It is, undoubtedly, true that colleges ought to recognize a broader fitting-school course of study than they do at present, but so long as they do not, it is criminal to make the Negro the peculiar sufferer from their exclusiveness and to deny the undoubted value of the present college curriculum to the finest Negro minds in Virginia.

2. It may be said that Hampton simply specializes on technical training and high school work and that students fitted for higher training can go elsewhere. This brings us to the second indictment against Hampton—her illiberal and seemingly selfish attitude toward other colored schools. She holds little or no fellowship with them; she has repeatedly loaned herself to decrying their work, criticizing and belittling their ideals while her friends continually seek to divert to Hampton the already painfully meager revenues of the colored colleges. Few schools can equal in its own field the efficiency of Hampton, with its millions of endowment, but certainly the splen-

did work of Atlanta, Fisk, Howard, and other schools, done in poverty and travail and in the face of hostile public opinion, deserves better recognition and less criticism than it gets from Hampton and her friends.

Moreover, the students who go to Hampton go for "education." They do not know their own bent and aptitudes. They come from homes where they can hope for little educational guidance. It should be the work of Hampton not simply to train but to sift and to send to colleges or other schools those fitted for work higher or different from that offered by her curriculum. This she never voluntarily does. She feeds no colleges or professional schools; she encourages no artists or musicians; she helps no writers, but apparently proceeds on the assumption that every Negro must be trained to farm, or to be an artisan or a servant. We have no silly illusions as to the number of talented Negroes who deserve higher training, but surely in fifty years it seems that out of tens of thousands of students Hampton might have found a few worthy of the highest training. Small wonder that educated Negroes resent this and demand that Hampton cease to bury talent and deflect genius.

3. The third indictment of educated Black Folk against Hampton is more difficult to express than the others, and one of which we are less sure, and yet it is a real grievance in our minds. We believe that an institution that professes to teach the Negro self-respect and self-control should give the Negro a larger voice in her government. We do not wish Hampton to be an exclusively Negro institution, but we do think that there should be Negroes on her Board of Trustees; that there should be a larger recognition of Negro achievement, instead of an almost exclusive emphasis of the white philanthropists; and that there should be a closer touch between the school and the body of educated Negro opinion. In fine, we think that Hampton should consider what we want and not simply what she wishes us to want. We do not feel, at present, that Hampton is our school—on the contrary, we feel that she belongs to the white South and to the reactionary North, and we fear that she is a center of that underground and silent intrigue which is determined to perpetuate the American Negro as a docile peasant and peon, without political rights or social standing, working, for little wage, and heaping up dividends to be doled out in future charity to his children.

Such a feeling as this may be wrong and ill-founded, but it is real and it easily lies within Hampton's power to disprove it.

These are the reasons why many educated Negroes are and have been "opposed" to Hampton. We have seldom voiced this opposition, and I voice it now only at your invitation. I reiterate my respect for the Institution and my firm belief that it has done great good, but I insist that no school which deliberately curtails the training of the talented, refuses to guide her apter students to their greatest development, save in restricted lines, and not only gives her beneficiaries little or no voice in its control, but seems even to harbor and encourage their enemies—no such school is reaching its greatest usefulness.

W. E. B. Du Bois.

~~ **40** ~~

The Common School

Much mist and misunderstanding has been consciously and unconsciously put in the colored public mind by recent discussions of the schools. We colored people must, however, keep one thing clearly before us: the first four years of a child's life, no matter what his race or condition, must be devoted by every modern country which wishes to survive and grow to a very simple program of study: (1) The child must learn to read so as to be able easily to understand what men have written; (2) the child must learn to write so as to be able to communicate with his fellow men; (3) the child must learn to count so as to be able to handle the extraordinary multiplicity of the world's things. To read, to write, to cipher—this is the program and the only program of the first four years of a child's school life. The neglect to do this work then means, in practically all cases, the fatal crippling of the child. This program of study is a matter of technique and difficult technique. It must be learned early and thoroughly or it may not be learned at all. It must be carefully drilled in and be made second nature to the child.

Whenever any person, country or age seeks to substitute for this work anything else, they are either themselves deceived or deliberately deceiving. Other things may appear in the program of the primary school but they are simply subsidiary to the main program and designed to make the main program more easily acquired. Play, for instance, is there as a matter of health and recreation; moral habits are always to be indirectly acquired in home and in school, but the technical business of the primary school is to teach the child to read, to write and to cipher.

No vocational training has any place in a primary school. Any attempt to turn the primary school into a place for teaching trades or teaching agriculture or teaching housework as such is absolutely wrong and should be fought bitterly by every advocate of democracy and human uplift. This does not mean that for recreation or as discipline little children may not sew and wash dishes and cultivate school gardens, but this work must not be vocational—it must be simply a means of interesting the child in this main work of learning to read, to write and to cipher.

The next four years of grammar grades are also mainly the carrying out of the work of the first four years, teaching the child to read for information as well as exercise; to write for self-expression as well as for mere communication; and to reason more clearly with mathematical correctness. It may be necessary at some times and places that a child from ten to fourteen be compelled to take some vocational work for self-support, but no country as rich as the United States or as enlightened can afford to make this necessary. It is becoming more and more fixed in our national thought that it is the business of a nation to educate a child up to fourteen years, that is through the grammar grades; and in addition to the three R's and the geography, history and language study that go with them we should add nothing to the curriculum which is not primarily for the helping of these students in this main work either directly or indirectly through inciting interest and correct habits of health and application.

After fourteen there comes an entirely different question—whether the child is to be trained directly for self-supporting work, as most children should be, or whether his talents are sufficient for him to be trained to greater service by longer methods of education.

∽ 41 ∽

Philanthropy

The Negro race in America owes a mighty debt, first, to that army of teachers that followed the emancipating hosts of the Civil War and taught the colored people until they were able in a measure to teach themselves; secondly, to the millions of people, some rich and some poor, who now for a half-century have been giving monies to support Negro education. It is not strange that the time is approaching and practically is upon us when the stream of financial help from this source is beginning to cease. We must frankly face the prospect that after the war when new calls for help and rehabilitation pour in from all sides and ask aid and succor from an impoverished world that the flow of Northern wealth to Southern colored schools will definitely diminish.

This is natural. No system of higher education for twelve million people can expect to be supported indefinitely by charity. If turning from individual donors we look to the great educational boards, foundations and endowments there is little to hope for. For the most part these foundations are either such as are hard-pressed for funds, as in the case of the church boards, or have ideas with regard to the education of Negroes with which thinking Negroes do not agree.

What, then, is the future of higher education among Negroes to be? Three universities, Howard, Fisk and Lincoln, are probably upon an assured basis; the last two by reason of small endowments, the first because the Negro vote in the United States will probably insure continued appropriations by Congress. Three universities, however, are ridiculously inadequate. We may then turn to those colleges under the control of the various denominational boards.—The Congregationalists can, if they wish, use enough of their endowment funds to support Talladega and Straight as higher institutions, and they may do so. The colored constituency of the

Methodist Episcopal Church will probably compel the maintenance at a fair state of efficiency of some schools like Claflin, Bennett and Clark. The Baptists are in a more debatable condition. Their Negro constituency has for the most part withdrawn to itself and is supporting its own schools, leaving the white Baptists with a small Negro constituency to support schools like Morehouse, Shaw and Virginia Union.

ᨀ **42** ᨀ

Self-Help

Negro universities and schools of higher training have got to be supported by Negroes or, for the most part, they will not be supported at all. If we black folk want college training for our children, we have got to furnish it out of our own pockets. This is a harsh conclusion and in many respects an unfair burden. If men were wise and if sociology were a science, it would be easy for Negroes to show the people of the United States that the safest and greatest investment that this country could make of a thousand millions of dollars during the next decade would be the establishment of a series of Negro universities and higher technical schools throughout the United States. But the nation does not see it and it will not see it for one hundred years. Human beings today have been educated to the point where they recognize the need of philanthropy for the hungry, the cripple, the grossly ignorant. Many have been educated also to see the just demand of philanthropy for the diseased, the weak and the half-trained. Beyond this, however, it is difficult to get philanthropy to go. Thorough education and higher training still seem to most people a luxury and an indulgence and we must recognize these facts. We ourselves, however, know that if the Negro is to survive in this world as a man of thought and power a co-worker with the leading races in civilization, a free, independent citizen of a modern democracy, then the foundations for this future must be laid in the Negro university. This much we know, but hitherto we have not realized that we have got to pay the bill for this education.

ᨀ **43** ᨀ

Awake, Put on Thy Strength, O Zion

We can support our own universities. We must do it. One little school in Virginia, supported simply by poor Negro Baptists, refused the help of philanthropists, paid back with interest the money that had been given to it, bought its own land and put up its own buildings, hired its own teachers and last year gave $25,000 cash to run the institution. The Virginia Theological Seminary and College is not a perfect institution. It does not meet the approval of all educators, but it does meet the approval of every independent, right-thinking colored man who believes that the day of passing the hat for Negro education is nearing a close and who is thanking God for it.

ᨳ 44 ᨳ

The Slaughter of the Innocents

Again the rolling of the years brings us to the annual Children's Number. Attention has been called this year especially to the child and the United States Government has been spreading widely the gospel of the preservation of child life. The death of some ten million men who would have been fathers of unborn children has made the world think of the horrors of peace as well as the horrors of war. And the greatest of the horrors of peace is the unnecessary and persistent slaughter of little children. It is a crime of every civilization and of every race, but we Negroes are among the guiltiest, among us from two hundred to five hundred of every thousand of our babies born die before they reach one year of age. We have pleaded poverty, prejudice and slavery as excuse, but the time is come not to excuse but to combat with our own available weapons this murder.

The remedy is, first, care and fore thought in bringing children into the world and, second, pure food and air for them when they come. We persist in keeping windows shut and living indoors; we persist in buying food carelessly and feeding all kinds of food indiscriminately to children. Outdoor life and simple, pure foods regularly fed would save the lives of a quarter million Negro children each year. Look on these pages. Are not these little lives worth the saving?

ᨳ 45 ᨳ

Save

We are earning money today. Never before in this history of the world has the Negro race enjoyed so large an income. Save! The fat years will not last forever. Save. Readjustment and reconstruction after the war will mean hard times for many a black laborer. *SAVE*. Saving is made easy and absolutely safe today for the small investor. SAVE. Buy Thrift Stamps regularly. Buy Liberty Bonds. Use the savings banks. Buy homes. SAVE! Do not waste and throw away the easily earned new wages. Do not increase your expense faster than your large earnings increase. Go slow with new furniture and new building and new clothes and fat food. SAVE!

⁓ 46 ⁓

Reconstruction

This is a program of reconstruction within the Negro race in America, after the revolution of world war. In *Education* we must take up the problem of the colored child in the white school. At present the tendency is to accept and even demand separate schools because our children so often are neglected, mistreated and humiliated in the public schools. This is a dangerous and inadvisable alternative and a wicked surrender of principle for which our descendants will pay dearly. Our policy should be to form in connection with each school and district effective Parents' Associations, composed of the fathers, mothers and friends of colored pupils; these associations should establish friendly relations with teachers and school authorities, urge parents to wash and dress their children properly, help look after truancy and poverty, arrange for homework and tuition for the backward, curb delinquency and be, in fine, a vigilance committee to keep the public school open to all and fit the Negro child for it.

In *Religion* we must, in the larger cities, stop building and purchasing new church edifices and begin to invest the money of the church in homes, land and business, and philanthropic enterprises for the benefit of the people. Individual home ownership in most large cities is today difficult; but a group of people who can buy and pay for a hundred thousand dollar church can purchase a hundred thousand dollar apartment house and run it. It is a simple business proposition and requires only elementary honesty and ordinary executive ability. Churches can easily begin co-operative buying of coal, bread and meat, using their own premises for distribution; churches in the country and small towns can buy farms and rent or run them; the church can purchase automobile trucks and help the Negro farmer market his produce independent of the railroads and thieving commission merchants; even simple manufacturing, sewing and building are not beyond the reasonable activities of church bodies. Indeed, unless the church extends its economic functions beyond the simple program of building bigger and finer edifices—unless it organizes the Negro laborer so that his entire wage will not go in rent and supporting

storekeepers who despise and cheat him—unless it thus helps the laborer, it will lose the laborer. The hope of the Negro church is character building through economic co-operation.

In *Business* the Negro must branch out into certain new lines where he
has long and foolishly hesitated: We must open drygoods and haber-
dashery shops, meat markets and clothing stores, shoe stores and hat
stores. We must gradually but persistently get into manufacturing. The
deft fingers of our young people are as easily adapted to machinery as
the fingers of whites. We are denied opportunity by white trade unions
and by lack of pioneering courage among colored capitalists and business men. Let us wake up. The era of manufactures in the United States
is just begun. The expansion of domestic and foreign trade is going to be
enormous. We raise the cotton—why not spin and weave it? We dig the
iron—why not weld it? We mine the coal—why not turn it to steam and
power? Do we lack brains and capital? No, we lack experience and
courage. Get them.

In *Politics* the colored woman is going to vote. This is our chance.
Away with the old regime, the pothouse politician and white bribery. Let
us form clubs and study government in city, county, state and nation. Let
us know the law and the officials and their duties. Let us keep continual
and rigid tabs on every candidate. Away with parties—what we want is
men. Away with promises—what we want is deeds. Study, learn, register and vote. Vote at every election and see that every friend of yours
votes. Pay your poll taxes and register. Do not vote for a party. Never
vote a straight ticket. Vote for men and measures—not for parties. But
above all, vote! Let every Negro man and woman, always and everywhere, *vote*.

～ 47 ～

Cooperation

Several cooperative efforts are starting among colored people. Probably
today, there are fifty or more local efforts. Most of them are sporadic, and
will fail. Some few are the efforts of individuals who use the magic word
cooperation for stores in which there is not a trace of the cooperation
principle.

There are a dozen or more which are largely cooperative, but not
entirely—for instance, they have shares, and the number which one man
may own is limited. The shareholders are obliged to buy a certain minimum amount of goods before they can share in the profits.

This is only partially cooperative. Full cooperation requires: cheap shares, of which anyone can own any number; BUT there is no temptation to own large numbers of shares, because PROFITS ARE DIVIDED ACCORDING TO THE AMOUNT THE PERSON BUYS.

Why, now, do beginners hesitate to make this last provision? Because having stirred up the people by the argument of race loyalty and opened the store, they say: "Why should I surrender the coming profits to a mass of people whom the driblets will not greatly benefit? Why not keep them and GROW RICH!"

Hesitate, brother, hesitate, RIGHT THERE! Remember that with the present chain grocery store and trust system, your individual grocery has a small chance to succeed, because the Trust can and will undersell you.

But with the true cooperative principle, your clientele is nailed down. Your shareholders are pledged by their own interests to trade with you, and to trade often and much. The more they spend the more they make. Your business is no guesswork. You know just how much to buy. If the chain store cuts prices below cost, your people will buy of you at the higher price, because they know that the low price is a temporary trick for which they themselves will eventually pay. Whatever happens, you CANNOT fail as long as your shareholders are true, and they will be true as long they share in the profits according to their purchases.

Don't be afraid. Try the whole co operative program. Write us.

～ 48 ～

Crime

We are not for a moment denying the existence of a criminal class among Negroes, who are guilty of deeds of violence. Every race in the world has such groups. No human efforts have yet been able wholly to rid society of crime. But if of all groups, the American Negro is to be singled out and punished AS A GROUP for the detestable deeds of its criminals, then this country is staging a race war of the bitterest kind, when the wronged and the innocent fight in desperate defense against the mob and murderer.

There is a curious assumption in some quarters that intelligent and law-abiding Negroes like, encourage, and sympathize with Negro crime and defend Negro criminals. They do not. They suffer more from the crime of their fellows than white folk suffer, not only vicariously, but directly; the black criminal knows that he can prey on his own people with the least danger of punishment, because they control no police or courts.

But what can Negroes do to decrease crime? Some white Southerners have but one suggestion, which is that when a Negro is accused of crime, other Negroes turn to run him down and hand him over to the authorities.

But hold! Is there no difference between a person accused of crime and a criminal? Are black folks accused of crime in the South assured of a fair trial and just punishment? We will let a white southern ex Confederate, Bishop B. J. Keiley, of Georgia, answer in the *Savannah Press*:

"Is it not the fact that fair and impartial justice is not meted out to white and colored men alike? The courts of this state either set the example, or follow the example set them, and they make a great distinction between the white and the black criminal brought before them. The latter, as a rule, gets the full limit of the law. Do you ever hear of a street difficulty in which a Negro and a white man were involved which was brought before a judge, in which, no matter what were the real facts of the case, the Negro did not get the worst of it?"

This is bad enough, but this is not all. We have criminals who deserve punishment. Now the modern treatment of crime and criminals, is built on carefully considered principles: one, old as the English Common Law, and older, declares that it is better for the community that ten guilty men should escape, rather than that one innocent man should be punished; moreover, it is beginning to be widely recognized that in crime, the criminal is not the only one guilty; you and I share in the guilt if we have not given him as a child an education, furnished him with a place to play, and seen that his body was nourished; we are guilty if as a man he was not allowed to do honest work, did not receive a living wage, and did not have a proper social environment.

This social responsibility for crime is so widely recognized that when the criminal is arrested, the first desire of decent modern society is to reform him, and not to avenge itself on him. Penal servitude is being recognized only as it protects society and improves the criminal, and not because it makes him suffer as his victim suffered.

What, now, is the attitude of the white South toward Negro crime? First and foremost, it would rather that ten innocent Negroes suffer than that one guilty one escape; secondly, it furnishes Negro children, for the most part, wretched schools and no playgrounds; it usually pays the adult low wages, houses him in slums, and gives him neither care nor thought, until he steals or murders. It has few juvenile reformatories, and herds all kinds of criminals together, selling them into slavery to the highest bidder, under the "Lease" system. Its idea of punishment is vengeance— vengeance of the cruelest and most blood-curdling sort.

Under such circumstances, what can an honest Negro do to stop Negro crime?

～ **49** ～

Two Methods

A Vigilance Committee in Des Moines, Iowa, under Mrs. L. B. Smith, has arranged the following program for the care of colored children in mixed schools:

   I. OUR POLICY:

      (a) To establish friendly relations with teachers and school authorities

      (b) To urge parents to wash and dress their children properly

      (c) Help with poverty and truancy

      (d) Arrange home work and tuition for the backward

   II. THIS VIGILANCE COMMITTEE which endeavors to fit the colored American child for the public school will deftly intertwine their effort in the mission:

      (a) To make colored children realize that being "colored" is a normal, beautiful thing

      (b) To make them know that other colored children have grown into beautiful, useful and famous persons

      (c) To turn their little hurts and resentments into emulation, ambition and love of their own homes and companions

      (d) To inspire them to prepare for definite occupation and duties with a broad spirit of sacrifice

      (e) To teach universal love and brotherhood for all little folks— black, brown, yellow and white

      (f) To teach them delicately a code of honor and action in their relation with white children

   III. WE ask the cooperation of all the teachers and principals in helping us to accomplish this splendid duty at this critical hour.

Mr. L. F. Artis, assistant secretary of the colored Y. M. C. A. writes us from Indianapolis:

It will interest you, I feel sure, to know of a piece of work that has just been completed here in Indianapolis, the effect of which is quite favorable.

Under the direction of the Industrial Department of the Colored Men's Branch of the Y. M. C. A. a vocational guidance conference was held with every colored boy who was graduated from the 8A grammar grades at the spring term. The hearty support and interest of the supervising principals of the colored schools and of the teachers of the schools concerned brought a full measure of success to the effort.

The purpose of the conferences was three-fold: To urge a continuance in high school of every boy; to guide those who MUST stop school and enroll them in a night high school; and to suggest high school courses in relation to future life-work. Each boy was carefully charted on a psychological analysis sheet. His temperamental and hereditary qualities were considered and his school history was added. The personal choice of his future vocation was secured from each boy and a thorough effort was made to correlate native endowments and vocational choices. Only two colored boys in the entire city failed to enter the local high schools.

A group of experienced men has been formed into a Vocational Guidance Committee which any boy in the city can consult and talk over the problem of his life-work. It is also purposed to carefully follow up the boys who were interviewed in this manner with the aim of guiding their young and fertile minds into profitable lines of endeavor.

This plan, we feel sure, could be put into operation in a number of our larger cities with marked success and with great potentialities for rendering a much needed service.

Finally, the Alpha Phi Alpha Fraternity during the week of June 6–12 put on an enthusiastic and nation wide "drive" to encourage colored boys and girls to go to High School and College. These efforts are the ones that tell. May they spread widely.

∽ **50** ∽

Thrift

A teacher writes us from Texas:

"Now that prices are on the decline and there is a consequent rise in the value of money, it occurs to me that this is an opportune time to start a national thrift movement among our people.

"Such a note should be sounded by our newspapers, magazines and periodicals of every kind. The preacher should proclaim it from the pulpit; the teacher from the lecture platform. It ought to be the watch word of every household.

"To have such a movement suggested by you in THE CRISIS, I think, would be timely and fruitful."

This is a wise word. During the last five years American Negroes have handled more money than in the preceding twenty years. With it they have bought millions of dollars' worth of property and invested other millions in business, insurance and education. But for every dollar thus wisely used, five dollars have been foolishly wasted.

We are not of those who decry the extravagance of the poor and see economic salvation in the luxury of the rich. Waste is waste whether in Harlem or on Fifth Avenue or in the poppy fields of Flanders, and the antidote for waste is not miserliness but wise expenditure.

Now, wise expenditure for Negroes today includes not simply good homes but good bank accounts. Money is rising in value. A dollar saved today means much more than a dollar tomorrow. We need to earn and control capital. All poor folk need to save and learn how to control capital. The capital which is today ruling the world is not the capital of the rich—it is the capital of the middle class and poor. The *control* of it is in the hands of the rich and that is the reason they *are* rich. The *control* must through democratic methods gradually shift to the hands of masses as the masses are taught or teach them selves the science of capitalistic production.

But the anger of the poor against those who control wealth must not, as it so often does, become anger against wealth. The world needs and must have capital if present culture is to be maintained. The Negro race needs and needs desperately larger and larger amounts of capital for its emancipation. While then we strive to learn to control capital, we must simultaneously strive to save it.

Thrift, saving, care and foresight are the watchwords for black folk today as never before. We are not going to be saved by high-powered automobiles and sables but rather by the canny savings balance, the wise investment, and the wide surplus of income over expense.

Much of what we save is thus put into the control of our white enemies. There are white banks in Texas, in Atlanta and in black Harlem that with millions of Negro money would sooner lend to the devil than to a Negro business enterprise. But the race is not to the swift nor the battle to the strong: our business enterprise is rising and thriving and it is a democratic business and not an oligarchy of millionaires. We are gradually learning as a race to control capital and therein lies salvation for us and the Poor. But to control capital there must be capital to control: Save then, brothers,—save and invest. Remember Poor Richard, how he said:

"A penny saved is a penny earned."

"Waste not, want not."

"Plough deep while sluggards sleep."

"Remember that time is money."

"A man may, if he knows not how to save as he gets, keep his nose to the grind stone."

"It is hard for an empty bag to stand upright."

～ **51** ～

The Drive

Again the pendulum has swung: it is no longer a question of educating the Negro to his just demands as an American citizen. He has ceased to be beguiled by the silly philosophy that a voteless, spineless suppliant who owns a three-story brick house is going to command anybody's respect.

But today comes the question of practical, efficient means of getting the rights which he has at last been persuaded he wants.

Into the field have jumped a hoard of scoundrels and bubble-blowers, ready to conquer Africa, join the Russian revolution, and vote in the Kingdom of God tomorrow. It is without doubt certain that Africa will some day belong to the Africans; that steamship lines and grocery stores, properly organized and run, are excellent civilizers; and that we are in desperate need today of organized industry and organized righteousness. But what are the practical steps to these things? By yelling? By pouring out invective and vituperation against all white folk? By collecting the pennies of the ignorant poor in shovelful and refusing to account for them, save with bombast and lies?

Or is it reason and decency to unite on a program which says: the battle of Negro rights is to be fought right here in America; that here we must unite to fight lynching and "Jim Crow" cars, to settle our status in the courts, to put our children in school and maintain our free ballot.

Far from being discouraged in the fight, we are daily more and more triumphant. Yesterday 1,650 Negro women voted in New Orleans. Never since 1876 have so many Negroes voted in the South as in the last election. Our fight for right has the enemy on the run. He has had to retreat to mob violence, secret and silly mummery, clumsy and hypocritical promises. Twenty-five years more of the intelligent fighting that the N.A.A.C.P. has led will make the black man in the United States free and equal.

Our enemies know this. They are scared. They are hastening to lay down a barrage of suspicion and personal bickering. They are encouraging and advertising any and all crazy schemes, to cut and run from the hard and bloody battle here, to Africa and the South Seas. Africa needs her children, but she needs them triumphant, victorious, and not as poverty-stricken and cowering refugees.

Are we going to be misled fools, or are we going to put a quarter of a million level-headed, determined and unwavering black men and women back of the N. A. A. C. P. to continue the battle so nobly and successfully begun? Answer, black folk of America, this month!

～ 52 ～

Negro Art

Negro art is today plowing a difficult row, chiefly because we shrink at the portrayal of the truth about ourselves. We are so used to seeing the truth distorted to our despite, that whenever we are portrayed on canvas, in story or on the stage, as simply human with human frailties, we rebel. We want everything that is said about us to tell of the best and highest and noblest in us. We insist that our Art and Propaganda be one.

This is wrong and in the end it is harmful. We have a right, in our effort to get just treatment, to insist that we produce something of the best in human character and that it is unfair to judge us by our criminals and prostitutes. This is justifiable propaganda.

On the other hand we face the Truth of Art. We have criminals and prostitutes, ignorant and debased elements just as all folk have. When the artist paints us he has a right to paint us whole and not ignore every thing which is not as perfect as we would wish it to be. The black Shakespeare must portray his black Iagos as well as his white Othellos.

We shrink from this. We fear that evil in us will be called racial, while in others it is viewed as individual. We fear that our shortcomings are not merely human but foreshadowings and threatenings of disaster and failure. The more highly trained we become the less can we laugh at Negro comedy—we will have it all, tragedy and the triumph of dark Right over pale Villainy.

The results are not merely negative—they are positively bad. With a vast wealth of human material about us, our own writers and artists fear to paint the truth lest they criticize their own and be in turn criticized for it. They fail to see the Eternal Beauty that shines through all Truth, and try to portray a world of stilted artificial black folk such as never were on land or sea.

Thus the white artist looking in on the colored world, if he be wise and discerning, may often see the beauty, tragedy and comedy more truly than we dare. Of course if he be simply a shyster like Tom Dixon, he will see only exaggerated evil, and fail as utterly in the other extreme as we in ours. But if, like Sheldon, he writes a fine true work of art like "The Nigger"; or like Ridgely Torrence, a beautiful comedy like "The Rider of Dreams"; or like Eugene O'Neill, a splendid tragedy like "The Emperor Jones"—he finds to his own consternation the Negroes and even educated Negroes, shrinking or openly condemning.

Sheldon's play has repeatedly been driven from the stage by ill-advised Negroes who objected to its name; Torrence's plays were received by educated blacks with no great enthusiasm; and only yesterday a protest of colored folk in a western city declared that:

"'The Emperor Jones' is the kind of play that should never be staged under any circumstances, regardless of theories, because it portrays the worst traits of the bad element of both races."

No more complete misunderstanding of this play or of the aim of Art could well be written, although the editors of the Century and Current Opinion showed almost equal obtuseness.

Nonsense. We stand today secure enough in our accomplishment and self-confidence to lend the whole stern human truth about ourselves to the transforming hand and seeing eye of the Artist, white and black, and Sheldon, Torrence and O'Neill are our great benefactors—forerunners of artists who will yet arise in Ethiopia of the Outstretched Arm.

∼ 53 ∼

Marriage

Among colored people, especially the advancing groups, marriage and birth are still slightly improper subjects which cannot be discussed with plain sense. The world has left us behind in this respect and we must needs rapidly catch up.

Here is a man and a woman. The natural and righteous cry of their bodies calls for marriage to propagate, preserve and improve mankind. But there are difficulties. First, as to ideals: the man—an educated Negro American of 1922—is himself a spoiled child. He has been catered to and petted by a mother. Coming up with small means, the family purse has been drained for his benefit. He has helped in his own support, but his work has brought him into contact with the luxury of the white rich; he has seen gluttony and tasteless splendor; futile women gorgeously gowned; royal homes, with yachts and automobiles. What does he think of marriage? He conceives of it as a very expensive indulgence, and for the enthroning of One Woman—which woman is to be His, and of him, and for him? And that woman must be not simply as someone has said, "A cross between a butterfly and a setting hen," but in addition, thinking of his own mother, he conceives his wife also as a trained, efficient Upper Servant, who can cook, serve, wash, clean, market and nurse; she must also be able to dance, play the piano, talk on politics and literature, entertain with daintiness, play tennis and drive an automobile.

To increase the complication the modern young colored woman has her own ideas and ideals. Her husband must have money and good looks. He must be a college graduate, a professional man, or at least a business man; hardly a mechanic, and certainly never a menial servant. He must have, ready for delivery on the wedding day: a well-furnished home in a good neighborhood, a servant or a day's worker, a car and a reputation that brings his picture to the pages of leading colored weeklies.

The result of all this theory is trouble. The best dancers are seldom the best cooks, and those who keep up with literature have little leisure to keep up with bad children. If a man's wife is chiefly for exhibition and entertainment, she cannot be expected to be an efficient business manager of a home, and mother, nurse and teacher of children. And, too, young men of marriageable age are not apt to be at once handsome, educated, talented, rich and well-known. Something must be sacrificed; the educated and talented must wait long if not always for wealth; the rich may come handicapped by a servile position and no education; while the handsome— well, fools are often handsome.

All these are of course types of a small but significant class. Down through the mass of laborers and servants we meet every human variation; men too poor, too undisciplined, too selfish to marry; women too ignorant, too lonely, too unfortunate to marry.

Thus, practically, marriage must be a compromise and if the compromise is based on common sense and reasonable effort, it becomes the center of real resurrection and remaking of the world. If it fails, then it should be dissolved—quietly and decisively in the divorce court. Any doctrine of marriage that conceives a quarrelling, unhappy, sordid and compulsory union of man, woman and children as better than peace and work even with poverty, is fundamentally wrong.

∼ 54 ∼

Birth

Yesterday I saw a young man and woman and their three children. And I was told: Four of their children are dead. I said: "That is a crime! It is not simply a misfortune—it is a deliberate crime which deserves condign punishment." No woman can bear seven children in ten years and preserve her own health and theirs. No man who asks or permits this deserves to be a husband or father.

Birth control is science and sense applied to the bringing of children into the world, and of all who need it we Negroes are first. We in America are becoming sharply divided into the mass who have endless children and the class who through long postponement of marriage have few or none. The first result is a terrible infant mortality: of every 10,000 colored children born 1,356 die in the first year, while only 821 die among whites. The second result is the senseless putting off of marriage until middle life because of the fear that marriage must necessarily mean many children.

Parents owe their children, first of all, health and strength. Few women can bear more than two or three children and retain strength for the other interests of life. And there are other interests for women as for men and only reactionary barbarians deny this. Even this small number of children should come into the world at intervals which will allow for the physical, economic and spiritual recovery of the parents. Housework is still a desperately hard and exacting occupation. It can and should be simplified and lightened by the laundry, the bakery, the restaurant, and the vacuum cleaner; but with all that it remains a job calling for strength, time and training. Social intercourse, which is largely in the hands of wives, is a matter of thought, effort and delicate adjustment. The education of children in the home calls for intelligence, study and leisure. To add to all this the physical pain and strain of child birth is to give a woman as much as she can possibly endure once in three, four or five years.

ᵔ **55** ᵔ

Childhood

Of the meaning of a child there are many and singularly different ideas. Some regard a child as a bond slave, born to obey immediately and without reflection or question; some regard a child as an automaton which absorbs advice and replies with action; some look upon a child as an Item of Expense until he can work and earn; some think of children as a kind of personal adornment of the parents, bringing them praise for beauty when young, for smartness when older, and for high distinction in wealth or brains when grown.

Meantime few people think of the child as Itself—as an Individual with the right and ability to feel, think and act; a being thirsty to know, curious to investigate, eager to experiment. Many folk while not knowing or dreaming these things at first, discover them later in some tense moment when father and "baby" face each other—grim, tense, angry; and father says, "You shall not!" and baby says, "I will!" The education of parents dates usually from some such soul-revealing moment. Blockheads who cannot learn usually try forthwith to beat the "stubbornness" out of the child by blows. If they succeed, they kill the spirit of the little man and leave little which the world needs. If they fail, they leave determination, without love or reverence.

Others learn. They realize with a start: Here is Somebody Else. I must inform, I must teach, I must persuade, I must direct. But if they are honest they soon learn that in a duel between two human wills even though one is four and the other forty, there is information to be imparted on both sides; and that youth can teach age some things; and that persuasion is a game that two can play; and that Experience, great as it is, is not all. Many people begin with trying to teach and persuade and end by commanding in anger, "instant" obedience, leaving the child with a tremendous and never-to-be-forgotten sense of being wronged and cheated. Only God's Few take this dialogue between Age and Childhood seriously and give to it as much time and money and study and thought as they give to their clothes and houses and horses. And some give more.

⌁ 56 ⌁

Education

Here is a widespread feeling that a school is a machine. You insert a child at 9 A.M. and extract it at 4 P.M., improved and standardized with parts of Grade IV, first term. In truth, school is a desperate duel between new souls and old to pass on facts and methods and dreams from a dying world to a world in birth pains without letting either teacher or taught lose for a moment faith and interest. It is hard work. Often, most often, it is a futile failure. It is never wholly a success with out the painstaking help of the parent.

Yet I know Negroes, thousands of them, who never visit the schools where their children go; who do not know the teachers or what they teach or what they are supposed to teach; who do not consult the authorities on matters of discipline—do not know who or what is in control of the schools or how much money is needed or received.

Oh, we have our excuses! The teachers do not want us around. They do not welcome co-operation. Colored patrons especially may invite insult or laughter. All true in some cases. Yet the best schools and the best teachers pray for and welcome the continuous and intelligent co-operation of parents. And the worst schools need it and must be made to realize their need.

There has been much recent discussion among Negroes as to the merits of mixed and segregated schools. It is said that our children are neglected in mixed schools. "Let us have our own schools. How else can we explain the host of colored High School graduates in Washington, and the few in Philadelphia?" Easily. In Washington, colored parents are intensely interested in their schools and have for years followed and watched and criticized them. In Philadelphia, the colored people have evinced no active interest save in colored schools and there is no colored High School.

Save the great principle of democracy and equal opportunity and fight segregation by wealth, class or race or color, not by yielding to it but by watching, visiting and voting in all school matters, organizing parents and children and bringing every outside aid and influence to co-operate with teachers and authorities.

In the North with mixed schools unless colored patrons take intelligent, continuous and organized interest in the schools which their children attend, the children will be neglected, treated unjustly, discouraged and balked of their natural self-expression and ambition. Do not allow this. Supervise your children's schools.

In the South unless the patrons know and visit the schools and keep up continuous, intelligent agitation, the teachers will be sycophants, the studies designed to make servant girls, and the funds stolen by the white trustees.

～ 57 ～

The Negro and the American Stage

We all know what the Negro for the most part has meant hitherto on the American stage. He has been a lay figure whose business it was usually to be funny and sometimes pathetic. He has never, with very few exceptions, been human or credible. This, of course, cannot last. The most dramatic group of people in the history of the United States is the American Negro. It would be very easy for a great artist so to interpret the history of our country as to make the plot turn entirely upon the black man. Thus two classes of dramatic situations of tremendous import arise. The inner life of this black group and the contact of black and white. It is going to be difficult to get at these facts for the drama and treat them sincerely and artistically because they are covered by a shell; or shall I say a series of concentric shells? In the first place comes the shell of what most people think the Negro ought to be and this makes everyone a self-appointed and preordained judge to say without further thought or inquiry whether this is untrue or that is wrong. Then secondly there comes the great problem of the future relations of groups and races not only in the United States but throughout the world. To some people this seems to be a tremendous and imminent problem and in their wild anxiety to settle it in the only way which seems to them the right way they are determined to destroy art, religion and good common sense in an effort to make everything that is said or shown propaganda for their ideas. These two protective shells most of us recognize; but there is a third shell that we do not so often recognize, whose sudden presence fills us with astonishment; and that is the attitude of he Negro world itself.

This Negro world which is growing in self-consciousness, economic power and literary expression is tremendously sensitive. It has sore toes, nerve filled teeth, delicate eyes and quivering ears. And it has these because during its whole conscious life it has been maligned and caricatured and lied about to an extent inconceivable to those who do not know. Any mention of Negro blood or Negro life in America for a century has been occasion for an ugly picture, a dirty allusion, a nasty comment or a pessimistic forecast. The result is that the Negro today fears any attempt of the artist to paint Negroes. He is not satisfied unless everything is perfect and proper and beautiful and joyful and hopeful. He is afraid to be painted as he is lest his human foibles and shortcomings be seized by his enemies for the purposes of the ancient hateful propaganda.

Happy is the artist that breaks through any of these shells for his is the kingdom of eternal beauty. He will come through scarred and perhaps a little embittered, certainly astonished at the almost universal misinterpretation of his motives and aims. Eugene O'Neill is bursting through. He has my sympathy for his soul must be lame with the enthusiasm of the blows rained upon him. But it is work that must be done. No greater mine of dramatic material ever lay ready for the great artist's hands than the situation of men of Negro blood in modern America.

⌇ **58** ⌇

Foreign Languages

One of the weak places in our high schools and colleges has been the teaching of languages. The dead languages have developed a teaching technique, usually a dry-as-dust, indefensible method of teaching human speech. For a long time the teaching of living languages followed the same path and today in most colored schools and colleges the persons who teach French, German and Spanish can neither understand nor be understood in those languages. They teach them, not as languages, but as crossword puzzles and the result is what one would expect. There are, however, a few institutions like Howard University and Livingstone College where men born on French soil are teaching French and persons who can speak and write Spanish are teaching Spanish; and these languages are being taught in the only way that languages can be taught and that is by having the classes speak, read and write them. The time must speedily come when any person who has studied French and cannot use the French language will be recognized as having done the impossible.

On the other hand, no man is educated who cannot speak, read and understand a foreign language. American Negroes ought to be able to visit Europe and the West Indies and talk to their fellows there. If our schools are not preparing for this, they are not schools.

~ **59** ~

Crisis Children

Again we come to the Annual Children's Number. Few magazines have tried to do more for the children than THE CRISIS. The space we have given them is indeed much too small and of this they have frequently complained; but at any rate, we have given them space every year and during the last years, with the help of Effie Lee Newsome, almost each month. This is as it should be, for the development of sound children and the youth among us is the astonishing thing of our history.

There are to be sure not enough children in families of the better class; and this is a matter for earnest thought among us. If children are not born to the family, why not adopt them? There are numbers and numbers of cases of adoption among colored folk today and THE CRISIS has helped in many cases.

Then beyond quantity of children there comes the matter of quality—a thing of much greater importance. We have still the spoiled and pampered child, over-protected and over-indulged, because the parent had so little of guarding and joy. Common sense and social education will weed these children out. Send your little girls and boys to summer camps and let them learn physical hardness and sportsmanship, and the glory of the great outdoors.

Schooling is still our grave problem. The colored child in the mixed public school has for the most part a hard road to travel. But he will be often stronger and sturdier for the experience, if he pulls through. The colored child in the better colored public schools has also the difficulty of contact with masses who have had small opportunity in this world. It frightens the careful mother and father to know what their children must meet here; but nevertheless, the masses of this world have always been unpleasant companions and only by contact with the better can they be made more pleasant and more useful. At least in your home you have a chance to make your child's surroundings of the best: books and pictures and music; cleanliness, order, sympathy and understanding; information, friendship and love,—there is not much of evil in the world that can stand against such home surroundings.

There is a real sense in which the world is growing young; and that is the reason we are paying more attention to the Youth, the Child and the Baby; and we are doing this because here we have glimpsed Eternal Life.

⤳ 60 ⤳

Boys and Girls

In lands of the East and in Africa a problem arises because the boys get all the current education and the girls none. In the United States and among this generation of American Negroes, the girls are getting longer and better education than the boys. In the Southern Negro colleges the women are outnumbering the men. It may be said truly that if either the mothers or fathers must be ignorant, better let it be the fathers so that the children may be well trained; but the difficulty is that there'll be few children if the college women cannot find true mates and if colored men cannot come up to the economic and cultural ideals of the new Negro women. The remedy is not less education for the girls but more for the boys. Do not so easily let the boy drop out and go to work. Do not reserve all the strings of discipline and guidance for the girls. Do not get the silly idea that girls must be coddled but that boys would best fend for themselves.

⤳ 61 ⤳

Our Economic Future

There can be no doubt but what the whole economic future of the Negro in America is ready for new thought and new planning. All the old slogans and old advice are worthless. To ask an individual colored man today to go into the grocery business or to open a drygoods shop or to sell meat, shoes, candy, books, cigars, clothes or fruit is competition with the Chain Store, is to ask him to commit slow but almost inevitable economic suicide, unless he has some unusual local or personal advantage.

The individual shopkeeper is disappearing in the American world, and his place is being taken by great country-wide organizations which sell food, clothes, cars, coal, coffee, furniture and hundreds of other things to meet the needs of men; and sell them at a price which makes attempted competition futile. The managers of these stores are appointed, and usually no colored men need apply. The workers in the stores and factories are hired, either in agreement with unions that keep out Negroes, or on an open shop basis, where Negroes are admitted only at the lowest wages.

In general industry, Negroes can become common laborers, underpaid and thereby ousting white competitors and thus engendering deep racial hatreds. Only in exceptional cases do Negroes get a chance in the higher ranks of skilled laborers or as Foreman or Managers.

In the credit world Negroes get bank credit with much greater difficulty than white men of equal honesty and ability. Negro banks are small and in any crisis they are dependent on the white banks of the city, and, of course, on the great white banking ring of the country. If for any reason, any influential part of any community wishes to crush a Negro bank, the bank is worse than helpless. The story of Memphis confirms this.

Nearly all of the old independent trades are now part of highly organized combinations, financed with large capital: like bakers, blacksmiths, fire men, jewelers, cigar-makers, painters, cabinetmakers, shoemakers, tailors, upholsters, tinsmiths, and any number of others. Men in the building trades are at the mercy of powerful trade unions, contractors backed endless bank credit and real estate combinations. In transportation, the Negro is absolutely excluded by the railroad unions and only has a desperate chance as longshoreman and laborer.

In the whole realm of manufacturing under the factory system, the Negro is excluded by the trades union and the deliberate and wide spread agreement of employers. Outside the cigar-making factories and the needle trades, there are practically no Negro operatives in cotton mills, candy factories, furniture factories, grain mills, leather factories, brass, copper, lead and zinc mills, paper mills, textile mills and hundreds of the like.

In the realm of personal service, the Negro has a chance as porter and servant, and in service for his own race. In professional service we have a first-rate record of desert in medicine, dentistry, literature, law, music and teaching, and a long tradition in the ministry; but these professions depend on a strong wage earning and income receiving mass and this we grievously lack.

In agriculture, thirty years training by Hampton and Tuskegee has decreased the proportion of Negro farmers in the colored population, and so few of their graduates have become farmers that they refuse to publish the figures. Hampton and Tuskegee are not to blame for this. They attempted the impossible. Farming for white and black today in the United States is a failing, unprofitable business; and the efforts to help it—farm credits and farm relief,—are not for Negroes.

In the face of this situation, there is no organized and thoughtful effort toward reform. The industrial school never accomplished the object which it had in mind, and which it widely advertised. It has not filled the land with Negro carpenters, bricklayers, wagon-builders, cooks and printers. Only to a limited extent are such schools training artisans today and all of the major industrial schools are being transformed into colleges.

What is to be done? There is to my mind only one way out: Manufacturing and consumers co-operation among the major part of twelve million people on a wide and ever-increasing scale. There must be the slow, but carefully planned growth of manufacturing trusts, beginning with the raising of raw material on Negro farms; extending to its transportation on Negro trucks; its manufacture in Negro factories; its distribution to Negro co-operative stores, supported by intelligent and loyal Negro consumers.

Such an organization is above and beyond race prejudice and trust competition. Once established on the basis of the English, Scandinavian, German and Russian co-operatives, it would insure the economic independence of the American Negro for all time.

Beside this could grow credit systems and co-operative banks which could bring the Negro-American group into carefully articulated co-operation with the West Indies and South America; with West Africa and South Africa.

It is more than idiotic,—it is criminal, for American Negroes to stagger blindly on, hugging the fond illusion that white philanthropy through industrial education is going to furnish them with future steady employment and economic independence. It is equally idiotic to hope that white laborers will become broad enough or wise enough to make the cause of black labor their own. These things will never be done in our day. Our economic future lies in the hands of carefully trained thinkers, technical engineers, and the unswerving will to sacrifice on the part of intelligent masses.

༨ **62** ༨

The City Child

The colored child, reared in the Northern large city, is so peculiarly a problem of parents that it deserves special thought. I am thinking of a community of perhaps 1,500 colored people, men, women and children, who occupy a city block. Their breadwinners are chauffeurs, post office clerks, porters and servants, with a few teachers and professional men. The median wage is $1,777 a year.

They represent; therefore, the upper laboring class of American city Negroes. They are well-dressed and make a favorable appearance upon the Street. There are probably very few among them who cannot read and write, and most of them have grammar and some high school and college educations. In noise and cleanliness, they are noticeably better than the average Harlem block, although there is some tendency to talk from windows and vermin is in some of the apartments.

There must be two or three hundred children belonging to this group, and it is with these children that the group makes the least favorable impression. The children are well-dressed; they go to school; most of them look well-nourished; they have a specially supervised playground. Nevertheless, as a group, these children are impudent; they are impudent, discourteous and noisy to a degree seldom equalled among similar classes of people. They are much more difficult to get on with than the children of the very poor in the East Side ghettoes of New York, although there is less actual delinquency. Possibly among the miners' children of England or of South Germany or in parts of Italy, one might find an equally undisciplined group, but certainly it could not be found in France, North Germany nor West Africa.

What is the cause of this? The cause is certainly not racial. It does not arise from any conscious lack of effort in economic lines on the part of parents, but it does undoubtedly lie in the fact that these children have not been taught to respect anything.

In home conversations, the characters of all persons are torn to pieces. Naturally, the good-will and objects of all white people are matters of the deepest distrust. But not only that: it is characteristic of the present transition period of the American Negro that practically all colored persons of whatever degree are despised and rejected. There is no respect for ministers or professional men, and, of course, even less for laborers.

The result is that these children are growing up without any teaching of courtesy, without any regard for age or essential humanity. They are not courteous to their own parents. How much less are they courteous to the parents of other children? The problem of their discipline in school and on the street and in the home is overwhelming in its complexity.

The cause of this is their parents' attitude. In the first place, the parents have little time for the home training of their children because they are hard-pressed to earn a living. Many of them are absent during the day, and when they return tired from work, they are only too willing to be rid of their children. The children are quite used to being outdoors after dark and they receive little formal home training in those things which the school cannot give. Girls are given a dangerous freedom, and license which no Youth Movement can defend. Moreover, in their desire to have their children self-respecting and not obsequious and fearful, parents encourage truculence and rudeness which they mistake for natural self assertion.

Not all of the children are thus rude and bad-mannered but naturally the best trained tend to approximate the manners not only of the worst trained of this community but of the bad children of all the surrounding blocks where standards are often the lowest. In the absence then of parental insistence and care, the greater part of the training of these children comes inevitably from the gutter.

The catastrophe of all this is two fold. First of all, the surrounding and dominant white world will put up with this impudence on the part of colored children to a certain point and then they will clap them in jail. The children will not deserve jail. They are not bad. They are simply untaught and their ideals are all awry. But in jail they will learn crime and thus a considerable proportion of them are destined to be driven into real crime almost before they reach manhood and womanhood.

In the second place, in their contact with their own colored people, they will, as they grow up, increase the inner hatreds, jealousies and feuds; the difficulties of attaining group action, the difficulties of maintaining proper and pleasant social intercourse. They will increase the present tendencies to boundless and ill-natured gossip, which is the conversation they are so often and largely reared upon. They will increasingly respect nothing and no body because they will believe that nothing is respectable. Their conversation today betrays a cynicism and belief in evil and lies and wrong, which leaves their childhood void of faith and romance and will make their adult life bitter and pessimistic.

Here is a problem. It is stated merely with only vague indications of the lines of betterment. But chiefly, this word emphasizes the tremendous problem of the next Negro city generation. A problem which one can easily see among the better colored people of New York and Philadelphia, of Indianapolis and Chicago, of Pittsburgh and Baltimore, and all of our larger cities. It calls for thoughtful individual and cooperative action.

∽ **63** ∽

The Negro's Industrial Plight

This number of THE CRISIS is given up mainly to our problem of earning a living. The Secretary of Labor gives us a few vague words of good will. The Communists declare that we cannot effectively use our consuming power; that we can not build a segregated Negro economy and that any at tempt to co-operate with white employers will subject us to Negro exploiters. In answer to this, Mr. Holsey tells us of an attempt by group co-operation to build up Negro retail business. How far do these things point to a way out?

We can only judge this fairly by the aid of additional information. Two books will supply much of this:

One is "The Coming of Industry to the South," published by the Annals of the American Academy of Political Science at Philadelphia and edited by William J. Carson. The other is Herman Feldman's "Racial Factors in American Industry," published by Harper and Brothers.

The first book is a tremendous exposition of the industrial revolution which has come over the South. The South of Booker T. Washington is disappearing. The South today is becoming industrialized with a speed that few Americans realize. Eight thousand million dollars worth of manufactured produce come out of the South yearly, consisting of tobacco, cotton and oil, furniture and other products, iron and steel, fertilizers and chemicals, paper, cement, railroad equipment, and hundreds of other things. Today, the South is one of the chief industrial centers of the nation. It uses 72% of all the cotton processed in American mills and has 53% of the active spindles. The South is one of the main centers of iron ore in the world and a center of steel production, not simply from its own but from imported ores. The coal industry of the South produces nearly half the bituminous coal of the nation.

But all this pales before the power production of the South;—the harnessing of water power for present and future production of electric power. The Southern Power province is producing today a greater proportion of total power by water than any states east of the Rocky Mountains. It has a total output of nearly thirteen thousand million kilowatt hours and by 1950 this will exceed sixty thousand million!

Add to this certain terrible facts: a working class, largely unorganized and to a considerable degree illiterate; this working class divided into two sections, of which the darker third has been disfranchised by the white workers, both in politics and industry, works for the lowest wages, is largely unskilled, and yet furnishes an enormous potential supply of industrial workers. To this, add the general well-known facts that the skilled worker in industry is being gradually replaced by the mass worker, working on machines and on materials owned by great aggregations of capital.

In other words, the South is growing in industry perhaps faster than any other part of the industrialized world. By the condition of its laboring class and by the power of its capitalistic exploiters, it is headed toward making every mistake and committing every crime that organized industry has committed in the past. It is unfettered by democracy, unappalled by considerations of law and order, and unafraid of poverty and crime. And all this is true despite the fact that education among black and white is increasing in the South and the forces of civilization and culture expanding. The point remains that industry is outdistancing everything.

What is the result of all this? Herman Feldman studies it in his excellent book. He writes that, to the Negro, "The whole South presents a series of rigid barriers, social, economic and political, influenced by actual regulations and supported by the almost united public sentiment." In the

North these formal measures are nominally less obvious and sometimes absent, but discrimination there is found everywhere. And the author concludes in regard to the Negro:

"Between the two extremes of hopeless resignation and unwarranted anticipation of trouble are found every degree of sanity and poise. It is in these middle ranges that the foundation for racial cooperation can be laid. But the sooner the causes for the more exaggerated reactions of the Negro are re moved, the firmer will that foundation be."

Considering these facts, what is the way out?

First of all, Negroes must realize the present crisis: no easy going optimism, no silly prayers, no idiotic dependence on white charity will avail. The initiative is with us. What shall we do?

THE CRISIS will welcome suggestions, and ventures here with all modesty to suggest its own.

1. Group effort to retain present employment, enter new fields of industrial technique, expand retail business, and live within our incomes; recognizing clearly that is only a transitional and temporary effort which does not attack the matter of our gaining real power and economic independence in the face of the organized monopoly of credit and concentration of power in transportation, mining, trade and manufacture.

2. Beyond this, definite and far-reaching effort to organize our consuming power. We are not as helpless here as some think. Twelve million people have a tremendous consuming power, even without direct voice or ownership in basic industries. We spend at least a thousand million dollars a year and probably twice that in rent, food, clothes, furniture, amusement and other things. The place, method, character and amount of this expenditure is not wholly but very considerably a matter of our own judgment and discretion. If we once make a religion of our determination to spend our meager income so far as possible only in such ways as will bring us employment consideration and opportunity the possibilities before us are enormous. This was shown in the Chicago Whip campaign last year and that was but a bare beginning. A nation twice as large as Portugal, Holland or Sweden is not powerless—is not merely a suppliant beggar for crumbs— it is mighty economic power when it gets vision enough to use its strength.

3. As we carefully organize our power as consumers, we must lend every effort to establish an economic General Staff. There is, for instance, no reason in the world why American Negroes, beginning with the cottonfield and working through the cotton gin, the cotton mill, the wholesale distributor and the retail store, should not furnish themselves with clothing in the face of the organized competition and discrimination of the surrounding economic world. This may mean some difference in fashions of dress and quality of material. It would mean undoubtedly a spiritual revolution in Negro thought and action. But it need not mean violence nor force, hatred nor economic war. The philosophy of Booker T.

Washington must turn toward wide intensive economic research in our colleges; repeated and determined actual and practical experiments; careful concentration and organization. It is a way out but it demands for its accomplishment the organization of education, the co-operation of the Negro church, without reference to creed, and the organization of intelligent sacrifice among masses of men such as the world has seldom seen but which is nevertheless patently possible.

ᨒ **64** ᨒ

Christmas Festivities

In the last years, there has arisen in the United States a new sort of Christmas celebration centering in the annual meetings of various Negro Greek Letter fraternities and sororities. I have read and heard echoes of them before. This year, I participated in the celebration at Cincinnati.

The oldest Negro fraternity, the Alpha Phi Alpha, held its twenty-fifth anniversary. A sorority, the Alpha Kappa Alpha, met simultaneously at the University of Cincinnati; and the local chapters of the Delta Sigma Theta and Omega Psi Phi, joined in the festivities. There must have been altogether four hundred delegates and visitors who, together with the local participants, made up at least one thousand persons. There were business meetings, lectures, balls, banquets, and a pilgrimage to the grave of Paul Laurence Dunbar. Looking at it all dispassionately, what can one say of the advantages and disadvantages of such meetings?

On the credit side must certainly be put: the meeting of young educated Negroes of both sexes from nearly every state in the Union and from all the leading institutions of learning.

The business of organization, election, and setting of aims and standards.

A peculiar sense of the possibilities of colored and Negro beauty. There could be nothing more marvelous than the dark skins and lovely gowns under the lights and music of Greystone Hall. From all this came a certain new joy and hope, a feeling of power and satisfaction, a determination to look forward.

On the negative side there was little visible drinking and few if any excesses or cases of unsuitable conduct.

These are certainly great and important advantages. On the debit side must be put, however, these things:

The cost of the meeting. It must have cost $1,000 in rentals for the various places of entertainment; the travel, board and hotel expenses for four hundred people and the expense of dress, particularly of the gowns for the women, added much more.

It is difficult to see how these conferences could have cost less than $7,500, and they probably exceeded $10,000.

The resultant problem is not a matter of saving all this expense and doing away with the conferences. That would be a calamity. They are valuable. They may grow to be of indispensable value to the Negro race in America. But there is a very grave question as to whether the same thing could not be accomplished at half or even a tithe of the expense.

Our racial problem of acquaintanceship and inspiration is so tremendous and calls for so much repeated effort on our part, that it is worth while studying gravely this question of economy and costs in order that we may even increase the occasions and the advantages of such meetings.

Finally, there is the problem of snobbishness and class distinctions. These organizations set apart from the mass, the educated and fortunate, is a closed clan. They say in defense that the line drawn is not the artificial one of birth or the accidental one of wealth, and yet in a day when education is not free and depends so largely on chance and money, how far can we make its lack a deadline?

On the other hand, will not our emancipation depend on united action of those of us who know and can think? Wherefore, the question stands: Are our fraternities and sororities growing centers of leadership and ideal or more matters of dress and gayety?

There were two answers at Cincinnati: the A.K.A. gave a girl a thousand dollars to study abroad. The Alpha Phi Alpha appropriated $1,800 for its educational campaign; but it was over the protest of a young gentleman who complained:

"I thought this was a social organization!"

~ 65 ~

To Your Tents, O Israel

With twelve million Negroes in America and at least ten millions in the adjacent West Indies, is the black race economically helpless? These two groups as consumers must at the very lowest estimate spend ten billion dollars a year. Perhaps the larger part of this expenditure is compulsory, and we have small choice as to where and how it should be spent. But there must be hundreds of millions where we do have choice in the direction of its expenditure. This expenditure can and must, if we survive in America, be so directed as to employ our own muscle and brains in the production of the goods and services which we need. Such production demands skill, but what skill, and how shall we gain this skill?

The way is clear. Our colleges are or may be centers of information and learning. They should study the facts concerning the consumption of goods by American Negroes and West Indians. They should measure and make clear our economic demands. We have industrial schools. Those industrial schools should train young people, so that they would have skill to do the kind of work which is necessary to satisfy our demands. Their aims should not be simply to do the work and make the goods which white folks demand. Their aim should not be simply to train for decadent and outworn trades where there is a lessening demand for workers. Their main object should be to train Negroes to supply Negroes' needs.

When we know just what our demand for goods and services is and when we have people trained in modern technique to furnish these things, we in turn can furnish the capital. That capital is simply a part of the money which we spend. We furnish such capital today to the white industrial world. There is no reason on earth why it should not be spent to establish a black industrial world.

There are wise and careful students who claim that no such racial economy is possible. I take no stock in their pessimism. It not only is possible but it is already beginning and it only needs scientific guidance and technical skill to make it spread. What has been done by separate nations, protected by tariffs, can be done by separate groups, protected by a vast sense of desperate need.

When these goods are made, they can be distributed by Negro business, built up like the C. M. A. stores. Such stores will meet increasing competition from white stores, and they are at the mercy of the owners of white capital. Nevertheless, they can meet this competition, and they can substitute colored capital for white capital, if they will start upon one path and that path demands the abolition absolutely of private profit: the willingness of voting Negro managers of brains and skill to work for low, definite wage, instead of trying to emulate the whites' desire for millions. We must embrace the ideal of poverty—not poverty that calls for dirt, disease and pain, but poverty that definitely and decisively puts aside the ideal of luxury, waste and inordinate wealth. To the ideal of poverty, we must add that of service, dedicated to the rescue of twenty-two millions of human beings who are bound to us by blood and tradition. Here is an economic program for times of depression, and it will work, if we work it.

To Your Tents, O Israel!

~ **66** ~

Young Voters

The Editor of the *Louisiana Weekly* writes:

"I shall appreciate very much a letter from you encouraging the young colored men of our city to increase their interest in politics. The older men have discouraged them and refused to act with them because of envy. A letter from you to the young men, urging them to carry on in spite of this selfish handicap, would go a long way toward kindling hope anew."

The situation of an intelligent, young colored man who wants to use his right to vote effectively in the South is exceedingly difficult. He is not admitted to the Democratic Party, and can not easily take part in their white primary. This is still true despite the continued efforts of the N. A. A. C. P. to stop it, and thus to break up one party government in the South.

On the other hand, the Republican Party in the South is not a party; it is mainly a group of selfish men, white and black, who are using the party organization for personal gain. Sometimes, under strong and honest leaders, like Cuney of Texas or Cohen of Louisiana, this group may be strengthened and organized so as to exercise some real political power. But when this group falls into the hands of mediocre self-seekers, or into the hands of local white politicians who use it simply for personal aggrandisement or who are in secret alliance with the Democratic Party, then the situation of the young and honest Negro voter is indeed difficult.

Nevertheless, there are certain clear lines of effort. First of all, the Negro must register and fight continually for the right of registration. The situation in Louisiana in this respect is disgraceful and the Negroes of Louisiana ought literally to pound the courts with cases until they get the right to register. One or two thoroughly arranged cases before the Supreme Court of the United States would show that of 415,000 Negroes in Louisiana in 1930, 21 years of age and over, less than 3,000 are registered, and this in spite of the fact that nearly 300,000 can read and write.

All Negroes who register should vote. First, they should seek to vote in the Democratic primary as this is the only voting that really counts. If they are denied this right, they should be especially careful to vote in those elections where the primary cannot function, as, for instance, in bond elections, and various referenda. In all bond issues, they should vote "no," unless they are able to get a categorical promise concerning the use of the money to be raised. They should especially vote for local officials and on local issues whenever and wherever they get a chance, and they should form political organizations with the specific object of equalizing taxation, stopping discrimination in civil life and stopping discrimination in appropriations for streets, schools and parks; increasing efforts in sanitation, and getting rid of venal and prejudiced public officials.

They should write strong letters of protest, regularly and often to the papers, to the Congressmen, and to the President of the United States. They should thus build up an active and interested political life and back it by just as many votes as they are able to cast.

⌒ **67** ⌒

Wilberforce

Wilberforce is not a university and has doubtful academic standing. It consists of two interlocked but really separate institutions. The State institution, supported by the State of Ohio, consists of 234 acres of land, some ten or twelve modern buildings, including an electric light plant, well-equipped shops, recitation halls, dormitories, an auditorium, a gymnasium, hospital and laundry. Its income from the state for buildings and current expenses, amount to nearly $300,000 a year, and it has thirty-four teachers.

The University is owned by the African M. E. Church, which bought the campus, now consisting of one hundred acres, in 1853, with help from the white Methodists. It has practically no endowment (less than $25,000), and depends on church appropriations, which fluctuate incalculably. It has three modern buildings and twenty-two teachers, most of whom receive the larger part of their salary from the State Department for teaching state students. The upkeep of the university campus, the lighting of the grounds and many of the current expenses, are borne by the state.

The President of the University is largely a figurehead, appointed by a church board of twenty-one trustees, and his only real power is his membership on the board which controls the state institution. This Board has a Superintendent, who has the control of the State Department, but his position is wholly without prestige and he is so hampered by the Church and the State that no first-class man can keep the position.

The State is in a quandary. Its funds in the past have been wasted and some times stolen. It can not give up the institution because of the millions of dollars which it has invested there, while the Church cannot support a real university separate from the State.

There are three possibilities: 1. To close the church school; 2. To close the state school; 3. To merge the two completely. To my mind the only solution is a merger of the State institution and the Church school into a great school of engineering and liberal arts, with secondary and even primary schools attached, which might serve the needs of the whole country. Such a program would meet opposition of those who would say that the State of Ohio is establishing a "Jim-Crow" institution. But that is exactly what the State of Ohio has already done, and the difference would be that the new university would be first-rate instead of third-rate. Next, opposition would come from the African M. E. Church, which would lose its leading institution of learning. But it deserves to lose it since it can not or will not support it.

Charles Wesley, the Howard University historian, was recently offered the presidency of Wilberforce. He looked over the situation and declined the office and he was wise. Richard Wright of Philadelphia has since accepted the presidency. Richard Wright is fifty-four years of age; he is a Doctor of Philosophy of the University of Pennsylvania and is a man of training and shrewdness. He has twice been a prominent candidate for the Bishopric in his church and has been one of its General Officers for twenty-three years.

He faces, in accepting the presidency of Wilberforce, two possible paths: He can, if he will, use the prominence which the position will give him and, like Bishop Gregg, make this position a stepping-stone to the Bishopric, leaving the Wilberforce problem substantially where it is now. Or, he can begin a far-sighted program to make Wilberforce one united university, supported by the State of Ohio, and equal in academic standing and the efficiency of its teaching force to any State university in the country. He can thus sever Wilberforce entirely from the dead hand of church control and from petty state politics which are today strangling it to death.

The carrying out of such a program will be no child's play; it may in the long run, kill Richard Wright, and one or more of his successors. The church will never forgive him but he will not need its forgiveness. Large numbers of American Negroes will antagonize him and accuse him of surrendering to segregation; but if he starts this program there will come generations, white and black, who will call him Blessed.

⌁ 68 ⌁

For Unto Us a Child Is Born

The man to whom the world is boredom and humdrum routine, easily forgets its miracles: the waxing and waning of the seasons, the marvel of sunrise and the glory of sunset. But even one who finds life tasteless or funny can not without trembling and amazement face the miracle of birth.

Comes, first, the ecstacy of the pain; the shattering, the tearing, wrenching physical agony, such as one reads of afar, but seldom in a lifetime hears within one's own doors. Then there is the new born child, an astonishing perfect microcosm of a bewildering universe; with lacework of fingers and toy toes, and great enveloping, disconcerting, unfathomable eyes. So fragile a bit of machinery yet working perfectly, rhythmically with blood, breath, heartbeat and moving muscle. What is Machinery to this Miracle? The cynic who is hard-boiled; who knows that life is cheating and singing and hating, stops whether he will or no and worships at a cradle.

We colored folk of this generation are foregoing the joy of children in wide degree. We recoil at the beastly pain, the primitive dirt, the endless work, the high cost. We remember in our own family hordes of unkempt, squalling brats; the slattern, haggard mother, the overworked, irritable father. When with discriminating care we choose the pleasures of life, in larger and larger numbers, we are choosing everything but children.

This younger generation,—not the youngest, but people of twenty-five, thirty, forty,—want comfortable homes; a small car; a chance to entertain friends now and then with cards and lunch; the theatre and the cinema; some travel, books and study. And yet those who have chosen this come singularly soon to recognize gaps. There is nothing like the tragedy of childless age. There comes rather suddenly to the man, and particularly to the woman of forty, a cutting off from present and future life which they cannot at first understand, and deeply resent. They are no longer young and they have fewer and fewer young companions.

Youth and children about them speak a new and unintelligible language. Strange antagonisms and petty criticism arises between them and children and youth. At last, as they grow still older, they realize that before death they are dead, because they are separated from a new and re-created world.

There is no need of deceiving one's self at the cost of children. Macy's advertises a baby carriage at $59. The young mother in my family is continually astonished at the time the new baby consumes in mere eating. She has no sooner fed it, than "Wow!", she must feed it again. There is washing and dressing and undressing and bathing. Nursemaids are for the rich and at that costly in more ways than one. Even laundries are dangerous to health and pocketbook. And this is but the beginning of trouble. "You will never sleep quietly again," said a mother to the mother of my firstborn, who had complained of the 5 A.M. waking habits of her child. Cost, care, work, worry, all these children demand and must get.

Yet those who would re-make the world; those who have within the unearthly joy and verve of the creative artist, can accomplish nothing that compares with giving birth to, molding and raising a generation of men. With thought and effort, with pattern and ideal, the world in these coming children becomes a new and possible and explicable thing. Not all men, not all women, either by heritage or inclination, are suited to this high task. Few mothers have the physical strength, and few fathers the time and money for the raising of more than one or two children. But those who have the vision and the power, and who can bring a few children into the world, and give those children what children ought to have, in food and manners, clothes, training and ideals,—these are the ones and the only ones whose eyes behold the Glory of the Coming of the Lord,— whether He comes in Papal Rome or Soviet Russia or the low swamps of Mississippi.

~~ **69** ~~

Toward a New Racial Philosophy

A college graduate came to me yesterday and asked: "What has the N.A.A.C.P. published concerning the present problems of the Negro, and especially of young Negroes just out of college?"

I started to answer with stereotyped remarks; and then I said suddenly, "Nothing."

The N.A.A.C.P., beginning nearly a quarter of a century ago, formulated on the basis of the problems which then faced Negroes, a clear-cut and definite program. This program we have followed ever since with unusual success for it has expressed during these years the aspirations and lines of effort among 12 millions and their friends.

Today the situation has changed enormously in its trend, objects and details, and there is both need and widespread demand for a re-examination of what is called the Negro problem from the point of view of the middle of the 20th Century. THE CRISIS realizes this and it proposes during 1933 to discuss the present Negro problems from 12 points of view. Tentatively, these points seem to us now to be something as follows, although we may change many of them:

1. *Birth.* The physical survival of the Negro in America is discussed in this number.
2. *Health.* In February, we shall ask: How can the infant mortality, the great loss from sickness and the general death rate among Negroes, be lowered? What is the duty of colored physicians toward Negro health? What is the extent of available hospitalization? How can we extend the life term and meet such enemies of our race as tuberculosis, pneumonia, syphilis and cancer.

Later, we shall treat our problems in something like the following order:

3. *The Home.* Should a Negro family live in the city or in the country, in the North or in the South, in a single house or in an apartment? And on what facts should an individual family base its decision? How can housework be reduced and systematized? Must paid household help be an ideal? Should Negroes seek to live in their own neighborhoods or in white neighborhoods?
4. *Occupations.* What kinds of work do Negroes want to do and what kind can they do and what kinds are they allowed to do? How far shall they be farmers, artisans, artists, professional men, merchants or financiers? What is their relation to the great economic and industrial changes going on now in the world of work? How far are they

being displaced by machines and technique and by new organizations of capital? Can they achieve a place of power and efficiency in
the present oligarchy of white capital or in the present labor union
or in any future industrial democracy?

5. *Education.* Should a colored child be sent to a white school or to a
colored school? Should it be educated in the North or South or even
abroad? What should be the kind and aim and length its education?
Should the boy or girl go to college? Should they go to technical
school? Should they go to professional school? Should they be
apprenticed to manual work? Should they depend for their education upon experience? How far is their education dependent upon
contact with the white group and its larger opportunities? How
shall the cost of education be met?

6. *Income.* What should be the ideal and standards of living among colored people? How much income must the average colored family
have and how should it be spent? How early can our people get
married? What things must they regard as luxuries and beyond
them and what as necessities? Shall we aim to be rich or make
poverty an ideal?

7. *Discrimination.* Accepting race color discrimination as a fact which
despite all effort is bound to last in some form at least through this
generation, if longer, what shall be our general attitude toward it?
How can we avoid in its face an inferiority complex? How far must
we be belligerent or acquiescent? Can we meet discrimination by
ignoring it or by fighting it? When shall we fight and how shall we
fight, and what is the cost of effective fighting? What types of organized effort are needed in this fighting? How much of co-operation
with the whites must be sought or accepted? How far must we be
willing recipients of white co-operation, philanthropy and charity?
How can we escape discrimination by emigration to other states,
countries or continents?

8. *Government and Law.* How far must we be obedient to government
and law when they are unfair to us? Can we adopt an attitude of
defiance? How can we change our legal status or reform evil administration? Is revolution by force advisable, possible or probable? Can
we use our right to vote, curtailed as it is, for our emancipation and
change of status? Should we vote for the Republican Party or the
Democratic Party; or for Socialists or Communists? Or should we
adopt a method of independent opportunism in our voting? In
states and cases where we are disfranchised, what shall we do about
it? Is it worth while to register, even though we cannot vote or cannot vote effectively? Should we join the Democratic White Primary
in the South? Should we in our voting keep our racial needs and
demands in mind, or should we have an eye upon the good of the

majority of the nation? And what shall we do in case these two ideals clash? How far are we criminal and anti social? What causes and what can prevent crime? How are our criminals treated?

9. *Race Pride.* How far shall American Negroes remember and preserve their history, keep track of their ancestry, build up a racial literature and a group patriotism? What does loyalty to the race mean? How far shall we have distinctively race organizations, and how far shall we seek to join organizations regardless of race? If we do have organizations, what sorts are needed for the various ends we have in view? How far do present organizations fill our need or how shall they be changed and what new ones must come? Shall we imitate and duplicate, on our side of the color line, the organizations that white folk have? Especially, of what use are secret fraternities and how can their functioning be made to help our general uplift? What is our relation to Africa, to the West Indies, to Asia, to the colored world in general? Is it profitable or advisable consciously to build up by race pride a nation within a nation, or races within the world?

10. *Religion.* We are by tradition a religious people and the "old-time religion" still has a strong hold on our masses. The present Negro church more nearly represents the mass of people than any other organization and its ministers are its spokesmen. Nevertheless, the number of colored people who do not go to church is large and growing. Is this right, and if not, what is the remedy? What should be the function of the Negro church? How far should there be churches divided along the color line? What is the present status of creeds? How far do we dare disturb simple religious faith, "evangelical" dogma and ordinary religious superstition? Should a man join a church and work with it if he does not believe completely in its dogma? Can the Negro church be made a center and unit of racial and cultural and social development? Will Creed and Culture, Reason and Faith, Science and Superstition clash as in other groups and ages? What should be the attitude of the Negro church toward white churches? How far should they co-operate in missions and philanthropy? How far is the white church, with its greater wealth and experience, pauperizing certain colored churches? What is the remedy? Will Christianity abolish or emphasize the Color Line? How can we, with or without religion, encourage courtesy, honor, unselfishness, sacrifice, self restraint, the ideals of the higher spiritual life, the recognition of beauty in Art and deed?

11. *Social Contacts.* Is the method of advance among colored people today a building up of social classes so that the educated, the rich, the well-to-do and the moral can separate themselves from the poor, the ignorant and the criminal? Can this class-building tech-

nique of civilization be ignored in our case and something better substituted? How far must colored people try to accumulate wealth and become the employers of other Negroes and even of whites? Must we have a bourgeoisie for defense in a bourgeois world? What should be our social standards in marriage? Should we encourage our children to inter-marry with white folk, or at any rate, to increase the social contacts between colored and white people with the ultimate ideal of marriage? And if not, where can the line be drawn? In the absence of social contact with more favored persons and races, is it possible for culture among us to grow or to grow as fast? Should we demand and practice social equality? Should we regard the development of lower masses among our people as inevitable, and if so, what should be our attitude toward these masses? What should be our attitude toward social questions beyond our own racial orders, toward world problems of peace and war, the labor movement, the status of women, education, health, social and economic reform?

12. *Recreation.* How can we get the relaxation of play and recreation without having it spoiled by discrimination along the color line? Should we travel, and if we travel, should we seek or avoid white people? Where can we spend our vacations? Where can we bathe in the ocean unmolested and not insulted? What should be our attitude toward discrimination in transport, rail road trains, buses and hotels? Where shall we be willing to sit in theatres and at concerts? If we seek recreation only in those places where there is no discrimination, will that help uplift by increasing our pleasure or will it encourage the growth of further discrimination?

The above is a tentative outline of 12 sets of problems. Further reflection will doubtless change and add to them. There are doubtless important omissions. THE CRISIS would welcome from readers suggestions as to these heads.

In the meantime, it is our present plan to publish a discussion of one of these subjects in each of the next 12 numbers of THE CRISIS, which will exhibit different points of view concerning the main problems suggested. We would be glad to have contributions or suggestions as to persons who might contribute to these symposiums. Of necessity, the contributions must be terse and to the point, and, of course, we cannot publish all. Beside the editorial statement of the problem, and papers discussing two or more sides of the problem, we are going to try to get hold of 12 pieces of fiction which will illustrate the problems humanly. We admit it is going to be a hard thing to do this.

What we want is suggested by the story this month,— "The Three Mosquitoes." Do you like it? Is it worth while? Such stories must be short,—not more than two pages of THE CRISIS,—and they must illustrate the difficulties and contradictions of each of these 12 suggested matters of thought. They must not be "defeatist:" we want them to be artistic; we want them true; but we do not propose to have every story end in a lynching or a suicide, for the simple reason that we do not believe that death is the necessary answer to any of these situations.

Finally, we welcome from everybody, terse, definite and pointed opinions, which we shall try to reflect and quote.

∾ 70 ∾

Our Health

Our death rate is without the slightest doubt a death rate due to *poverty* and *discrimination*.

What little racial factor is present is too small to be taken into account. The scientific validity of such studies is utterly vitiated by ignoring not only the social condition and environment of those measured, but by classing all persons of Negro descent as belonging to the "Negro" race no matter what their percentage of white or Indian blood. Moreover, the majority of such "scientists" has been distinctly prejudiced and determined to prove an already assumed case.

As a problem of poverty our death rate can ultimately be brought down to normal size only as our income is increased. There are no reliable figures as to the average income of Negro families but it is certain that their average is far below the minimum which social agencies have from time to time established. What shall we do about our low wage? Our inadequate income?

Meantime, there are certain matters we can stress even in our poverty:

1. Fresh air.
2. More nourishing food with less hot bread and fried greasy meat; with more vegetables, eggs, milk and greens.
3. Cleanliness in body and in crowded homes; in clothes.
4. Sleep, adequate in length and quiet.
5. The systematic use of physicians, dentists and hospitals; not simply to recover from disease but to prevent illness; especially the use of hospitals for births, severe illnesses and necessary operations.

On the other hand, an improvement in our present habits with regard to air, sleep, food, clothes and medical attention, and even increased income will not entirely settle our problem of sickness and death, so long as race discrimination continues on the lines in which we see it today. Even for those of us who are able to pay, hospital doors are today half-closed in our faces; parks, swimming pools and recreation centers often will not admit us; projects for improved housing seldom include us; and available food supply, particularly in cities, is vitiated by the custom of dumping the worst food at the highest prices into Negro districts; and police and sanitary control of our dwelling districts is universally neglected.

Finally, there can be no doubt that the atmosphere of discrimination and insult and dislike acts as a general depressant, particularly on the young people of the Negro race. In such competitions as the Atwater-Kent auditions and the national oratorical contests and the competitions for scholarships and prizes, Negroes are continually made to realize that merit with a dark skin has great difficulty in winning. The resultant inferiority complex and even counsels of despair make for lack of stamina and resistance.

Here, then, is our problem: Better income; better use of our present income; a frontal act upon race discrimination and a gospel of defiant hope.

～ 71 ～

Our Class Struggle

In the Marxist patois, the "class struggle" means the natural antagonism and war between the exploiter and the exploited; that is, between those persons who own capital in the form of machines, raw material and money, and who can command credit, and that other large mass of people who have practically nothing to sell but their labor. Between these two classes, there can be no peace because the profit of the capitalist depends on the amount of surplus value he can extract from the work of the laborer.

One no sooner states this than the expert would say immediately that there is no trace of such class struggle among American Negroes. On second thought, however, he might modify this and say that the occupational differences of American Negroes show at least the beginnings of differentiation into capitalists and laborers.

Of Negroes, 10 years of age and over in gainful occupations, there are:

Skilled laborers	331,839
Semi-skilled laborers	734,951
Farmers	873,653
Common laborers	3,374,545
Trade and Business	52,957
Professional	119,827
Civil Service	15,763
Total	5,503,535

Of the farmers, 181,016 were owners. The others were tenants. We may, therefore, say that the capitalistic class among Negroes would be among the following:

Trade and Business	52,957
Professional	119,827
Farm Owners	181,016
Civil Servants	15,763
Total	369,563

Most of these however depend for their income on labor rather than capital. Those in trade and business, include clerks, as well as about 30,000 investors of capital. And the professional men are not capitalists, except as some of them have saved money. The same thing can be said of the civil servants. The farm owners are by vast majority peasant proprietors, most of whom hire a little or no labor outside the family.

The most that can be said is that many of the people in this group have the American ambition to become rich and "independent;" to live on income rather than labor, and thus their ideology ranks them on the side of the white capitalists. On the other hand, the laborers, skilled and semi-skilled, and the tenants, are all a proletariat, exploited by white capital. One has, therefore, a rather curious arrangement, with the real class struggle not between colored classes, but rather between colored and white folk.

There is, however, an inner division that calls for attention because it emphasizes and foreshadows class distinctions within the race. And that is the existence of delinquency and dependency, of criminals and paupers. What is the extent of this class among American Negroes and what is the relation of the class to the workers and the more prosperous elements who have begun to accumulate property?

During the earlier history of the colored race, there was a natural social and class difference that came through the existence of mulattoes. In the West Indies, by French law, these mulattoes were free and often inherited wealth from their fathers. In many cases, they were carefully educated and formed a distinct social class, whose rank depended upon wealth, education and personal freedom. In the later history of the French colonies, and even more in Spanish and American colonies, persistent effort reduced this class to a semi-servile position, and it was the resentment against this that led the mulattoes to unite with the blacks in the Haitian Revolution and overthrow the whites.

In the United States, this color caste was dealt a death blow by the law that made children follow the condition of the mother, so that white fathers sold their colored children into slavery, and the mulatto ceased to be, in most cases, a free man. He inherited no property from his father and lost his right to education; although so far as he was free, he promoted schools, in centers like Washington, Charleston and New Orleans.

The color caste idea persisted after Emancipation, but was gradually driven out by the new economic organization. In this new economy there arose the criminals and paupers;—the direct result of the poverty of a suddenly emancipated class who had little or no capital.

The apparent criminality, however, of the Negro race is greatly exaggerated for two reasons: First, accusation of crime was used systematically in the South to keep Negroes in serfdom after the Civil War; and secondly, Negroes receive but scant justice in the courts. Most writers, today, have assumed on the basis of statistics, that because the Negro population in jails and penitentiary is proportionately much larger than the white population, that, therefore, the Negro is unusually criminal. But as Thorsten Sellin has pointed out in his note on the Negro criminal, "The American Negro lacks education and earthly goods. He has had very little political experience and industrial training. His contact with city life has been unfortunate, for it has forced him into the most dilapidated and vicious areas of our great cities. Like a shadow over his whole existence lies the oppressive race prejudice of his white neighbor, restricting his activities and thwarting his ambitions. It would be extraordinary, indeed, if this group were to prove more law-abiding than the white, which enjoys more fully the advantages of a civilization the Negro has helped to create."

On the other hand, the peculiar result of the assumed fact that Negroes are criminal is that within the race, a Negro accused or convicted of a crime immediately suffers a penalty, not only of ostracism, but lack of sympathy. Negroes make comparatively little effort to defend the accused; they do not systematically look after them; the churches take little interest in delinquents, and the general attitude of the race is one of irritation toward these members of their groups who have brought the whole race into disrepute. This makes a peculiarly bitter feeling among the unfortunate of the race and the more successful.

So far as dependents are concerned, again the material which we have to measure the amount of dependents is inconclusive and unsatisfactory. There are such differences in policy in various states, such difference in treatment that it is hard to say what the condition is. It would seem, by a study of states where there is a substantial uniform policy toward the feeble-minded and paupers, regardless of race, that there is a higher rate of institutionization among Negroes than among whites. And this would be natural unless corrected by taking into account the unequal economic and social condition.

Here again within the race, there is a certain resentment against a colored person who fails to progress as rapidly as the Negro thinks a black man must. When, therefore, such a person becomes a subject of charity and must be put into an institution, he is regarded not so much as unfortunate as in some vague way blame worthy. He hinders the general advance and even if he is not at fault, his existence is a misfortune. The real question, then, in the Negro race, is how far the group can and should assume responsibility for its delinquents and dependents, and cultivate sympathy and help for these unfortunates, and how far in this way differentiation into class can keep economic exploitation from becoming a settled method of social advance.

ꙮ 72 ꙮ

Our Music

If a trained Negro singer gives a concert in New York, or a trained colored chorus sings there or else where in the North, there is a type of comment, always made concerning their singing which is stereotyped and inevitable and repeated from year to year ad nauseum. For instance, Olin Downes, of The New York Times, voiced it after hearing the Fisk University Choir at Carnegie Hall; and asks the listener to "compare last night's singing of spirituals with the manner of the singing in the drama of 'Porgy,' or the performances of the Hall Johnson Choir in 'Green Pastures,' which contributed so memorably to the effect of that production. Or let him attend a real religious revival in Harlem, as the writer has done. He will hear hymns and spirituals, but they will have an emotion that was not to be felt last night. That was one thing. Quite another thing is the wildness, the melancholy, the intense religious feeling communicated when Negroes sing in the sacred spirit and the uncorrupted manner of their race."

All this is to our humble opinion pure and unadulterated nonsense. What it really means is that Negroes must not be allowed to attempt anything more than the frenzy of the primitive, religious revival, "Listen to the Lambs" according to Dett, or "Deep River," as translated by Burleigh, or any attempt to sing Italian music or German music, in some inexplicable manner, leads them off their preserves and is not "natural." To which the answer is, Art is not natural and is not supposed to be natural. And just because it is not natural, it may be great Art. The Negro chorus has a right to sing music of any sort it likes and to be judged by its accomplishment rather than by what foolish critics think that it ought to be doing. It is to be trusted that our leaders in music, holding on to the beautiful heritage of the past, will not on that account, either be coerced or frightened into taking all music for their province and showing the world how to sing.

~ **73** ~

The Negro College

*This is part of an address on "The Field and Function of a Negro College", deliv-
ered at the annual alumni reunion during commencement week at Fisk
University last June. The complete address has been issued in pamphlet form by
the University.*

It has been said many times that a Negro University is nothing more
and nothing less than a university. Quite recently one of the great leaders
of education in the United States, Abraham Flexner, said something of
that sort concerning Howard. As President of the Board of Trustees, he
said he was seeking to build not a Negro university, but a University. And
by those words he brought again before our eyes the ideal of a great institution of learning which becomes a center of universal culture. With all
good will toward them that say such words—it is the object of this paper
to insist that there can be no college for Negroes which is not a Negro college and that while an American Negro university, just like a German or
Swiss university may rightly aspire to a universal culture unhampered by
limitations of race and culture, yet it must start on the earth where we sit
and not in the skies whither we aspire. May I develop this thought.

In the first place, we have got to remember that here in America, in the
year 1933, we have a situation which cannot be ignored. There was a time
when it seemed as though we might best attack the Negro problem by
ignoring its most unpleasant features. It was not and is not yet in good
taste to speak generally about certain facts which characterize our situation in America. We are politically ham-strung. We have the greatest difficulty in getting suitable and remunerative work. Our education is more
and more not only being confined to our own schools but to a segregated
public school system far below the average of the nation with one-third of
our children continuously out of school. And above all, and this we like
least to mention, we suffer social ostracism which is so deadening and
discouraging that we are compelled either to lie about it or to turn our
faces to the red flag of revolution. It consists of studied and repeated and
emphasized public insult of the sort which during all the long history of
the world has led men to kill or be killed. And in the full face of any effort
which any black man may make to escape this ostracism for himself,
stands this flaming sword of racial doctrine which will distract his effort
and energy if it does not lead him to spiritual suicide.

We boast and have right to boast of our accomplishment between the
days that I studied here and this 45th Anniversary of my graduation. It is
a calm appraisal of fact to say that the history of modern civilization can-

not surpass if it can parallel the advance of American Negroes in every essential line of culture in these years. And yet, when we have said this we must have the common courage honestly to admit that every step we have made forward has been greeted by a step backward on the part of the American public in caste, in tolerance, mob law and racial hatred.

I need but remind you that when I graduated from Fisk there was no "Jim Crow" car in Tennessee and I saw Hunter of '89 once sweep a brakeman aside at the Union Station and escort a crowd of Fisk students into the first-class seats for which they had paid. There was no legal disfranchisement and a black Fiskite sat in the Legislature; and while the Chancellor of the Vanderbilt University had annually to be re-introduced to the President of Fisk, yet no white Southern group presumed to dictate the internal social life of this institution.

Manifestly with all that can be said, pro and con, and in extenuation, and by way of excuse and hope, this is the situation and we know it. There is no human way by which these facts can be ignored. We cannot do our daily work, sing a song or write a book or carry on a university and act as though these things were not.

If this is true, then no matter how much we may dislike the statement, the American Negro problem is and must be the center of the Negro American university. It has got to be. You are teaching Negroes. There is no use pretending that you are teaching Chinese or that you are teaching white Americans or that you are teaching citizens of the world. You are teaching American Negroes in 1933, and they are the subjects of a caste system in the Republic of the United States of America and their life problem is primarily this problem of caste.

Upon these foundations, therefore, your university must start and build. Nor is the thing so entirely unusual or unheard of as it sounds. A university in Spain is not simply a university. It is a Spanish university. It is a university located in Spain. It uses the Spanish language. It starts with Spanish history and makes conditions in Spain the starting point of its teaching. Its education is for Spaniards,—not for them as they may be or ought to be, but as they are with their present problems and disadvantages and opportunities.

In other words, the Spanish university is founded and grounded in Spain, just as surely as a French university is French. There are some people who have difficulty in apprehending this very clear truth. They assume, for instance, that the French university is in a singular sense universal, and is based on a comprehension and inclusion of all mankind and of their problems. But it is not so, and the assumption that it is arises simply because so much of French culture has been built into universal civilization. A French university is founded in France; it uses the French language and assumes a knowledge of French history. The present problems of the French people are its major problems and it becomes universal only so far as other peoples of the world comprehend and are at one with France in its mighty and beautiful history.

In the same way, a Negro university in the United States of America begins with Negroes. It uses that variety of the English idiom which they understand; and above all, it is founded or it should be founded on a knowledge of the history of their people in Africa and in the United States, and their present condition. Without white-washing or translating wish into fact, it begins with that; and then it asks how shall these young men and women be trained to earn a living and live life under the circumstances in which they find themselves or with such changing of those circumstances as time and work and determination will permit.

Is this statement of the field of a Negro university a denial of aspiration or a change from older ideals? I do not think it is, although I admit in my own mind some change of thought and modification of method. The system of learning which bases its self upon the actual condition of certain classes and groups of human beings is tempted to suppress a minor premise of fatal menace. It proposes that the knowledge given and the methods pursued in such institutions of learning shall be for the definite object of perpetuating present conditions or of leaving their amelioration in the hands of and at the initiative of other forces and other folk. This was the great criticism that those of us who fought for higher education of Negroes thirty years ago, brought against the industrial school.

The industrial school founded itself and rightly upon the actual situation of American Negroes and said: "What can be done to change this situation?" And its answer was: "A training in technique and method such as would incorporate the disadvantaged group into the industrial organization of the country, and in that organization the leaders of the Negro had perfect faith. Since that day the industrial machine has cracked and groaned. Its technique has changed faster than any school could teach; the relations of capital and labor have increased in complication and it has become so clear that Negro poverty is not primarily caused by ignorance of technical knowledge that the industrial school has almost surrendered its program.

In opposition to that, the opponents of college training in those earlier years said: "What black men need is the broader and more universal training so that they can apply the general principle of knowledge to the particular circumstances of their condition."

Here again was the indubitable truth but incomplete truth. The technical problem lay in the method of teaching this broader and more universal truth and here just as in the industrial program, we must start where we are and not where we wish to be.

As I said a few years ago at Howard University, both these positions had thus something of truth and right. Because of the peculiar economic situation in our country the program of the industrial school came to grief first and has practically been given up. Starting even though we may with the actual condition of the negro peasant and artisan, we cannot ameliorate his condition simply by learning a trade which is the technique of a passing era. More vision and knowledge is needed than that. But on the other hand, while the Negro college of a generation ago set down a defensible and true program of applying knowledge to facts, it unfortunately could not completely carry it out, and it did not carry it out, because the one thing that the industrial philosophy gave to education, the Negro college did not take and that was that the university education of black men in the United States must be grounded in the condition and work of those black men!

On the other hand, it would be of course idiotic to say, as the former industrial philosophy almost said, that so far as most black men are concerned education must stop with this. No, starting with present conditions and using the facts and the knowledge of the present situation of American Negroes, the Negro university expands toward the possession and the conquest of all knowledge. It seeks from a beginning of the history of the Negro in America and in Africa to interpret all history; from a beginning of social development among Negro slaves and freedmen in America and Negro tribes and kingdoms in Africa, to interpret and understand the social development of all mankind in all ages. It seeks to reach modern science of matter and life from the surroundings and habits and aptitudes of American Negroes and thus lead up to understanding of life and matter in the universe.

And this is a different program than a similar function would be in a white university or in a Russian university or in an English university, because it starts from a different point. It is a matter of beginnings and integrations of one group which sweep instinctive knowledge and inheritance and current reactions into a universal world of science, sociology and art. In no other way can the American Negro College function. It cannot begin with history and lead to Negro History. It cannot start with sociology and lead to Negro sociology.

Why was it that the Renaissance of literature which began among Negroes ten years ago has never taken real and lasting root? It was because it was a transplanted and exotic thing. It was a literature written for the benefit of white people and at the behest of white readers, and starting out privately from the white point of view. It never had a real Negro constituency and it did not grow out of the inmost heart and frank experience of Negroes; on such an artificial basis no real literature can grow.

On the other hand, if starting in a great Negro university you have knowledge, beginning with the particular, and going out to universal comprehension and unhampered expression, you are going to begin to realize for the American Negro the full life which is denied him now. And then after that comes a realization of the older object of our college—to bring this universal culture down and apply it to the individual life and individual conditions of living Negroes.

The university must become not simply a center of knowledge but a center of applied knowledge and guide of action. And this is all the more necessary now since we easily see that planned action especially in economic life, is going to be the watchword of civilization.

If the college does not thus root itself in the group life and afterward apply its knowledge and culture to actual living, other social organs must replace the college in this function. A strong, intelligent family life may adjust the student to higher culture; and, too, a social clan may receive the graduate and induct him into life. This has happened and is happening among a minority of privileged people. But it costs society a fatal price. It tends to hinder progress and hamper change; it makes Education, propaganda for things as they are. It leaves the mass of those without family training and without social standing misfits and rebels who despite their education are uneducated in its meaning and application. The only college which stands for the progress of all, mass as well as aristocracy, functions in root and blossom as well as in the over shadowing and heaven-filling tree. No system of learning—no university can be universal before it is German, French, Negro. Grounded in inexorable fact and condition, in Poland, Italy or elsewhere, it may seek the universal and haply it may find it—and finding it, bring it down to earth and us.

We have imbibed from the surrounding white world a childish idea of Progress. Progress means bigger and better results always and forever. But there is no such rule of Life. In 6000 years of human culture, the losses and retrogressions have been enormous. We have no assurance this twentieth century civilization will survive. We do not know that American Negroes will survive. There are sinister signs about us, antecedent to and unconnected with the Great Depression. The organized might of industry north and south is relegating the Negro to the edge of survival and using him as a labor reservoir on starvation wage. No secure professional class, no science, literature, nor art can live on such a sub-soil. It is an insistent, deep-throated cry for rescue, guidance and organized advance that greets the black leader today, and the college that trains him has got to let him know at least as much about the great black miners' strike in Alabama as about the age of Pericles.

We are on the threshold of a new era. Let us not deceive ourselves with out worn ideals of wealth and servants and luxuries, reared on a foundation of ignorance, starvation and want. Instinctively, we have absorbed these ideals from our twisted white American environment. This new economic planning is not for us unless we do it. Unless the American Negro today, led by trained university men of broad vision, sits down to work out by economics and mathematics, by physics and chemistry, by history and sociology, exactly how and where he is to earn a living and how he is to establish a reasonable Life in the United States or elsewhere—unless this is done, the university has missed its field and function and the American Negro is doomed to be a suppressed and inferior caste in the United States for incalculable time.

Here, then, is a job for the American Negro university. It cannot be successfully ignored or dodged without the growing menace of disaster. I lay the problem before you as one which you must not ignore.

To carry out this plan, two things and only two things are necessary,—teachers and students. Buildings and endowments may help, but they are not indispensable. It is necessary first to have teachers who comprehend this program and know how to make it live among their students. This is calling for a good deal, because it asks that teachers teach that which they have learned in no American school and which they never will learn until we have a Negro university of the sort that I am visioning. No teacher, black or white, who comes to a university like Fisk, filled simply with general ideas of human culture or general knowledge of disembodied science, is going to make a university of this school. Because a university is made of human beings, learning of the things they do not know from the things they do know in their own lives.

And secondly, we must have students. They must be chosen for their ability to learn. There is always the temptation to assume that the children of privileged classes, the rich, the noble, the white, are those who can best take education. One has but to express this to realize its utter futility. But perhaps the most dangerous thing among us is for us, without thought, to imitate the white world and assume that we can choose students at Fisk because of the amount of money which their parents have happened to get hold of. That basis of selection is going to give us an extraordinary aggregation. We want, by the nicest methods possible, to seek out the talented and the gifted among our constituency, quite regardless of their wealth or position, and to fill this university and similar institutions with persons who have got brains enough to take fullest advantage of what the university offers. There is no other way. With teachers who know what they are teaching and whom they are teaching, and the life that surrounds both the knowledge and the knower, and with students who have the capacity and the will to absorb this knowledge, we can build the sort of Negro university which will emancipate not simply the black folk of the United States, but those white folk who in their effort to suppress Negroes have killed their own culture.

Men in their desperate effort to replace equality with caste and to build inordinate wealth on a foundation of abject poverty have succeeded in killing democracy, art and religion.

Only a universal system of learning, rooted in the will and condition of the masses and blossoming from that manure up toward the stars is worth the name. Once builded it can only grow as it brings down sunlight and starshine and impregnates the mud.

The chief obstacle in this rich land endowed with every national resource and with the abilities of a hundred different peoples—the chief and only obstacle to the coming of that kingdom of economic equality which is the only logical end of work, is the determination of the white world to keep the black world poor and make themselves rich. The disaster which this selfish and short-sighted policy has brought, lies at the bottom of this present depression, and too, its cure lies beside it. Your clear vision of a world without wealth, of capital without profit, of income based on work alone, is the path out not only for you but for all men.

Is not this a program of segregation, emphasis of race and particularism as against national unity and universal humanity? It is and it is not by choice but by force; you do not get humanity by wishing it nor do you become American citizens simply because you want to. A Negro university, from its high ground of unfaltering facing of the Truth, from its unblinking stare at hard facts does not advocate segregation by race; it simply accepts the bald fact that we are segregated, apart, hammered into a separate unity by spiritual intolerance and legal sanction backed by mob law, and that this separation is growing in strength and fixation; that it is worse today than a half century ago and that no character, address, culture or desert is going to change it in our day or for centuries to come. Recognizing this brute fact, groups of cultured, trained and devoted men gather in great institutions of learning.

⤳ 74 ⤳

Organization

The American Negro has not begun to use his power of organization or to conceive what he might accomplish if he did. His best and most educated elements seek to evade the social leadership of their people under the impression that their best opportunity to advance lies in separating themselves from the Negro race and finding a place in white civilization. They call this "settling" the Negro problem.

As a result, the American Negro's success in business, in fraternal organization, and even in the church, has been mainly the success of the great mass of unlettered people, led to a large degree by untrained devotees whose enthusiasm has far outrun their knowledge. There have been exceptions to this, but they but prove the rule. The educated leadership which today knows the facts of this civilization and has ability to think clearly and logically, is standing aside, criticizing and even escaping the bonds of race or trying to. This philosophy of escape is dominant. We do not want to live in Negro neighborhoods. We do not want to attend Negro colleges. We sneer at Negro business. We declare that there is no such thing as "Negro" science, and as a result of this, some of our finest opportunities are being missed.

For example, in the North, with enlarged opportunity, we continually run across the utter futility in the efforts of Negroes. Let us take, for instance, the Chicago Fair. The Negroes of Chicago have large and effective political power. If they had wished, they could have had set aside for them a building in which they could have shown the history of the Negro race and the accomplishment of American Negroes in such an effective and scientific way that it would have attracted the attention of the whole world. Instead of being an instance of segregation, it would have been an unanswerable argument for the humanity and mentality and adaptability of a great section of the Negro race.

It would be no greater instance of admitted inferiority than the Spanish building or the French building or the American Indian exhibit; but no, any such movement was not only not proposed, apparently no one thought of it. Nothing was done, until, at the last moment, there was some small, half hearted suggestion of Negro participation among the Makers of America.

On the other hand, in the South, where there is continued frustration of Negro effort through custom, law and lawlessness, we find mass movements and organized accomplishment which are extraordinary when we remember that even here the best trained leadership is not taking hold. The other day, out on the new North Drive of Atlanta, I rode by a little Negro settlement; simple, pretty houses, on high ground, facing this thoroughfare which is destined to develop. But who were these Negroes? Not the graduates of the colleges, not the experienced leaders, but ordinary laborers, able to read and write, but knowing little about the world and its ways. What will result? They will be cheated and driven out of this lovely little settlement within ten years because they do not know how to organize and hold it. Or again, we could organize and develop Negro country life and land-holding, and hitch it up with small industry and manufacturing and commerce. But those who can plan this, are not interested. They are trying to lose themselves in New York or in the West or any place where it is possible to escape the Negro problem and the resultant disabilities.

We refer again to the explanation of remarkable Japanese co-operation which J. Max Bond explains in the June CRISIS: "Go to the Japanese, thou sluggard. Think on his ways and be wise!"

INDEX

slothfulness, 23, 40, 51, 53, 88, 103, 116, 124, 149, 151, 182, 190
social reform, 19, 39, 159, 208
Souls of Black Folk, The, xxii, 17
Stewart, Maria, xx
suffrage. *See* voting
summer camps, 235

Talented Tenth, 100, 212
theft, 51, 88, 105, 201
thrift, xviii, 80–84, 104, 129–30, 132, 136–37, 149, 156, 168, 184–90, 203, 219–20, 225–26
toil. *See* work
training, 19, 24, 52, 91–102, 104, 123–33, 136, 147, 150–56, 161, 179–80, 204–6, 217–18, 239, 245
Trotter, William Monroe, xix
truancy. *See* children

uplift, xxiii, 147, 184
urban cities, xxiii, 181–84, 238–39
utilitarian writing, xix–xx, xxiv–xxv, 13

vagabondage. *See* crime
vagrancy, 32, 85, 87, 161
Voice of the Negro, 17, 171
voting, 8–10, 22–23, 42, 104, 148–50, 212, 221, 245–46

Washington, Booker T., xx, 15, 45, 104, 109–10, 112, 242–43
wealth, 7, 182, 184–92
Wells, Ida B., xix
World To-Day, 17, 148, 190
World's Work, 17, 68, 181
work, 7, 114–26, 147, 156, 171, 176, 178–79, 183–84, 190, 202–3, 206–7, 250, 255–56

ABOUT THE EDITOR

Brian Johnson is professor of English at Gordon College and non resident fellow in the W. E. B. Du Bois Institute of African and African American Research, Harvard University.